A Killing Cure

A KILLING CURE

Evelyn Walker
Perry Deane Young

HENRY HOLT AND COMPANY | NEW YORK

I DEDICATE *this book to those people
who have stayed by me all these years,
who continued to believe in me when
I no longer could.*

*To Perry Deane Young, who suffered my nightmare
for two years while writing this book.*

To Joy Harris, my agent, who became my friend.

To Channa Taub, my editor, who cared and understood.

*To my sons and certainly not last
my friend, my love, my husband, Earl,
who helps to mend the broken pieces.*

Library of Congress Cataloging in Publication Data
Walker, Evelyn.
A killing cure.
1. Walker, Evelyn — Trials, litigation, etc. 2. Parzen, Zane — Trials, litigation, etc. 3. Trials (Malpractice) — California — San Diego. 4. Psychotherapist and patient. 5. Psychotherapist patients — Abuse of. 6. Psychotherapists — Sexual behavior. I. Young, Perry Deane. II. Title.
KF228.W28W35   1986   345.73'0268   85-24785
                         347.305268

ISBN 0-03-069906-1

First Edition

Designer: Ann Gold   Printed in the United States of America

10   9   8   7   6   5   4   3   2   1

ISBN 0-03-069906-1

Preface Evelyn Walker and I first met in our agents' offices, a glass-walled corner suite in the last tall building of Hollywood's raucous Sunset Strip, overlooking the first neatly trimmed lawns of the more sedate Beverly Hills estates. Outwardly, Evelyn seemed as confident as any woman I had ever known. Her luxuriant black hair was brushed back as if styled by the wind. Tall and broad-shouldered, she looked like a younger version of the dancer Ann Miller getting ready to go on stage and hoof it for another few hours. Inwardly, she was a very different person, but it would take time for me to learn just how complicated she really was and how genuinely tragic her life had been.

At this first meeting, Evelyn was the one who reduced our polite get-acquainted chatter to the important questions involved. Could I understand how somebody who now looked strong and healthy would have submitted to all she had at the hands of her psychiatrist? No, I had to admit, maybe no one who hadn't had that experience could ever know and understand it completely.

But in the writing of this book, my job, I felt, was to hear Evelyn Walker's story in as much detail as she could possibly relate it, and then describe what happened as closely as possible to how she had lived it. The problem was that Evelyn was mentally ill during much of this time and there were important scenes that she simply could not remember clearly. There were also vital medical and legal documents that she was never shown because of her very unstable mental condition.

That is why we decided that the most accurate and honest approach for this book would be for Evelyn to tell her story in her own voice and for me to write the rest in the objective third person. (Prior to beginning work on this book, I had never been to La Jolla or San Diego and I had never met or even heard about any of the people involved in the story.) While it is true that much of the most critical material comes down to Evelyn's word against that of her former lover and psychiatrist, Zane Parzen, it is important to remember that Evelyn's testimony has withstood intensive cross-examination by very aggressive lawyers in a complex, two-part trial by jury and also in two medical society hearings before committees of Parzen's fellow psychoanalysts. Parzen or his attorneys were present every time Evelyn testified, and they were given plenty of time to refute everything she said. They could not do that because she was telling the truth.

Although by the time we met she had testified many times about what had happened to her, I could not expect Evelyn to remember her past with the fine detail necessary for this book, or to remember precise dates for events that had occurred ten years earlier. In that regard, we were privy to a writer's goldmine. The official records in this case are voluminous. They include not just the transcript of the two-part trial, but also thousands of pages of pretrial "discovery" documents. In civil cases in California, the lawyers for both sides must make available — months in advance of the trial — any and all personal, private, and confidential records that might bear on the case. The usual privilege of confidentiality between doctor and patient was thus waived by both sides. Evelyn Walker's entire medical history over a twenty-year period became part of the public record — from the routine notations of visits to the family doctor to the more detailed notes of the analysts who treated her. Likewise, the records of Zane Parzen's own state-ordered analysis were subpoenaed as evidence. In addition, both sides were allowed to examine the opposing witnesses in officially recorded sessions that lasted anywhere from one hour to two days. Much of the material in these remarkably detailed depositions was never entered as evidence in the trial itself, but all of it is part of the official record.

Unless otherwise identified, all of the private letters and the confidential personal, medical, and legal documents quoted in the book were subpoenaed as evidence in *Walker v. Parzen,* and all are public records. These official documents helped corroborate everything Evelyn told me, but I also visited every place described, interviewed most of the major figures in the story, and offered the others the chance to meet with me and give me their views of the events here described.

The names of nine people involved in Evelyn Walker's story have been changed in this book. The following are not their real names: Bill Higgins, Robert Fournier, Bob Simmons, Pat Stern, Mary Sutton, Carl Anson Walker, Michael David Walker, Carole Shepherd, Connie Martin. Everything else about these people is factual and true.

In recalling her story for me, Evelyn was forced to relive in painful detail the horrors of that earlier time in her life. Having read in one of Sigmund Freud's early case histories that a person can be pushed to recall something he swears he's forgotten, I tried to push Evelyn to remember. By "restaging," as I naively called it, the more traumatic scenes, Evelyn was able to recall all kinds of details she thought had passed from memory. In one terrifying experience of what Freud had labeled "transference," I became in Evelyn's mind the psychiatrist whom she still loved with such confused intensity. She was crying to me as she had to him. "Don't you see?" she asked. "I had nobody else—no place to go but back to him. He had become my whole life."

Yes, I was beginning to understand — not only how she could have been manipulated so viciously, but also how easily a doctor with problems of his own could get carried away with having such extraordinary powers over another person's life.

Perry Deane Young

Prologue Off by herself at the back of the courtroom, Evelyn Walker sat waiting for the verdict. She was forty-one years old, the mother of two teenage sons. She had been married and divorced twice.

What was visible in her that day, however, was not a mature adult, but a pathetic, helpless little girl, an abused child pleading for explanations about why she was being punished when she'd done nothing wrong. Her clothes—an open-necked sailor's blouse and a simple full skirt—only added to this impression. Her bleary eyes and the pale puffy skin of her face reflected the months and years she had spent in a wretched—often drugged—state of anguished days and desperate, sleepless nights.

As she sat there, she tried not to think of what might happen if she lost this case: Was she a bad person, she wondered, always in the wrong, as her mother had made her feel? She had been looking for answers, looking for help, when she went to this psychoanalyst named Zane Parzen—and then his "treatment" had almost killed her more times than she could remember, or, in truth, was ever aware of. Others had talked her into bringing suit for malpractice against the man. But, once in court, she found that she was as much on trial as he.

The jurors would be deciding not only whether Evelyn Walker would have any money to live on for the rest of her life; they would be confirming whether anybody believed she was telling the truth. On the first day of the two-month-long trial they had been told by her lawyer, Marvin Lewis, Sr., that they would not see much of her in court. The day-to-day testimony about what had happened to her would be too upsetting for her delicate mental condition. She would be there for her own testimony, of course, "and she will be here to hear your verdict."

A flamboyant San Franciscan, Lewis was of the old school of law-yers more taken with the language of Shakespeare than that of Black-stone. With his literary and theatrical bent, and with more than a half century before the bar, Lewis presented a case — from the selection of the jury through the final argument — with the meticulous crafts-manship of a fine playwright.

Lewis may have oversimplified the case of Evelyn Walker for the jury's understanding, but that was exactly how he saw it. He depicted Evelyn as the innocent Trilby to her psychiatrist's Svengali. Like George du Maurier's fictional hypnotist, the doctor had gained con-trol of Evelyn's mind and then proceeded to change her life com-pletely.

True, she did have a troubled childhood. But Evelyn had married well and at the time her serious mental problems developed, she was a successful woman by anybody's definition. Her husband, Bruce Walker, was a brilliant young engineer in the space program and had gone on to a lucrative career in computer sciences. He was tall and athletic, a fine match for her own dark good looks. Later, Bruce Walker interrupted a vacation with his present wife to testify in court that Evelyn had been "a good wife and a good mother" until she started seeing Zane Parzen.

Parzen was known to his colleagues at the San Diego Psychoanalytic Institute as a dedicated scholar, teacher, analyst, parent, husband. He had studied under some of the most distinguished names in the world of psychiatry and analysis. Parzen's training had been carefully con-sidered by Evelyn's neighbor, Gary Shepherd. Shepherd was one of Parzen's psychiatric peers at the Institute, and he had recommended Parzen to Evelyn.

If Shepherd was the one who introduced Evelyn Walker to Zane Parzen, he was also the one who stepped in and saved her from the man's clutches when he realized she would soon be dead if she stayed under Parzen's "care." Slowly, ever so slowly, Parzen had convinced Evelyn that her marriage — even her children — was all wrong for her. He was the only one who really cared for her, he alone understood her wants and needs, and he would always be there. She was starved for such concern and for the real physical affection (however strange) that the doctor soon provided on the couch in his office. She was paying him a dollar a minute, $55 a visit, twice a week. But when she would say, "If you love and care about me, how can you charge me?" he would insist on the money and tell her: "You're paying for the time, not the caring."

A healthy woman would have sensed that none of this was right, and would have walked out the first time he touched her leg. But Evelyn Walker was not healthy; that is why she went to Parzen in the first place. Although the news reports about this case would speak of Parzen's "seduction" of female patients as if it were no more serious than a little hanky-panky on the couch, what he was doing was far more sinister. "There is no delicate way of putting it," Parzen's colleague Gary Shepherd would testify. "He was killing these women." For Evelyn, it would eventually be revealed, was only one of at least four patients Parzen had abused.

For many years, Parzen maintained a busy professional schedule and a lucrative practice in La Jolla (pronounced "la hoya"), a picturesque enclave of the very rich situated on the rugged coastal cliffs just north of San Diego. Parzen's fellow psychiatrists, in their offices in a glistening new white-marble-and-tinted-glass building overlooking the Pacific Ocean, either did not see or refused to see what was wrong with him and the irreparable damage he was doing to certain patients. After she beame involved with Parzen, Evelyn Walker would lose everything she had ever cared about. She became a woman possessed, living out her days in a one-room studio apartment, her whole being focused on the brief phone calls and the twice-a-week office visits with Parzen.

She began seeing him in September 1974, and — sinking deeper and deeper into a drugged oblivion — she continued to see him until January 1977. She had made numerous attempts at suicide by the time Gary Shepherd stepped in and had the president of the Psychoanalytic Institute order Parzen to transfer her to another doctor.

Meanwhile, Parzen continued to practice — and to abuse other female patients — long after the psychiatric community was alerted to his behavior with Evelyn Walker. It would be another two years before his fellow doctors would finally begin the difficult and — for them — threatening process of bringing the formal charges that would remove him from the profession. This action was more or less forced on the doctors by the bizarre behavior of another Parzen patient, who had been even more abused than Evelyn Walker had been. In one "acting-out" session, Parzen had thrown the other woman against a wall; in another session, he ordered her to duck-walk across the room, unzip his pants with her teeth, and then perform oral sex on him. This was his way of helping her overcome certain problems in dealing with sex.

Parzen had also taken nude photographs of the other woman, who by then was suffering so severely from anorexia nervosa that she herself said she looked like a concentration camp victim. In addition, the woman had become pregnant by Parzen, and he helped her to get an abortion. Nonetheless, the woman wore a big Z around her neck as a symbol of her undying love for her tormentor. Although her closest friend provided these details for investigators, the woman herself remained under Parzen's spell. She vehemently refused ever to testify against him, and she threatened to kill anyone who took action against him.

Evelyn Walker alone agreed to speak for the record about Parzen's abusive behavior behind the locked doors of his office. But even she took action only because it was explained to her that she would be helping Parzen. In fact, if he had listened to his colleagues at that stage and declared himself an impaired physician, the case might well have remained within the medical community. He might not have lost his license to practice, and there might have been no malpractice suits against him. But Parzen turned on his fellow analysts and threatened to sue *them* if they tampered any more with his private practice. It was only the latest in a succession of traps Parzen seemed to have laid for himself. As Gary Shepherd saw it, "He was playing a cat-and-mouse kind of game, saying catch-me-if-you-can." As it was, an incredible number of years passed before action was taken against Parzen — and at any step, he could have stopped it if he had really tried. A simple phone call or brief note from him to Evelyn Walker would have stopped everything — and he knew that better than anyone.

At the urging of Shepherd and others, Evelyn did finally initiate a suit against Parzen. But since she filed suit years after the malpractice occurred, the chief issue in the ensuing trial was never Parzen's guilt or innocence (since by the time of the trial Parzen had already signed a line-item statement acknowledging his illegal and unethical acts) but whether *she* had filed within the one-year period set in California as the statute of limitations for malpractice cases. In this trial, Parzen was represented by his insurance company's lawyer, Michael I. Neil.

He was a perfect foil for Evelyn's lawyer, Marvin Lewis, the man who quite literally wrote the book on psychic injury cases.

With his heavy brows and mane of white hair, Lewis looked like a figure out of history. Expertly trained at his mother's elocution school, he was a fine orator — and a convincing one because he refused to take a case unless he believed in it. In contrast to Lewis's Shakespeare, Mike Neil told Irish jokes. But he, too, cut a striking figure, especially in San Diego, where the U.S. Marine Corps and the U.S. Navy are the major employers. As a young lieutenant in Vietnam, Neil had been a hero under fire and had been awarded the Navy Cross, the second highest award for bravery in combat. Edging into middle age, he had remained the lean, tough Marine, his hair still almost shaved to pass inspection. Because of his position as a colonel in the Marine Reserves the trial of *Walker v. Parzen* would be interrupted for two weeks so he could go to summer camp.

The two-part trial was long and unusually complicated. With the jury still out at the end of the second part, who could say how much they had understood or what kind of decision they would bring back. "She will be here to hear your verdict," Lewis had intoned in his final argument. Whatever the jurors' decision, they would have to face Evelyn Walker when it was all over.

After all those weeks of argument and testimony about her, the woman herself seemed to have been forgotten as the moment of truth drew near. She sat alone, clutching her face in her hands, trying not to think of the worst. In truth, she was destitute at the time. She hadn't even been able to hold down a counter job in a fast-food restaurant. If Marvin Lewis hadn't taken her case on the contingency that he would be paid only if sufficient damage payments were awarded by the jury, Evelyn could never have afforded a lawyer.

The jurors deliberated for less than four hours before sending word at 3:20 P.M. July 7, 1981, that they had reached a verdict. A bailiff opened the corner door and the members of the jury filed in.

The ritual questions were asked and answered. Had they reached a verdict? "Yes, sir, we have." The bailiff took the verdict sheet from the presiding juror and handed it to the judge. He read it and passed it down for the clerk to read. The jury had found in favor of the plaintiff, Evelyn Walker, and had awarded her the sum of ". . . four—." Here, the clerk stumbled over the long figure, as everyone in the courtroom strained to hear how much. It was $4,631,666, the largest amount ever levied in damages against a psychiatrist in the United States and the second-largest medical-malpractice award in any category at that time. One older woman juror later embraced Evelyn Walker and muttered to a reporter, "A hundred million dollars wouldn't be enough."

But what everybody in that room would remember was not any sort of celebration on the plaintiff's side. It was a chilling wail that pierced the silence as soon as the verdict was read. Evelyn Walker did not react with shrieks of joy and laughter, as some had anticipated. She cried out as if in pain and then collapsed in bitter, hurtful tears. She faced the gut realization that the long court fight might be over but her personal struggles would continue. She knew that no amount of money could ever restore the years she had lost or heal the mental wounds she will carry to her death. The jury had arrived at that odd figure because they felt she might require medical and psychiatric treatment for the rest of her life — and that was the projected amount it would cost.

I. The Caring

Chapter I

I picked Zane Parzen from a list of three psychiatrists my next-door neighbor recommended because I liked the sound of his name. That might sound like a casual way to make so important a decision, but it really wasn't. I didn't know anything about any of the three doctors. More important, I didn't know anything at all about the whole field of psychiatry or psychoanalysis. My neighbor was a psychoanalyst himself, so I just had to trust his recommendation.

Other doctors had not been able to find any physical cause for the headaches and periods of depression I was having, so I had no choice but to look for help from a doctor of the mind. I had gone to another psychiatrist for a brief time a few years earlier, and I felt that talking with him had helped me a great deal.

Doctor Parzen's office was located on a small, enclosed walkway among one-story offices of real estate people and young lawyers. The place itself was small and unpretentious, but it was located in the heart of downtown La Jolla, a prestigious address.

As with most psychiatrists, Parzen's office was designed to give the patient the maximum privacy. There were two outer doors. One opened into the waiting room, the other opened from the doctor's inner office. This way, patients coming and going never saw each other — and there was no need for a receptionist. I remember there were two pen-and-ink drawings by the actor Lionel Barrymore on the wall of this tiny room. And, as with every other psychiatrist I would later see in La Jolla, there was a radio speaker always softly playing the local classical music station. The announcers all have those soothing voices and they all seem to be saying, *Don't worry dear, everything's going to be all right*. I now connect those gentle voices with my hellish experience with psychiatrists — and I cannot bear to hear the classical music station anymore.

Because my husband, Bruce, had been involved in the decision for me to see a psychiatrist, he went with me on that first visit to Doctor Parzen's office. The doctor came out and introduced himself to us and then we went through a small outer room — with a corner full of African violets in full blossom — and into the main office. A couch was against the wall on the left. It was covered in beige leather. The whole room was done in nice masculine shades of off-white, beige, and brown, and the upholstery was brown leather. There were four chairs — and how we were arranged in them explains a lot about that first meeting. Behind the desk was the doctor's chair, and in front of the desk was a chair for the patient undergoing face-to-face therapy instead of on-the-couch analysis. Behind the couch, but diagonally across from the patient's chair, was another chair for the doctor. On a table beside it was his extra pipe and an ash tray. That is the chair the doctor took; Bruce sat closest to him in the patient's chair; and I — the subject of the meeting, after all — had no choice but to take the fourth chair, across the room at the foot of the couch.

Bruce chain-smoked cigarettes as he talked; the doctor lit and re-lit his pipe and listened. I sat watching and listening as if none of it had anything to do with me. I don't remember anything Bruce said. I just remember that he did all the talking. When Bruce finished speaking, the doctor said he wanted to see me alone the next time, and we agreed on a time and date a week later.

▬

After two meetings with the new patient, Parzen wrote a report for his own files, dated September 16, 1974. "In the initial interview," he wrote, "she was in the room with her husband, and he did most of the talking, and basically portrayed a long-standing history of depression with severe exacerbation at times." After talking with her alone, Parzen noted: "She feels she is not needed nor respected, even though she feels there is a good relationship with her husband. At this point it would seem appropriate that twice-a-week therapy would be indicated, but pending insurance availability, I will see her on a once-a-week basis." Although Evelyn told him she was having migraine headaches, Parzen said, "These sound more like tension headaches."

He noted that he would "go cautiously" in treating her for the head-aches, experimenting with mild tranquilizers at first to see how she responded. In two concluding sentences, he contradicts himself on whether Evelyn is or is not opening up to him. "Exactly what the therapeutic goals are going to be are certainly not clear but it seems that when she was alone with me she could talk freely and could open up." But then he adds: "Until she can really relate more about herself, other than her paranoid suspiciousness of everything, I will have to hold off with more definitive statements."

In those first weeks and months, the whole idea of becoming emotion-ally involved with my psychiatrist was totally foreign to me. I would no more have fallen in love with him than with a filling-station attendant. Ours was a purely professional relationship. And besides, I felt my husband was everything I ever wanted in a man. At the time, I saw nothing wrong with our marriage.

Doctor Parzen was an interesting man, and I did not find him unattractive, but I simply didn't think about him in those terms. Later, however, I would look back on those first sessions and realize he had been thinking that way from the start. He would always ask me what I thought about when I was getting ready to come to his office. I didn't really understand the question. I certainly didn't think about him, and I didn't realize at the time that that was what he wanted to hear. I thought nothing about calling up and cancel-ing an appointment if something more important came up — and virtually everything I was involved with was more important to me then.

I remember a particular incident that puzzled me at the time. Doctor Parzen was planning to move into the top-floor offices of a new building on Prospect Street. He had given up the lease on his old office before the new one was ready, and for a few weeks he had to use a hotel room as his office. I arrived at the hotel room for my appointment one day and took my place as usual. Something seemed odd about the room, I felt, and I kept looking around, trying to figure out what was wrong. Finally, I realized that although it was a regular hotel room, the bed had been removed. When I commented on this, Doctor Parzen said: "I didn't want anybody to get the wrong idea." I was so surprised by his explanation that I smiled and almost laughed out loud. But the doctor didn't think it was funny at all.

By "the wrong idea," he had to mean sex. I just couldn't picture anybody ever thinking about sex with Doctor Parzen. But I didn't attach much importance to the words then. Only years later, on reflection, would I look back on those words as a kind of signal for all that was to come.

For six months, I went nearly every week to a fifty-five-minute session with Doctor Parzen. I would sit there, as rigid and reluctant to talk as a child called in before a school principal. I never once took my sunglasses off; and there were, in fact, long silences. The doctor pulled and pulled, trying in vain to get any kind of details out of me about my childhood, especially about my mother.

I remember once — this was at the old office — I asked him about a color photograph in a frame standing on a cluttered shelf behind his desk. It was the only picture in the room, and apparently it was his son. I asked if this was his only child. He answered bluntly, "No." Just kidding, I asked: "Don't you like your other children?" Zane answered coldly, "He's dead." I froze then, saying nothing. Zane asked, "What are you thinking?" I answered: "How terrible it must be to lose a child." Although the son was not mentioned for almost another year, I never got over the jolt of that moment and my feeling of sadness for the doctor. But this was a rare personal exchange between us. I didn't think anything more or less about him: He was the doctor and I was the patient. And he didn't seem unusually interested in me, either.

One thing that did bother me was his persistence in questioning me about my husband and my children. I didn't feel there were any problems at all involving them; if there were problems, they were all mine. A great deal of my time was spent talking about how guilty I felt paying $55 a week just to sit and talk. I felt somewhat better when Bruce was able to get most of it paid through his insurance. In the end, I guess I rationalized that if the sessions with Doctor Parzen weren't helping that much, they weren't doing any harm either.

Then, one day in late February 1975, I was very upset over something specific that had happened at home. On the surface it was just another silly family squabble, but I had a feeling it was much more than that. And, after all, wasn't this the kind of thing I was paying a psychiatrist for — to listen and to explain?

What bothered me so much about this particular argument was not that there was anything new and different in it. It was the same one I had been losing all my life. No matter what happened, it seemed, I was made to feel I was always wrong. First, it was my mother who made me feel that way. Then when I would go to my father, he would always support my mother. When I met and married Bruce, I thought everything would be different from then on. I had someone who loved me, someone I could trust.

But, as Doctor Parzen kept digging into my past and asking me over and over about my family, I found I was in the same predicament all over again with my husband. Whatever Bruce said was the law, whatever I thought that disagreed with his words was just not important.

When our sons Carl and Michael were babies, they were ours. I was left alone with them many times, but Bruce loved them and loved to spend time with them. We shared all the responsibilities and loved doing it. I was too busy taking care of the children to be plagued by the old doubts and fears of my childhood. I felt fulfilled in the most basic motherly way. One time, my mother came over and tried to tell me I was holding Carl too much. For once I talked back to her: "He's mine and I can do whatever I want with him."

But when the boys started going to school, my role in their lives was shifted to the point where it often seemed that I had no say at all in the decisions affecting them. They were no longer *our* sons, they were Bruce's. It seemed that once the boys stepped out the door into the public eye at school, Bruce took charge and claimed full ownership and responsibility. Carl, the oldest, not only looked like his dad, he had early developed a similar personality. Doctor Parzen explained to me that I would soon have not one but two Bruces to deal with.

On that particular February day, I got a call from Carl's history teacher at La Jolla Country Day School. The teacher said Carl was not doing the work he was capable of doing. The teacher had already dropped him a full grade in hopes of shocking him into working harder. I talked with the teacher for a long time, trying to understand just what Carl was doing wrong so I could discuss it with him.

When Carl got home from school, I told him about the call and everything the teacher had said. But, every other sentence, he would interrupt and say, "That's just not true."

I kept trying to talk to him, but we became more and more angry with each other. Finally, Carl said, "You don't know what you're talking about." I was so mad that my son would be talking back to me so rudely, I broke off and said, "We'll talk with your father when he comes home."

Bruce and I did talk privately, and then Carl came in and gave his side of the story. Gradually, it dawned on me that Bruce was siding against me, even though I was the only one who had talked to the teacher, the only one who knew what the man had said. It was the kind of heart-to-heart talk that should have ended with both parents saying, "Now, son, we know you can do better work. Just go back in that class and show them what you can do." But no, that wasn't it at all. It was another way of putting me down, of telling me I was all wrong.

First Carl and then Bruce picked up the line that I didn't know what I was talking about. I was so angry and hurt with my husband and my son that I grabbed the keys and ran out to my car. Nobody came running after me. I have no idea where I thought I was going to go or what I was going to do. I just wanted to be away from that place where I was always wrong. Somewhere in the back of my mind I was thinking that maybe I would just get a hotel room and spend the night alone and see if anybody missed me back at home. That was, of course, no real solution, but at least it would be quiet in a room by myself and there would be nobody to talk down to me.

I got to the parking lot around the Summer House Inn, a high-rise hotel at the northern edge of La Jolla, but I didn't park or even stop. I just drove around and around in circles. I was so confused I didn't know what to do. Of course, I did finally go back; what else could I do? I loved my husband and our two boys. I couldn't seriously think of leaving them and I knew it.

There was only a sullen silence in the house when I returned. Nobody ever asked where I had gone or said, "I'm sorry." The argument was never mentioned at home again.

But the next day, February 21, 1975, I had an appointment with my psychiatrist. Maybe Parzen could tell me what was going on here. This was the first time I had ever come to him with a specific problem to talk about. At least it was the first time I had ever thought about it that way. Before, he was always probing for explanations in my past. Now, I had this very upsetting incident in my present and I wanted him to explain it to me.

I came into the office and sat down in the patient's armchair. In the new office, Doctor Parzen had put the desk at one end of the much bigger room; the couch was over against the left wall. And at the opposite end from the desk were two armchairs, for patient and doctor, with a big footstool or ottoman between them.

My sunglasses were still in place at this stage. And I remember I was wearing a pair of wide-legged slacks because I had my right foot up on the ottoman, my knee bent. I have no idea what I had expected from the doctor after I had told him my story. Obviously, I was looking for support and approval, but mainly for some explanations. But since I had never found that in my life before this, I had no reason to think Doctor Parzen could now provide it.

I told him in detail about everything that was said and done the night before. Much to my amazement, as the details unfolded, Doctor Parzen didn't just shake his head and say I was wrong or I didn't understand. He agreed with me and said I was right in what I had told my son. And he said the boy was wrong and my husband should have supported me no matter what. He said the boy was at fault, and, further, he said the boy obviously was talking to his mother that way because he knew he could get away with it.

For the first time in my life, I was hearing somebody say that something was not my fault, that I was not to blame. It is difficult to describe how overwhelming that feeling was to me. Maybe it is impossible for someone who is not me to know just how emotional such a moment could be. I felt that I was on the verge of breaking down, a whole lifetime of tears was bursting to get out. But I fought it with all my might. I held onto the arms of the chair so tightly that my arms and shoulders ached for hours afterward. But the more I tried to force back the tears, the more determined they were to flow. I was under such strain, I could feel my hair and blouse getting wet with sweat.

Finally, the dam burst and I sat there sobbing out of control. My face got so wet that my sunglasses slipped down my nose and I had to take them off. The moment I started to cry, Doctor Parzen got up and sat on the ottoman. He pressed his leg against mine and held my upraised knee between his hands. All I could think about was how horrible it was to be breaking down in front of a stranger, how awful I must look to him. I gripped the arms of that chair in a death lock. I didn't know why the doctor was rubbing my leg. I was hardly even thinking about that. I could not take my eyes away from his eyes. I could not turn my face away from his face.

As he was massaging my leg, he talked in soothing tones. He said it was very important for me to know I was not crazy, I was not insane. (I had never thought I *was* insane.) He said all these people in my life — my mother, my husband, my son — were not always right. I was just as intelligent as they were.

Then he said something that really bothered me later when I thought back on it. He said it was not uncommon for a divorce to take place when people were in therapy. I didn't react to what he said at the time, but I couldn't forget it, either. An idea had been planted in my mind. It had never entered my mind before this. I had never seen anything wrong in my marriage. Bruce was the perfect husband, I thought. After all, I had nothing else to compare our marriage to except my parents' very troubled relationship. I had seldom dated in high school; I had rarely even kissed a man before I started dating Bruce. I had never had sex with any other man. Once we were married, I assumed we would always live together. If there were problems, they had to be mine. I made no connections at all between my headaches and anybody else. I firmly believed that it was all inside my own head. I wondered why this doctor would even suggest that anything was so wrong with my marriage that I should consider a divorce. But I couldn't bring myself to say anything to him that day. I just stared into his eyes and listened to him talk.

Both his hands were moving up and down my leg. Reflecting later on those minutes, I realized that the strangest part was that I kept thinking it would not be "appropriate" for me to move my leg away from Parzen or to tell him to stop stroking me. It was all part of my confusion and discomfort over breaking down in front of somebody I hardly knew — and in an office in a professional situation. I asked him if my hour wasn't about up. I just wanted to get out of this embarrassing situation. I was so concerned about losing control I didn't even think about how improper it was for him to do what he had done.

Before I left, the doctor told me once again that I was not crazy, I was not insane. "There is nothing wrong with your thinking," he said, "and don't let anybody tell you you are crazy."

At my session the next week, my sunglasses were back in place and I was determined not to break down again. I told Doctor Parzen I was very upset about losing control the last time. We talked in general terms and stayed at a professional distance from each other. I don't know what led up to it, but Parzen said he thought it would be a good idea if Bruce came to the next session. He had already talked with him once or twice on the phone and he said he would make all the arrangements.

Bruce left work the day of the appointment the next week and met me at the doctor's office. We went in, and the two men took the doctor's and patient's chairs — leaving me with only the couch to sit on. When I first thought about going to a psychiatrist, I knew I could never endure analysis on the couch. If I was going to talk with somebody about my life and my problems, I had to be able to look them in the face. This was the first time I had ever sat on Doctor Parzen's couch, and my husband and my doctor had put me there. I could not know it that day, of course, but this couch would soon become the focus of my life — and, as others later explained to me, would also lead me to the very edge of death time and time again.

The doctor lit up his pipe; Bruce smoked his cigarettes. I sat in my place, waiting quietly, letting the men do the talking once again.

Bruce hadn't told me anything about it, but he had prepared a long, handwritten memorandum on what he thought my problems were. In the past, every time he had had to deal with my problems, Bruce would tell me: "If you were a computer, I'd know what to do with you." Now, it was as if he had brought his car into a mechanic with a long list of everything that was wrong with it. But with the cars, I knew, he got rid of them if they kept causing him trouble.

This list of all my problems took up four pages of a legal pad. As I had during that first session, I sat in silence while the men discussed what to do with me. But as Bruce read on and on, I became more and more upset. I was hurt, embarrassed, and ashamed as I sat hearing this man coldly describing me — this man I had lived with, slept with, and loved all those years. Doctor Parzen smoked his pipe, listened, and said nothing.

Finally, I had had enough of hearing myself put down, point by point. It wouldn't do to break down and cry in front of either man at such a moment. But my voice was cold as I told Bruce he didn't have to stay the full hour; he could leave right then.

Bruce looked up from his list, shocked at hearing me talk back to him — and he promptly got up and left. His lower lip was sticking out, his head was tilted the way it always was when he was in an uncomfortable situation.

That was the first time I realized Doctor Parzen's doors were double-locked from the inside. After Bruce left, Parzen carefully closed and locked the door behind him. He stood looking down at me on the couch. I was hugging my knees, my head down. I felt totally dejected. The only man I had ever loved had just denounced me in front of another man we hardly knew.

Doctor Parzen sat down close beside me and said, "I want you to hold on to me. Lean on me. I am the one you will turn to. I am the one who cares for you." He kept telling me to hold on to him, so I put my face on his shoulder, a little girl in her daddy's arms. I was upset about crying again, but what I was doing with the doctor just seemed to come naturally. He kept whispering that he was the only one who cared about me, he was the one who knew what was right for me. Then we were kissing as he slowly and gently moved us down on the couch so that we were lying side by side. He was talking to me the whole time. I couldn't say anything. The truth is, I wouldn't have known what to say even if I could have gotten in a word between his.

Doctor Parzen held my head so tightly I could not look away. I had never felt this way with any man other than Bruce. Ever since we were married, I had never so much as kissed any man besides Bruce. But I had also never felt so close to anybody in my life. I needed Zane Parzen desperately, and he seemed to need me, too.

After some time, I said, "You know, I'm not a little girl." That sounded silly when I thought about those words later. I must have been trying to tell Doctor Parzen that he shouldn't play games with me, that I was a grown woman with the feelings and responses of a woman.

Smiling lovingly into my eyes, the doctor answered that day, "You certainly are not a little girl."

Driving home from this session, I was so upset I had to pull off the road and just sit there for a long time until I could control the shaking and trembling. I was so confused. I could not understand why this man wanted me that way. I could not understand why it felt so good to me.

When Bruce came home that afternoon, I went up to our bedroom to talk with him in private about this psychiatrist. I went over to him and asked him to hold me close. He put his arms around me, but it was more like a duty, not something he wanted to do. I told him I thought that Doctor Parzen liked me. He said, "Why shouldn't he like you? That's very nice."

No, I said, I mean he *really* likes me.

Bruce still didn't seem to understand what I was trying to say. He said it was very good for me to have somebody who liked me, somebody I could really talk to. Talking to Bruce then, I felt the way I had as a child, trying to get through to my father. I didn't think my father understood what I was trying to say about the way my mother treated me. And if he had understood, and if Bruce now understood, then they couldn't really care about me or they would react differently.

That whole week I tried to put out of my mind what happened in the doctor's office. But I couldn't help wondering what I might have done to cause this to happen. There was only confusion in my head and no answers, no solutions at all.

At my regular session the following week, I went straight for the patient's chair and sat stiff and proper with my sunglasses back in place. I told Doctor Parzen I did not understand what had happened between us the previous week. I was shocked by my own behavior. I had never before done anything like that. I just did not know what had come over me.

Doctor Parzen started soothing me again with his words. There was no reason for me to apologize, he said. There was nothing wrong with what had happened. I asked him if this were some form of therapy. He said no, he had been married for more than twenty years and I was the first woman other than his wife he had ever been interested in. "I care about you." He kept telling me that.

Getting up and moving over to the couch, Doctor Parzen stood holding out his arms, gesturing for me to come to him. I was determined not to move. He said, "Come on, I want you to be with me." I remember thinking that my body was like lead. I could not, I just would not move. But the doctor kept beckoning me, his eyes locked on my eyes. I could not look away. It was only a matter of seconds, but it seemed like hours to me. I was so intensely confused. I could not move, it seemed, and yet I could not *not* move either.

Finally I put out my hand. Parzen grabbed it and pulled me toward him. From that moment on, we were never again doctor and patient, Doctor Parzen and Mrs. Walker. We were Zane and Evelyn, two people involved in a way that had nothing to do with anybody's profession. I never thought of him as my doctor after that day.

Zane pulled me down onto the couch beside him so that we were again lying beside each other. Somehow, he moved around under me and locked his legs so I couldn't move. He held my face in both hands so I had to look straight into his eyes. I was numb with confusion. It was wrong, bad, but it felt so good. I was resisting and he was saying, "No, no, no, it's okay." Everything would be all right now, because I was in his care, in good hands. I was to stay right there beside him and never, ever go away. He had become a man who had fallen in love with a woman, and I was that woman.

For some reason, I was thinking of my Uncle Eric. There was the same nice smell of leather and tobacco, the big, protective body. I felt safe with Zane, as I had with Eric.

▄▄▄

In direct contradiction to Evelyn's account of the actual events, Parzen's notes show that Evelyn was the one who kept urging him to have sex with her and (according to his notes) he never once responded to her "advances." As early as December 17, 1974, he noted: "Doing well, bought some more sensual clothing. Was thinking about she would like to have sex with me. . . . "

Parzen's notes also contradicted the facts about the kinds of drugs he was prescribing for Evelyn, drugs to which she was gradually becoming addicted. As Parzen wrote it for his records, Evelyn was the one who wanted more and more drugs. However, Evelyn remembers distinctly that Parzen was the one suggesting new and stronger medication. He had started out with a mild prescription for Empirin and then went on to experiment with fairly weak tranquilizers and sleeping pills. Although Parzen's notes list only a small part of the drugs he gave Evelyn, they were sufficient for experts in the field to document in court that they were not proper for her condition. They were clearly addictive, and she did in fact become addicted — her eventual withdrawal from them could have killed her. In the beginning, Evelyn got all of her medication from Parzen in the usual way: He would write a prescription and she would have it filled. But as she came more and more under the influence of Parzen and of the drugs, he would just tell her to help herself to the pills in the bottles and boxes in his office. Evelyn eventually would be taking forty to sixty pills a day; by that time she did not know the names of any of the drugs, much less what they should have been prescribed for.

In the later malpractice trial of Parzen, Evelyn Walker's lawyers would suggest that the psychiatrist might have doctored the daily notes that were subpoenaed as evidence in the trial. There were some minor discrepancies in the nearly illegible handwritten notes and the typed copies submitted with them. However, on careful examination, the notes appear to be genuine — the dates all coincide with other documents in the case. The "doctoring" was probably not a case of Parzen's making changes later on, but rather of his altering the facts from the very beginning and on a day-to-day basis.

Parzen's notes also offer numerous examples of his planting destructive ideas in Evelyn Walker's head. In his notes on his first interview with her, for example, he wrote: "At no time did she ever really evidence psychosis, although there had been a number of suicidal attempts, one more recently." In sworn testimony, Evelyn and Bruce Walker would both say that — except for a childhood incident she had not mentioned to Parzen at this time — she had never attempted suicide before she became involved with Parzen. In light of what happened later, this inaccurate note of Parzen's has sinister implications. Was it possible that the man planned even this — her suicide attempts — from the very beginning?

Nobody could foresee at that time, in late 1974, that Evelyn would ever reach the severe mental state that would push her to seek death's solution. In fact, three months after the first visit, Parzen wrote a very hopeful note about Evelyn to the Walkers' family physician: "This is a note to let you know that I am still seeing Mrs. Walker in psychotherapy on a once-a-week basis, and that she is doing quite well. She seems to have a little more self-esteem and self-confidence, and feels more comfortable in talking spontaneously about herself and her various problems."

One of the most persistent "problems" in Evelyn's life that Parzen consistently refers to in these notes has to do with her husband. As the doctor recorded it, Evelyn was slowly but surely turning against her husband and he was a major source of all her other problems. As Evelyn remembers it, she absolutely refused to speak against Bruce until long after she and Parzen were more intimately involved. Still, Parzen notes as early as December 31, 1974: "Anger at husband." And again on January 12, 1975: "Anger at Bruce re: being left.

Feels shouldn't be away." She would, of course, eventually turn against Bruce — but only because the doctor she loved had guided and shoved her in that direction.

According to Parzen's notes, the meeting with Bruce Walker in his office took place three months after that February session when Evelyn first cried — and not two weeks later, as she remembers. His notes for that day include yet another theme he would build on in his step-by-step destruction of everything Evelyn held dear: "Bruce with Mrs. Walker. Recommended martial [sic] therapy and individual therapy for both. Then I just saw her and she verbalized a fear that she was afraid he will harm her." Even in the worst days of the nightmarish months ahead, even after her husband actually had struck her, Evelyn would never believe that Bruce would ever harm her. But, as with his words of love and caring for her, the doctor would repeat his warnings again and again and again — trying to make her see that her husband might hurt her, trying to make her see something that was not there.

On that day when he first touched her leg, Parzen made these notes: "Cried in the session for the first time. Need for object love." (These two meager sentences are his notes in full for February 21, 1975.) Three weeks later, his notes for their weekly session together consisted of two words: "(wiggly) — flirtatious." This suggests the doctor now had her where he wanted her. He no longer had to ask her what she thought about when she was getting ready to come to his office. He could see she was beginning to think only of him. As Evelyn saw it, they were just two people becoming more and more attracted to each other. It would take months and years before those around them could see that what was taking place between them was a far cry from sexual attraction or love. And Evelyn Walker herself would never fully accept that her Zane was out to destroy her, not to make love with her.

Evelyn Walker, of course, knew next to nothing about the whole field of psychiatry — which is why she kept asking Parzen if his caresses were some kind of therapy. But he most certainly knew that the relationship between a therapist and a patient is fraught with dangers enough, even without an intimate, physical relationship. In fact, such an awareness is basic to any effective understanding of the profession of psychiatry. From the beginning of the development of psychiatry, analysts knew that there was a clear and present danger of emotional involvement between them and their patients. The woman generally acknowledged as the first analysand (person to be analyzed) was called "Anna O." by Josef Breuer and Sigmund Freud, but her real name was Bertha Pappenheim. She had been suffering from an extreme case of hysteria when Breuer discovered that talking with her helped to get at the root cause of her fears and delusions. In particular, she had developed a deathly fear of drinking water from a glass. Under hypnosis, she told about seeing her governess allow a dog to drink from a water glass. Discovering through hypnosis the source of her phobia, she promptly overcame it. She called it "the talking cure." Freud himself saw analysis as a means of treatment, but rarely as an absolute cure. He was fond of quoting the words of Heraclitus: "The soul of man is a far country, which cannot be approached or explored." And one of his most famous observations on analysis was published in his 1895 *Studies on Hysteria,* which he wrote with Breuer: "Much is won if we succeed in transforming hysterical misery into common unhappiness."

One can best appreciate the new humanity expressed in Freud's studies in the context of medical treatment of that time — when hysterical women especially were dismissed as "malingerers and malcontents." Prior to this time, psychotics were locked up like criminals and the more-numerous neurotics were considered lazy no-accounts and ne'er-do-wells wasting doctors' time with imaginary illnesses.

In his later case history of Anna O., Breuer included the naive observation: "The element of sexuality was astonishingly undeveloped in her." But, as Freud related the untold story of Anna O. to his colleague Ernest Jones, sexuality was very much present between the doctor and the patient. The last time the two saw each other, Breuer was summoned to his patient's bedside, where she was in the throes of an hysterical (imagined) childbirth (pseudocyesis), and, yes, she felt her doctor was the father of that child. After seeing that she was cared for, Breuer fled the house and never saw her again.

Jones, who wrote the authorized biography of Freud after his death, told of a similar situation Freud encountered with a patient: "One day a patient suddenly flung her arms around his neck, an unexpected contretemps, fortunately remedied by the entrance of a servant. From then on he understood that the peculiar relationship so effective therapeutically had an erotic basis, whether concealed or overt; twenty years later he remarked that transference phenomena had always seemed to him an impregnable proof of the sexual origin of the neurosis. Unlike the scared Breuer on a similar occasion, Freud regarded the problem as one of general scientific interest."

Freud saw "transference" as one of the most important of his discoveries and a valuable tool in analysis. Transference is the process wherein the patient forgets the professional situation and sees the treating doctor as the object of love, anger, hate, or whatever emotion applies to the person being described. "Countertransference" is the matching emotion that occurs quite naturally in the doctor when he encounters such an outpouring of feeling from a patient. No one can be certified as a psychoanalyst without a thorough education in the benefits and possible dangers of such involvement between patient and doctor.

In his 1912 "Recommendations to Physicians Practicing Psychoanalysis," Freud said: "The doctor should be opaque to his patients and, like a mirror, should show them nothing but what is shown to him." But that was the ideal and one that Freud himself never lived up to — or he would never have discovered transference. His most famous exchange on this subject was with a former patient, Sandor Ferenczi, who would become a distinguished analyst in his own right and who was an early advocate of having therapists show physical comfort and affection toward patients. In a letter to the younger analyst, Freud wrote:

You have not made a secret of the fact that you kiss your patients and let them kiss you. . . . Now I am assuredly not one of those who from prudishness or from consideration of bourgeois convention would condemn little erotic gratifications of this kind. And I am also aware that in the time of the Nibelungs a kiss was a harmless greeting granted to every guest. I am further of the opinion that analysis is possible even in Soviet Russia where so far as the state is concerned there is full sexual freedom. But that does not alter the fact that we are not living in Russia and that with us a kiss signifies a certain erotic intimacy. We have hitherto in our technique held to the conclusion that patients are to be refused erotic gratifications. . . . Now picture what will be the result of publishing your technique. There is no revolutionary who is not driven out of the field by a still more radical one. A number of independent thinkers in matters of technique will say to themselves: why stop at a kiss? . . . the new adherent, however, will easily claim too much of this interest for himself, the younger of our colleagues will find it hard to stop at the point they originally intended and God the Father Ferenczi gazing at the lively scene he has created will perhaps say to himself: maybe after all I should have halted in my technique of motherly affection *before* the kiss. . . .

One of Zane Parzen's most distinguished instructors in the department of psychiatry at the University of Chicago Medical School was Heinz Kohut, a world authority — although somewhat controversial — in the study of narcissistic personality disorders in childhood, such as those of Evelyn Walker. (In psychiatric terminology, narcissism has to do with self-esteem and self-worth rather than the popular definition of a preoccupation with one's own image.) In his most famous work, *The Analysis of the Self,* Kohut warns that an analyst's reactions (or countertransferences) "in the analysis of narcissistic disorders are rooted in the analyst's own narcissism and, especially, in the area of his own, unresolved narcissistic disturbances. These phenomena do not, in essence, differ from those which occur in the analysand. . . ."

Another famous analyst in Chicago whose name Parzen would invoke in one of his more bizarre office incidents was Bruno Bettelheim. (After knocking the patient against a wall, Parzen had explained to her that he was following the teachings of Bettelheim. That strange assertion would eventually lead to his public disgrace.)

Bettelheim, in his book *Freud and Man's Soul,* criticizes the many students who passed through his courses in Chicago. He writes that the new generation of analysts have failed to understand that Freud began his studies of others by first writing about his own

arduous struggle to achieve ever greater self-awareness. . . . in a way, all his writings are gentle, persuasive, often brilliantly worded intimations that we, his readers, would benefit from a similar spiritual journey of self-discovery. . . . for nearly forty years, I have taught courses in psychoanalysis to American graduate students and residents in psychiatry. . . . Almost invariably, I have found that psychoanalytic concepts had become for these students a way of looking only at others, from a safe distance — nothing that had any bearing on them. They observed other people through the spectacles of abstraction, tried to comprehend them by means of intellectual concepts, never turning their gaze inward to the soul or their own unconsciousness. . . . Psychoanalysis as these students perceived it was a purely intellectual system — a clever, exciting game — rather than the acquisition of insights into oneself and one's own behavior which were potentially deeply upsetting. It was always *someone else's* unconscious they analyzed, hardly ever their own. They did not give enough thought to the fact that Freud, in order to create psychoanalysis and understand the workings of the unconscious, had to analyze his *own* dreams, understand his *own* slips of the tongue and the reasons *he* forgot things or made various other mistakes.

The life and career of Zane Parzen offer a clear illustration of Bettelheim's point. From all outward appearances, Parzen was a model student, teacher, analyst, citizen of the community. But he had never turned his gaze inward to the soul of his own conscience — a failing that would have tragic consequences for all those he was involved with.

This failing is dealt with bluntly by "Aaron Green," the fictional name of the psychoanalyst profiled by Janet Malcolm in her widely acclaimed book, *Psychoanalysis, The Impossible Profession.* Malcolm seems appalled that Green agrees with the treatment received by two doctors (one a former president of the American Psychoanalytic Association and the other a leading instructor at the New York Psychoanalytic Institute) who married former patients. The doctors were dealt with "ruthlessly" by the analytic community. They were stripped of all committee positions and both left New York in disgrace — although the scandal was kept quietly within the profession.

Malcolm's Dr. Green explains:

There have been many times when I've entertained fantasies of dating and marrying patients and having sexual intercourse with them. These are common countertransference reactions. Yes, I have had these fantasies. Every other analyst has had them, too, and they're not the issue. The issue is whether the analyst is in an emotionally desperate situation that prevents him from analyzing his reactions and causes him to do something dire. . . . Analysts who sleep with their patients are usually people in desperate psychological straits. It isn't the attractiveness and seductiveness of the patient; rather, it's that the analyst is in horrible shape in his own life and turns to the patient for help.

Green's general analysis closely fits the facts about Parzen as they eventually emerged. Parzen would become the embodiment of the old joke about the psychiatrist who is sicker than his patients. But there was nothing funny about what happened to Evelyn Walker, who had only sought help from Parzen.

In reality, our time together was strictly limited to the fifty-five minutes of my paid appointment. But Zane never made me feel like I had only so many minutes left. I could see the little red light go on on his desk when the next patient came into the outer waiting room, but otherwise there was no such thing as time when I was in Zane's arms. There were only the two of us, and nothing else mattered.

Week by week our lovemaking advanced into greater sexual intimacy. At first, Zane sometimes would lie on top of me, covering me, protecting me. He knew I needed that; I felt so safe with him over me. But usually, he would move around and under me so that I was on top. The first time he started to undo my blouse, I twisted back, crossed my hands over my chest. Shaking my head no, I said he shouldn't do that. I shouldn't be doing that; nice girls didn't let men feel their bodies that way. But he held me with those warm, loving eyes and asked, "Why not?" I couldn't think of any reason why not at that point.

Zane liked to feel my breasts. He said I had a nice body and especially nice breasts. I loved dressing up for him. I liked to dress up for Bruce, too, but with Zane — the way he would touch me and look at me with those penetrating eyes of his — he just made me feel pretty.

I had always liked colors, yet I guess I dressed fairly conservatively — I didn't want to draw too much attention to my body. Perhaps this was due to my being gawky and tall as a teenager, but more likely it was an overreaction to my mother's vanity. She would stand in front of a mirror for what seemed like hours at a time, obsessed with her own good looks and clothes. I had never thought of myself as pretty and I never liked to look in mirrors. Zane understood all of this and he was trying to help me overcome it.

"Do you know you are a very pretty woman?" Zane would ask me. I would shake my head shyly and say, no, I didn't know that.

Then he would tell me I had a good mind. Nobody had ever talked to me like that. But Zane was a professional. He knew my weaknesses and my strengths. And with this knowledge, his influence over me continued to grow, slowly but surely.

I think it was about a month after our first kiss that I was lying on top of Zane on the couch one day. I had unbuttoned his shirt and was kissing his chest. (This was as far as we had ever gone, although the last time we met, as we were lying there holding each other and rubbing our bodies together, he started to have an orgasm. He arched his back and acted as though he were losing control, about to scream or something. That was the first time I'd ever seen a man react like that.) But this day marked a turning point in our sex life on the couch. At first I had no idea what Zane was doing. He started pushing my head and shoulders down the length of his body. I kept kissing him as he eased my face farther and farther down. I had never done anything like this, so I did not know what to expect. He maneuvered my face even with his crotch. He took one hand and held the back of my head, and the other hand he used to put his penis in my mouth. Then he took both hands and moved my head down and up, down and up. I had never had oral sex with my husband. In my mind, that was something a man went to a prostitute or a mistress for. Wives didn't do things like that. But by this time, I was beyond any feelings of right and wrong when it came to Zane. If he wanted me to do it, then I would do it.

I no longer asked him if this were some form of therapy. At first, I had questioned him about it, but he would grow angry, as if the question were an insult. He would tell me that it was not therapy, that I was the only patient he had ever been involved with, the only woman he had been with other than his wife. But if we were no longer doctor and patient but two people in love, why was I still having to pay him? His answer was always the same: "You're paying for the time, not the caring."

From then on, the pattern was established. I would come in for my appointment. The office he had moved to — a glass-walled penthouse — was much more open and elegant than the old one. There was more sunlight for the flowers — African violets against one wall, potted roses outside on the wide, rooftop terrace. We would sometimes talk for a while, then we would end up lying on the couch. As I remember it, he would always have an orgasm, but only occasionally would he satisfy me — sometimes orally, but usually with his finger.

We never once met outside Zane's office — and it wasn't because I didn't want to. As with everything else, he never explained why we couldn't see each other freely elsewhere. He would never give a direct answer to anything I asked; he was a master at evading the question. But I was more and more blinded by love.

Chapter 2

Many long months would pass before Bruce Walker fully understood what his wife meant when she said her psychiatrist *really* liked her. By that time, Evelyn was so deeply involved with Parzen there was nothing anybody could do to turn her back to her husband and family. By that time, also, she became convinced that her doctor was right in saying her husband was cold and indifferent to her wants and needs.

Bruce's training as an engineer and his background as an engineer's son had produced a clear-cut technical outlook that made few allowances for the vagaries of human behavior. At work, the complicated problems he faced always had solutions. At home, solutions eluded him. His wife was not a computer or a car that just needed a tune-up. She didn't seem to be getting any better, and there didn't seem to be anything he could do about it. Even if he didn't always show it, Bruce was concerned about Evelyn, especially in the early days of her involvement with Parzen.

That he was a man who didn't always know how to express his feelings did not mean that he didn't have such feelings. That he seemed outwardly cold didn't mean there wasn't a great deal of warmth and caring inside him. Evelyn would complain about the lack of physical affection from Bruce, but she never once felt that he did not love her. It was, after all, Bruce's concern for her that had led her to a psychiatrist in the first place. In light of the way things developed, there is a touching note attached to an early letter Bruce wrote to Parzen about insurance coverage for Evelyn: "Please take good care of Evelyn. Despite the feelings she may express, I really *do* love her very much."

Most people who knew Bruce and Evelyn Walker up to this time would have been amazed to learn that there were any serious problems in their lives. They seemed the picture-perfect fulfillment of the American dream. Everything was beautiful and successful in their lives — children, house, pool, yard, career, and social life. They were attractive, upwardly mobile suburbanites who seemed securely headed for the top.

Sometimes at parties, Bruce would be so happy and content, so full of himself, that he'd pose proudly beside Evelyn and swear he was going to become "president" of California and she was going to be First Lady. By anybody's definition, he was a solid, stable man. Step by methodical step, it seemed, he had achieved everything he had set out to do. He was born September 24, 1936, in North Attleboro, Massachusetts. His father was a native of Canada, an electronics engineer who had settled into a big, comfortable house in a small town southwest of Boston. Bruce's parents continued to live in Massachusetts until his father's retirement, when they moved to San Diego.

Evelyn always felt Bruce's father was a far more intelligent and creative man than the bare facts of his life indicated. But he had made his choices early in life and he stuck by them — including a rigid faith in an unusually narrow brand of evangelical Christianity. Even as a grown man, Bruce Walker did not smoke or drink in front of his father. Yet, for many years, the elder Walker drove a bright red Lincoln convertible. The car contrasted with the rest of his life; perhaps it was an expression of the livelier spirit hidden beneath the drab exterior.

While he showed no adult interest in his father's religious bent, Bruce did follow him into the field of engineering. He earned a B.S. degree at MIT and then an M.S. in engineering at UCLA. Bruce's record as a student was good enough to give him his choice of jobs when he finished school. This was an extraordinary moment in history for a bright young engineer to be stepping into the job market. The leaders in American business and government were caught up in a post-Sputnik panic. The Russians had launched the first space satellite and the Americans were determined to catch up at all costs. Bruce Walker was situated in one of the most lucrative and glamorous positions a man could hold at that time and place in American history. He was not one of the astronauts, but he was the next best thing.

He worked with and for them at the Convair Astronautics plant in San Diego, designing the rockets and vehicles that would carry the first Americans into outer space.

The work at Convair involved computers, placing Bruce Walker in yet another pioneering field of technology, one that soon would be affecting nearly every area of American life. As the rapidly developing computer science business progressed, Bruce moved with it. Later in his career he worked for a corporation called Systems, Science and Software, which was later bought out by the larger electronics and aerospace conglomerate, TRW. By the late 1970s, San Diego was second only to the famed "Silicon Valley" farther north in the number of computer-based corporations. By 1980, Walker was an executive with Logicon, in charge of a fifty-person team that was developing a system for the Federal Aviation Administration to provide automated weather and other service information to pilots.

It was at Convair that Bruce met his future wife, Evelyn Barbara Gordon. She had gone to work there in 1958, not long after finishing high school. She was a glorified clerk, doing typing and filing and going for coffee. Although she was beginning to do some drafting, she scoffs at the idea that she got the job because of her ability as an artist. "Are you kidding?" she laughs. She got the job for one reason only: her father — himself an engineer at Convair — had gotten it for her.

Bruce fit nearly every woman's idea of an ideal husband. He was clearly headed for the upper echelons of one of the highest-paying and most important fields in America. In addition, he looked like one of the Kennedys, and with his bright, blue eyes, he was even more handsome than most of the astronauts. Evelyn herself was tall, but Bruce was much taller, standing well over six feet, with a solid athletic build. In the early 1960s, he wore his light brown hair in a short, military crew cut, which only added to his youthful look. Later, changing with the styles, he would let his hair grow into longer curls and would grow a moustache, as well.

As a hard-working student, Bruce had had little leisure time. He had not indulged in any kind of social activism or in any sort of raucous partying. The decade of his high school and college years was that of the laid-back 1950s, the calm before the storm of the next decade. Bruce was a Republican, but not out of any deep-felt philosophical commitment. As with his father, the free spirit under the studious exterior expressed itself in the car he drove. Bruce owned a succession of fine sports cars. When Evelyn first started dating him, he was driving a classic square-cut MG convertible. By the time of their honeymoon, his Porsche — long on order and very costly at that time — had finally arrived.

Evelyn and Bruce had seen each other in the hallways at the office and even at parties for several months before they met. Theirs was no mad, passionate love-at-first-sight. But, once they started dating, there were no other romantic interests in either of their lives. The little differences that would cause so much trouble between them in later years only added spark and interest to their first months and years together. Bruce had never dated a Jewish woman before, and Evelyn had no idea what it was like to come out of the old puritanical New England experience.

Evelyn had a lively artistic eye, which Bruce was lacking and could appreciate in her. He had furnished a small two-story apartment in a complex not far from where Evelyn's parents lived on Point Loma. The furnishings were nice and sturdy, but everything was in inconspicuous shades of brown and beige. Evelyn planned bold flashes of color — throw pillows and spreads — as she began to think of his place as theirs.

She remembers no dramatic moment when they decided to get married; it was just assumed that they would, since they seemed to get along so well and spent all their free time together. They were married July 14, 1961, in Las Vegas. Evelyn had a terror of needles, and Nevada was one place she knew where a blood test was not required for a marriage license. A few of their family members were happy to have an excuse to go to Las Vegas, and since neither of them had strong religious ties, they saw no reason why they shouldn't be married by a justice of the peace there. Their honeymoon started right then and there. After taking in the casinos and the shows of Las Vegas, they drove the new Porsche north along the back roads to Yosemite National Park, where they spent a few days before going on to San Francisco.

Bruce liked to drive his new car fast, but once he got to a place, he loved nothing better than to park and just walk around as if they had all the time in the world. This delighted Evelyn, who had disliked the rushed trips that were her parents' idea of a vacation. In San Francisco, they went shopping in the galleries and bought their first oil painting together. It was an abstract city scene that they kept throughout their marriage. Taking the scenic coastal road south toward Los Angeles, they stopped at San Simeon, William Randolph Hearst's castle. They were about midway through the house tour when Evelyn became faint in the stale, hot air. She asked Bruce to help her, to take her outside. "What!" he exclaimed, "and miss the tour?" A guard helped her out to a resting place and got her a Coke. They would laugh about that line from then on, but when Evelyn related this story to her lover-psychiatrist Zane Parzen, he seized on it as historic evidence that her husband really didn't care for her.

After a few days in Los Angeles, they returned to their place in San Diego and went back to work at Convair. They worked in different departments and Evelyn didn't know enough about what Bruce was doing to ask questions, but at home they shared every project. They hung their first painting as if it were a treasure from the Louvre. And Bruce came to appreciate every splash of color Evelyn added to his bachelor quarters.

Bruce traveled a great deal while he was working with the space program, and the day Evelyn found out she was pregnant, he was at Cape Canaveral. She was so excited she turned to a total stranger in the elevator and announced: "I'm pregnant." Later that night she waited for Bruce to come home. She would always remember that it was raining heavily. She had the shades up and the curtains pulled back and the bed next to the window so she could lie back and enjoy the rainfall, something unusual in San Diego.

When Evelyn was 7½ months pregnant, she and Bruce were driving to a friend's house for dinner one night when a man in a big Ford sedan smashed into the front of their Porsche. Evelyn was not hurt, but after an examination, her doctor said it was time she stopped working. With time on her hands, she made an artistic showcase out of the baby's room. She designed all kinds of brightly colored wall hangings, stuffed animals, quilts, and coverlets. Her enterprise was so strikingly successful that friends who saw her work would beg her to create things for them to give as gifts. Many years later, this would grow into a lucrative sideline for her — so much so that Bruce would jokingly say she was putting them in a higher income bracket.

The baby was born February 9, 1962, and named, by his father, Carl Anson Walker. Evelyn had wanted to name the baby Aaron or Shepherd — a premonition, she would later think, that those names would have great significance in her life. But Bruce's choice prevailed.

As a young mother, Evelyn had days when she was so utterly content she thought she was the luckiest woman in the world. She had Bruce for a husband and Carl for a son. After the first two weeks, Carl slept all night. He was such a good baby that Evelyn couldn't believe he was hers. She fed him by bottle because she had seen too many of her friends breast-feed their babies and end up with colicky, sickly children. Also, she wanted to know exactly how much food her child was getting.

The many psychiatrists who saw Evelyn later in her life would all agree that these were Evelyn's happiest years. She was totally fulfilled in the most basic ways. She was busy at all times, she was needed, and she was loved. She didn't hesitate to hire a sitter when she and Bruce wanted to go out, but she also loved to take the baby wherever she went. He had a poochy kind of face like his dad, she thought, but unlike his dad, he would let his mother caress and pinch his cheeks, and they would laugh together as if they were both babies.

Carl's baby book reflects his parents' delight with every little gift he received and each new movement he made. Many of the notations also reflect his father's involvement with the space program and his love of cars. Under "My Loot," Evelyn has listed: "clown doll, stuffed dog, monkey, plastic clown doll, octopus dolly, yellow sweater, blue sweater, candy-striped sunsuit, crib and mattress, cuddle chair, horsey wagon." Under "The World Around Me," his parents have written that when Carl was born the President was John F. Kennedy, California's governor was Pat Brown, and the mayor of San Diego was James Dale. "History-Making News of the Day" was obviously supplied by the father: "Shepard, first in space—Glenn, first to orbit (three times around earth), USA's first." "New Inventions and Gadgets of My Era": First communications satellite launched, first U.S. lunar impact, optical maser. . . . "The Hottest Cars on the Road": Jaguar XKE [With his growing family, Bruce would have to trade in the Porsche for a more practical four-door Jaguar sedan]. "The Fastest Plane in the Sky": North American X15. "The Foremost Entertainers in My Generation": Frank Sinatra, Elizabeth Taylor, Leonard Bernstein. "The Brains Behind the Ideas": Wernher von Braun, James Van Allen, Jonas Salk.

Little Carl had "quite a bit of blond hair" in the first month. At three months, he laughed for the first time; at six months, he was rocking on his hands and knees; and he crawled at seven months. . . .

When he was a year old, Carl went with Bruce and Evelyn on a long vacation to Lake Tahoe. Babysitters were included in the price of the cottage they rented, and it seemed as though they were on a second honeymoon — going to shows and staying out late. But all was not bliss in the Walkers' marriage. The main problem, as Evelyn saw it, was that Bruce traveled too much. She didn't like being alone, especially with a new baby. But there was a deeper, more serious problem that tore at the very heart of their marriage.

The first time Evelyn and Bruce tried to have sex after Carl was born, Evelyn was in such pain that she asked Bruce to stop. It was the first time she had ever used a diaphragm, so she thought it might not be inserted right. She went into the bathroom and checked, and everything seemed all right. She went back to bed, and again Bruce tried to enter her. This time he pushed so hard she began to cry. But he wouldn't stop. She began to push at him and beg him to stop. Finally he did pull out of her. She saw blood on herself and even more on the sheet, which seemed to confirm that there was something wrong.

The next night, Bruce wanted to make love again, but again Evelyn was in such pain she couldn't stand it. Bruce yelled at her for "being a baby." Evelyn cried that she couldn't help it. Bruce said it did not make sense. Evelyn didn't know why — all she knew was that she felt like she was being torn apart.

In the next few days and nights, Bruce continued to try to have sex with Evelyn. If anything, the pain became worse and the problem hung like a dark cloud over their marriage. For the first time, Evelyn began to dread the evenings, because she knew Bruce would want to have sex again. Then one afternoon Bruce came home from work and said he had asked one of his friends if he had ever had such an experience with his wife. The man laughed about what Bruce told him. He said that his wife was so anxious to make love they did it in the hospital the day after she had the baby. This convinced Bruce that Evelyn was carrying on — there was no real reason why she should be having such pain. Evelyn could barely stop crying over this. It seemed as if her marriage was ruined, her life over at the age of twenty-two.

In desperation, she called their family doctor and tried to explain the problem to him. He sensed what was wrong immediately and asked her to come in that afternoon and to be sure to bring Bruce with her. Evelyn was still very sore, but the doctor examined her carefully and said there was nothing physically wrong with her. The stitches from childbirth had healed, but she was still very tender, that was all. Perhaps, Bruce had been too forceful with her. The doctor explained — more to Bruce than to Evelyn — that there was nothing wrong with Evelyn. He said she had had a great many stitches and it was only natural that she would have some pain until the muscles had fully healed. He told Bruce that he had to be more gentle and more patient. He also said Bruce's friend must have a great imagination and a very shaky ego.

At the doctor's suggestion, Evelyn and Bruce went away for the weekend to relax and enjoy being by themselves. From then on, Bruce was more careful with Evelyn, and they would continue to have sex, of course, but she never overcame her fear that it would hurt when he first entered her. She was never able to forget the way he yelled at her and called her a baby and continued to push himself into her while she was crying in pain.

Years later, the first time she had intercourse with Zane Parzen, she couldn't help but notice that with him there was no fear at all.

Parzen no doubt knew exactly what Evelyn was describing when she told him about the initial pain she felt during intercourse with Bruce. It was a fairly common condition known as dysfaurenia, though this term was never used, nor was the condition properly explained to Evelyn. In fact, she and Bruce both had been right. She was, indeed, experiencing pain; and he was right that the source was not biological. Dysfaurenia arises when a person is subconsciously resisting her mate. For whatever reasons, the natural lubricants that should form with arousal and ease the process of intercourse do not form, and the resulting dry intercourse can be very painful. Although Evelyn resented Bruce's frequent absences and his failure to provide the physical affection she needed, she was not capable of rejecting him on any conscious level. But her body resisted him on a more basic level.

Of course, Evelyn was not aware of this. As she saw it, nothing was wrong with Bruce or with their marriage — if there were problems, they were all hers. The Walkers were both young and naive, and going to a marriage counselor was the farthest thing from their minds. In those first minutes Parzen saw them together in his office, he must have sensed that there was friction between them. Furthermore, there can be no question that he knew how to deal with dysfaurenia from his extensive training. (In fact, one of his colleagues had made a joke about dysfaurenia in his mock history of Parzen's class at the University of Chicago Medical School.) But saving the Walkers' marriage was the last thing on Zane Parzen's mind when he began treating Evelyn.

By Carl's third Christmas, there was a new baby in the Walker household. Michael David was born September 26, 1964. If anything, Michael's baby book reflects an even happier childhood than Carl had. It was all designed by Evelyn, with elaborate and colorful lettering on each page. But from the beginning, the two boys had strikingly different personalities. Michael was as rambunctious and restless as Carl had been calm and quiet. What was most troubling to his parents was that Michael would have horrible nightmares when he was too young to understand what was happening or to explain why he was so scared. He would wake up in the night, leap out of his bed, and run down the stairs, screaming and crying, and stand there stamping his feet. He would never say anything; his parents could never get him to explain what frightened him so in his sleep. Evelyn talked with the pediatrician about this, but she never considered taking him to a child psychiatrist.

All this was after the family had moved into a big, old house on the grounds of an old estate in Riverside, fifty-eight miles east of Los Angeles and 108 miles north of San Diego. When they moved to Riverside in early 1965, the oldest boy had just turned three and the youngest was not yet one. That winter, Evelyn remembers, it seemed like it rained every single day. And to make matters worse, Bruce had a new job that kept him out of town even more than when they lived in San Diego. It seems possible that young Michael was only responding to his mother's fears and anxieties, which had become very intense after several months in Riverside.

As long as she was married to Bruce, Evelyn would have a recurring dream when he was away from home for any length of time. In the dream, Bruce has left town, saying he will call and let her know where he is staying. He does call and says, "I want you to come and be with me." Evelyn goes to his hotel, goes up in the elevator, and finds herself in a long, stark-white corridor. She starts looking for Bruce's room number, but she finds that none of the doors have numbers on them.

In a panic, she starts walking down the endless corridor, looking at blank doors, searching for a number that isn't there. As she walks, she hears people laughing. The laughter gets louder and louder — until she wakes herself up, screaming in confusion and terror.

Evelyn was particularly frightened in that strange house in Riverside. Nobody had told them when they moved there why such a fine house had sat empty for many years. Evelyn found out that it was because the previous tenant had killed himself there. Once, when she was in the shower, Evelyn looked out the window and saw a man staring at her. She stood frozen with terror, then wrapped herself in a towel and ran for Bruce. He went outside but could not find anybody or see any tracks beneath the window. The police also came and searched, but they found no trace of the peeping Tom. But from that moment on, Evelyn would look up and see those eyes, that face, staring at her as she moved about her daily chores.

When Bruce was away, she tried to develop outside interests to keep herself from being tied to the house and children. She was in charge of acquisitions at the local art gallery and was very proud of the exhibitions she staged. One artist she met there did a fine portrait of the two boys that would become one of Evelyn's prized possessions. But she still was very unhappy in Riverside, and the miserable weather only made her feel worse inside.

After a thorough physical examination showed that there was no biological explanation for her headaches and depressions, her family doctor suggested she see a psychologist. The first psychologist met with a quick rebuke from Evelyn. He was probably only trying to explain to her in simple terms the process of transference, but what he said and what Evelyn heard was: "It is quite natural that you may fall in love with me." Evelyn was outraged. She snapped, "You should see my husband," and stormed out of his office.

Bruce and Evelyn talked a great deal about her headaches, which seemed to be getting worse and worse. Finally, a friend recommended an older psychiatrist who had offices in an old house near them in Riverside. His name was Philip Lawler. Much later, when Evelyn's psychiatrist and lawyers tried to locate Lawler and his records, they could not find him. However, the 1977 biographical directory of the American Psychiatric Association lists a Philip Wendell Lawler, then living in Pismo Beach, California, and his biography fits everything Evelyn remembered about the doctor in Riverside. He was born January 16, 1903, in Los Angeles and got his M.D. at Stanford University in 1931. He went into psychiatry much later and did his psychiatric residency at the state hospitals in Warren, Pennsylvania, from 1957 through 1959, after which he returned to California and resumed private practice in psychiatry.

Evelyn remembers mainly that the old doctor had big, raw red splotches of acne on his hands, which he was scratching constantly. But she also remembers that he was a gentle, kind human being who seemed genuinely concerned about her and wanted to help her. He didn't confuse her with the technical language of the profession; he just listened and let her tell what was bothering her — at least what she thought was bothering her. And then they discussed calmly what it might mean. At that time, Evelyn felt her parents possibly were the cause of her problems. She was deathly afraid of her mother, and was nearly hysterical after a telephone call or visit from her mother. Even as an adult, Evelyn would feel belittled by her mother — as if she were still a child.

What Lawler told Evelyn was the most simple, sensible observation — but it was one that Evelyn had never been able to arrive at on her own. Lawler told Evelyn that she shouldn't feel guilty about not liking her mother. He explained that her mother probably didn't really dislike her. Perhaps her mother had problems of her own that she couldn't deal with, so she was taking them out on Evelyn. Above all, Evelyn shouldn't be upset that all this made her nervous and angry — her response was only natural. Anybody in her shoes would be upset.

Evelyn liked talking with Lawler and she felt these talks did help her during this time. But neither she nor Bruce was particularly happy in Riverside, so they moved back to San Diego on December 12, 1966.

The Walkers were hardly alone in looking for health and happiness in the ideal climate of San Diego. They were in the vanguard of a massive influx of new residents who would make this small, obscure Navy and Marine port town the eighth most populous city in America. It has many of the advantages of a small town and few of the disadvantages of a major city. If the more sophisticated cities of Los Angeles and San Francisco exist in a "bicoastal" axis with New York, San Diego has a more unpretentious connection with the Midwest. Most of the older and more prominent families — such as the newspaper owners Scripps and Copley — came from Detroit, Chicago, Cleveland, Kansas, and Missouri.

In a very small space, the weather of Arizona is combined with the picturesque scenery of Monterey, Hawaii, and Palm Springs. It's rarely too cold for the beach — and if it is, the deserts and mountain ski resorts are only a short drive away. "ANOTHER HO-HUM DAY IN PARADISE" is the most popular slogan on local T-shirts; "THERE IS NO LIFE EAST OF I-5" is another.

In their tenacious clinging to the small-town mood, San Diegans seem to be trying to hold on to the innocence they left in Nebraska. After one early financial empire in San Diego collapsed in the 1970s, the *Wall Street Journal* called San Diego "the flim-flam capital of America." A deputy district attorney says, "It's like an overgrown midwestern town." Another lawyer who was formerly head of the district attorney's fraud investigations unit says, "I don't know if it's the environment or the beauty or the little bit of laid-back. The people in San Diego are a little more gullible. It's a safe city; they're kind of lulled into feeling that everything goes right — there's an automatic trust. . . ."

So great has been the gullibility problem that in 1985, the San Diego Crime Commission would begin staging seminars to educate the people about scams and con artists. At one of these, psychiatrist Thomas N. Rusk said, "The con artist and the con victims are mirror images of one another. . . . The person being conned is insecure about himself. He walks down the street and hears a rumor about a person who can make him rich. The con man offers a dream, but you don't want to look at it too closely. If you do, the dream may blow up." The con artist, on the other hand, Rusk explained, "can't permit himself to legitimately succeed" because of "tremendous self-hatred."

Where money is involved, of course, there are specific laws to protect the investors being duped. But where the scams involve mental health — the spirit and soul — there seems to be little the law can do to protect the naive and innocent. A major industry in California has been built on the quick-and-easy answers of pop psychologists. During especially low points in their lives in the coming years, Bruce and Evelyn Walker would both seek help in this direction. Bruce would be among the 500,000 going through the "est" training of Werner Erhard, and Evelyn would briefly be among the thousands seeking prosperity through God and a female evangelist named Terry

Cole Whittaker. But in the beginning, they would put their faith in legitimate psychiatry.

The Walkers moved from the big house in Riverside to a little yellow frame cottage at the edge of La Jolla. Although it is within the city limits of San Diego, La Jolla has a separate postmark and a decidedly separate identity. So great is the snob appeal of this Palm Beach West that residents for many miles around claim it, and many people drive fifteen or twenty miles to use post office boxes there. Until very recent times, La Jolla was a little village of fishermen, artists, and some wealthy residents. The rough waters had carved weird caves and coves into the high sandstone cliffs and the ocean was visible from nearly every office and house in town. By the 1980s, all that had changed; the village had been transformed into a small town complete with walls of glass and steel and molded concrete. The long-time manager of the old Valencia Hotel walked the length of the town, "looking for something I know." And in 1984, a contractor was hired to build a ten-story building after tearing down the three-story structure he'd built when he first came to town five years earlier.

But La Jolla still had the ambience of a village when the Walkers arrived there in 1966. On sunny days, Evelyn would take the boys down to the little, protected family beach. And she liked being close to the fancy shops and art galleries in the village itself. She was happy in their cozy cottage, but it was only a temporary home. Before their year's lease was up, their new house was finished at the edge of Clairemont Mesa, southwest of La Jolla. From the front it looked like an ordinary tract house in any modern suburb in America. There were only narrow walkways between it and the houses on either side. But the real value of the house lay in the back. A tiny little backyard went right up to the edge of a cedar wood fence, which was all that separated the yard from a sheer drop of several hundred feet at the western edge of the mesa. Below was Pacific Beach and Mission Bay, and beyond was a clear blue horizon of ocean and sky.

In the yard, Bruce built a small lava-rock pool in the style of Japanese gardens. Up the street was a house with an interesting lat-ticework enclosure, which Evelyn was interested in copying. She walked up there one day and began talking with her neighbor. Inside the woman's house, Evelyn quickly forgot about the lattice and asked about the unusual wall hangings of fabric and other materials. She was instantly drawn to the work. She asked the woman if she gave lessons, and the woman said she would be happy to do so. From then on, Evelyn's artwork took a radical turn to this kind of abstract expression in weaving. Evelyn took great pride in decorating Bruce's office. In fact, his office often looked like a gallery of her work. Once, he sold a piece right off the wall.

At home, you would never have known there was any trouble in the marital bed. In fact, the bed seemed to be the central focus of the entire house. Evelyn had designed a dramatic yellow canopy that went up to the ceiling from behind the bed and then draped down and over.

The Walkers liked their house with a view, but after a few years they decided they needed more room inside and outside. They found the ideal place under construction in a new development north of La Jolla, in University City, which was just being laid out around desert canyons where locals still hunted rattlesnakes, near the new campus of the University of California at San Diego. Along with their next-door neighbors, a psychiatrist named Gary Shepherd and his family, they were the first residents in this huge development, which in ten years would become a small city. Bruce paid $53,000 for the house and lot; he sold it less than ten years later for many times that amount. By the 1980s, this former desert wasteland would be called "the golden triangle" — a center for medical, scientific, and computer-based technological research and development.

Evelyn took an even more active role in the construction and design of the new house. By comparison, it was huge, and built on three different levels, with a deck in back overlooking a large, kidney-shaped swimming pool. Inside, Evelyn decorated in such a lavish manner that all of the neighbors' interiors looked ordinary by comparison. She put a billboard-sized Peter Max design across one wall, and the entrance was lettered DOOR in huge box letters. In the living room were several of her own pieces of pottery, drawings, and wall hangings. But, again, her main effort went into the marital bed. It was a king-size bed, and Evelyn ordered hand-turned high, wooden posters. She and Bruce built a six-foot-high headboard and covered it in an intricate, elegant design of suede, fabric, and imitation fur.

Outside, landscaping was needed in front and up the hillside in back. Evelyn exhausted herself almost daily, creating a formal arrangement of rocks and shrubs in front. In the back, she laid out a vegetable garden. One year, she grew enough beets to preserve several quart jars, and enough zucchini to supply half the neighborhood.

The two boys, Carl and Michael, were both in school, and they remember those first months in the new house as a busy, happy time. Bruce went along with Carl to meetings of the Indian Guides and Evelyn was den mother to Michael's Cub Scouts. One summer they borrowed Bruce's father's van and went on a camping trip along the rivers in the national forests north of San Francisco.

Their closest neighbors were Gary and Bettie Shepherd. The two couples first met one day while they were inspecting the lots where their houses would be built. Despite their different backgrounds and careers, the four of them seemed to like each other from the start.

By the beginning of their second year (1974) in the new house, Evelyn's headaches and depressions had returned — and they seemed to be lasting longer. It had been seven years since Evelyn had last felt the need to seek help from a psychiatrist. Her mind wandered back to those days when she had taken her problems to the psychiatrist in Riverside. She had the usual lay person's embarrassment about such problems and although she knew Gary Shepherd was a psychiatrist, she was reluctant even to mention to Gary that she had problems. She approached the subject warily, at first in casual conversations with Bettie Shepherd. Evelyn was amazed to find that not only had Bettie been trained as a psychiatric nurse, she also admitted to having problems of her own, which had caused her to begin intensive, classic, five-day-a-week psychoanalysis. Evelyn had never known anybody who talked about therapy, much less as easily and openly as Bettie Shepherd did.

In fact, Bettie Shepherd was in therapy with Sanford Izner, a teacher of her husband's at the San Diego Psychoanalytic Institute (although she and he had never met before her first day in his office). Bettie never told Evelyn who her doctor was, nor did she describe to Evelyn what her sessions with Izner were like. But Bettie remembers being so nervous during her first hour with Izner that she sat on her hands to keep the doctor from noticing that they were trembling. He told her she was obviously "very depressed." For some reason, those words released a flood of tears — and she didn't have to worry about being nervous in front of the doctor any more.

Bettie Shepherd describes herself as "a fairly classic analytic case, with the kind of problems for which analysis was developed." Her problems had not been totally debilitating, but they had been causing her a great deal of pain and unhappiness. She went to Izner five days a week for four and a half years. She lay on the couch and talked; the doctor sat behind and listened. She never knew if he took notes; sometimes he worked a crossword puzzle.

With only an occasional comment or observation, Izner allowed her to steer her own course. He never asked for any kind of detailed history or family background; he let her free-associate with whatever she wanted to tell him. The value of that, Bettie felt, was that the doctor didn't have to do so much "winnowing" — just by the way the patient tells something, he knows what is "weighted" and what is not important.

There was no problem of any kind of erotic involvement with her doctor — at least partly because Bettie brought to these sessions her own background in the profession and her own code of doctor-patient decorum. But it was an intense relationship all the same, and not one to be broken off casually. When he felt it was the proper time, the doctor began scheduling fewer and fewer sessions, "weaning" the patient over a period of months.

Today, Bettie Shepherd no longer has the periods of depression and anxiety, but she cannot explain just how or why analysis helped her overcome them. "I had expected him to take it out and tag each thing and put it back together. But, it's much more a gut-level experience."

Although at the time she met Evelyn, Bettie Shepherd had not worked as a nurse in several years, she was the same person who had been drawn as a young woman to the specialized training of a psychiatric nurse. That specialty was where she was most comfortable, where she felt she could do the most good. "It utilized the traits I have. I'm not very talkative, but I am a good listener. When you are psychologically minded you tend to look for those kinds of intangible causes — as opposed to medicinal causes and cures. It's being able to say, 'It seems to me.'" The psychiatric nurse has to be constantly aware of what she is doing and saying, because an important part of her job is to serve as a "healthy guide" to the disturbed patients. "I learned not to say 'good morning,' because you would get into a confrontation over whether it was really good or not. You need to be honest and direct with the patients."

In the coming months, Bettie Shepherd's psychiatric background would be put to the test as she saw at close range that Evelyn Walker's mental condition became worse and worse and worse. And in the troubled years that would follow in Evelyn Walker's life, Evelyn would find in Bettie Shepherd not just a good neighbor but also a patient nurse and a loyal friend.

After their long talk that day, Evelyn went home feeling better about the prospect of going back to a psychiatrist. She felt that the doctor in Riverside had helped her and now she was having similar problems; maybe another doctor could help her overcome these difficulties. She and Bruce discussed it and came to the conclusion that she should begin seeing a psychiatrist again. Since they didn't know anyone appropriate, they asked Gary Shepherd if they could have a serious talk with him. During their discussion, Shepherd explained that because of their friendship it would not be proper for him to treat Evelyn. But he asked them to give him some time to think about it, and he would come up with a list of two or three doctors who would be especially well suited to treat what seemed to be Evelyn's problems. By this time, Shepherd knew about her childhood and about her problems with her mother. Although he did not have the necessary details to make a firm diagnosis, he felt that Evelyn's adult problems stemmed from some kind of narcissistic injury sustained as a child. Shepherd had been around her enough to know that while Evelyn sometimes had the aggressive and active personality to go with her statuesque appearance, she also had a very insecure side that seemed to stem from some traumatic experience in her past.

The next day, Shepherd gave Evelyn a typed list of three names — Robert Nemiroff, Alvin Robbins, and Zane Parzen — all three were doctors with education and training in the areas of narcissistic injuries to children.

Evelyn's eyes scanned the list and stopped on *Zane Parzen*. She liked the sound of it. She called and made an appointment for her and Bruce to go in for a preliminary interview with Parzen.

Much later, when Evelyn's problems had become so severe and seemed so hopeless, Bruce would appear to be a man who simply wanted out of a dreadful marriage. But in the beginning, he was as concerned and caring as he knew how to be.

Less than a month after Evelyn's first kiss with Parzen on the couch, Bruce proposed that they take a vacation in Mexico City and Acapulco. It would do them both good to get away, and they could leave the children with his mother. Neither of them had ever been in Mexico City, so maybe they could get a new start in a new place.

Evelyn was only slightly preoccupied with Parzen at this time, so she began making preparations for the trip with Bruce uppermost in her mind. She made him an elaborately embroidered linen shirt, and in March of 1975 they flew off quite happily with great expectations for their time alone.

They took snapshots of the major scenic attractions in Mexico City and Bruce climbed to the top of the Pyramid of the Sun at Teotihuacán. In the spectacular National Museum of Anthropology, Evelyn was entranced by the art objects of the ancient Aztecs. Much later, in San Diego, she bought an elegant coffee-table book about the museum's collections.

It was a pleasant time, all in all; Bruce and Evelyn were happier than they had been for many months. But even in Mexico, Evelyn felt there was something missing—something she was beginning to feel only Zane could give her. They continued on to Acapulco and had a good laugh when a waiter at one restaurant was wearing a shirt almost identical to the one Evelyn had made for Bruce.

Back home in San Diego, they resumed the routine of their lives—and Evelyn went back to the weekly visits to her psychiatrist's couch. The trip to Mexico took on greater meaning for Evelyn later that year when Parzen also took a trip to Mexico. After his return, they spent many hours talking about the things they both had seen there. As it turned out, the picture book that Evelyn bought in San Diego was not a souvenir of her second honeymoon with her husband, but rather a Christmas present for her lover.

Chapter 3
I know that anyone reading this will naturally wonder why I kept going back to Zane when — on reflection, at least — it seems so clear that our relationship was never going to be what I wanted it to be. I did not understand what was going on then, so I cannot presume to understand fully and explain it now. However, there are some explanations. To begin with, I was confused, in need of help, or I wouldn't have been seeing a psychiatrist. I did not know where I was weak and vulnerable, but Zane certainly did.

The events described here in paragraphs and pages actually took place over several weeks and months. I had been seeing Zane for six months before I ever broke down in front of him. It was another two weeks before we held each other the first time; and it was another month after that before we had any kind of sexual contact.

And, in fact, I did question everything that was going on as it was happening. And, always, Zane was reassuring. No, he would say, this was not some form of therapy. I was special; I was the first and only woman he had been involved with besides his wife; I was not the kind of person a man just had an affair with. Meanwhile, I could never get any straight answers to my questions about where all of this was leading or why we never could see each other outside his office.

This should have been warning enough, I know that now, but I was becoming so dependent on Zane that I could no longer see things clearly. And as I became more and more in need of him and his affection, I was also becoming more and more dependent on drugs. In the first weeks of treatment, he would prescribe only a small number of pills of this or that medication until we could see how I responded to it. However, as we became emotionally involved, the pill-taking also got out of hand. The prescriptions overlapped, and then he would just tell me to help myself to all those he had in a cabinet in his office. I took the pills because Zane told me to, and then I simply needed them in order to get through the day. It got so I didn't know the names of any of them, much less what they were for. Along with this were any number of physical problems — my head, my stomach, my back, my chest, my digestive tract. The doctors I was seeing for those physical ailments were prescribing still other drugs for me. I was eventually taking the whole spectrum of the rainbow — forty to sixty tablets a day — and sometimes I didn't even know how many I had taken.

But the most explicit warning I received — and today I wish I could have heeded that warning then — came one day when I was sitting in the waiting room while Zane finished with the previous patient. As I waited for Zane to come out of his office, suddenly I heard very frightening noises from inside. It was like a tornado coming out of a clear sky on a quiet day. There was complete silence, and then I could hear the awful, terrifying sounds of a woman screaming and crying hysterically. I never knew, of course, what had happened, but it sounded like someone stumbling about in confusion — dropping her purse, her keys, crying and wailing all the while. Finally, doors were opened and closed.

It sounded as though someone needed help, so I opened the outer door just in time to see a thin blonde woman running down the hall, disappearing around the corner toward the elevators. I sat down again, and soon Zane opened the inner door and told me to come in. He didn't look the least bit flustered. I asked him what had happened. He said it was nothing. He asked me if the noises had frightened me. I told him they had. "Don't you think you should go after her and be sure she's all right?" I asked him. I was so shaken by what I had heard I went to the patient's chair instead of the couch. "How do you know she's going to be okay?" I asked. Something in the woman's screams made me think she was desperate. "Would she try to hurt herself?" I asked him. No, Zane assured me, the woman was all right, I shouldn't worry.

"Do you know where she's going right now?" he asked me. And of course I didn't, so he answered his own question. "To get retread tires for her car. That is how serious her suicide threats are." But, he said, if it would make me feel better, he would promise to give the patient a call later to be sure she was okay. Then he told me more about the woman. He gave me her first name — which for some reason stuck in my memory. She and her predicament would come back to me much later at a turning point in my life.

Zane also said that the woman had been a patient of his in Chicago. When he moved to California, she had followed him. I thought it was a little strange for a patient to make such a drastic move for a doctor, but it never entered my head that Zane was involved with her in the same way he was with me.

By the summer of 1975, I was totally involved with Zane. Our sexual relationship had gone from light caresses and hugs to more intimate fondling and petting on the couch. (We would not actually have intercourse until we had been intimate with each other for more than eighteen months.) We always lay on the couch and held each other; when Zane wanted it, I would satisfy him with oral sex. Sometimes, Zane would arouse me with intense sexual teasing. He would have his orgasm, but would stop before I was satisfied. I would leave the office feeling shaken and frustrated.

Every time we would be together, he would say things that left me hurt and bitterly confused. So much of what he said to me was beginning to sound like a broken record. I would say I didn't ever want to lose him, and he would say, "There is no reason for you to think you will ever lose me. We have the rest of our lives together." I would say, "You mean this way?" And he would say, "You know the answer to that." Or he would say, "You can't lose something you don't have." I would ask, "Do I have you?" "Don't you know? I'm here, aren't I?" He would always use double-talk and answer my questions with questions of his own — neatly avoiding the real questions in the process.

One day in May of 1975, I had asked Zane point-blank, "Will it always be like this?" I wanted a definite answer to that question, but all I got was, "I will always be here for you." That particular day, we had been lying on the couch in our usual lovemaking position — Zane on the bottom, me on top — when suddenly we began arguing. Zane got very cold, got up from the couch, and stood glaring down at me for a long time. Then, just as suddenly, he turned me on my back, pulling down my slacks as he did that. He unzipped his trousers, pulled them down, and lay on top of me. He had his hand inside my panties, and then he pulled them down. He had never gone this far with me before, and I fully expected after so many weeks of foreplay that we were finally going to have intercourse. He pulled his pants all the way down — another thing that had never happened before — and he was rubbing up and down with his penis on my stomach. He spread my legs apart and kept moving up and down on top of me. Anticipating that very moment, I had already been fitted for a new diaphragm. (I hadn't needed one for a long time with Bruce, because he had had a vasectomy.) As Zane got more and more excited, he kept pressing down on me, harder and harder, with his body, and his penis was getting more erect than it usually got. I was lying there, full of love and excitement, waiting to be fulfilled. But Zane was almost ready to enter me when he reached his climax and pulled back. And that was the end of that. His cold, professional manner took over again — and never mind about my feelings.

"Why did you do that?" I asked him. He didn't answer. "Aren't you ever going to make love to me?" I asked again.

"Never is a strong word," he said.

"What does that mean?"

"We have our whole life together."

"What about my feelings?" I cried. He had no answer.

With that, I pulled my clothes back on and glared at Zane. Without knowing what I was saying or why, I hurled these parting words at him: "You'll be sorry."

▬

Parzen made these notes on this same scene: "Wants to internalize me but eroticize and anger. States at the end of the session. Stated that I wanted to have intercourse with her, yield [*sic*] threatening not to come back, threatened, 'You'll be sorry.' (Expect gesture of some form.)"

▬

I was so angry I could hardly think to get in my car and drive home. All I could think about was Zane and how mad I was at him. I was fed up with his double-talk and the confusion in my head about my life with him and my life with my own family. I wanted out.

I do not remember clearly planning anything. I just went straight for the medicine cabinet as soon as I got home, and I lined up all of the bottles of pills I had accumulated. For no reason that makes sense to me now, I removed all the labels first and flushed them down the toilet. I got a big glass of juice from the kitchen, because I knew I would need it to swallow pills, and then I emptied them into my hand and swallowed them a handful at a time.

After I had done it, I had the most marvelous feeling. Maybe it was the peace of mind I had originally sought through therapy. Whatever the source, I lay on my bed and felt light, peaceful, calm. I remember thinking that nobody would ever hurt me again. . . .

Slowly, slowly, I came through a haze, blinking my eyes onto a world of white. Nothing was familiar to me and I could not figure out where I was or what I was doing in such a place. There were white sheets on the bed and other sheets were strung up as dividers all around the bed. On either side of my arms and shoulders, the white sheets still had red-brown stains on them. My arms were black-and-blue with bruises, and a tube was coming out of one of them. My stomach hurt and I hurt between my legs, where I could feel a catheter tube.

A big, friendly nurse named Marty pulled back one of the partitions and came in. I had some vague memory of Bruce getting me into the car and bringing me to the Scripps Hospital emergency room, but it was like being told about something that had happened a long time ago to somebody else. When I came to in the intensive care unit, Marty was there beside me. She was so good and strong and comforting — and that caused me to start crying. Marty told me to relax, everything was going to be all right; I was safe now. I was in good hands; they would look after me. Later, Marty would tell me how I had fought the people who were trying to save my life.

I had gone to sleep peacefully because I felt the confusion and the hassles in my life were all over. Then I must have come to as they were strapping me down and sticking needles in my arms. I didn't want help, I didn't want to live. "For a skinny thing, you sure did put up a fight," Marty laughed. Every time they would try to put the tube in my veins, I would rip it out. I was so thin and weak that they had trouble finding a strong-enough vein.

In and out of consciousness that night, I could hear them discussing my case. A young doctor came in once and explained to me that they were going to make an incision. Then they decided not to do that. Much later, Marty took out the catheter and I was more comfortable and able to sleep. She told me that in my delirium, I kept asking for somebody called "Zane." She knew from the admitting report that this was not the name of my husband, so when I was able to talk the following morning, she asked if this was somebody who should be notified. "Oh, yes," I explained, "that's my doctor, Zane Parzen." The nurse told me Zane had already been called and he would be in to see me later that day.

Zane did not arrive until 9 P.M. I was trembling because I was so afraid of what he would say. He closed the curtain behind him and walked over to the bed. He glared at me. He was cold; he was angry. He said he never thought I would be the kind of person who would hoard pills that way. What I probably needed, he said, was a good screwing. This was not said playfully. In his office, he often used those kinds of words to shock me.

I couldn't think of anything to say — I felt I had been very bad and Zane had every right to be angry with me — but he didn't leave room for me to talk anyway. He just kept scolding me — not the way somebody who loved you would, but with the disinterested manner of a schoolteacher.

━━

Parzen made these notes for May 20, 1975, on Evelyn's first suicide attempt: "6:25 P.M. Phone call from Bruce Walker (rational — no emotionality, what to do). At 4:30 – 5:00 wife took Gynergen pills #18, Phenaphen, unknown amount, and Hydrodiuril — 2 or more. Now trouble breathing; stomach hurts (ergotamine — with stomach and lungs). Rx: push fluids, caffeine, do not allow to sleep until 11:00 P.M. Call me if necessary. Hysterical episode — feel no pressure re acute episode."

The hospital records also show that Evelyn took 50 Valium pills in addition to the drugs mentioned in Parzen's notes. Valium, of course, is the most popular tranquilizer prescribed in America. Gynergen is the Sandoz company's brand name for ergotamine, a drug usually prescribed for migraine headaches and — in Evelyn's case — for stomach pains as well. Phenaphen is the Robins company's brand name for a mild analgesic used for headaches or to reduce fever. (Tylenol and Excedrin are other brand names for this. Phenaphen with codeine is also commonly used, although Parzen's notes do not specify whether this was what Evelyn took.) Hydrodiuril is the Merck Sharp & Dohme company's brand name for hydrochlorothiazide, a drug used to eliminate excessive fluid retention and reduce high blood pressure.

On May 21, 1975, after his visit to Evelyn at the hospital, Parzen made these notes: "I called her at 9 A.M. Just doing okay, does not feel well. Bruce [Walker] in L.A."

▬

When Bruce arrived at the hospital to take me home, I started crying. He tried to comfort me by saying nothing else mattered except that I was going to get well and be all right. When we got home, Carl and Michael came running out to the car to meet me, and I started crying again and blubbering apologies for what I had done. The boys were hardly old enough to understand what was going on, much less why their mother should be saying "I'm sorry" over and over to them. I felt like the lowest person in the world, a mother who had deserted her children. They seemed so good and I seemed so bad. They deserved better than what I was able to give them.

Inside the house, I went straight up to our bedroom and went to bed. My mother-in-law came in and sat on the bed beside me. She surely meant well, but she only made me feel worse. She said she just could not understand why I would do something like that. How could I possibly be unhappy? After all, I had a beautiful home, two fine healthy sons. And her son Bruce was all any woman could possibly want in a husband and father. What on earth was wrong with me?

I had no answer to any of her questions. I didn't know what was wrong. I didn't know why I was so unhappy. I only knew that the perfect marriage that Bruce's mother saw from the outside was not all it seemed. Zane had tried from the beginning to get me to recognize certain things that were not right in my marriage. Bruce was a healthy, handsome man and a good provider, but he had never given me the affection I so desperately needed. But I had loved him so much all those years, I would never see or admit that there was anything wrong with him or our marriage — until I had been talking with Zane for several months.

The first time I went back to Zane after the suicide attempt, I was sure he would be angry with me and I would be subjected to another lecture about how bad I had been. He sat there puffing on his pipe, not saying anything. I was on the couch, waiting for him to resume our relationship where it left off. After a long silence, he got up from his chair and came over to me. He grabbed my head and held it, his eyes digging into mine. "Don't you know you hurt me when you hurt yourself?" he asked. "Haven't I lost enough people whom I love?" He held me in his arms and we had never seemed so close. He told me he would forgive me for what I had done.

From then on, he said, I should come to see him twice a week instead of once. He also increased my medication. To save me from having to go to the drugstore with a prescription, he gave me pills from the jars and boxes in a low cabinet beside his desk.

▬

Evelyn Walker remembers little of what happened to her in the months following her first suicide attempt. During much of that time, she was in a drugged zombie-like state in which she was barely aware of what she was doing or saying. There were numerous times when she overdosed on drugs and she did not remember whether she had deliberately attempted suicide. Her neighbor Bettie Shepherd said that taking Evelyn to the emergency room became almost as routine as taking the kids to school.

▬

From the very beginning, Zane had tried to get me to talk against Bruce. Later I would realize that from the start he felt our marriage was no good and divorce was the only solution. I had resisted violently when he would try to get me to criticize Bruce: I had not come to him to talk about my husband; I wanted to know what was wrong with me.

During one session, Zane told me that Bruce was trying to "gaslight" me. I had never heard that expression, although he would use it many times after that. I asked him what he meant by that. He said it came from the movie of that name, starring Ingrid Bergman and Charles Boyer. In the movie, a husband tries to make his wife believe she is insane so that she will be put in an asylum and leave him free to ransack their house, where he knows some priceless jewels have been hidden.

I did not contradict Zane when he would say these things about Bruce, but I would never believe that Bruce would have tried to hurt or harm me. I was so in love with Zane and so confused about everything,

I wasn't sure how I felt anymore. Zane would tell me I had to see that Bruce was wrong for me, that he was cold and uncaring. I could see that Bruce had reasons to be annoyed with me, but I knew for certain he would never be or do what Zane was suggesting.

One day in September 1975, Bruce came home from work and announced that he had to go to a business meeting in Geneva, Switzerland. He wanted me to go with him. I had always dreamed that we would go to Europe together. For one thing, I wanted to see the house in Vienna where my father was born and reared. But this did not seem like the right time. Lately, Bruce and I had argued about everything that came up, so I didn't think it would be much fun traveling with him. More important, I didn't like the idea of being so far from Zane.

But I talked it over with Zane. At first, he didn't say anything. Then, after a while, he said maybe it would be good for me, since it was only for two weeks. He would miss me but it wouldn't be for long and then we'd be together again.

I felt pulled in every direction, but Bruce seemed so serious about wanting me to go — and deep down I still lived as though things would work out between us and we would go on living together. In the back of my mind was the dark fear of taking our troubles with us. But we were so busy getting shots and passports, packing, and planning the rest of our trip after Geneva, I was able to look forward happily to a real adventure.

It was a long, tiring flight, and we arrived so late at night that we checked into our hotel room and immediately went to bed. I didn't even need to take any sleeping pills.

The next morning, we ordered breakfast sent up to the room and pulled the curtains back to take in the magnificent view of Lake Geneva, just across the street. I could see the swans and the small boats, and there was a fountain spurting up from way out in the lake. It was an elegant old hotel, furnished in heavy, ornate, carved wood furniture — everywhere there was the glitter of real crystal and here and there a touch of satin and lace.

We had that first day to ourselves. We walked along the lake toward the center of the city. We didn't talk very much, but it seemed like we were both enjoying the beauty of the place in our separate ways and we didn't need to talk. Several times, Bruce became impatient with me because I couldn't keep up with him — I was slowed down by all the medication I was taking. About midafternoon, we returned to the hotel bar. It looked like the drawing room of an old castle — huge oil paintings in gilt frames on the walls, richly crafted wood tables, comfortable overstuffed chairs, and couches covered in velvet. We sipped our drinks and talked about the coming evening. Bruce said he would go ahead so he could register; then I would join him at a cocktail party before dinner.

The party, it turned out, was not a social event. I was the only wife there who wasn't involved in the conference — and it was strictly business from the beginning. The opening speeches began immediately after dinner, and Bruce told me to go back to our hotel. I felt like he'd thrown cold water in my face. This was not my idea of a good time, and I could not fool myself about being happy any longer.

I decided it was much too early to go to bed, and I didn't want to spend all that time alone waiting for Bruce, so I went into the bar and ordered a cup of coffee. I was sitting there feeling lost and left out, and I must have looked it. The waiter soon brought over a note from a man sitting on the other side of the room. All I could think about was how nice it was to have somebody on hand who could speak English. His note asked if he could join me for a drink. I saw that the sender was a nice-looking gentleman; when I looked up, he was nodding at me. From a distance he seemed harmless, and certainly this was a safe place where nothing strange or dangerous could happen to me. So I wrote him a note back saying, yes, please join me.

He was a broad-shouldered, heavy-set man with thick red hair. I was struck by the hair, thinking I had never met anybody with red hair before. He introduced himself and said he was in Geneva on a business trip from South Africa. He said he had noticed me the day I checked in with my husband. Where was my husband? Why was I alone?

I told him that Bruce was tied up with business meetings, but I sensed that this man understood a lot more than that. We chatted for a while, until I excused myself, saying that my husband would be coming in shortly.

The stranger asked about my plans for the next day. I told him I would be with my husband when he wasn't involved with the conference. The man walked me to the elevator and said good-night. Bruce did not get home until after midnight. He talked a few minutes about the conference and then went to sleep. The next morning, Bruce said he'd be busy all day. He handed me $20 and said he'd see me that evening. That amount would have paid for a Coke and a sandwich, but little else in our expensive hotel and most of the places we'd seen.

I had saved some pieces of bread from our breakfast, so I took them over to the lake to feed the swans. It was all so beautiful, but that only made me feel more alone, abandoned, because I didn't have somebody special to share it with.

I wandered about for a while, but I spent most of the day in our room. Late in the afternoon, I went down to the hotel and had another cup of coffee. The South African businessman came in, ordered a drink, and sat down beside me. He said he had had a busy day and asked about mine. Fortunately I didn't have to admit how bored I'd been, because at that moment I spotted Bruce going to the elevator in the hotel lobby. I went out and stopped him and brought him back to meet my new friend. The three of us sat talking for a while, then Bruce announced that he had to go up and change for the dinner session of the conference. The message was clear to me: I was to be left alone again.

Back in our room, I cried and told Bruce I was not having a good time; I wanted to go home. He said that was nonsense. If I would just be patient, he said, the conference would soon be over and we could go ahead with our trip, just the two of us.

But after he left, I felt so low that I sat down and wrote a letter to Zane, trying to tell him how much I missed him:

Dear Zane:

Things are just not going well at all. I really can't even relate in a letter the various reasons why. Geneva is lovely, but can be truly seen in one day — that's it! Besides the fact that I am not sleeping, I have had a headache for four days. I try to tell myself that tomorrow will be better. I have decided that I am a liar! This isn't as good as a three-minute phone call would be, but at least I know you'll have to think about me for one-half minute, anyway, before throwing this letter away. Zane, I miss you. Please miss me just a little. My love goes to you.

Evelyn

I was sitting there wondering what I was going to do all evening when the telephone rang. I assumed it would be Bruce calling, but it was the man I had met in the bar. He asked if I would like to join him for dinner. I didn't think I should do it, but I also didn't think it was right that I was having to spend the evening alone. So I said I would like very much to join him for dinner.

We talked mainly about our families. He had two sons who were older than my two boys. He never mentioned his wife, and I talked less and less about my husband. The man said he traveled a lot, including twice a year to visit the United States. He wanted my address and phone number, but I acted as if I didn't hear him when he asked.

For the next few days, he was my tour guide around Geneva. Bruce said he thought it was nice I had made a friend. The last day we were to be in Geneva, my new friend invited me to lunch. He said that since it was our last time together, it would be nice to be alone, so he had ordered lunch to be sent up to his suite. He had been such a pleasant companion all week that I didn't want to be rude and tell him no. And, once I was there, he made me feel at ease and comfortable in his room. I was thinking about how much I had enjoyed his company and how much I would miss him.

After lunch, he said he wanted to keep in touch. Wouldn't I give him my phone number? I resisted again and he moved around and kissed me. This time I didn't resist. In fact, it felt good, and we were soon on the bed having sex. At the time, I didn't feel guilty about it. I didn't feel much of anything. We just seemed like two people who had met, enjoyed a nice time together, and would never see each other again. He had changed a miserable stay in Geneva into a pleasant experience—and there seemed nothing wrong with saying goodby this way. I never told Bruce about the man in Geneva, but I later felt obligated to tell Zane all about it. It was a painful ordeal for me to tell Zane; I begged him not to think less of me because I had done this.

We finally left Geneva and went on to Vienna. On a tour of the city, I gave the address of my father's birthplace to the guide, and he knew exactly where it was. We stopped and took snapshots of the fine palace and two office buildings on either side of it. Bruce and I tried to keep up appearances, but there was growing tension between us. I was aching inside, miserable because I was so far from my children and even more miserable because I was so far from Zane. I took more and more pills to get through each day, and that only made me more of a drag for Bruce. I tried to be good company, but I knew inside that I was not having a good time and neither was he. Once we tried to make love, but we both seemed to realize it was no use.

A violent argument grew out of one of our disagreements in a hotel room. I was screaming and crying. Bruce shoved me around and then held me down on the bed, trying to restrain me. As loud as I could, I screamed: "I want to go home!" We decided to leave the next day — four days earlier than we had originally planned.

We first sent a telegram to Gary Shepherd, telling him to call Zane to let him know I was coming home early and would like to see him as soon as we returned. On the flight home, Bruce and I talked as we never had before. For the first time, he seemed to understand how seriously disturbed I was. He still did not know to what extent I was involved with Zane. I blamed myself for all the problems we had been having in our marriage. I told Bruce I was sorry everything had worked out badly, but I didn't seem to be able to work out anything. I wanted him to understand that I couldn't get better without his support and love. I talked a lot about how sorry I was that my problems were costing him so much money — and I kept apologizing for ruining this expensive trip to Europe. But Bruce told me not to worry, everything would be all right once we got home. He said, "Doctor Parzen will help you."

Once the long flight was over, it seemed to take hours to get through customs. But I felt so good being home. I had missed the boys. They wasted no time digging through our baggage to find all the goodies we had bought for them. They had enjoyed their stay with their grandmother, but they had missed us and were happy to see us.

My mother-in-law fired a barrage of questions: Why had we come home so early? Had I tried to overdose again? Why was there a message for me to call Doctor Parzen as soon as I got home? That was all I needed to hear. I went up to the bedroom and called Zane's answering service immediately, and he promptly called back. I felt calmed just by hearing his voice. He asked if I was all right. He said he had arranged for a special appointment for me the next morning. He was glad I was home safely.

I was so happy to see Zane that I could hardly wait for him to be with me on the couch. I had brought him a very special present from Geneva, a blend of pipe tobacco I knew he liked and couldn't get in this country. He was so pleased he thanked me with a long, warm, and loving kiss. He held me very tightly — and I felt safe again, home at last.

Zane said that after Gary Shepherd called him about our telegram from Vienna he had worried that I might have tried to kill myself again. He said when he got my letter he was sure something very bad had happened between me and Bruce. I told him about some of the friction that developed between us on the trip, but mostly I just talked about how lonely I had been without him.

"What about divorce?" Zane asked me. Was I finally thinking about going through with it?

"No!" I was not ready to think about that. Maybe I knew that Zane was the only one I truly loved now, but I still couldn't think about breaking up my marriage. Maybe Bruce had told me some things by now that had hurt me beyond healing, but still a part of me held out hope that we could hold our marriage together for the boys' sakes if not our own. I didn't want to think about this unpleasant subject — not then, maybe not ever. I changed the subject.

One night, not long after we returned from Switzerland, Bruce called me from a business trip in New York. He mentioned that he had been at a conference with a woman he worked with back in San Diego. He also said they had slept together. By then, Bruce was aware that I was romantically involved with Zane, even though we had never discussed it in calm, rational terms. It had just come out in our constant arguing that Zane cared more for me than Bruce did and that I loved Zane, too. Considering what I was doing myself, my reaction to Bruce's infidelity was totally irrational. It helps explain to me now how completely confused and insane was the struggle inside me. I loved Zane, yet I also wanted everything to be okay with my husband and family. When Bruce returned from New York, we had a ferocious argument about what he had done. I was utterly unaware of the hypocrisy of my position as I raged that if he could not be faithful to his wife, he had no business remaining in the house with me and the children. I suggested a trial separation, with the understanding that he would be the one to move out. But Bruce let me know in no uncertain terms that it was *his* house, they were *his* sons, and if anybody moved out, it would be *me*.

▬

Meanwhile, Parzen's notes reflect the steady dissolution of Bruce and Evelyn Walker's marriage. After her first session with Parzen in September 1974, he wrote: "Won't talk against Bruce." In April 1975, he noted that Evelyn was "more self-assertive with husband." On May 30, 1975, he wrote that she was "confronting husband more."

On September 9, 1975, Parzen noted that Evelyn's other doctor, a general practitioner, had "posited separation" between Evelyn and Bruce. And, after the session on October 9, 1975, Parzen noted: "Bruce came home. She told him to get out angrily." And on October 13, 1975: "To lawyer tomorrow for information." Once again, Parzen's script was getting ahead of the actions he was directing. Several months would pass before Evelyn would take the drastic step of consulting a lawyer about a divorce. The Walkers would continue to share the same bed and live under the same roof for another nine months, although in every detail but that, their marriage was finished by this time. In her mind, Evelyn was already married to her Zane.

During one of her sessions that fall, Evelyn had told Parzen how supportive of her Gary and Bettie Shepherd had been. Gary's office was right next to Zane's; in fact, they paid their rent together as joint tenants. (The San Diego Psychoanalytic Institute moved into the Prospect Street office building at a special rate, with the proviso that the member psychoanalysts would also rent space for their private offices. Shepherd and Parzen both rented penthouse office space.) But Parzen became very angry over Evelyn's innocent comment about her good neighbors. He shouted at her that he was the only one in the world who cared for or understood her. He grabbed her head in his hands, as he always did at moments like this, and made her stare into his eyes and tell him she believed him: *he* was the only one.

Parzen also reacted strangely every time Evelyn mentioned her other doctor, Robert Fournier. Fournier had become the Walkers' family doctor one summer after he successfully diagnosed some allergies in Carl that were so bad that the boy had to be pulled out of summer camp. The whole family went to Fournier after that. Tall and handsome, Fournier looked like the older Paul Newman. Yet at that time, Evelyn would no more have thought about having sex with him than she would have thought about it with Parzen the first few months she was seeing him. Still, a kind of sexual jealousy clearly was aroused in Parzen every time she mentioned Fournier's name to him. Just how upset Parzen was over Fournier's role in Evelyn's life is documented in a letter Parzen wrote to Fournier on October 8, 1975. It is a very long, rambling letter, but it is quoted here in full because, in its convoluted way, it reveals and documents just how confused and troubled Evelyn's psychiatrist was.

Dear Doctor [Fournier]:

Mrs. Walker called me on Sunday after I had seen her last week upon her return from the trip, and she stated that she was feeling a lot of mixed pressures and confusion. She felt that she was being told by you to take certain actions while at the time, she felt that she was not ready to take such actions. I think that for the last several months, as the crisis between Mr. and Mrs. Walker has heightened, particularly as she has gained strength psychologically, that she has been experiencing more and more contrasting messages between you and me.

In addition, on Sunday, she told me that she was confused because you had prescribed some types of psychiatric drugs for her, and that when she had asked if you should call me, you felt that it was too difficult to get hold of me. Furthermore, she feels that seeing me on Tuesday and Thursday and then having to go to your office to see you for which she feels are psychological sessions, makes it only more confusing for her.

I would tend to agree with her, and I think that with a woman that has tended to live in terms of what other people tell her to do, that any such messages that are conflicting become very very difficult. In addition, I think that she has a particular type of system that responds to psychiatric drugs very idiosyncratically, and these have to be used with caution and awareness of the particular paradoxical side effects that can occur with them. In this regard, when she called me on Wednesday, she was having a fairly typical type of physiologic reaction to Sinequan [the Pfizer company's brand name for doxepin, an antidepressant that carries specific warnings that it can increase the effects of any number of other drugs if taken concurrently] that is not that rare, particularly when given at nighttime.

I am aware that this is a favorite drug used by many people today but I think that the literature is becoming more loaded with these types of adverse paradoxical reactions which are unfortunately more common than not, particularly with this drug. In any case, I think it ought to be decided as to how the management of this case is going to be.

My own particular prejudice is that I should deal with the psychological issues, and insofar as I do have communication with Mr. Walker and he called me Monday morning, with in essence the same type of confusion in message, it seems that I have an adequate relationship with him, even though somewhat strained to say the least. I did feel that on Monday at his bequest, that I give him the name of a psychiatrist who does marital counseling. My work with Mrs. Walker has been basically in terms of her internal psychic makeup that responds to the external crisis, and insofar that I am not trained to do marital counseling, even though I am well aware of some of the parameters involved with it, I felt that I should refer them to someone far more appropriate than myself. To this end, I have referred them to a Dr. John Hassler, who I know does this work quite adequately. I think that it would be advisable to leave the marital decision at that level rather than trying to deal with the pressures that have been brought on Mr. Walker both by his wife, and some of the conversations with you, are for the first time in his life resulting in some fairly serious psychic decompensations, which I am afraid might be quite serious. In this regard, he is not only beginning to experience insomnia, but also impotency and temper outbursts which are basically ego-alien to his overall functioning.

In summary then, I think it has to be focused on that one thing that must be carefully guarded in terms of Mrs. Walker is that she not get conflicting messages from anyone. I think that even with excellent rapport between two doctors, that since recommendations have to come more in terms of the flow of the material at the moment, that no one can develop an adequate degree of correlation of advice. Thus, for example, we have recommended that either she, or another time, he move out, and at the same time, I have been telling her that she has to think through each subject very carefully, that she should see a lawyer and that she should not act rashly on any of this. In this regard, even though the problem has been there for a long time, I have told her that her ability to move out and to separate is something new, and therefore is relatively rash. She does not consider all factors. This has been certainly one of the conflicting messages that have made her more anxious and decompensated even a little bit more at times. I think that it is striking that psychologically she has been strong enough to go on these trips, and at the same time has not decompensated despite increasing pressures in many ways.

I do not think that there is anything in this letter that is not already within the awareness of Mr. and Mrs. Walker, and therefore, in terms of the particular psychiatric issue of the confidentiality of all communications in terms of relationship with the patient, I will let Mrs. Walker see a copy of this, although since Mr. Walker is not a primary patient of mine, he will not see this.

Sincerely yours,

Zane D. Parzen, M.D.

Of course, Parzen never showed this letter to Evelyn and never discussed its contents with her or Bruce. He was remarkably quick to judge Bruce Walker, who was not his patient at all. And even as the husband of one of Parzen's patients, Bruce — by this time — was hardly communicating the kind of intimate details about his life that would allow for such harsh judgments on the doctor's part.

Parzen's sage advice about a marriage counselor went unheeded by the Walkers — perhaps because they never received this advice from Parzen. Neither of them ever heard of the other doctor Parzen claims to have referred them to in this letter. Instead, Parzen continued to push Evelyn farther and farther away from her husband and children and to urge her to get out and get a divorce.

As for Parzen's words of wisdom on the use and misuse of certain drugs, would that he had followed his own counsel. In the end, the incident that would lead to his undoing would be his flagrant mishandling of drugs.

On October 30, 1975, Parzen wrote one of his periodic reports on Evelyn. These reports indicate that Parzen was creating what appeared to be legitimate "documentation" that might serve as a cover for his own misconduct behind the locked doors of his office.

Even though Parzen introduced many fictitious details, these office notes and reports do not reflect patient Evelyn Walker's progress, but rather her steady decline. In the end, they would be subpoenaed and introduced as evidence not of the doctor's day-by-day care of the patient, with a cure in mind, but to show how Parzen himself was overseeing and directing Evelyn Walker's slow but certain destruction.

The entire October 30, 1975, report reads as follows:

Mrs. Walker has been seen in therapy on a twice-a-week basis almost since the beginning on September 16, 1974. [In fact, Evelyn did not begin seeing him twice a week until June 1975.] At this time she has been seen a total of 64 hours, and the treatment has certainly been quite tumultuous and erratic. There have been multiple suicide attempts, and over-idealization and fixation to the therapist, and a tendency to withdraw from her husband. Divorce issues are paramount at this point, and yet when she gets faced with the issue of what she wants to do with herself, then she begins to decompensate.

After her last decompensation and suicidal threat, which did not lead to anything, I have taken complete charge from Doctor [Fournier] as regards handling her medications. The initial rage that I wouldn't give her enough to kill herself subsided, and she was beginning to direct some energies elsewhere. I would feel certain that the diagnosis at this time is not only chronic depressive personality disorder, but many borderline features with some paranoia. It is significant, however, that in the trusting situation of therapy that she has been able to open up, and in spite of ongoing resistance has been able to relate much more.

I think the prognosis is still guarded, but I think there is evidence that she could respond positively to therapy, and significantly enough even her husband is making some moves as he has developed symptomatology, such as transient impotency, and himself may be interested in therapy. The future of both the marriage and the patient still remains in doubt, and I think there is an awful lot of supportive therapy and ego strengthening techniques that are going to have to be used, prior to any degree of stabilization being reached.

Zane D. Parzen, M.D.

Evelyn's growing dependence on drugs — and her abuse of Parzen's prescriptions — is clearly documented in Parzen's notes. What isn't always noted is that after every suicide attempt, he would renew and often increase the same prescriptions that had almost killed her. On July 1, 1975, Parzen wrote: "Call from Bruce Walker in Scripps Emergency Room: took an OD of Gynergen and Phenaphen at four —

conscious — no problems — no vomiting — indicates approximately 150 Phenaphen. Last prescription for Phenaphen April 8, 1975, with one refill. Last Gynergen January 20, 1975, #50, with five refills in six months (had a headache on Saturday, tranquilizers fine)." These were some of the same drugs Evelyn took in her first suicide attempt in May 1975.

On August 10, 1975, Parzen noted: "Dr. [Fournier] called as regards Mrs. Walker. She was in tears, very anxious, with the feeling she could not do anything right and was depressed. A trial of therapy was given with Triavil 4-25 [a combination of strong tranquilizers used as an antipsychotic] and she was sent home, even though somewhat suicidal. . . ." On September 7, 1975, he noted: "Od'd with Tranxene [the Abbott company's brand name for clorazepate, a tranquilizer], Hydrodiuril [an antihypertensive given with the warning that it can increase the effect of similar drugs if taken together], Pro-Banthine [the Searle company's brand name for propantheline, an antispasmodic given to relieve spasms in the digestive tract with numerous warnings on the dangers of taking with other medication]. To Clairemont Emergency Room, OK." Two days later, he wrote: "Did not want to do it, 100 pills, combination same, took only handful. . . ."

Evelyn Walker was in a drugged state during most of the summer and fall of 1975 and is understandably vague in her memories of those months. Often she could not remember things she had said or done. Friends would tell her about her rambling, desperate phone calls — calls she could not even remember making. The details in the scenes described here, thus, come not only from her sketchy memories, but also from other witnesses, and from legal and medical documents that were subpoenaed as evidence in her later trial.

At some point during the late summer or early fall of 1975, Gary Shepherd's sister, Carole, came to live with her brother and his family. After a while, she moved out and got an apartment of her own in Pacific Beach. In Carole Evelyn found not only a sympathetic ear for her emotional difficulties, but also an intelligent and witty companion. Carole was careful not to be judgmental when Evelyn told her in gory detail about her involvement with her psychiatrist. In the past, Evelyn had always been shy and reticent about her personal life. She would hardly discuss her problems with her husband, much less with a total stranger. And it would have been absolutely unthinkable for her to divulge intimate details of her marriage to even the closest of friends. But now she had reached a state where she just could not stop talking. Parzen seemed to have opened up a Pandora's box inside her. Once he got her started talking about herself, there was no stopping her. It had become a very real physical need. She just had to talk with somebody, anybody. She had a list of friends she would call up every day and talk for hours at a time. They would later tell her about how many times she would call up and just rattle on about herself and Zane. But she didn't remember the calls. She does remember that all she thought about in those months was Zane.

Her friend Connie Martin would later give a dramatic account in court of how she watched in helpless horror as Evelyn went from a fun-loving, outgoing, creative person to a reclusive woman obsessed by her love for her psychiatrist. Martin had known Evelyn from the time they both lived in the same apartment complex in San Diego. Evelyn was a happy new mother then. Martin would tell the court that Evelyn had been devoted to her husband: "She adored Bruce." But, later, Martin — who by then had moved away from San Diego — would get long, sometimes incoherent, phone calls from Evelyn talking endlessly about her psychiatrist and whether or not he loved her.

One night at home with Bruce and the boys, Evelyn thought she was going to fly into a million pieces. Because she couldn't handle conflicts with her sons and her husband and her lover, Evelyn decided she had to get out of her own house. If Bruce would not move, then she had to do it.

She drove to Carole Shepherd's apartment. Carole was clearly frightened by Evelyn's state, so she called her brother, who was concerned not only about Evelyn but also about his sister. Shepherd then called Parzen and asked him to talk with Evelyn and get her calmed down.

Carole was especially disturbed about all the pills Evelyn had brought with her. Evelyn flushed most of the pills down the toilet, but she managed to keep a small part of her supply.

While at Carole's, Evelyn got a call from her husband's old friend Bill Higgins. When he was later required to testify, Higgins would say that Bruce had called him and said he was very worried about Evelyn. He wanted Bill to see if he could talk Evelyn into getting rid of the pills and coming home again by telling her that her family and friends loved her and cared for her.

Higgins came by and took Evelyn for a drive in his car. He tried to get her to go to a bar so they could talk, but she refused, nor was she willing to return to her apartment. Evelyn was getting so nervous that she asked Bill to stop somewhere so she could get a Coke with which to take some pills. He pulled into a motel and got her the soda, then he went in and rented a room for them for the night. Evelyn was so disoriented that she went along. She just wanted to be left alone to go to sleep and forget about everything and everybody.

Evelyn remembers that there were twin beds in the room, but she does not remember getting undressed or going to bed with her husband's friend. She woke up the next morning — lying beside him — and then she panicked. What would Bruce say if he knew? She was sure Bruce would kill her when he found out.

She got dressed and told Higgins to take her back to Carole Shepherd's. Once there, Evelyn grabbed her things and drove off in her car. She was too scared of what Bruce would do to go straight home, so she went to the house of another couple who had been friends of theirs for many years. She poured out what she could remember of the night to her friend and told her she could not face Bruce alone. Evelyn returned home that afternoon, but her friends came over in the evening to be with Evelyn when she told Bruce what had happened.

Much to Evelyn's relief, Bruce was understanding and gentle with her about what had occurred. If their group of friends did not know just how sick she was, he certainly did. But he was furious with Bill Higgins. Higgins later testified that Bruce called him and shouted into the telephone, "You're nothing but scum."

The next day, Higgins's wife arrived for her own confrontation with Evelyn. She wanted Evelyn to deny everything that had happened, but Evelyn told her she could not do that. "You know, Evelyn," the former friend said as she shook her head, "you are a very sick woman." But Evelyn stuck to the truth; that she was sick did not mean she couldn't see the truth.

It was the final break in a close group of friends. The wives had met regularly for bridge for several years, and all the couples had shared the chores for a great many picnics and parties. In earlier years, Bruce and Evelyn had been busy and sociable. But since Evelyn had become involved with Parzen, they had stopped going out altogether.

This is how Parzen recorded the preceding events in his office notes:

October 15, 1975: Phone call. Evelyn left home at 3 P.M. Moved to [Carole] Shepherd's. Gave me number. Had 48 pills. I called her. Will come in tomorrow. In P.M., call from Dr. Shepherd. He is concerned about his sister. Told her to flush the pills away.

October 16, 1975: Call from Carole Shepherd. Patient drugged. Should not drive. Insists on coming. Patient obviously sedated. Wants more from me. Wants me to love her, give to her, angry that I won't. Resisting to talking about what to do. Question of hotel tonight. (I gave her Nembutal 100 mg., #6 [the Abbott brand name for pentobarbital, a barbiturate, "sleeping pill" or sedative], for four nights, and hydrochlorothiazide, #14, 25 mg. [the generic name for Hydrodiuril, anti-hypertensives, given to reduce body fluid and lower blood pressure], two a day for a week prior to her periods) 3:45 P.M. pharmacist called. She wanted chloral hydrate [the generic name for "knockout drops," or "Mickey Finns"], etc. She called and raged and gave it to me, stating that she needs it (I said no). Last menstrual period October 5, 1975.

October 17, 1975: Discussion with Mr. Walker at 9:45 A.M. Evelyn totally preoccupied with suicide. Talking to everyone. Question of hospitalization came up. I concurred. Recommended he contact Doctor Shepherd for referral. Someone who does hospital work.

October 20, 1975: Phone call, Mr. Walker. Evelyn said that man took her out to talk her out of the suicide, took her to a motel. . . . Evelyn was angry, did not want to tell me herself. Calmer. Wants from me to stabilize her. Has Nembutal, #700 mg. [sic]."

▬

When I had first started seeing Zane, I would talk nearly every session about the cost involved. I felt very guilty about spending $55 on myself. I had always been very proud of the way I managed our spending at home, and this seemed like such an extravagance. But I had come so far from that kind of thinking that the $110 I was now paying Zane each week was only a small fraction of my overall medical bills each month.

At first, Zane thought my headaches might be caused by some kind of hearing problem, so he recommended all kinds of tests on my ears. Then, my stomachaches and digestive problems got worse and worse, so I went into the hospital for tests on my stomach and my upper and lower digestive tracts. During the last of these tests, complications developed, and it turned out I had a cyst on my ovary. Just before Thanksgiving in 1975, I had to go back into the hospital to have it removed. Bruce drove me to the hospital and picked me up when I was ready to go home. But Zane never came. He never even called. When I got back home, I should have spent more time recuperating in bed, but all I could think about was meeting my appointment with Zane. I was still very weak and sore from the operation, but I got up, got dressed, and made it to his office on time.

Zane said he had been thinking about me and he had wanted to call and come see me, but that he couldn't handle seeing me in the hospital. What mattered to me was that we were in each other's arms again. He could hold me real tight, and I could forget about all the problems in my life outside his office.

By this time, of course, I had given up on the rest of my life. I lived the twenty-four hours of every day for the five- or ten-minute phone conversations with my Zane. If it hadn't been for my appointments with him twice a week, I would never have gotten out of bed. When he would answer my calls in the mornings, he would tell me to get up and take a shower so that I would feel better. I would take a shower, put on a clean nightgown, and go back to bed. For a while, I tried to keep up with the housework and the cooking. I would prepare food and leave it out for Bruce to warm up for himself and the boys at night. But it got so I couldn't face them anymore. I almost never ate. My weight dropped by thirty and then forty pounds in a matter of weeks. For a time, also, I tried at least to do the laundry and have clean clothes for everybody. But this also became too much for me. Bruce would wash and dry the clothes and then bring them up to the bedroom for me to fold and put away.

I had always done all the grocery shopping for the family, but this came to a sudden halt one terrifying day in the supermarket. I had picked up my cart and was getting things we needed, as I had always done. Then I got to the shelves of canned potatoes. I looked at the stacks of white potatoes and then I looked over at the red potatoes. I looked back and forth, back and forth, trying to decide which ones I wanted to buy. Suddenly this silly moment of indecision created an overwhelming panic. I couldn't decide; I couldn't figure out whether I wanted white or red potatoes — and I felt that I couldn't go on until and unless I made that momentous decision. I knew I couldn't cope with anything like that anymore. I left the cart where it was, ran out of the store, and got in my car, sobbing and crying out of control. I couldn't make up my mind about a little thing like that; I couldn't do anything. From then on, Bruce did all of the shopping.

I had withdrawn to the point where I spent all of my time, except for when I went to see Zane, in the bedroom with the shades drawn. I never knew when it was night or day, whether Bruce was at work, or downstairs, or somewhere on a trip. I kept the television on because I couldn't stand the quiet.

Once, I pleaded with Bruce not to leave me alone so much, and he hired a girl to be a kind of companion for me. But I was so ill and she was so young that it didn't work out.

Zane insisted on my keeping every appointment with him — and that was all I lived for. I remember thinking that Zane had become like a puppeteer, with me as his puppet. I didn't see this as anything evil or sinister. He held all the strings; he had total control of my life — and I was so removed from reality that I liked it. He owned everything about me. I felt — as he had told me time and again — that nobody else knew or cared about me as he did. I had been lied to by everybody but him; I felt he truly loved me. He would always be there; he told me he would be.

Chapter 4

In those intimate sessions on the couch, Evelyn Walker would often talk about her past and about the other people in her life. This, of course, is precisely what one would expect of a patient in psychiatric treatment. How can a doctor treat you if he doesn't know who you are and what is bothering you?

However, Evelyn recalls that during the doctor-patient stage of her relationship with Parzen, she held back and divulged very little about her own background beyond the superficial generalities. Parzen seemed to have his ready-made formulas — not just about her husband, but also about her parents and her childhood. He insisted that her parents must have scared her as a child by saying the Nazis would get her if she didn't behave, but Evelyn assured him her parents had never done that.

It was not until long after they had become intimate that Evelyn started to open up. In fact, she remembers that it was a session sometime after her first suicide attempt when she told Parzen something about her childhood that she had never talked over with anyone before.

▬

I had never been able to talk about this with anybody, yet somehow I knew it had marked an important turning point in my life. That day, in Zane's office, he sat in his big armchair smoking his pipe. I took off my shoes and curled up between his legs, sitting on the floor, leaning back, looking up into his warm, understanding eyes.

The story I told Zane was about a time when my mother had beaten me one day after school. I was about eight-and-a-half years old. (Later,

73

when I heard my parents arguing, I realized this was the day my mother learned she was pregnant again, and that was why she was so angry. That day, however, I had no idea what was going on, why she was so mad at me.) When I came home from school, it was as if my mother had been waiting for me just inside our apartment door in that narrow hallway where my parents stored their two rollaway beds. As soon as I closed the door behind me, my mother started screaming at me and pulling my hair and sort of wildly flailing the air. She slapped me hard and knocked me back against the wire springs of the bed, and I cut the back of my head. My mother was, in fact, not very tall, but to me, a skinny sticklike kid, she seemed huge. I described to Zane how my mother had seemed to me then like a terrifying beast looming over me in the small, enclosed space of that hallway, while I cowered, trying to get out of the way as she kept swinging her arms and saying things that made no sense to me.

I never had any broken bones or bad bruises from those times when my mother would hit me, and I never missed school because of them. But I told Zane that what I remember most about my mother is her low attitude about me and everything I did — it was how she looked at me and talked to me that hurt so much. It was the browbeating that hurt more than the actual hitting or slapping. And that's what left the enduring marks on me.

I described to Zane how my mother had told me that when I was a baby, she dressed me up and treated me like a doll. Sometimes she would change my clothes six or seven times a day — the way a child would play with a doll. But from the time I can remember, my mother never made me feel like I belonged, much less that I was loved and needed. She would always say she loved babies but she couldn't stand children. Zane explained that as I grew older — another mouth to feed and body to clothe, and another female in competition for the attention she wanted — my mother resented me more and more.

I told Zane that I was so terrified of my mother that I never dreamed of doing anything wrong. I came straight home from school and did my homework and whatever housework I was told to do. The browbeating would get so bad at times that I would ask my mother, "Do you really love me?" And she would always answer, "Only if you are good." Since she was always mad at me and never seemed to love me, I came to feel I must be bad or she wouldn't be treating me that way.

But after this particular beating, I waited for my father to come home from work so I could talk to him and see if he could protect me. I did manage to get in a few private words with him, and I begged him not to say anything to my mother, not to tell her that I had asked him to help me. I told him I wasn't doing anything wrong, yet my mother was punishing me all the same.

The next day, I found out that my father had betrayed me. My mother slapped me again because I had talked with him behind her back. I vowed never again to tell my father or anyone else anything that was bothering me — and I stuck to it — until I told all this to Zane.

A day or two later, I took steps to get myself out of that awful situation. I didn't consciously think of what I was doing as a suicide attempt, but Zane agreed with me that that was what I had done. I went into the bathroom we shared with another family in the next apartment and took down a bottle of vitamins and a bottle of aspirin. Then I swallowed all of the pills in the two bottles. All that gave me was a very sick stomach. In a matter of minutes, I threw up all the pills and had to go to bed because I was so sick.

My mother and father never sat down and asked me why I would do such a thing. My mother just screamed at me for being wasteful. "Why are you doing this to me?" she would cry. "Are you crazy? Why are you putting me through this?" I told Zane that it seemed I was always the cause of my mother's problems, the reason for all of her unhappiness and discomfort.

That whole incident of being slapped against the bedsprings and taking pills had gotten buried inside me, because from that moment on I never confided in anyone — that is, until I came to Zane. Nestled between his legs that day, I told him he was finally somebody I could trust. He said he cared about me, he said that he loved me. I knew by then I loved him, too. It was so quiet in that room, and I felt so safe with Zane. I felt that nothing was ever going to hurt me again. Zane said I belonged to him; he would look after me. Our relationship was only going to get better and better as we became closer and closer over the years.

▬

Today, there are so few items left to remind Evelyn Walker of her childhood that she can keep them in a little gray satin bag. There is one snapshot, "the only one I ever saw of us together," of her at about six or seven with her mother. Two other pictures show her smiling happily with her Uncle Eric. The most impressive photograph shows her forebears in Vienna — an elegant formal portrait with her father, a young Lord Fauntleroy, lounging in front of the stout and prosperous-looking elders.

A photostat of her birth certificate reflects the bare facts about her parents at the time she was born. Evelyn Barbara Goldschlager was born at 4:55 A.M., January 13, 1940, in William Booth Memorial Hospital at 2345 Broadway in New York City. Her father is listed as Paul Harold Goldschlager; color, white; age, 33; birthplace, Vienna, Austria; occupation, handyman; address, 7 East 43rd Street. The mother is named Rita Ann Karp; color, white; age, 18; birthplace, Vienna, Austria; occupation, housewife; same address. A stamp across the top of the certificate reads: "NAME LEGALLY CHANGED MAY 4, 1943," and Goldschlager has been marked out and "GORDON" written over it. The father's occupation has also been crossed out and upgraded to "sound engineer." Evelyn never asked why they changed the name or where the new one came from.

At the time this book was written, Evelyn Walker had severed all ties with her family. It was a painful decision, but one she and her doctors felt was necessary if she were ever to live at peace with herself. Her collaborator requested a meeting with her father to verify certain facts that only Evelyn's parents could confirm. Paul Gordon said he would be happy to talk; he had nothing but time. He was alone most of the time; he was sick and not able to leave the house. His wife was another matter. She would never talk about Evelyn; she would not even be present for his interview.

The nice little gray corner house the Gordons were able to begin buying with war reparations money in 1958 is in a less-expensive area of Point Loma, once San Diego's most fashionable address. It sits about midway across and halfway out the long peninsula that protects the entrance to the oldest, deepest natural harbor in California.

Paul Gordon answered the door somewhat awkwardly. He was extending one hand while reaching behind with the other to straighten out a long line of plastic tubing. This was connected to a small oxygen tank behind his chair in the living room and to a light plastic harness over his head, holding the two-pronged outlet into his nose. A frail, gentle man, he stood a head shorter than his oldest daughter, Evelyn. He moved with the natural grace that suited his princely upbringing.

Outside, it was another of those clear, dry, sunny San Diego days. Inside the Gordon home, it was almost dark. There was nothing bold or unusual about the decor, but over to the left, facing into a small dining alcove, was a striking, almost life-size oil portrait of a young girl in a brilliant turquoise dress. The visitor's eye would come back continually to this extraordinary painting.

Gordon was asked to talk about his parents and the life they lived in Vienna and how and why they came to this country. "My father was Julius Goldschlager and he came from Ismail, which was then Turkish. My mother was Irene von Mangold, and her mother was a von Posner. Two very famous families and very rich. My father was a genius, a very complicated man. He was blond. His father, my grandfather, was a tobacco merchant, and he was about eighty when I was born in January 1907. My father was born very poor. He worked his way up and then he married my mother, who was worth millions. My father studied architecture and he built sixty-four houses in Vienna before World War I. He was friends with the mayor; he was well known. He liked the women and wine; the money came second. He had a lot of money at one time but he didn't know how to invest it. He didn't like to be employed, so he would build something and then sell it. In 1914, he completed an office building, one of the biggest buildings in Vienna at that time. He gave the whole thing to the army for a hospital from 1914 to 1918. He was able to put in his brother as chief surgeon. After the war, the Socialist regime wanted to employ him as city architect, but he refused. From then on, they wouldn't let him have his permits and just made it difficult for him. He built a movie theater and he built an automat. He got fat and he started to lose money."

Originally, the Goldschlagers had lived in a huge palace at the back of an open courtyard flanked by two taller buildings of offices and apartments, also built and owned by Julius Goldschlager. These were — and are — at Numbers 30, 32, and 34 Prinzeugenstrasse in Vienna. (These are the buildings Evelyn saw on her visit to Vienna with Bruce.) Gordon said that when he and his wife went back to Vienna in the 1960s, they found that the three buildings his father had built were still there, but a few blocks away, the magnificent Rothschild mansion had been torn down and replaced by a modern office building. His family wasn't quite on a level with the Rothschilds, Gordon said, smiling, "but it was a very good neighborhood."

After graduating as an engineer from the technical school in Vienna, Gordon worked first in Poland and then in Berlin and London before he returned to Vienna in 1938. He was a bright young engineer in a brand-new industry. He worked for Tobis-Tri-Gon, the company formed by the three inventors of sound film.

That fateful March of 1938 when Hitler took over in Austria was also when Gordon met and married Rita Ann Karp. She was sixteen years old, fifteen years younger than he was, but Gordon says there was nothing unusual about their courtship and marriage. Evelyn's mother always told her they met on the street, but he said they met "the usual way, through friends."

Gordon was fiercely reluctant to talk about the Nazis. "Whatever happened over there is in the past and over with." But his interviewer persisted. Didn't his family suffer in any way after the Nazi takeover? Did none of them end up in concentration camps? "My oldest brother, Eric, was in a concentration camp for a while and then he went to London. My youngest brother went to London and stayed in England and became a commander in the army and he died a few years ago there. But I or my wife did not suffer. All those cruel things they did I only know from what people tell me. [Hermann] Goering's brother was my boss at the film company. I had worked there for six years and he was like family to me. Many times he would help me locate some friends who had disappeared. People would disappear from the street, but we did not suffer. My father died in a hospital and the attending physician was one of my tutors."

But what about others in his family? What about his mother? "My mother disappeared, so we never knew what happened to her." What about his wife's parents? "They disappeared and we never knew for sure."

Wasn't his father's property seized by the Nazis? "No. His property was *sold* when I was there." But if there was nothing wrong about that transaction, why was the family paid reparations after the war? "All I know is the property was sold to the Nazi government direct. And after the war, my younger brother in England handled all that. We got $2,000 each, I think it was. All I know is we got the money and bought this house in 1958."

In 1939, Gordon said, he and his wife finally were able to emigrate to America, using affidavits supplied by his cousins in Chicago. They were allowed to take only $54 with them, and $8 of that went immediately to pay for a week's rent in New York. His dream had been to get to California and pursue a career as a sound engineer, but that was out of the question, because there was no money and little prospect for it. His alien status kept him away from any kind of technical job; he had to take what he could find. He worked as an elevator man at the Arthur Murray Dancing School and, for a time, repaired jukeboxes. "One day in New York," Gordon recalled, "I got a postcard from Goering [Hermann Goering's brother, for whom Gordon had worked in Vienna] from Italy. I guess I should have saved that." Also in New York, his daughter Evelyn was born at the Salvation Army Hospital. "All I remember is that the whole thing cost $60."

Although Evelyn had not seen her parents in some time, they were described in an article about Evelyn published in a San Diego newspaper. Two points that the reporter had made had particularly galled Paul Gordon, and an opportunity to contradict them seemed to be the real reason he had granted this interview. (Evelyn did not speak about her parents to this reporter. The reporter got her information from court testimony and other sources. Evelyn, in fact, requested a correction from the newspaper.) The reporter in the story had described Evelyn's parents as "Austrian Jews, concentration camp survivors." And the reporter claimed that Evelyn "says her mother constantly accused her of being ugly and stupid, would make it clear her daughter provoked her frequent anger, but wouldn't explain how." The Gordons had also learned that there had been testimony in court that Evelyn had described physical abuse from her mother.

"Why is Evelyn feeling so Jewish now?" Gordon asked. "In Austria, nobody was talking about the Jews until Hitler came. We never were Jews in Austria. I would have been in the army if I had stayed. We were the typical *not Jewish* family in Vienna. I was *never* a Jew; Hitler *made* me a Jew. Jewish is a religion and it is not real. But anti-Semitism is real." Gordon explained his concern that none of their neighbors in San Diego had known they were Jewish. And, yes, he and his wife were afraid it would make a difference.

In Evelyn's little memory bag is a curious certificate that her father was asked to explain. It is a "confession by faith" in the South Shore Presbyterian Church in Chicago, Illinois, for Evelyn Barbara Gordon, dated April 30, 1944. Evelyn remembers passing by that church after her family was living in Chicago, but she does not remember being baptized there or attending church there. Again, she never asked her parents what the document meant or why it had been preserved so carefully all these years.

Her father explained: "The reason why we were baptized in Chicago was to get out of what Hitler once did, so that our children will never have to go through what we did. In Vienna, it never occurred to us what would happen. We had no Jewish friends in Chicago. At that time, I said why should our children go through the same thing again? It was purely a business deal. That is the realistic world. I am not an atheist. I believe in nature. But I think all religions are too old for the life we live now. No, what I did in Chicago was purely a business deal. We don't know this cannot happen again. We don't know how many generations in America it takes to get another Hitler — if it goes on with Reagan, it may be very fast."

Changing the family name from Goldschlager to Gordon was another practical decision. The old name was just too difficult for Americans to pronounce or spell, Gordon explained. The new name was one his younger brother Bobby had used when he was playing with a jazz band in Vienna. Gordon reacted as if he'd been slapped when told that the old name hadn't been erased from the books but had merely been crossed out and written over.

The other point in the newspaper article that had upset the Gordons had to do with "this whole childhood thing. . . . She has these things in her head — some of it is true and some of it is constructed." He introduced these comments with an odd tirade about Evelyn: "She is a *perfectionist*!" He spat out that word with contempt. "With Evelyn, everything has to be perfect. She does not understand other people. You should have seen her house: It was perfect. I bet her house now is *immaculate*. Some other things she says are not true. She was not slapped. She was never beaten. Do you know why she was never beaten? Because she *never* did anything wrong. She was a coward and she still is. The other child [Evelyn's sister Beverly], now she knew what she wanted. She was an unlucky person but she lived. She coped with it. Evelyn had everything. I would take her husband's side even if I am her father. Bruce is an engineer. He was educated in Boston and he is very cold and very selfish, but he was a very good man and he did take care of his family.

"In Vienna, we had a friend who studied psychoanalysis, and we discussed all that. What Freud talked about were theories, not what these people are doing. There are some who are good, but these people Evelyn has seen are quacks. This last time I was in the hospital, one of them came in with a tape recorder and started asking me all kinds of questions. He said this problem I had with my breathing was all in my head. But my mother had this same problem and so did her mother. I threw that guy out. He was so cheap, he wouldn't even buy his own tape. He expected me to pay for it.

"If a psychiatrist wants to talk with somebody, he should talk with their whole family. A good psychiatrist will talk with everybody involved. I never believed in those people and I know exactly what they do to Evelyn. When a person thinks about herself all the time, naturally she will have problems. She was never disturbed before. She was a coward all her life. She was not disturbed when she got married."

In the months before her trial against Parzen, Evelyn Walker's lawyers were fearful that her parents would be subpoenaed as witnesses by Parzen's lawyer and would, in effect, testify against their own daughter. This never happened, possibly because Parzen's lawyer could sense that such a move might well backfire. There is something chilling about a parent who would speak of an ailing daughter as a coward. At one especially low point in Evelyn's years in and out of hospitals, she was forced to borrow some money from her father. When she was not able to repay this on time, her mother wrote her a vicious letter on dainty, flowered notepaper — calling Evelyn a "bitch" and a "yellabelly," among other cruel remarks. Evelyn's psychiatrist at the time of the trial passed on one page of this letter to her lawyers. It was never needed to counter her parents' testimony, since they were never called, but it remains a vital document in her story, confirming everything Evelyn said and felt about her mother.

But Gordon's feelings for his absent daughter are complicated. "I miss her, you know," he concluded after his bitter talk. "I wish she would come see me. I don't know what has happened to her children, they never come around. I can't go anyplace because I have to have oxygen all the time. . . ."

As the interviewer stood to say goodby, his eye was caught again by the brilliant colors of the oil portrait in the corner. The bright turquoise alone was enough to hold one's attention, but the young girl herself looked remarkable. There was a faint resemblance to Evelyn, the dark hair and the features of the face. But here was something else again — something Evelyn did not have. Here was a voluptuous, tempestuous woman in a child's body. Who is the girl in the portrait? Gordon was asked. Was that Evelyn or one of his two other daughters? He smiled, "Oh, no, that's my wife when she was eight years old. The father of a friend of hers did that. They always said I had four daughters instead of three."

And then, as if he were reading the interviewer's thoughts about that last sentence and how it related to everything involving Evelyn and her mother, Gordon added, "I have to tell you one thing. My wife never liked children."

Evelyn remembers being a child herself and hearing her mother say time and again that she didn't like children. She liked babies, but not when they grew into young adults. Actually, Evelyn's mother acted more like her sister — with a strong feeling of sibling rivalry. Evelyn was always made to feel unwelcome, unwanted, in the way. The mother was the young princess, the daughter was the ugly stepsister. The mother refused to see herself as an adult. She had gone from being the adult in a child's body — at the time of that oil portrait — to being a child in an adult's body as she grew older and had children of her own. She was always complaining to Evelyn that she had been denied her youth because she got married when she was sixteen.

In December 1943, when Evelyn was almost four, the family made a Christmas visit to relatives in Chicago, and Paul Gordon found work in that city as an electrical engineer. Evelyn's family moved into three small rooms above a block of stores and shared a bathroom across the hall with their next-door neighbors. There was a tiny room for Evelyn, but the parents slept on either side of the dining table on rollaway beds that they would pull out at night. Gordon was still holding down two, and sometimes three, jobs, so his wife usually was left alone with little Evelyn. The mother confided everything to the child, because she had nobody else to talk to. On Saturday, they would go to the movie theater at the end of the block. There were three shows for twenty-five cents, and they sat through all three nearly every Saturday.

School offered no escape for Evelyn. She was humiliated when they would call her out of the regular classes to take her place in the

remedial courses in spelling and English. She spelled *window* with a V
because that's the way she and her relatives pronounced it. She was, in
fact, a pretty little girl, but that was not how she saw herself. In her
own eyes, she was awkward and gangly, and she held back from
making friends and from joining in any kind of group activity. She
was not allowed to bring home any of her playmates, even for a brief
visit. She did not date until she was in her late teens.

There was one bright place in Evelyn's childhood. This was where
the roles were reversed — where she was the precious darling and her
mother was all but ignored. Her relatives all said that she looked just
like her paternal grandmother, the wealthy heiress.

Going from the drab, cramped rooms the Gordons lived in to their
cousins' house a few blocks away was not just a journey back to the old
country, it was also an extraordinary shift in mood — quite literally
from darkness into light, tense anger into joy.

Paul Gordon's first cousin, Senia Greve, and his wife, Mitzi, had
come to Chicago from Germany in 1937. Greve was a voice teacher
who no longer sang professionally. But his wife, who used the stage
name Maria Hussa, did sing occasionally in Chicago, and every summer she would go to Hamburg to sing with the Hamburg State Opera.
Unlike most opera singers of the time, Maria Hussa was a slight,
delicate woman. To little Evelyn, Mitzi was the perfect embodiment of
all that was elegant and refined. In Germany, Mitzi had known the
composer Richard Strauss, and she had sung in the premiere of his *Der
Rosenkavalier* in Chicago. Although she had dreams of singing with the
Metropolitan Opera or another major company in the United States,
Mitzi finally was reconciled to teaching voice, along with her husband, at the Sherwood School of Music in Chicago.

Mitzi and Senia had been able to carry with them a number of the
Goldschlager family pieces — huge, gilt-framed oil paintings, crystal
chandeliers, and heavy baroque furniture, and the Greves' household
provided Evelyn with a connection to a happier world than the one
she knew at home. They introduced her to the real world of music and
romance in Chicago and Europe. Several times a year, Mitzi would
buy a bag of chocolate-covered orange peel for little Evelyn to munch
on, as they rode the train on their way to the opera. There was *Hansel
and Gretel* every year at Christmastime, but Mitzi also took Evelyn to
several performances of *Aïda* and many other Verdi operas. Mitzi
would explain the stories as if she were telling fairy tales to the

child — and Evelyn was utterly entranced. In her mind, this cousin became her lasting ideal of what a true lady should be.

The holidays, mainly Christmas and Easter, were always celebrated at Mitzi and Senia's house. In the corner there would be a huge tree decorated with real candles. The food was a rich feast created with recipes from old Vienna. The conversation was always loud and joyful, and at a certain point everyone turned to one of the two grand pianos. There was one downstairs and another upstairs in what had been the attic. Evelyn's Uncle Eric lived in the attic, which he had converted into his own apartment — complete with a very modern deck built out into the branches of a huge, overhanging tree.

In the troubled years ahead, those pleasant moments with Mitzi and especially those with her father's brother Eric would become more and more important to Evelyn. Every man she would ever care about would be measured not by her father but by her Uncle Eric. He was not very tall, but he was very broad, and Evelyn saw him as a huge, loving bear of a man — always squeezing, pinching, hugging, always smelling of tobacco. Back in Vienna, he had been an orchestra conductor, but in Chicago he pursued his second profession of architecture. Working with the firm of Epstein and Sons, he designed several major buildings and some very prominent houses in the suburbs. At Christmas, Uncle Eric would be stationed beside the candlelit tree with a bucket of water, and Evelyn would scrunch up beside him as they ate their Christmas dinner together. There were also some few but very special times when Eric would come to get his "little Avie" and take her to Block's Restaurant, a block away.

One Christmas, Evelyn's parents managed to save enough to buy her a very special frilly dress that she had been longing for in the window of one of the nearby shops. It seemed such a fabulous dress that she never thought it would be hers. It was blue with a white organdy pinafore and a big embroidered butterfly for a pocket. Long after it was too small for her, it was her favorite dress, because it seemed to say to her that maybe her parents did love her after all. Years later, as a grown woman, Evelyn would be administered a sequence of psychological tests, and in one of them she would draw a simple sketch of how she saw herself: still a little girl in that pretty dress.

When Evelyn was nine, her mother twenty-seven, and her father forty-two, her younger sister Beverly Ann was born in Chicago. Not long after that, the family moved into a bigger apartment, at 8055 Merrill Avenue, a few blocks away. The second daughter was born into a very different situation from what Evelyn had known. Evelyn's mother was more Americanized and relaxed. The new apartment was also much larger and offered more space — even a backyard to play in. But Beverly was a wild child almost from the very beginning. As Evelyn's charge, she was a constant worry. She was always running off, not just down the street but so far away that the police often had to be called to find her. Evelyn begrudgingly admired her little sister's spirit. She would take guff from no one, including their mother. Beverly thought nothing of telling her mother to go to hell. To Evelyn the incredible thing was that her mother seemed to respect and like Beverly more because of this.

By 1955, Paul Gordon had a very good job as an electronics engineer at the Standard Business Machine Company in Chicago, but he was tired of the harsh winters, so he jumped at the chance to work for similar wages at the Convair Astronautics Company in San Diego. Others who had made a "Little Vienna" of this South Shore neighborhood in the late 1930s and 1940s would also be leaving. Evelyn's Uncle Eric would get married late in life and move to the suburbs, where he died in 1976. Senia Greve had died in 1952, but his widow lived in the little house with her costumes and memories long after Little Vienna had become Little Harlem. She was knocked down and beaten up on two occasions, yet she stayed on until her death at 87 on April 19, 1980. By that time, Evelyn's problems would be so overwhelming that she had no time to think about the once-beloved relatives she left behind in Chicago.

In 1955, the Gordons rode west in a bright red Pontiac convertible. The trip was like their vacations: Evelyn's father seemed to be in a contest with himself to see how many miles he could cover in a single day. Once in San Diego, they lived in a small house in an inexpensive area of Point Loma, just up the hill from the U.S. Navy boot camp. But in 1958, when Evelyn's father received his war reparations check from Austria, they were able to buy a larger house in a nicer area farther up the hill.

At Point Loma High School, Evelyn found the work even harder than what she had back in Chicago. After taking some entrance examinations, she was put back a full year, a humiliating experience. She only excelled in one course: art. She had been interested in drawing and painting since she was a child — she would copy the illustrations from a little Uncle Remus book and also from a wonderful book of German fairy tales, which had come from her old-world relatives.

One art instructor at Point Loma was especially helpful to Evelyn. He understood and appreciated her talent, although they didn't always get along. It was the one area where she could assert herself, and she always wanted to be different — at least in her artwork. She and the instructor would argue about what was and wasn't art, what she should and should not be doing. Once, she was taken to the school counselor because she was not going along with the program. However, the instructor did help her put together a portfolio, which won her a scholarship to the Coronado Art School.

After graduating from high school, she went to work at the job her father had gotten for her at Convair, but she took art courses off and on for several years after that. She was dating some, and she was halfheartedly engaged to an older man. Then she met Bruce Walker, and the other man was quickly forgotten. In every way, Bruce seemed the ideal match for her. Once they met and married, she couldn't imagine that there would ever be another man in her life — until she started seeing psychiatrist Zane Parzen.

In those sessions on his couch, Zane Parzen would talk to Evelyn about his past almost as much as she talked about her background. This was a clear violation of proper psychiatric treatment, but Evelyn did not know this. Even if she had realized it, she would have explained it as the sharing between two people in love, not the discussion between a doctor and his patient. In fact, psychiatrists are taught never to let details about their own lives interfere with what a patient has to tell them. Their offices are supposed to be barren of any kind of personal mementos, such as photographs or other objects that would arouse the patient's interest in their private lives.

In the trial, Evelyn's lawyer would point out that this was a classic case of role reversal — the doctor was playing the patient, in effect using Evelyn as his own sounding board or analyst. Parzen told Evelyn about his real father and his death; his stepfather and how he hated him; his mother and only brother; his wife and four sons. The birth and death certificates of certain of Parzen's family members demonstrate that Evelyn's memory of details he told her about them was remarkably accurate. These details served another function at a key point. When she first began to tell people about her involvement with Parzen, most of them dismissed it as another patient falling for her doctor — with no basis in fact. However, Gary Shepherd deduced that at least part of her story must be true, because suddenly she was telling him exact details about Parzen's family background (which Shepherd knew from other sources), which could only have been divulged in the most intimate of situations.

To understand why and how Zane Parzen abused this whole process of transference and countertransference with Evelyn Walker and other patients, it is necessary to delve into his own history. All those years of education and training unfortunately had not changed who he was when he entered the profession. None of that could take away the mental scars he bore from his own unhappy childhood, nor could it resolve the awful confusion in his own mind about his mother and father and stepfather, his wife and sons — his own confusion about himself. It is a classic case of the psychiatrist's failing to heed the ancient warning: "Physician, heal thyself," which can be translated into the psychiatric concept: "Physician, know thyself." But, perhaps like Evelyn Walker and many of his other patients, Parzen didn't know or understand what was wrong with him, so he could not know what to do about it.

Zane Dribin Parzen was born July 26, 1933, in South Bend, Indiana. Both his parents were born in Russia. His father, Louis Aaron Dribin, was born January 23, 1902, the son of Zalman and Slavia Staradusky Dribin. His mother was Ethel Levy, born June 16, 1902, the daughter of Joseph and Anna Levy. The Dribins had one other child, a son named Sheldon, who was born April 18, 1938, five years after Zane.

On July 7, 1941, just before Zane turned eight, his father died at Epworth Hospital in South Bend. Louis Dribin had been ill for several months with terminal cancer (lymphosarcoma). Rabbi Maurice Parzen conducted the funeral service at the Dribin home. Two years later, on October 26, 1943, in Chicago, the rabbi would marry Dribin's widow. He would also adopt her two sons, giving them his own last name but maintaining their father's surname as their middle name.

During his father's painful illness and after his death, Parzen's mother stepped in as a partner at her husband's furniture store. (Louis

Dribin and a partner had opened a store they called Radio Mart, at 763 South Michigan Street in South Bend. This was at a time before television, when radios were also furniture. Although the store continued to be called Radio Mart into the 1970s, it would evolve into a discount furniture store.) She worked long hours and would come home irritable and exhausted. One way she would relax would be to have her oldest son, Zane, rub her back. Parzen's own psychiatrist, James T. Thickstun, would later refer to this as one source of Parzen's central problem.

Parzen's treatment by Thickstun was one of several conditions Parzen had to meet after his medical license was suspended. In a report on Parzen, written at the end of one year of therapy and dated October 10, 1980, Thickstun observed:

> The most important figure against whom he [Parzen] was defending himself was his mother, seen as a powerful, pre-Oedipal, phallic, controlling, needy, self-centered, spider woman. . . . Dr. Parzen's mother appears to have been a dominating, self-centered woman. His relationships were largely dictated by her own needs and desires. . . . The patient's father was an architect-engineer with creative abilities who acceded to the mother's desire that he work within the family retail furniture business. He appears to have provided understanding, warmth, love, and support for the patient and, in the eyes of the patient, protected him from the dangerous demanding mother. There were conflicts between the parents, which apparently included the danger of the father leaving the mother. (The father's "irritability" was later explained by the mother as due to his illness.) These resulted in the patient's fantasies and the mother dominating and destroying the father because he had opposed her and failed to meet her needs. The patient identified with his weakening and dying father, but also with the stronger, creative, intelligent, supportive and forceful father (before his debilitating illness — lymphosarcoma). . . .
>
> The patient became, before the father's death, when he was seven years of age as well as after, a caretaker for both parents — with the fear that he would be destroyed by the mother as the father had been if he did not satisfy her. A screen memory typifies this: When the mother returned from the hospital and announced the father's death to the patient, he said, "Don't cry, Mommy" — his role in life

was already to meet her needs and to deny his own. The sacrifice of himself and meeting the needs of others became characterological and his self-esteem was maintained by self-sacrifice (and his guilt over his hostility relieved). The guilt to his father was over his anger at the father for abandoning him (through illness and death) and for the demands he felt placed on him as a child to be with his father and sacrifice his own play with other children to his father's long, depleting, and ultimately painful illness. The father's hospitalizations, ambulances taking him away in the night, his splenectomy, etc., all added to the tremendous burden of fear, grief, anger, guilt, helplessness, etc., that the patient suffered as a child — and to the depressive mood so much a part of his life.

After the father's death (and after the father's deathbed admonition to take care of the mother and to do what she wanted), the patient's desire (and fear!) of being the man of the house was confirmed in fantasy, and to some extent in fact, by the mother's request for massages by the patient when she returned fatigued and needy from the day's work (and probably from lack of fulfillment of her sexual needs). Oedipal triumph and guilt from the father's death and Oedipal sexual fantasies with consequent guilt added to the patient's core of conflictual constellation. The role of meeting the mother's needs now involved meeting her physical, sensual and sexual needs, but with uncertainty about how far he could go with the massages, awareness of his sexual arousal, desire to satisfy his needs, and fear of what his mother would do if she were aware of his sexual desires.

His own desires and needs were largely unacceptable to him and seen as dangerous. His character structure revolved around meeting the needs of others, while sacrificing himself. Through this he could gain safety, self-esteem, defense against underlying depression, relief of guilt and some sexual satisfaction insofar as this could be to meet the needs of others. He became a doctor in response to the mother's conscious suggestions, but also an unconscious identification with the mother's wish to be a doctor herself. His mother's desire for him to be a doctor also negated the patient's identification with his father, established prior to his illness and death. He should not be *like* his father but should *take care of* his father, his mother and others. This was like the creation of a second identity, concealing the original one the mother wanted him to deny. After the mother's remarriage, as a matter of fact, his surname was changed to that of his new father. . . .

Zane's new father was such a formidable figure in his life that many years later he would refer to him not by name or even as his stepfather, but always as "The Rabbi." The son of Samuel Parzen, Maurice Parzen was born December 22, 1910, in Poland. He had four brothers (all doctors) and three sisters, and he was descended from fifteen generations of rabbis. In 1936, Parzen became rabbi at Sinai Synagogue in South Bend, a congregation founded by twenty families in 1932. In 1949, Parzen broke ground for a $250,000 building that is still the congregation's home.

Due to ill health, Parzen resigned as rabbi in 1966, but he lived another ten years, dying March 4, 1976. Only fourteen days later, the rabbi's younger adopted son — Zane's brother, Sheldon — would die of Hodgkin's disease. Sheldon Parzen had begun a career as a biochemical geneticist, but he had resigned his academic position when his stepfather became ill, so that he could return to South Bend and take over the family furniture store. Like Zane, Sheldon had named his only child, a son, Louis Aaron, for their real father. Ethel Levy Dribin Parzen would live until January 19, 1979, a week before the first psychiatric hearing that would set in motion the legal proceedings to remove her sole surviving son from his chosen profession and bring public disgrace to the surname that Zane had always despised but never had the courage to change.

Zane Parzen always created the impression that he was a Harvard graduate. Harvard records show, however, that he went there from 1951 to 1953 but was never graduated. Records at the University of Indiana, in Bloomington, show that Parzen was graduated from there in 1954. Indiana, of course, is not Harvard — and Indiana is not mentioned in any of the biographies Parzen provided about himself for the various medical society directories in which he was listed. When Evelyn's lawyer asked him about his undergraduate schooling during pretrial examination, Parzen said only, "I first went to Harvard," and left it at that.

From Indiana, he went to medical school at the University of Chicago. Even in the dull context of the class pictures at Chicago, the face of young Zane Parzen stands out. His features are delicate, birdlike, the mouth a fine line, the nose small and pointed. What is most striking about the face are the eyes — deep-set, dark, and brooding. It reflects the personality his colleagues would all describe: aloof, distrustful, a loner.

Parzen married Judith Bailie, the plain but very bright daughter of another prominent Jewish family in South Bend. Their first child was a son, born November 2, 1956, in Chicago during Parzen's second year in medical school. He was named Aaron Louis for Parzen's real father (although reversing the names). The Parzens would have three other children, all sons. In the 1980 psychiatric report on Parzen, his doctor would say that this marriage "was designed to continue the relationship with his mother — his wife, in many respects, being like his mother."

Although his mother had wanted him to become a surgeon, Parzen chose psychiatry instead. Years later, his psychiatrist would explain this move: "He occasionally could take steps opposing his mother, but always at some cost to him."

Parzen did his internship at Cook County Hospital and his residency at the University of Chicago Clinic, becoming a full-fledged psychiatrist in 1962. In addition to his private practice, Parzen would also be associated with the Michael Reese Hospital as associate attending psychiatrist from 1964 to 1968. Parzen began studying toward becoming an analyst in 1964 at the Chicago Psychoanalytic Institute; he completed the program in 1971. He was consultant at the U.S. Federal Attorney's Office from 1966 to 1971, and the Cook County State's Attorney's Office from 1969 to 1971 — according to biographical information he supplied to the American Psychiatric Association.

None of the brief biographies supplied for professional directories by Parzen give a date for his leaving the Michael Reese Hospital. However, Daniel Offer, the chairman of psychiatry at that hospital in 1984, says that Parzen's last year, according to hospital records, was 1968. Offer also says that Parzen did "have trouble" at Michael Reese, and he was restricted in his practice. But he left of his own accord and his trouble had nothing to do with sexual involvement with female patients. Offer also says that there is no record in Parzen's file to indicate that anyone at the Michael Reese Hospital recommended him for a position in California, although he adds that any one of the doctors could have done so independently. Parzen's colleagues in California would later swear that he was highly recommended by his fellow doctors in Chicago, claiming, furthermore, that the doctors there had to be aware of his problems with female patients. Offer counters this by saying that the California doctors are only "trying to blame us for their problems." If there had been problems of that serious nature for Parzen at the Reese Hospital, Offer explains, Parzen would never have been able to pursue his studies at the Chicago Psychoanalytic Institute. The hospital and the Institute work so closely together that such a serious matter could never have been kept secret.

In 1971, Parzen met two psychiatrists from the new San Diego Psychoanalytic Institute on a plane trip to a professional meeting in San Francisco. There is no record of what Allan Rosenblatt and Sanford Izner told Parzen, but obviously the three men got along very well. Parzen was impressed by what they told him about San Diego and they were equally impressed with Parzen. Within a matter of months, he responded to their enthusiastic invitation to move to San Diego.

By the time he got to California, Parzen had mastered the role of the frumpy, Ivy League professor. He smoked a pipe and knew about the best blends of tobacco. He wore comfortable old tweed jackets with suede patches on the elbows. He was self-deprecating enough to seem real. But along with this was an aloofness, even an arrogance, that said this was a man of depth and substance who had no time to waste on trivial pursuits or foolish people. The public persona Parzen so carefully built for himself over the years made it extremely difficult for anyone to get at the truth of what he was doing in his office, much less find out who he really was. He was rarely guilty of outright lying, but he was a master at suggestion and innuendo, which always made him seem far grander than he ever was. This was all accomplished mainly through his manner and gestures. It was not so much in anything he said, one colleague explained — it was more in what he did not say.

The Parzens moved into the heart of picturesque, affluent La Jolla. Parzen's office was in a fairly unpretentious little enclosure downtown, but it had that magic postmark. The family home, at 6004 Avenida Cresta, had a broad ocean view that was worth a fortune. And the house itself was a fabulous low, rambling, Spanish-style structure, which they gutted and completely redesigned at a cost even greater than the initial purchase price. Parzen drove a chocolate brown Jaguar XJ6 with "ZDP" on the license plates. "Zane Parzen, M.D., a

Professional Corporation" earned more and more each year. By 1974, he was reporting gross receipts of $78,191 from his practice; by 1978, that figure would rise to $102,993.

When the Parzen family moved to La Jolla, Parzen's son Aaron was an immediate hit among the teenagers at the local high school. He was a member of the soccer team and a superstar in his father's eyes. Very early on the morning of March 28, 1972, just eight months after the Parzens arrived in California, Aaron and a friend were driving on Interstate 10, just inside the California border with Arizona. At 6:52 A.M., near the exit for the town of Blythe, they collided with a huge tractor-trailer truck. The friend, who was driving, was not hurt, but Aaron's skull was fractured, and he never regained consciousness. He was flown to University Hospital in San Diego, where he died eight weeks later, at 8:20 P.M., May 30, 1972. He was fifteen. Aaron was buried in the Orthodox Jewish cemetery, Home of Peace, in East San Diego.

Parzen would later say that his personal problems began with his inability to cope with his son's death. The facts contradict him: Long before he left Chicago, he had been involved with at least one patient, a patient who followed him to California. But Parzen's psychiatrist, James Thickstun, noted the significance of Aaron's death.

At the time of the tragic traumatic death of his son Aaron . . . a serious regression began. The loss caused great grief and sadness but also great anger, loss of self-esteem (he had failed to be the caretaker he needed to be in a crucial relationship), and fear (iden- tification with his son, reviving the identification with his dying father when he was equally helpless and useless) — followed by deepening depression. The tremendous stress of that time was compounded by the disturbances it produced in other members of his family. His rather fragile, needy and self-centered wife was unable to cope with the situation, or to give him or their children much measure of the support they all needed. . . . These traumas resulted in a characterological regression to an increased need to satisfy the wants of his patients — particularly needy, demanding, disturbed women.

Only Parzen's closest colleagues knew how utterly devastated he was by his son's accident and death. To others, he presented the same smug, arrogant façade he always had. But Evelyn Walker knew. None of his patients could help but know about Aaron, since the color picture of him was on display in the office—contrary to rules of psychiatric practice. But this was only the least of the rules Parzen was breaking by that time.

Parzen had a reputation in San Diego for being involved in scholarly research that was not merely interesting and important but also fairly exotic. In yet another manifestation of his grandiosity, he listed himself in the professional directories as the author of three scholarly articles. In fact, he was not the sole author of any of them, and two of the "articles" are mere transcriptions of roundtables or seminars in which he participated.

The most unusual studies Parzen was involved with had to do with the treatment of male-to-female transsexuals, who represented a large percentage of his patients. More than one of Parzen's psychiatric colleagues has suggested that he was drawn to these studies for personal rather than purely scientific motivations. It is a fact that during most of the sexual play with Evelyn Walker, Parzen took what many would consider the traditional feminine role, lying on the bottom, with her on top. A psychiatrist who treated another of the female patients after she had been abused by Parzen said, "I can't discuss it because that is confidential and privileged, but I can tell you this: you cannot go too far in saying he was taking on the female role in his relations with these women." In other words, he was seeking out the woman in himself, or the woman he might have been—tall, needy, whiny—and, as his actions proved, that woman was someone he despised.

Male transsexualism was the subject of a seminar Parzen participated in at the School of Medicine, University of California/San Diego, in September 1973, a transcript of which was published in the May 1974 *Western Journal of Medicine*. At one point, Parzen introduced a transsexual patient and attempted to interview her. The failure of the interview was clearly Parzen's fault, but he took none of the blame. "Although there are patients from whom you can get a feeling for what their transsexualism is all about, I could not get such a feeling from this patient. . . ." He spoke of these patients as others would later speak of him: "Transsexual patients classically tend to be very manipulative and very secretive. They tell you what they want you to know, and they have learned from much experience to read and to manipulate medical staff."

In light of the revelations about Parzen's own problems with sexual identity, the eloquent conclusion to this seminar seems a chillingly prophetic warning. This was delivered by Arnold Mandell, who was then chairman of the UCSD Department of Psychiatry. Not only is Mandell highly regarded in the scholarly field of psychiatric research, he also is a very popular lecturer and author. In 1984, he was awarded one of the much-coveted MacArthur Foundation Life Study grants. Mandell said:

To deal with a person who has this conviction that "he" is really a woman in a man's body, we must learn to empathize with this form of human behavior, and to do this effectively, we have to be aware of our own hang-ups, our own psychosexual defenses. In a sense, it involves getting in touch with the opposite sex that is in every one of us, and that can be pretty threatening. Essentially what these people are struggling with is a problem of identity — an overwhelming need to find an identity with which they can be comfortable, and in which they can relax. And when we go in to try to help them, we have to do it with a feather, gently. We are not public prosecutors — we do not enforce any law that says the way these people behave is illegal — we are physicians and the first rule, always, is do no harm!

Those last words are taken from the physician's oath attributed to Hippocrates. Zane Parzen was oblivious to the ethical rules of medicine, so he would live to face the curse that is contained in the second part of the Hippocratic oath: "I swear . . . I will prescribe regimen for the good of my patients according to my ability and my judgment and never do harm to anyone. To please no one will I prescribe a deadly drug, or give advice which may cause his death. . . . If I keep this oath faithfully, may I enjoy my life and practice my art, respected by all men and in all times; but if I swerve from it or violate it, may the reverse be my lot."

Chapter 5 At Christmastime 1975, I made every effort to keep the family holiday. I managed to buy presents for the boys and decorate the house. On Christmas Eve, as always, we went over to my parents' house for dinner. Ever since we had moved to California, we had always used this occasion to make a call back to all the relatives gathered at Mitzi's house in Chicago.

I learned only then that my beloved Uncle Eric had been in and out of the hospital for some time and nobody had told me just how seriously ill he was. I didn't need to be told that when I heard his voice on the telephone. He had always been a pillar of strength and love in my life. But what I heard that Christmas Eve was the thin, weak voice of a very sick old man. I was crushed. Whatever else might have happened in my life, I had known in the back of my mind that my Uncle Eric would always be there.

As the other men in my life continued to hurt, frustrate, and disappoint me, the image of Uncle Eric loomed larger and larger in my mind. Although I had grown even taller than he was, in my eyes he remained big, strong, bright, witty, and, most important, caring. Even his smell of cigars stayed with me as something a man should have. It would never be offensive to me, because it reminded me of so many nice moments with my uncle.

I had seen Eric only twice in the twenty years since our family left Chicago for California. He hated flying, so the only time he ever came to see us was when he thought my father was dying of Hodgkin's disease. And Bruce, the boys, and I had stopped in Chicago once because I wanted the boys especially to get to know their Great-Uncle Eric. Watching him with them, I recalled those happy times in my own childhood when Eric had taken my hand and led me off for a few hours' peace away from my parents.

Eric did not like to write letters, so our only communication was by telephone, and as the years went by and I became busy raising my own family, even those calls dwindled to the ceremonial one every Christmas Eve. I never knew whether anybody had told Eric about my problems in those years, but he never heard a word about them from me.

When my turn came to talk to Eric on Christmas Eve, I was shocked by how weak and old he sounded. He said a faint "helll — ooo," as if it pained him to pronounce the words. He had always been heavy, so when he told me his weight was down to 127, I knew how desperately sick he must be. The family had known how serious his illness was for some time, but nobody had told me because they knew how much it would upset me.

Until that moment, I had never thought of Eric growing old and dying, as everybody must. Somewhere in the back of my mind, I just felt that he and his love for me would always be there. It had been the purest kind of love — totally accepting and trusting, expecting nothing in return — and, of course, there was no element of sexual expectation, which had caused so much friction between me and Bruce and now me and Zane. I was feeling utterly alone and lost. All I could think about was getting to Chicago to be with Eric when he needed me.

When Bruce told me that a business trip would be taking him to Chicago the next week, I thought it was the answer to my prayers. But Bruce didn't feel I was able to make such a trip. So he convinced me that he should go alone — and he promised that he would go to visit Eric, who was back in the hospital, and report back to me on his condition.

When Bruce got back, he told me he had gone out to dinner with other relatives of mine, but he had not gone to the hospital to see Eric. I was furious. It was only the latest of his betrayals and broken promises. From that moment on, something inside me changed toward my husband. I felt that I had stood by Bruce when his father had been dying of cancer, and the least he could have done was to make this final visit to Eric for me.

Zane said Bruce was a "hateful bastard" for doing this. When I explained to him that my uncle had cancer of the pancreas, Zane was especially kind and understanding. He prepared me for the worst.

This kind of cancer, he said, was known among doctors as "the silent killer," because by the time they discover it, it's usually too late to do anything about it.

At my next regular session, January 30, 1976, I was still hoping I could get to Chicago to see Eric. But when I got home at 5 P.M. that day, my mother called to tell me that Eric had died at 9 that morning. I immediately called Zane. There was a long silence after I told him, and then he asked me how I was taking it, if I was okay. I said I was all right. Zane said, "I love you." He said we would see each other at my next regular session Monday morning, three days later.

That Monday, February 2, 1976, Eric was being buried in Chicago while I sat talking with Zane in his office. I was on the couch, feeling totally dejected. Zane came over and handed me a long letter he had received from his son's best friend after the son died. We had never talked about this tragedy in Zane's life; now Zane described to me how his son had died after lying in a coma for weeks after a hideous car accident, and how this death had devastated him.

It was an intensely personal and private gesture, and I was moved to tears by Zane's sharing this letter that meant so much to him. The son's friend said what a terrible loss he would feel with Aaron Parzen gone, but he said it had been the most wonderful experience of his life to have known such a fine person and to be able to call him his friend. The memory of that, the friend said, would never die as long as he lived.

I had never asked Zane and he had never told me about the details of Aaron's death. Now he poured out the whole story — the shock of first hearing about the accident, then the agonizing days of sitting beside his bed, knowing he would die. He said he had cut out the tongue of one of the athletic shoes the boy was wearing that day as a lasting reminder of him, so alive and young.

Zane took the letter from me and put it on his desk. Then he came back and held me in his arms. I was so distracted at that moment that I didn't see anything odd about his behavior. After hearing about my uncle and telling me about his son's death, Zane became teasing and playful with me. He unbuttoned my blouse and then lay down on the couch, pulling me down on top of him. He joked that I was never, ever going to get rid of him. He said I belonged to him and we would be in each other's lives forever. We had never been so close or intimate as

this — and I remember the question just seemed to come out naturally: "When are you going to marry me?"

Zane stopped cold. He was livid with anger. His face grew pasty
white. The expression on his face was so fierce I was frightened of what
he might do to me. "What do you mean?" he shouted.

"Aren't you planning to leave your wife?" I asked.

"Why should I do that?"

"How do you expect to keep me and stay with your wife? You can't
have two wives. Don't you plan to marry me?"

By now Zane had shoved me off of him and was pacing about the
room. When I repeated my question about when he planned to marry
me, he shouted: "Why would I do that? I have a wife now."

"Is this just an affair to you?"

"You are not the type of woman a man just has an affair with."

"What does that mean?"

"I'm a married man."

"Well, this is a fine time to remember that," I said. "Does this mean
you don't really want me?"

"Of course I want you."

"How can we do this and not be married?"

It was the same kind of dialogue we had gone through many times
before. I would ask these heartfelt, pleading questions and he would
come back with this cold double-talk that offered no answers, no
solutions at all.

But this day was different. Somehow the death of my Uncle Eric had
brought all my problems to a head. In truth, I think it finally shocked
me into seeing the reality of the situation with Zane. I was tired of
these hopelessly confused arguments, tired of Zane's anger at me. I
was tired of feeling guilty about failing Bruce and the boys. I was just
plain tired.

I suddenly turned and left, ending the dialogue in midsentence. I
swore to myself that this was the last time I would ever see this awful
man, and I left him without one word of goodby. I had made up my
mind. My life now had a quick, sure focus.

I had remained true to a promise I had made to Zane not to hoard
pills, and I had only the medication for my stomach, a few tranquilizers, and eight or ten sleeping pills. I knew from past experience that
this would never be enough.

I drove first to a drugstore and browsed, not knowing exactly what I was looking for. I knew I couldn't just ask for something over-the-counter — especially since I didn't know what to ask for.

Next I went to a supermarket and found the shelf for insecticides. Most of them came in spray cans, but I finally spotted a pint bottle that was marked clearly with a skull and crossbones to show it would kill you if taken internally. This time, I would make no mistakes.

I went home and locked all the doors of the house so that when the boys got home from school they would not be able to get in and find me. Then I started to drink the poison. I gagged on the taste and smell of it and couldn't swallow any of it.

In the refrigerator I found a pitcher of lemonade, and I mixed the poison in that. Then I was able to drink the whole bottle fairly quickly. The poison burned all the way down, but I didn't cry. Instead, I remember letting out a piercing, primal scream, my last goodby.

I did remember that the boys had to be picked up at school. Trying to sound calm, I called Bettie Shepherd and asked her if she would mind going and getting them for me. I remember nothing else about that day. I lay down thinking all my troubles were over — I would go to sleep and never wake up.

———

Bettie Shepherd remembers getting her two toddlers into the car and driving halfway to the Walker boys' school before she realized that it wasn't yet time for school to be out. This seemed strange, so she turned around and drove home quickly. When she got there, she saw that two of the neighbors had called an ambulance. Evelyn vaguely remembered crying out for help, but she did not remember making the phone call that brought the neighbors running. (Bettie Shepherd felt that Evelyn consciously wanted to kill herself in these several suicide attempts. However, once her consciousness was put aside by the pills or the poison, the subconscious instinct for survival took over — and Evelyn would reach for the phone to save her life, not even knowing she was doing it.)

Parzen made these notes about Evelyn that day, February 2, 1976: "Denial of mourning in some ways. Wants from me — full blown fantasy that if I love her and she gets well, I will divorce my wife and marry her (this was masochistic activity on her part to push it now). I said, 'No.' She 'it can't be. You will.' Angry. Rx: Nembutal Gr. 3/4 #8. She said she had no other sleeping pills. (? Suicidal?)"

At 3:30 P.M. on the same day, Parzen notes: "Call from Scripps E.R. — brought there by police. O.D. Seconal and Nembutal. ? also Chlordane rat and roach poison (? of this being a fantasy of 'if I am good, I'll get anything I want' versus borderline personality with narcissistic grandiosity as self importance. Certainly denial and disavowal of reality that does not fit with her wishes occur, and at other times good reality testing is present.)"

Although he was careful not to blame anyone specifically, the doctor who admitted Evelyn to the emergency room on this occasion did make a definite connection between her visits to Parzen's office and these suicide attempts.

B. Kim, M.D., wrote:

. . . this 36-year-old Caucasian lady . . . was admitted with acute intoxication of Seconal and Chlordane ant killer. The patient was previously admitted July 1975, at which time she was admitted with a barbiturate overdose and hospitalized in the Intensive Care Unit and stayed for three days for observation. At that time she was also seen by Dr. Parzen and treated for personality disorder and 24 hours after she saw Dr. Parzen in the office she took Valium, 50 tablets. She was observed in the ICU for three days and was discharged, and the final diagnosis was acute barbiturate poisoning and reactive depression. At this time it is difficult to obtain a history from the patient. However, some history is obtained from the husband. The patient was apparently extremely depressed and visited Dr. Parzen today and got Seconal, and afterwards she ingested the Seconal and also the ant killer, which is apparently Chlordane chemically. When the patient was seen in the Emergency Room she was drowsy but not depressed from a respiratory point of view and was easily awakened. The patient was immediately lavaged with 5 liters of saline with charcoal, and there was no episode of aspiration during this procedure. By the time I saw the patient in the E.R., the patient was wakeful and drowsy and was asking whether the doctor had notified Dr. Parzen, and also whether her husband was informed. . . ."

Once again, I woke up in a sterile white enclosure at the Scripps Hospital emergency room. This time, I was in excruciating pain. The poison had burned my esophagus and stomach lining. I felt as if my insides had been rubbed raw with sandpaper. I cursed myself, my fate. How low could anyone sink who couldn't even succeed at killing herself?

When a nurse came in to check on me, I asked if Marty were still working there. The nurse said Marty would be coming on duty in about an hour. When I saw my old friend, I started crying. Marty put her strong arms around me and said — once again — "Everything is going to be all right now." We sat up most of the night. Marty told me about her husband and children and how happy they all were with the new camper they had just bought. At one point, I was even able to joke about not knowing how to kill myself properly. I couldn't swallow anything — not even a glass of water or a cup of broth. But after several hours, Marty brought me some Jell-O, and I was able to swallow a little bit of that. It would be weeks before my digestive system worked without awful pain. I took it as part of the price I had to pay for being a failure — a failure at life and a failure in attempting death.

After forty-eight hours, I was moved into a private room. Bruce was there waiting for me. He told me he had talked on the phone several times with Zane and that Zane was very upset with me for taking the poison. My guilt and shame over what I had done were only made worse by Bruce's coldness toward me. I could not explain to him that I was not a child pulling stunts to get attention. But neither could I explain to him that I really wanted to die. By now Bruce had lost all patience with me.

Although it had been obvious for some months that I was totally involved with Zane, Bruce had refused to recognize it or deal with it. He prided himself on not being jealous; he had always told me that before. He would tell me that jealousy was totally childish behavior. But when he finally acknowledged that I was involved with Zane, he said I was Zane's responsibility — not his.

Bruce became more restless, sitting beside my bed that day so I finally told him to go home and relax. The nurses had told him that I was not to be left alone, but he leaped at the chance to leave, gave me a quick kiss on the forehead, and was gone.

I was now alone with nothing to do or think about except the impending visit from Zane. I had a gut feeling that it was going to be an ugly, very unpleasant meeting. I didn't consciously think he would hurt me — not then, or ever — but for the first time I think I was frightened about seeing him. There was no other word for what I was feeling but fear.

I had a terrible headache, and I was feeling generally miserable all over, inside and out. I turned out all the lights in the room and turned on the radio to some nice, peaceful music. I was resting like that when suddenly the door flew open and Zane burst in and switched on the lights. I begged him not to do that because the lights hurt my eyes. But he coldly said he needed to see me clearly.

"Why should I waste my time on you?" he snarled at me. My worst fears were coming true. He was mean and angry with me, not loving and supportive, as I needed. But I wasn't the docile lamb I was before. I was hurting, and I had no time for his games. "How dare you hold yourself blameless!" I shot back at him. I didn't have the strength to carry on a real argument with him. But I kept telling myself not to cry, not to cry; I would not give him that satisfaction.

"Maybe I should just throw you out," he said, as if he'd been doing me such a great favor all this time. "Go ahead," I told him, "you're costing me $110 a week." I was sure he'd miss that, if not me. For the first time, cutting remarks came flying out of my mouth toward Zane; I had never thought about him before in those terms, much less talked to him that way. I was thinking that he had his nerve, coming in there as if he were God, with no fault of his own. I wasn't the one who started this relationship. I hadn't been looking for another man. I didn't know what was happening, but he certainly did.

Then he said something so cruel I found it hard to believe: "You didn't even know how to kill yourself — you used the wrong kind of poison."

"I'm very sorry," I said bitterly, "I'll try to do better next time."

"I should think so," he said.

At that, I could no longer hold back the tears. I was so angry at myself, but even in my confused state I knew he should have been supportive of me at that moment. If he had to talk rough to me, he should have waited until I had recovered enough to deal with it. He knew what a struggle I had had in recent months just finding the desire to live. He had convinced me that he was the only one who could help me. And he had convinced me that I wasn't crazy, that I could get better. But I wasn't getting any better — and I wanted to die.

"I'm not coming back to you," I told him.

"Well," he said, "if you're going to be a coward, you can leave me and go to another doctor — I'll even give you a name."

I was feeling so bad, and he was making me feel so much worse, that I wouldn't even look at him. Out of the corner of my eye, I could see him tilting back in the straight chair he was sitting in. Incredibly, he was swaggering even while he was sitting — he had his hands in his pockets and he was moving back and forth as he talked tough. And I was hardly able to move on the bed in front of him. I was thinking how much I'd love it if the chair slipped out from under him and he had to pick himself up from a humiliating position.

But he had control of me, and we both knew it. I wanted desperately to get out of bed and away from him, but I knew I didn't have the strength to get up. I would have to ask him for help — and I wasn't about to let him know I needed him. I reached for a glass of water and turned away from him to drink it — I didn't want him to see how painful it was for me to swallow. I just wanted him to leave me alone, but I could tell he was settled in for a long visit.

Finally, I asked if he had meant everything he said to me in his office. "What exactly do you mean?" he asked.

"Do you intend to stay with your wife?"

"Yes!"

"Then you don't love or really want me."

"That's not true."

"In other words, you want to have your cake and eat it too," I said.

"I'm surprised at you saying such a thing," he said with that older, wiser schoolteacher air of his. "That's crude."

He began a kind of low yelling at me — not loud, but forceful, controlled. He said he was very upset with me, that he did love me and intended to be with me. I was too weak and confused to question him more.

Zane said he would authorize the hospital to release me the next morning. Then he asked where Bruce was. I told him Bruce had been there with me, but he had left several hours earlier. Then he started raging about Bruce. Bruce was not to leave me alone any time I was in the hospital; I was never to be left alone. Zane repeated that he was the only one who cared for me; Bruce didn't care anything at all. I was getting so upset by all this that I thought I was going to throw up — but, of course, there was nothing inside me to regurgitate.

When Zane had said he would release me the next day and then arrange for an appointment in his office the day following that, I had said, "I'll think about it."

"There's nothing to think about," he said. If I didn't come, he would call me; he would always find me.

Finally, he was gone and I was left wringing wet with sweat. I rang for a nurse to come help me into the shower. I stood there a long time, letting the water cool me off and ease my mind. It felt so good that I left my hair wet and brushed it into a ponytail, feeling fresh and clean again. I felt that the worst was over with Zane. I still wasn't sure I'd go back to him. But I had failed him, and therefore I guess I deserved his angry words. I just wanted to go to sleep and not think about any of it.

The next morning, when Bruce came to take me home, I refused a wheelchair. I made a vow to myself that I would walk out of that place on my own two legs and I would never be carried back in there again.

After we were home, Bruce said he wanted to have a heart-to-heart talk with me about a lot of things that had been bothering him. He said when we first met he was quite taken with me. I was different and he liked that. For one thing, I was Jewish and he had never known a Jewish woman before. He said he had been attracted to me sexually in the beginning, but he had not loved me. He had married out of obligation, feeling he owed it to me because I seemed to love him so much. He said he grew to love me, but also grew to resent me. He liked having a home and children and the respectability that gave him in the community. He liked all the things that went with marriage — except being tied to a wife. Considering my condition, this was a brutal revelation at the time. I know it sounds totally irrational — since I had been having a relationship with Zane for almost a year at that point — but I had never questioned my love for my husband or his love for me.

I sat there stunned by everything Bruce was telling me. I felt totally abandoned now — by everybody except Zane. If Zane could and did hurt me, that was a risk I had to take. I had sometimes wondered what was missing in my marriage — and now Bruce had explained everything, filled in the missing piece of the puzzle in my head.

Deep inside, I knew I would go back to Zane. I had reached a point where there was nowhere else to go. When I got to his office the next day, I sat there for a long time not saying anything. And then I started telling Zane how disturbed I was by the way he had treated me in the hospital. I told him bluntly that I had been frightened about coming back to see him.

He was calm and reassuring. He said he was glad I had come back to him. He reminded me of his warning that if I hadn't come back, he would have come after me.

Sitting on the couch, I asked Zane to come to me. I was afraid he was still so angry with me that he had stopped loving me, that he would hate me now. But he came to me and put his arms around me, held me tightly. Once again, he said he would always love me and I had nothing to be afraid of. He would always be there.

"I couldn't stand it if you ever stopped loving me," I said.

"That's something you never have to worry about," he answered.

As before, Zane increased my medication when I came out of the hospital. I resumed my life in the darkened bedroom, getting up only for the daily telephone call to Zane and a morning shower, leaving the house only for the visits to Zane's office twice a week. Now, however, I made a special effort to stay away from Bruce. I didn't know how to behave around him now that I knew how he felt about me.

One evening a friend of mine brought over a casserole for our dinner. As she was leaving, I overheard her telling Bruce that he ought to do more to help me around the house. She said he should hire somebody to come in and help me with the housework. Bruce angrily told my friend that it was none of her business; he would handle his home his own way.

One day in March 1976, I came home from my session with Zane to find Bruce and his mother talking in the living room. My mother-in-law politely began by asking me how I felt. She went on from there to say I should try harder to snap out of these problems I kept having; it was too hard on Bruce and the boys. She just couldn't understand what could possibly be wrong with me.

I was in no condition to explain or justify my existence at that point. Couldn't they see that the worst part of my problem was that I didn't know what was wrong or what to do about it? I got up and was walking toward the kitchen when I realized that Bruce and his mother were closing in on me. Both of them are taller and heavier than I am. All of a sudden, I felt like a tiny animal with two huge monsters crowding in on me, cornering me and forcing me to consider questions I could not answer.

I yelled back something at them but I can't remember what. Those big forms and all those words were swirling about my head in total confusion. I went into the kitchen. I guess I thought a drink of water would help me talk better. I picked up a glass, but it fell out of my hand and shattered on the floor. Impulsively, I reached up and started grabbing all the glasses, one after the other, and smashing them on the floor. I was laughing and crying; the glasses seemed to be dancing. Somewhere in my confused mind I was thinking that this would keep Bruce and his mother away from me, although even in that state, I certainly didn't want to hurt them. I just wanted them to stay away from me and not hurt me.

Then Bruce grabbed my wrist and twisted me around so that he could pick me up and carry me up the stairs. He threw me on our bed and shouted: "Are you completely crazy? What are you trying to do?" I was out of control now. I screamed at him, "I hate you! Your mother should know what you really are. You are nothing but a liar and a selfish bastard."

Bruce stormed out of the room. I was finally alone, so I could call Zane. I was blubbering and babbling out of control, but he let me talk on and on, describing everything that had happened. I was so embarrassed about causing such a scene in front of my mother-in-law. But Zane told me I had no reason to be ashamed or feel guilty. I had reacted in a natural way to a nagging situation.

Bruce and his mother never mentioned the incident again. I guess they had come to expect that kind of behavior from me, and it was obvious that there were no solutions in talking things out.

In the weeks that followed, my condition went from bad to worse. I would have horrible dreams and nightmares about my Uncle Eric. The deck off our bedroom reminded me of the deck off Eric's apartment in Chicago. Some nights, I would wake up confused and think I was back there. Other times, Bruce would find me walking in my sleep. I thought Eric would come to get me, if I could just get down the stairs to meet him. I was never fully awake at these times, of course, because I was always in a drugged haze — I had to keep taking pills, one after the other, just to make it through the day and night.

By April 1976, Bruce and I were arguing almost every time we were together. In all these months, Bruce had held me down and restrained me a few times, but he had never hit me. But one night the tension was too much for him, and he lost control. As usual, it was a petty family squabble that mushroomed into a major confrontation because of my mental condition.

Our son Carl had been watching television, and I told him to turn it off. When he refused, I reached over and turned it off myself. He and I were arguing on the stairway when he angrily pushed me aside so he could get by. I almost fell down the stairs.

When Bruce came home that night, Carl and I were telling our separate sides of the story. I guess the anger — maybe real hatred — stored up over all those months finally spilled out. Bruce and I started arguing in the kitchen. I said something that caused Bruce to knock me against the wall. I fell down and he grabbed my wrists and roughly dragged me through the kitchen and dining room and up the stairs, bouncing me off the steps and walls. Finally, he threw me onto our bed. The next morning, Bruce left on a business trip and I had big black-and-blue bruises all over my body. I called a friend and she came over and helped me get to a doctor. This doctor sent me for X-rays and treated me for all the bruises and swellings. There were no broken bones, but I was sore for several days.

When I went in for my next session with Zane, I wore a long-sleeved sweater. I didn't know how to begin telling him about what had happened. After a long silence, I just took off my sweater and let him see all the bruises.

Zane was furious. He said something had to be done; I couldn't go on living like this. Zane took out a legal pad and told me to describe every detail of the fight with Bruce. He turned suddenly cold and professional, and I was very upset about his clinical attitude. I asked him why he was taking such detailed notes on what I was saying; I wanted him to stop writing. No, Zane said, he needed the notes, "in case the divorce goes to court."

"What divorce?" I cried. "What court?"

Zane said, "I might have to testify in court on your behalf." Then he told me I should learn how to defend myself. He said that if Bruce ever came at me again, I should kick him in the groin. I told him I would never do anything like that and he shouldn't talk to me that way.

As he was saying goodby to me that day, Zane told me to be very careful and to call him immediately if I needed his help. He held my face very tightly in his hands; his eyes glassed over with feeling for me. "You don't deserve this," he said.

I continued to try to talk to Bruce about a "trial separation," but his response was always the same. It was his house and his sons; he was the one who had worked hard and earned all the money for everything we had. What had I ever done except cause problems? Bruce felt I didn't deserve anything, including the children. He assured me that he was far more able to take care of the boys than I was.

Zane kept bringing up my divorce, but I couldn't bear to speak to him about the loss of my marriage and my children. When I once told him that I couldn't stand to live without my sons, he answered, "You lost them a long time ago."

On June 1, 1976, Parzen made another of his sporadic reports on patient Evelyn Walker's condition. It is quoted here in full:

The patient has now been seen for a total of 120 hours on a twice-a-week basis, and even though many crises continue, to say the least, things have stabilized pretty well.

Suicide attempts have been gone through recently, and she has been able to "keep her word" and not take any overdoses. Her difficulty in wanting to act out in the transference persists, although it seems that she is able to tolerate the affectual state of being cared for without having to have it acted out sexually.

She has been able to complete a course in interior decorating and now has a job, although this itself presents problems. Since October there have been many marital difficulties, including her husband losing his temper to the degree that she has had to have X-rays and has had severe bruises on various parts of her body. She had an episode which occurred in March of 1976, and her husband's basic response was not to contact me for a little while and really not talk about his losing his temper. He is still manipulating, totally unaware of what he is doing in terms of his acting out of hostility toward her, using hyperhonesty, accusing me of seducing his wife, telling his wife things that will make her want to leave treatment, and in many ways still persists in trying to push her into suicide.

I think we have stabilized things enough such that this will not occur, and the question of separation occurs. He is taking a course in transactional analysis which is used by him in terms of interpreting her behavior, never looking at the relationship between the two, but at this time he may be feeling a little more pressure. His intellectual and obsessive defenses are still quite potent to say the least, but the rage begins to be acted out but he can block it off and repress the content later.

The prognosis is still guarded, but it looks like we are making some headway in terms of her capacity to internalize the positive self representation, even though she is still highly susceptible to either her mother or her husband giving her negative input about herself.

Zane D. Parzen, M.D.

In these semifictional notes and reports on Evelyn Walker, Parzen became more and more vindictive in his depiction of Bruce Walker as the villain. In a matter of months, Walker — in Parzen's notes — progressed from being merely a cold, unresponsive husband to being an impotent psychotic who was out to kill his wife. In that connection, Parzen constantly referred to the 1944 film *Gaslight*. Over and over, Parzen would tell Evelyn that Bruce was "trying to gaslight you." Evelyn would ask what he meant. And so would her lawyers in court much later. It is possible that here, as in many other patterns of his behavior, he was attaching his own faults and problems to someone else. In fact, in one scene in that film, the husband uses language almost identical to that Parzen used with Evelyn in some of their scenes together. The film husband used a similar brand of double-talk with his wife, answering questions with questions, and he would also go into rages against her, as Parzen did once or twice with Evelyn. After one of these, the film husband asks threateningly of his wife, "Do you want me to get angry with you again?", the very same words Parzen would use in a dialogue with Evelyn.

On one level, Parzen seems to have been aware of the fact that he was to blame for Evelyn's disintegration, but, on another level, he could not cope with that fact. He had to blame somebody, so he blamed Bruce Walker. Word for word, line for line, he was accusing Bruce of doing to Evelyn what he, Parzen, was doing to her.

—

Early one morning in June 1976, I decided to take things into my own hands. While everyone was still asleep, I got up and went out looking for an apartment. I found a nice little studio just a few minutes from our house. It was furnished, and the rent was only $240 a month.

When I told him, Bruce was delighted with the idea of my moving out and said he would help me with rent and other living expenses. I signed a six-month lease, thinking my problems surely would be resolved in that time.

Although Bruce was happy to see me go, he was not going to make it easy for me. When I reached for a blender that a friend had given me, Bruce said that it was his and I could not take it. This argument was just too absurd for me to deal with, so I didn't even ask for anything else. I moved out with only my clothes and a few pictures. And there I was in my own apartment: thirty-six years old and living alone for the first time in my life.

—

About one month after she moved into the apartment, Evelyn had a visit from her friend Ellen Hayes. Ellen knocked at the apartment door and got no answer. Then she went around to a window closer to the bed and knocked longer and louder. Finally, Evelyn got up and let her in. Living alone, Evelyn had been taking even more drugs. She had stopped eating altogether, existing on an occasional glass of juice or cup of tea. She moved about in a dreamlike state, never quite conscious of who she was with or what she was saying and doing.

Ellen Hayes remembers that this particular night, Evelyn insisted that they go swimming. But Ellen hadn't brought a bathing suit. Never mind, Evelyn said, she would just go swimming in the nude. They went down to the apartment complex's pool. Ellen went in first and then watched in horror as Evelyn seemed to melt, going totally limp as her body eased into the cold water. Ellen grabbed her and pulled her out of the water, but Evelyn seemed to have no control of her muscles. She was awake, but glassy-eyed, and she couldn't sit or stand up.

After struggling back up the stairs with the dead weight of her friend, Ellen Hayes put Evelyn to bed and determined to do something about all the drugs Evelyn was taking. Without telling Evelyn, she called Parzen. She knew that Evelyn would never have allowed her to do this. But she felt something had to be done. She asked Parzen if he was aware of how many drugs Evelyn was taking and of what effect they were having on her. Parzen was not merely cold and professional, he was downright rude. He bluntly answered no, he did not know how many pills she was using, and yes, he would do something about it. Parzen's office notes are just as cryptic, making no mention that he received the call or that Ellen Hayes's warning was the reason for his action. For the record, he wrote only this: "She passed out and I discontinued all drugs."

Later, in the trial, Parzen would offer this as further evidence of how well he had been looking after Evelyn, ignoring the fact that he had been the one who gave her those drugs to begin with — and he probably never would have stopped if it hadn't been for the call from her friend. Evelyn would not know about Ellen Hayes's call for another two years.

━━

That Thursday in July 1976, I went in for my regular afternoon appointment. Nothing seemed different between Zane and me. But slowly he brought the conversation around to the medication I had been taking. He said he was concerned about all the pills I was using. He said he didn't think I needed any of them anymore. It was very important to him that I stop taking everything. He told me to go home and throw away all the pills.

"Well," I said, "if you think it's that important, I'll do whatever you say. I'll do it just for you."

"Yes," he said, "it is important to me, and I want you to do it. You may lose some sleep for a few nights, but that will be the extent of it. It will take maybe a week or two for the drugs to get completely out of your system, but eventually you will get back to normal and start sleeping again at night."

Zane reassured me that I would only lose a little bit of sleep. In fact, he made a joke about my going out and buying some magazines and stocking up on ice cream and potato chips and other junk food because he said I'd be watching the late, late shows.

Once I was back home in my little apartment, I gathered up all the pills. I knew by the labels that some were for stomach pain, some for sleep, some for drowsiness, backache, headache, shakiness. There were red ones and green ones and blue-and-yellow and white-and-pink ones. I knew them by colors, but the truth was I didn't know what any of them really were. By that time, I was taking forty to sixty pills a day, and I had on hand about 200 of them.

I first thought about flushing them all down the toilet. But I wanted to show Zane that I would do anything he asked me. So, I decided that since his birthday was coming up, I'd give him a nice surprise. I'd prove to him just how much I cared by showing that I had kept the pills in the apartment and forced myself not to take any of them.

I kept my studio apartment immaculate, and it was only a small space, so there was not much work to keep me busy. I didn't notice anything different for the first several hours that first evening. I kept the television on for company and worked on a piece of needlepoint that would be my main present to Zane for his birthday.

I had not gone so many hours without pills in years. Whenever anything upsetting had happened, I had always reached for pills to calm me down or pick me up — but especially to help me get to sleep every night.

Very late that night, the restlessness began. I got tired of switching the television channels and turned off the set. But I couldn't stand the silence, so I turned it back on. I couldn't focus on any particular program. I couldn't focus on anything. I walked back and forth like a prisoner in a small cell. There wasn't that much room to walk in, but I couldn't stay still. Walking around didn't seem to calm me either.

I tried to lie down and relax, but that was just as bad as sitting up. Try as I might, I could not find any place or position that was comfortable. When I tried drinking a glass of juice, I got about two sips down before it all came up. A little while later, I fixed some clear soup, thinking that might stay down better, but it was the same thing all over again. I would try to eat or drink something and then have to rush to the bathroom and stand there retching and retching, long after there was nothing in my stomach. Slowly, I began to realize that it was going to be more than a matter of not being able to sleep.

The retching led to coughing, and then my nose started running as if I had a bad cold. I would go from hot to cold sweats and shiver and shake in convulsions. For a time, I think I passed out. Nothing seemed to make me comfortable. It was as if my very skin were hurting. I felt I would be much better off if I could peel off my skin. I was aching all over, as if I were bruised inside and out.

Once, I pulled a blanket up over me, and it felt like sandpaper rubbing my skin. I was losing control, but I vowed to stick with it. I had to prove to Zane I could do it; in my mind, I had no choice but to suffer through it for him, no matter how bad it got.

As Friday dawned, I found some relief under the shower, but that was only temporary. I would shower and wash my hair and dry off, and a little while later I would go back and do it again. The hours and days seemed to meld together into one long-drawn-out nightmare of soreness and discomfort. Friday came and went, and then Saturday, and then Sunday.

By Monday morning, I felt so weak and was trembling so badly that I did not think I would be able to make it to Zane's office for my appointment that afternoon. I had been desperate to talk with him, but it was always understood — even though he hadn't spelled it out in so many words — that I should never call him at home on weekends. Even in such desperate straits as these, I never would have risked making him as angry as I knew he would be if I called him at home.

As soon as I knew he would be in his office on Monday morning, I called the answering service. He returned my call immediately.

"Evelyn," he said, "are you all right?" He rarely called me by my first name, so I took that as a sign of his genuine concern for me. He did care, he did love me. I asked him why he had not told me it would be so rough. Again, he asked how I was feeling. I told him I was better than I had been over the weekend, but I was still feeling pretty bad.

"Don't worry," he said, "we will be seeing each other in a few hours." Then he said he had to get back to his patient, and he hung up.

I fixed a cup of warm tea and sipped on it very slowly. I managed to keep that down, but I still didn't know whether I had the strength to get up, get dressed, and drive to Zane's office. Nothing could have kept me from it, however, and I did somehow manage to get in my car and make it to downtown La Jolla.

Zane was just coming back from lunch, and he had gotten on the elevator in the underground garage. I got on at the first floor. For a moment, I was shocked at seeing him. We never met outside his office, except in the hospital of course, and I didn't know how I was supposed to respond. We just nodded at each other and looked away. Neither of us said anything. As far as the others in that elevator knew, we were two strangers just nodding politely to each other.

In the office, we were locked inside our private world — and everybody and everything else was locked out. I fell into Zane's arms and he held me the way I liked. He said he was very proud of me for what I had done. He said he had thought about calling me to see how I was, but he just didn't get around to it.

I joked that maybe the next time he shouldn't think about it, he should go ahead and do it. He also said he would have come to me if I had called and told him I needed him. I didn't want to argue about anything, I felt so weak. I just wanted to be held, to be told he cared about me. Zane said the worst was over; I would start feeling better now.

In fact, in the following months I did start feeling better without all those drugs in my system. But it would be a very long time before I was truly clearheaded. During this time, I would often get disoriented going down streets I was familiar with. I'd end up lost, even following a route I'd taken a hundred times before.

━

It would be three years before Evelyn would learn that what she had gone through was severe withdrawal. Parzen knew it very well, however. He also knew that she could easily have died from abruptly stopping so many strong drugs. His office notes for July 19, 1976, document his knowledge that she went through withdrawal, even though he didn't call it that. He wrote: "Had tremors without deliria. Was hot and cold, sweating, nauseated, and had occasional tremors, shaking with some agitation. . . ."

━

Zane's birthday was the next Monday, July 26, 1976. I walked into his office and held out a small package, keeping my real present hidden behind my back. I had wrapped up the box of pills in fancy paper with a nice ribbon and bow around it. Zane looked shocked when he saw all those pills. Then he said once again how proud he was of me for what I had done. He said he didn't know where I found such strength. I knew I could always find the strength for him; I was living only for him now, and he knew that as well as I did.

Then I presented him with my main present, the needlepoint piece I had framed for his wall. It was a quotation attributed to Mark Twain, and I thought it had very special meaning for Zane and me and our love for each other. Zane smiled proudly, pleased with the gift and the thoughts it expressed. He waved his hand toward a wall of psychiatric textbooks and other books. "You know," he said, "that one quotation says more than all those books up there."

It read: DON'T PART WITH YOUR ILLUSIONS. WHEN THEY ARE GONE, YOU MAY STILL EXIST, BUT YOU HAVE CEASED TO LIVE.

Chapter 6 In August 1976, I went to work at an interior decorating shop located just across the street from the building where Zane had his offices. I had not worked in fifteen years, but it was a matter of simple arithmetic that I had to have a job. Bruce had agreed to give me $600 a month, but my rent was $240 and I was paying Zane $440 a month.

I worked hard at the shop and did complete some design jobs. I even designed the interior of the home of one of San Diego's wealthy clothing-store owners. But I never felt well, and I was constantly afraid of losing my job. Zane and I had some nice moments during this time. I would take my design plans over to show him and we would spread them out on the floor and go over them together. In this small way, he was getting to be the architect he had always wanted to be. Apparently Zane had a workshop at home where he spent a great deal of time. He had some woodworking books on his shelves in the office, and once he showed me the plans for a fine piano bench he was building.

During this time there were also some odd moments when Bruce and I were as close as we had ever been. He would come to my apartment and we would talk in a way we had never before been able to talk.

One night, however, Bruce stopped by in such a disturbed state that our roles were reversed. For the first time, I was concerned about his emotional condition. Bruce had just gone through the first phase of est training, and he seemed totally unhinged by it. As Bruce told me about this experience, he began to cry. I had never seen him cry or lose control, and I was very disturbed at seeing the strong man in my life fall apart this way. But this experience told me that maybe he had changed; maybe there was some hope that we could get back together and have a happy normal life again. I was so desperate that I would have agreed to anything, so I went with him to a session of est. But what I saw at this meeting seemed brutal to me, and I was frightened by it. The cold, hard manipulation was too much for me. These people were saying and doing brutal things, and there seemed to be no affection at all. I asked Bruce to take me home, and that was the end of that experiment.

In September 1976, Bruce filed for divorce. It was a long, slow, agonizing process for me — we would be legally separated for a year before the divorce became final. I already felt such guilt over what I had done to my family that I could only say yes to everything Bruce demanded. And, in the end, I got nothing. I lost custody of our sons. Bruce said I was unfit and he was right — I didn't want them to suffer any more because of me. I did have visiting rights, but after Bruce and I were legally separated, I found it increasingly difficult to make contact with Carl and Michael — or to arrange meetings with them. Bruce would insist on being present, so we always had to suit his schedule. There was a complicated divorce agreement wherein Bruce signed a promissory note to give me half of the amount he paid for the house — which, of course, was only a fraction of what it was worth and what he would eventually sell the place for. The note wouldn't come due until he sold the house, so the agreement didn't do me much good. I had to sell the note, at a loss of $18,000, because I was so desperate for money.

My lawyer made me sign a release holding him blameless for what I was agreeing to — he said it was a "dirty divorce." In the end, I signed away everything out of guilt. I didn't want my children involved in a public fight over property and custody.

Throughout the agonizing process of divorce, Zane was my only comfort. But there was something missing in our relationship, and I knew it. If I lacked the healthy awareness to understand exactly what Zane was doing to me, I did perceive on the most basic, instinctive level that he was getting fulfillment out of our sexual relationship. But for me it was far from being everything I needed in a loving relationship.

Just exactly what Evelyn and Zane were doing sexually was the subject of lengthy and detailed questioning during the later court proceedings. Evelyn explained that during most of the eighteen-month period following the first time she performed fellatio on Parzen, she would have oral sex with him at least once a week. She also said that he would sometimes try to satisfy her either with his hand or, on rare occasions, with his mouth. She said he always had an orgasm; she rarely did. In his own pretrial examination, Parzen said he started having sex with Evelyn only because it was something she wanted so much from him. Yes, he knew it was a clear violation of psychiatric procedure. No, he had never been taught that it was ever proper for a psychiatrist to engage in sex with a patient. However, he had been taught that it was all right to hold a patient — and that was how sex with Evelyn got started. She had said she wanted to make him feel good; she had coaxed him onto the couch. Parzen insisted that he had only performed cunnilingus with Evelyn "once or twice," and then only because she had forced him to do it. He estimated that she had engaged in oral sex with him twenty times and that toward the end of their relationship they had intercourse eight times.

Parzen swore that he had strongly resisted Evelyn's "advances" from the beginning, first by saying, "That's not what we're here for." But, he added, his "problem manifested itself when I was seeing a particular type of female patient who was depressed, needy, whiny, who felt she needed to be given to in order to feel decent. I could not say 'no' to her whether that was in terms of sex, drugs. I didn't set the limits."

Parzen had no explanation for the court, or for Evelyn at the time, as to why — after eighteen months of only "oral or manual" sex — they suddenly began having intercourse. But Evelyn clearly remembers that important turning point in their relationship.

——

It was an afternoon in late September or early October of 1976. We were having such a pleasant quiet hour together, and Zane told me he had an hour free the next day for me to come in. I told him I couldn't afford a third hour, but Zane said, "It's on me."

The next day, as I crossed the street from the design shop where I worked, I looked up and saw Zane watching for me from the terrace outside his office, as he often did. I didn't wave and neither did he, but seeing him only added to the tension and excitement I was feeling over this bonus meeting. I closed the door behind me and Zane had me in his arms immediately. Then, almost in one movement, we were down on the couch and he had his legs locked around me. We were kissing and whispering affectionate words to each other when suddenly he stopped and told me to get up and take off my slacks. At first I didn't move, so he told me again to get up and take off my pants. Then he pulled down his pants and underwear. We lay there as we had so many times before — with me on top. I was so surprised by this new turn that I asked him "Why?" At that point we had been seeing each other for more than two years; we had been having sex during more than eighteen months of that time; but Zane had never once entered me in the regular way. Of course, the way we were finally doing it was not exactly the old missionary position, but to me it was true love at last.

I sat astride him and slowly moved his penis inside me. The great moment had finally arrived. We were truly making love; he really did love me — this proved it. I was overwhelmed by the spiritual meaning of the act. I have no memory of how it felt in a physical sense. I don't think I had ever been so nervous or excited, not even when I had sex with Bruce the first time when I was a virgin. I was trembling so much I was afraid my legs might give way underneath me. Even after it was over, I still lay there shaking all over from excitement. Zane asked me why I was reacting that way. I asked him, "Why did you suddenly decide to make love to me?" He answered, "I thought it would be fun. Didn't you want me to?"

I felt like a young girl in love as I floated out of his office, down on the elevator, across the street, and back to work. It was so sudden and such a surprise — such a happy, wonderful surprise.

Later that night, alone in my apartment, I relived that moment in the afternoon with my beloved Zane. I trusted him so completely that I had never once considered that he might have any kind of problem when it came to sex. I was the sick one, the one with problems. That night I came to a rather stunning conclusion — I felt amazed, then delighted and more than greatly relieved — I now knew that there was nothing wrong with me sexually.

▬▬
▬

When the divorce settlement with her husband was being finalized, it became clear that Evelyn would no longer have the money to pay Parzen his $440-a-month fee for her visits. In his longer reports and daily notes, and later in his court testimony, Parzen would attempt to make the record show that it was an act of kindness on his part that he brought up the subject and volunteered to stop charging Evelyn Walker for her twice-weekly sessions with him. The truth was much more complicated. In fact, it was only for a few weeks that he did not charge Evelyn — a mere fraction of the total amount she paid in the two years and three months she was seeing him. Also, it was no act of kindness on his part to stop charging her; it was a matter of necessity. Evelyn had no money.

One day Zane was pressuring me with questions about my divorce proceedings. I kept turning away from Zane in an effort not to answer his questions about the divorce agreement. Finally, he grabbed my face, kept my chin in his hands, and forced me to look into his eyes. He wanted to know all about the divorce agreement, what property I had signed away to Bruce. I confessed that I had signed away virtually everything. I also blurted out that I would not be able to continue paying his bill.

Zane sat there in silence for a long time. After some minutes, he asked me if all the papers had been filed. I said I understood that everything had been settled; it was only a matter of signing the papers. Zane wanted to know how much money was involved, but I told him I had no idea how much money Bruce had or how much our house was worth — or anything else about our community property. That ended the conversation, but a week or so later, Zane returned to the question and said he appreciated what I had given up for him. He asked, if I had it all to do over again, would I do it?

"Do you mean fall in love with you?" I asked.

"Yes," he said.

My love for him had become my only reason for living by this time, so I said yes, of course I would do it all over again. I would do anything for him, anything he asked me to do.

Zane then told me not to worry about his bill, he would try to work something out. But I explained that I had no money and I wouldn't be able to pay him, even if that meant not seeing him again. Zane was quiet for what seemed a long time. His fee had been a sore subject between us from the very beginning. I had felt guilty that I was taking money from my family to pay a doctor to listen to my problems. Later, when I became sexually involved with Zane, I felt more and more confusion and guilt about paying — in effect — for love and affection. I was not paying for it anyhow, he would add; the bills were going to my husband. But that only made me feel all the more guilty.

Zane told me I had paid enough; then the subject was dropped. But just a week or so later, we were chatting in his office over some coffee while he was going over his bank book, getting ready to go to the bank. The subject of my paying or not paying never came up, and I still do not know what was on his mind. But suddenly he looked up from the bank book — his eyes were glassed over, his face had turned deep red, and he was screaming at me with a kind of violent anger I had never seen in him before. All the veins in his neck seemed to stand out. At first, I tried to soothe him. I said I didn't know what I had done wrong, but I was sorry for whatever it was. But he grew more and more angry, and I became very frightened of him. I stood up and backed against the wall. But seeing how terrified I was only seemed to make him more angry with me. He shouted, "Why are you doing that?" And he motioned for me to move away from the wall. I said he must not love me or he wouldn't get so angry with me. He yelled back that he did love me very much and wanted to run away with me, but he couldn't do that; he had a family to think of, people he cared about.

I felt pushed and pulled in every direction, totally confused by what was happening. I just wanted him to hold me and stop being angry, but he kept yelling, and I was so frightened I couldn't move away from the wall. I was a child again, cowering in fear of my mother's flailing arms. In desperation, I cried, "If you don't leave your wife, I will lose you."

"You will never lose me," he shot back. "How many times do I have to tell you that?"

Even in our shouting, we were still saying how much we loved each other. I moved over and put my arms around him. "I love you," I said, "I don't want to hurt you." I told him I wouldn't want to live if I ever lost him.

With that, Zane shoved me away from him and said, "Go kill yourself then." I was stunned by the violence in his eyes and by his words. I grabbed my purse and ran out of the office. I sat behind the wheel of my car, trembling, unable to get enough control to start the car and get home.

When I finally got out onto the highway and headed toward my apartment, I had to pull over to the side of the road and sit there for a while to calm down. At last, safely in my apartment, all I could hear were Zane's words going over and over in my head: "Go kill yourself then." I could still see the fury in his face, the wild look in his eyes. This was a part of the man I had never seen before.

I was struggling against the impulse to end the confusion, to get it all over with, when the telephone rang. It was Zane. "Evelyn, are you all right?"

I said nothing.

"Are you frightened?" he asked.

I lost control then, trying to talk through heavy sobbing and crying. I said I wouldn't be going back to him. I told him he hurt me too much. I didn't understand what was happening; I didn't think he really loved me.

He stopped me with a loud question: "Do you want me to get angry again?"

"No," I cried.

"Then don't say I don't love you, because I do." He said he just wanted to make sure I got home safely. He would see me in the office for my next appointment. His next patient was waiting; he had to hang up.

I said, "I'll think about it."

Zane said, "I'll see you at the office."

At my next appointment back in the office, Zane sat smoking that damned pipe of his as if nothing had ever happened. I sat on the couch, unable to speak. I felt numb, frozen; even my mother had never hurt me so deeply. I tried to talk, but the words wouldn't come out. He sat there, smoking his pipe, letting the tension linger. Finally, I called him to come to me on the couch. The minute he touched me, I started crying. I tried to explain how awful I felt about what had happened. But I didn't know what had made him angry.

Zane kept saying that everything was all right. I said I loved him so much I couldn't bear it if I had ever hurt him. Zane made no attempt to explain himself or to take any of the blame for the outburst that had caused me so much confusion and pain. I left him that day still feeling guilty about having made him angry. He had succeeded once again in shifting the blame, making me feel it was all my fault, when in fact I had done nothing wrong.

Although my parents had enrolled me as a member of the Presbyterian Church as a child, they were not converts in any sense of that word, and I was not reared with any kind of religious training. Religion was a subject that was never discussed in our household. However, it was something that I felt was lacking. I feel that whatever the religion, a family should have a faith. That was why I was the one who insisted that my sons be members of my husband's family's Presbyterian Church back in New England; and why, on occasion, I had gotten Bruce to go with me and the children to a Presbyterian church.

I had never thought of myself as Jewish, but now I was in love with a psychiatrist whom I knew to be a devout Jew — and I had every hope of some day being the perfect wife to him. Religion, or being Jewish, was something Zane and I rarely talked about. But it was something I shared with him, a historical tie that bound us. More important, it was something that set me apart from my husband — and from his father's evangelical Christian preachings. In that long heart-to-heart talk in which Bruce had laid out the things he didn't like about me, my "Jewishness" was another negative point.

Whatever the conflicts in Zane's public and private lives, his faith had remained intact. I knew it was something I wanted to know about and learn if I was ever going to be the ideal Jewish wife he deserved. After all those years, I would finally become a Jew.

In looking for a synagogue, I was careful to choose one I knew Zane and his wife would never attend. I went to see Rabbi Michael Sternfield, intending to prepare myself for marriage to Zane Parzen. Sternfield gave me a list of books to read — about the Jewish festivals, the history of Judaism — and a copy of Milton Steinberg's *Basic Judaism*.

I was never well enough physically to attend the regular series of instructions at the synagogue, but I read the books. I made some notes from the books and my talks with Rabbi Sternfield: *shabbos* was Friday night, *n'tilas yodayim* means you should wash your hands three times before eating. *Purim,* I noted, was the feast of Esther. *Mazel tov* meant congratulations; and, most important, *ketuvah* meant marriage contract.

My most important question about Judaism seemed to be answered on page seventy-three of Rabbi Morris N. Kertzer's book *What Is a Jew?* The most relevant words about Zane and me were these: "Divorce has always been rare in the Jewish community. It is still well below the national average in the United States. Nevertheless, when differences between husband and wife make living together intolerable, Judaism not only permits divorce — it encourages it. A love-filled home, our teachers tell us, is a sanctuary; a loveless home is a sacrilege."

Divorce would come to both Zane's and my homes; however, this would not, as I then hoped, bring the two of us together in a happy, love-filled Jewish home.

▄

The strangest of Zane Parzen's longer "psychiatric evaluations" of patient Evelyn Walker was also to be one of his last. Neither he nor she could have known this at the time, but perhaps Parzen sensed that he might soon be confronted with outside evidence of his behavior in his office. In this report, dated November 29, 1976, Parzen's vitriolic feelings about Evelyn's husband are almost out of control.

Again, it seems that the anger that Parzen should rightly have turned on himself for what he was doing to Evelyn is turned to her husband. In fact, Evelyn never believed that she was in any physical danger from her husband (as Parzen states repeatedly in his notes and reports). This was clearly Parzen's invention. Even as Parzen tries to conceal the truth, he reveals it. For example, in the report, "the man" Evelyn "had sex with in September" is Zane Parzen himself, which is why he writes in such garbled confusion about her fears that she may be pregnant by "this man." And Parzen is clearly being self-serving when he talks about loving his own wife and implies that the patient is suffering from a state of unreality when she asks to run off with him. Parzen must have felt that this official-looking evaluation, stamped confidential, would support his contention that his sexual involvement with Evelyn was strictly Evelyn's fantasy. But, carefully considered, this document seems damning of the doctor: It confirms that the major "unreality" involved in this situation was the doctor's own.

The evaluation written November 29, 1976, is quoted here in full.

This is the first week in some time that I had only seen her once a week, due to the Thanksgiving holiday, and over this period of time, apparently her husband threatened her in many different ways, including financial, and stimulating the fears that I will desert her. She became aware of how much more she wants from me, and felt that she was always being scared now that I was going to desert her. Her attorney had suggested that she not have any contact with her children until the divorce is settled, and her husband would not be able to have any leverage on her, and she seemed to almost accept this without very much affect.

When I expressed my concern about her husband's anger, and his tendency to act out towards her and to "gaslight" her, she responded that she felt that that was not her problem, but only the fear that I would desert her. She then parenthetically mentioned that she had not menstruated in two months, and felt she was pregnant, and that I would be mad at her. She felt that she did not know how she was pregnant, as she was taking the birth control pill, but there was in fact a relationship with a man approximately two and a half months ago when she was first on the pill.

She then went into a borderline decompensation in which she wanted more and more from me, felt I did not love my wife, and yet therefore I was only treating her as if she was a kept woman, and even though I was currently seeing her without her paying, insofar as her husband was withholding money, this meant nothing to her. She no longer wanted to see me here in the office, but wanted me to leave my wife and run off and marry her. I told her no, that I love my wife and I was not going to run off and marry her, as I had told her many times in the past, and that I was only going to see her here in the office. She then began to shake and talk about how unfair I was to her and how much she had given up for me, and only wanted me to love her, and this was the only meaningful part of her life.

She then called me approximately one hour later, basically obviously having decompensated more. Whether or not there is any suicidal risk at this point is somewhat up in the air, but I think therapy has advanced to the point where this will hold. She is able to handle her anger a little more without splitting the object as much, but the negativity towards me at this point because of again confronting her with her unrealities, may not be as much as she feels she can take.

I think at this point it would be unwise for me to contact her to try to persuade her, because it would only be used by her as how much I really care for her and not for my wife and family, and then will perpetuate the delusions even more. It is striking how much this becomes extremely delusional at some times and at other times is either repressed or else is not cathected. It always gets much worse after her husband has any extended contact with her, and he apparently knows that withholding money and threatening her with my not really caring about her at all is the thing to make her decompensate.

I have some feelings that this man has basically a psychotic flaw within him with a tremendous amount of rage, and that she is probably in danger for her life, both directly and indirectly. I would doubt that she is pregnant at this time, but this is more related to her pathology that she has going on in her ovaries that initially had her seen by Dr. Wenzel, but she is going to use it in her own particular way, and probably will get her husband to act out more towards her. I think that if all his leverage is taken away from him, he will go to work more diligently on her to destroy her as he has in the past.

Zane D. Parzen, M.D.

By this time, Parzen was probably aware that at some point he might have to defend his actions with his patients. If Evelyn (and other patients) did not know that what he was doing was unethical and illegal, he surely did. He also knew that Evelyn was talking to any and everybody about their relationship in long telephone calls and conversations she didn't always remember—the subject in those days was always her and Zane.

Oddly enough, Parzen himself had encouraged Evelyn to talk with Gary Shepherd if anything bothered her. On two occasions, Parzen told Evelyn and another female patient that he would be out of town and they should call Shepherd if they needed help. Even though Parzen told the women this, he never told Shepherd himself—he didn't even know if Shepherd was going to be in town those weekends. When Shepherd found out that this was going on, he confronted Parzen and told him never to refer a patient to him without telling him in advance. Perhaps Parzen was pushing—as guilt-ridden people often do—to get caught.

Much later, Parzen's lawyers would attempt to depict Gary Shepherd as a man propelled only by guilt. They said Shepherd had gone after Parzen because he felt guilty for having recommended Parzen to Evelyn in the first place. If Shepherd was that seriously concerned about Evelyn, they asked, why hadn't he taken steps to get her away from Parzen before two years and three months had elapsed?

Actually, it was difficult at first for anyone to know how best to deal with Evelyn and Parzen. Evelyn's involvement with Parzen had been a slow and gradual process. It had gone beyond the danger point before anybody around her knew it was happening.

As neighbors, the Shepherds would have liked to maintain a polite and safe distance from the Walkers' personal problems, but as Evelyn's condition worsened, they were drawn into her life out of necessity. Bettie Shepherd was the one Evelyn called when she would accidentally overdose or deliberately try to kill herself. Whenever Bruce would find Evelyn passed out from another overdose, he would run next door to the Shepherds and ask for their expert advice and professional help in dealing with his wife. Sometimes, the Shepherds would sit up with Evelyn for hours at a time until they were sure she could be left alone.

When Evelyn first told Bettie Shepherd about her involvement with Parzen, Bettie reacted with her usual calmness. She didn't quite believe it, although she reasoned to herself that these things do happen, people do fall in love — even doctors and patients. When Evelyn first began to mention her involvement with her doctor, it was more in the form of hypothetical questions, such as, Is it normal in analysis for a patient to fall in love with the doctor? Does this often happen in an analytic situation? Were you ever attracted to your psychiatrist?

Evelyn had spoken with Gary Shepherd about her involvement with Parzen at a very early date. As Gary Shepherd watched his neighbor's descent into a kind of mental oblivion, he had on several occasions asked Parzen about her, and every time the answer was the same: She was "just neurotic," suffering from delusions about love and marriage with her doctor. This answer of itself was a red flag to Shepherd, because he knew perfectly well that Evelyn's condition was far more serious than "just neurotic." With time, Shepherd came to realize that Evelyn had to be telling the truth about her relationship with Parzen. Her revelation of intimate details about Parzen's personal life confirmed that she was not getting proper treatment and also suggested that she was telling the truth about other aspects of her relationship with Parzen. Shepherd knew it was possible for a true love relationship to grow up between a doctor and patient, but he also knew that if such a thing did occur, it was the doctor's responsibility to shift roles. The doctor is the professional, the one who has spent years getting the education and training to understand and handle precisely these situations with patients. If true love had developed, then Parzen should have transferred Evelyn as a patient to another doctor and dealt with her as a nonprofessional.

Bruce Walker was the one person who could have done something about Evelyn's situation. But, for him, too, the situation was complex and confusing. Bruce must have found it humiliating to know his wife had become interested in another man. If Evelyn and Parzen were truly "involved," it could not be a one-way relationship — his wife had made her choice. And if he falsely accused this doctor, what kind of legal trouble would he bring on himself?

As early as July 4, 1975, Gary Shepherd had advised Bruce Walker that he should do something about Evelyn and Parzen. Shepherd remembers the date because it was the annual Gourmet Club picnic. This was a casual association of six or eight couples who would meet at each other's houses or in a public park for a picnic.

After eating that day, the couples were lying back talking and watching the children play when Bruce asked Gary Shepherd if he would go with him for a private chat. They rented a sailboat and moved out onto Mission Bay. Bruce said he was very concerned about Evelyn and her psychiatrist. He asked Gary Shepherd if he thought Parzen was actually having sex with Evelyn or if this was just a fantasy on her part. Shepherd said yes, he definitely thought something was going on; he thought it was wrong and he felt Bruce should do something about it. Shepherd does not recall the conversation exactly, but he remembers that Bruce was very concerned and worried about what he could do to help his wife. Neither of them, however, had any concrete ideas about what to do.

Gary Shepherd was caught in a more difficult bind than Bruce. He had not only his friendship with the Walkers to consider, but also his professional relationship with Zane Parzen, who had been his teacher and colleague all these years. To try to interfere between Parzen and his patient would be walking on very treacherous ground — legally, professionally, and in many other ways. Furthermore, Shepherd realized that the only thing keeping Evelyn alive was the delusion that

Parzen was going to marry her. Had he been able to take her away and convince her of the awful truth about that man, Shepherd felt certain that she would kill herself.

But by Christmas of 1976, Evelyn's condition had deteriorated to the point that Gary Shepherd feared she might soon be dead if he didn't do something to get her away from Parzen. On December 30, 1976, he made his move.

By his own description, Gary Shepherd is an odd-man-out in his chosen profession of psychiatry. Unlike most of his colleagues, he is not an urbanite, a Jew, or an intellectual. He looks like a somber American version of the jolly, English country squire — thick salt-and-pepper beard, hairy barrel chest, ham-sized fists — but his looks hide a man with serious convictions. If he feels a colleague is a god-damned asshole, that's what he calls him — and he has felt that way about a number of doctors he's worked with. In fact, more than a few of Shepherd's fellow doctors feel his harsh judgments have been expressed too frequently and too often without just cause. Shepherd unashamedly uses the word *crusader* to describe himself.

Even as a young intern in Arizona, Gary Shepherd had moved against a colleague who was negligent with a patient. Shepherd had admitted the patient and diagnosed the case properly. However, the patient had died because the physician had failed to give the proper treatment. All his fellow interns and the other doctors looked on Shepherd as the guilty one for causing trouble. But Shepherd persevered — and the doctor was barred from the hospital because of his actions.

Still later, when Shepherd was a young psychiatrist beginning his career in San Diego, he brought charges against another psychiatrist to stop him from treating patients at one particular mental hospital. This time he felt the doctor's treatment had been so improper it could have caused the patient's death. In private conversations with the hospital's director, Shepherd had been assured of a proper hearing. However, during the actual confrontation in the director's office, he says, "The son-of-a-bitch just sat there and lied." And no action was taken against the other doctor.

Gary Shepherd was born and reared in Texas and Oklahoma, and finished medical school at the University of Oklahoma. He did a general rotating internship at Good Samaritan Hospital in Phoenix, and then returned to Oklahoma and completed his residency requirements for an M.D. This was at the height of the Vietnam War, and doctors were a high priority for the draft. Through one of his professors, Shepherd arranged to go into the Navy and be assigned for his entire tour of duty to the Balboa Hospital in San Diego, one of the largest and best equipped military hospitals in the world. After he got out of the Navy, he and Bettie decided to settle in San Diego — that's when he began taking courses at the Psychoanalytic Institute and bought the lot and house next door to the Walkers in University City.

The eventual showdown between Parzen and Shepherd was a classic confrontation between extrovert and introvert. Here was the fast-talking Ivy League intellectual being brought to task by a plain-speaking plowboy from Oklahoma. A colleague of both men says the reason it took so long for Shepherd to move against Parzen was that "he was totally intimidated by the man." However, Shepherd says that this is simply not true. He explains that he waited so long because of the serious nature of the charges. But the fact remains that when it came right down to it, Shepherd "confronted" Parzen through an intermediary and never told him face-to-face what he thought about his mishandling of patient Evelyn Walker.

Still, taking such action is a deadly serious matter — it affects a man's reputation in the community, his whole career, his means of earning a living. One does not take such actions lightly. Shepherd well knew that if he acted in haste or accused Parzen falsely, he himself could be charged with falsely accusing and defaming another doctor.

Shepherd first talked with his friend Al Robbins about what could be done to get Evelyn away from Parzen. Robbins had been on the psychiatric staff at the naval hospital with Shepherd, and the two had enrolled in the first class of the new San Diego Psychoanalytic Institute. In fact, the two men had together attended a course given by Zane Parzen on the history of psychoanalysis. By his own description, Shepherd had felt he was out of his league at times. During the course, Robbins and Parzen would routinely get into lengthy discussions on the fine points of Freud's life and work, for example, and Shepherd would sit there wondering why any of it mattered to them. "A lot of it was Greek to me," he recalls. "I felt stupid. I was in the midst of my own analysis [analysis is a requirement that must be fulfilled in order for a candidate to become a certified analyst], and I was just beginning to figure things out. I don't feel stupid now. I feel that Al Robbins is smarter than I am, but I'm smart enough."

During their discussion about Parzen's treatment of Evelyn, Shepherd and Robbins came to the conclusion that the confrontation with Parzen should be handled by Sanford Izner, a founder and then director of the Institute. On the morning of December 30, 1976, Gary Shepherd met with Izner and laid out the case against Parzen. Izner asked Shepherd if he thought Evelyn was telling the truth. "Absolutely," Shepherd replied. But for some reason of his own, Izner would later insist that it hadn't mattered to him whether Evelyn was telling the truth or not. She should have been transferred to another doctor simply because she was telling people these things about Parzen — that alone would be damaging to Parzen's reputation and effectiveness.

In the later hearings involving Parzen, Izner would be questioned at length about why he didn't do more than just call up Parzen and advise him to transfer a patient. Izner insisted, "I didn't know and I didn't want to know" if Evelyn's stories were true. If Izner didn't know for sure, then he could feel he had done his duty. But action taken at the Institute just a few months later confirmed that Parzen's colleagues did believe that he had been wrongly involved with a patient. Parzen had applied for the final and highest designation of senior training analyst at the Institute. He was strongly advised to withdraw his application because certain members of the committee had already said they would never vote for Parzen.

While Shepherd was talking with Izner the morning of December 30, 1976, Evelyn and Zane were carrying on as if it were just another day in their relationship. Parzen's notes on her for that session consisted of only two words: "Anxiety down." Later that same day, however, he got the call from Izner and made this note to himself in Evelyn's file: "Dr. Shepherd notified Dr. Eisner [sic] that she has been telling someone (Dr. Shepherd) that I have been having sexual relations with her. Dr. Shepherd contacted me and recommended transfer even with the suicidal risk. I will contact Dr. Olenik as he has a hospital practice."

Evelyn, of course, was completely in the dark about all of this; Shepherd had not told her anything about seeing Izner or about the fact that her next visit to Parzen, on January 3, 1977, would be the last time she would ever be alone with him. It was her 175th hour with Parzen.

—

I don't remember anything special about that day before I arrived at Zane's office. I went in as usual and smiled as usual and asked, "How are you?" or some such innocent question. But Zane didn't move from his chair. He glared at me and said, "I am angry!"

"Why?" I begged him to explain.

"I am very mad at you."

"What have I done?"

"You told someone that I was going to bed with you."

"No," I cried, I would never do anything to hurt him. If I had talked with anybody, it was only because he said it was all right.

"I got a call from someone from the Institute," Zane said.

But now I was really confused. I didn't know anyone there; I'm not sure I had even heard about the Institute before that.

"I was told that someone was informed that I was supposed to be going to bed with you."

I knew that the only person I had talked with who might have anything to do with the Institute was Gary Shepherd — and I would not believe he would do this to me. I pleaded and explained to Zane that I would never do anything to hurt him, but he still made me feel as if I was to blame.

I asked Zane what he told this person who had called from the Institute.

"I told him that you fantasized the whole thing because it was something you would like to have happen."

"You made a liar of me!" I cried. "A sick liar!"

"What could I do?" Zane asked. "I had to say something. I have my career to think of."

At the time, the significance of those words didn't sink in; I didn't stop to think about what he had said or what it meant; I just thought he was angry and saying whatever came into his head.

After a time, I moved over to him, sitting on the floor in front of him. My face was wet with tears that wouldn't stop. I was terrified of what he was going to accuse me of next.

"Evelyn, I want you to listen to me," he said. "I can't see you for a while."

"No!" I cried, and buried my face in his legs. I couldn't believe he was saying this. Surely he meant he wouldn't be able to see me in the office.

"No," he said, "I can't see you at all. But just for a while. I want you to see a doctor who I feel is very good. I've already talked to him and I want you to let me make an appointment for you to see him."

All I could hear was that I wouldn't be seeing my Zane. I didn't want to hear about any other doctor. I tried to put my arms around him, but Zane pushed me away. He gripped my arms and shoved me back so that I couldn't get near him. I begged him, I pleaded with him not to do this to me. I didn't care any more what I said or what I looked like. Zane was my whole life. I couldn't possibly live without him. I was screaming all this, and out of control.

Zane ordered me to stop screaming, and I did stop. I hadn't even realized how loud I had become.

"But," I cried, "how long will it be before I get to see you again?"

"I will see you in six months," he said. "Then we will be back together."

Then he called up the new doctor's answering service and left a message. He stood up and pulled me roughly to my feet. He shoved me toward the door. I was screaming and crying, "No, please don't do this to me," as he pushed me closer and closer to the door. He stopped suddenly and told me he would miss me very much.

"But how are *you* going to be without *me*?" I asked him.

He told me not to worry about him. He could handle all this better than I could. Zane kissed me. I asked him if he loved me. He said he did. He kissed me one last time on the forehead, opened the door, shoved me out, and locked the door behind me.

I was blinded by confusion and despair. I managed to get on the elevator and down to the street, where I walked right into heavy traffic. Cars screeched to a halt, but I kept walking to the shop where I worked. My boss was not there at the time, but the two other women I worked with were there, and they could see how upset I was. They told me to take the day off and go home. But before I did that, I reached for the phone and called the one man who for fourteen years had always been there when I needed him. I told Bruce that something terrible had happened. I was desperately confused and frightened to be alone. Would he please meet me at my apartment? He said he would.

When Bruce arrived, I put my arms around him and cried hysterically. I had never seen Bruce so gentle and concerned about me. But then, I guess he had never seen me as utterly distraught as I was then. As I was telling him about all that had happened, the telephone rang. I was frightened that it might be more bad news, but I reluctantly picked up the receiver. It was Zane. He told me he had made an appointment with Doctor David Olenik, a nice man and a good doctor. I was to see him at 9 A.M. the next day, a Tuesday.

Bruce stayed with me all that afternoon, comforting me and hearing me pour out my story, telling me that everything would somehow be all right. He said I should go to this new doctor and do what Zane told me to do. But by evening, Bruce had to leave. He had a date and he didn't want to break it. In my despair, I had forgotten that we were legally separated. His life didn't include me anymore.

━

Gary Shepherd was in his office next door during Evelyn's last session with Parzen, and he would later explain in court what he heard that day.

It was lucky for me that I didn't have a patient that hour. The wall between our offices was pretty well soundproofed, as you can imagine why it would be, and all of a sudden I began to hear a woman's voice that was very upset and tearful. It was Evelyn Walker's voice. It was loud enough that not only could I hear the voice, but I could hear the words clearly and recognize the voice.

And for about — it seemed like forever — I would guess maybe thirty minutes, there was a sort of wailing, crying on her part, "Please don't do this to me. I love you. You can't let it end like this. You can't do this to me. Please don't. For God's sake, don't do this." And it went on like that for some time. And then his door opened and closed rather loudly a couple times and that was it.

Parzen's notes on that final scene with Evelyn reflect his own state of mind at the time. In one note he says that it was Shepherd who called him, in another that it was Izner. In one, he says she arrived at 2:05 P.M.; in another, it was 1:15 P.M. However, Parzen continued to lie about his sexual involvement with Evelyn, and he was absolutely consistent in denying any wrongdoing with Evelyn Walker. His final report on her is quoted here in full.

Dr. Eisner [sic] notified me that someone had called him and told him that I had been having a sexual relation with a patient of mine. Dr. Eisner notified me, and we discussed the situation, and he recommended that unless I was planning to hospitalize such a patient, that it would probably be better to transfer this patient to another therapist who will be able to hospitalize her, and to that end, I contacted Dr. David Olenik, as he also has a hospital practice.

I saw her at her scheduled time of 1:15 on Monday, January 3, 1977, and told her that someone had told one of the senior analysts at the Institute that I was having an affair with her, even though that she knew I was not, and since this was the type of thing that could be problems to me in terms of her reputation, that he recommended that I should transfer her to someone else. She begged for me to get a divorce then, and marry her, stating that I did not love my wife, etc., that is my wife and family were only responsibility to me, and that on the other hand, she would be good for me because she loved me.

I told her how we had talked of this many times in the past and that I was not going to have an affair with her, nor was I going to marry her, and that she has asked (begged) me to do this before, that in the past I said I would not, and that I could not do what she wanted; and that it was not a reflection on her, as I was her doctor and not her lover that she wanted.

I told her that the senior analytic people advised that I transfer her to another doctor in order to protect my own reputation, and that therefore I was referring her to Dr. Olenik, with whom I had already talked. I told her I saw no value in waiting at this point, and gave her Dr. Olenik's name, address and phone number, and I told her I would make the appointment for her. She expressed a lot of anger affectively with "You can't do this to me." When I told her I had to and that this was reality, she would then shake, and would then repeat everything as if it had not been said before. She stated that she has only worked at getting well in order to please me, that I would not do this to her, "Get a divorce and marry me." "You don't love her, you only love me — ." With each pattern I again told her what the reality was in that she had a wish that had become a fantasy, and that she believed it as a fact but that it was not reality, that we had not had a sexual affair, that I was not madly, passionately in love with her, and that even though I have a caring and concerned response toward her on my part, that I was not going to have the affair, divorce, etc. — that she would like me to do. She would then shake, pause, and then start over again.

I think there could be a suicidal risk, but I think she had some reality testing now so that this will make her go through with seeing Dr. Olenik. I emphasized the gains to her that she had made, and I think she may have heard that.

At 4:15 I was able to make an appointment with Dr. Olenik for her, and I talked to her on the phone, and she was much more settled down, but again wanted to focus on my feelings, and how much I loved her rather than what she was experiencing, and what the realities were. She was to contact Dr. Olenik to confirm the appointment for her tomorrow morning, January 4, at 10:15 A.M.

Zane D. Parzen, M.D.

This report was not just another page in the files of patient Evelyn Walker. This was Parzen's report on her case to her new doctor. It is difficult to imagine how this new doctor could have been expected to treat her properly when he was beginning with a set of such outright lies about her. Most of Parzen's colleagues now say that they did believe at that time that Parzen had been having sex with Evelyn Walker. None of them, however, except Gary Shepherd, seems to have understood just how serious and dangerous this involvement could have been. And even he did nothing beyond seeing that Evelyn was removed from Parzen's care.

After he had transferred Evelyn Walker, Parzen continued as an instructor of other analysts at the Institute. He remained an active member of the Peer Review Committee of the California Psychiatric Association, and he continued to treat women patients in private practice. Nobody seems to have considered that what Parzen had done once, he might well do again. Two years more would pass before Parzen's psychiatric colleagues would be forced to face the full extent of his misdeeds. Eventually, the message would be brought home literally to at least two of them: Parzen, it would be charged much later, had also been having sex with the wife of a fellow psychiatrist. She was just one among four patients other than Evelyn with whom he was said to have been involved.

Evelyn Walker, meanwhile, was floundering about in hopeless, helpless despair. She was not so much like a boat set adrift without a rudder or sails as she was like someone brutally shoved out of an airplane without a parachute. Everybody could see she was going to crash — the only question was when. For almost two years, her only reason for living had been to be with Zane Parzen. However sick their relationship, however tenuous that connection of life, it was the only one she had. All for him, she had broken her ties with family and friends. And when she did talk to any of her former friends and relatives, it was only to talk about her Zane. Bruce had helped her through those first hours after she was thrown out of Parzen's office, but his concern only went so far. He had a life of his own now, and he was not going to cancel or postpone a date in order to be with his ailing former wife. Crying and sobbing throughout the night, Evelyn tried not to think of the worst. She could not imagine life without Zane; it never entered her head that she would never see him again. She was thinking only of how she would get through the next six months until, as he had promised, she would be with him again.

Chapter 7

Tuesday morning, January 4, 1977, at 9 A.M., I walked into the office of David Olenik. I was terrified about what I might do or say. I had no idea what Zane had told him about me, much less about us. All I could think about was that Zane said I had told somebody about him and me, and that had caused all the problems. I wanted desperately to stay quiet, but I was so hysterical I just started sobbing and babbling sentences. I remember the main point I seemed to want to make was that my relationship with Zane had not been a fantasy. Zane had told me he had told the other doctors that. "I am not a liar," I told Doctor Olenik. I had not made all this up about me and Zane.

I couldn't hold back. I told him all about what happened in Zane's office and a little about our relationship. I was afraid this new doctor would think I was either a fool or completely insane, from the hysterical way I was trying to tell my story. And I just couldn't stop crying.

Doctor Olenik said I should try to calm down. He also said I could trust him; he believed I was telling the truth. He said I should think about going into a hospital, and he mentioned Mesa Vista. "But that's a psychiatric hospital!" I cried. He said it was a good hospital and I should think seriously about going there. Then he said something else just as disturbing to me. He said I needed to take a tranquilizer to help calm me down. I told him I would not take any medication of any kind, but I was determined not to explain why. He assured me that the medication he wanted me to take could only help me, that it wouldn't harm me in any way. It must have been a very frustrating hour for him—I didn't want to talk; I refused medication; I turned down his suggestion that I go to the hospital. And I was crying the whole time. But he made another appointment for me two days later, Thursday. I

told him I had no money and couldn't afford that. He said we would
work out something later regarding my payments; the important
thing was that I get treatment.

I went back to work and somehow managed to make it through the
rest of the day. That night, I got to thinking about my visit with Doctor
Olenik and I decided I couldn't go through with another appointment
with him. I just could not risk saying something that might harm Zane
further. I wrote Zane a letter explaining this.

▬

Dear Zane,

Tuesday morning I saw the doctor as you asked me to. I fully
intended to see him at least three times, also as you asked. But after
meeting him and a great deal of thinking about it, I realized this is
something I just can't and won't do.

I feel no trust and will in no way take a chance that harm can
come to you. This is all I care about.

There are no words to describe what this is doing to me inside.
All my love and thoughts are with you.

                                                    Evelyn

When Olenik's files were later subpoenaed for the trial against
Parzen, this and several other letters would be included. Evelyn was
mortified that her most intimate and heartfelt messages would be so
coldly passed around. Parzen usually mailed her letters on to Olenik
the day they arrived, and they always carried a small note from
Parzen. The first one read: "Dave, Got this today—Obviously she
can't deal with the rage at me, & the destructive impulses, & thus
projects them (the lack of trust) upon everyone else, & thus she can be
'good' & 'protect' me. Z"

▬

After I wrote to Zane, I sat there alone and desperately confused. I
tried and tried, but I couldn't stop crying. The constant strain was
causing a dreadful ache in my neck muscles—and that, of course,
wouldn't go away either. I called a friend and tried to talk with her,
but I could hardly talk because I was crying so much. She tried very

hard to be supportive. She told me to look at all the positive things Zane had said and done for me. She assured me that he would not let me down now. I hung onto the phone, desperately hoping that conversation would never end, but of course my friend had to break off at a certain point.

I had never felt so hopeless and lost. I told myself over and over that Zane did love me and he would not forget me and in six months we would be together again. I kept trying to reassure myself that way, but another part of me just wanted out of all the pain and confusion. Every time those thoughts of suicide crept into my mind, I pushed them back, but they were always there in the background. I told myself it was dangerous for me even to think about dying — I had promised Zane I would never try to kill myself again.

I was so tired I felt I could hardly move, yet I could not go to sleep. Everything Zane had said to me kept flashing through my mind. It seemed so deathly quiet in my apartment. I hated the place and didn't want to be there, but I had no other place to go.

I called Doctor Olenik and told him I didn't think I could come to see him on Thursday. He said I needed to come in and he wanted to help me get better. I tried to explain to him that I had a reason for not coming; I was frightened about what I would say and what that would do to Zane. But I wasn't thinking clearly, and I have no idea what I actually said. I just wanted to hang up and not have to deal with explaining any more. Doctor Olenik finally gave up trying to change my mind, but he said if I did decide to come in or just wanted to talk with him, I shouldn't hesitate to call him right away.

Wednesday and Thursday went by somehow. I have no memory at all of anything I did or said or thought during those two days. I must have gone to work and come home and then gone to work again and come home again. But Friday morning was a different story. I was so tired I had to force myself to get out of bed, and then it took every effort to get my clothes on. I dreaded going to work, but it didn't seem as if I had any choice. I had hardly slept at all since Monday, and I couldn't even remember when I had last eaten anything solid — was it Sunday or Saturday? As I was getting dressed, I began to cry again. I felt sick to my stomach and I didn't even bother with eye makeup or lipstick.

When I got to work, I went straight to the bathroom and threw up. That made me feel even worse, and I sat down at my desk feeling dizzy and very sick. My boss came over and asked me to deliver a footstool she had made a needlepoint cover for. The thought of having to get back in my car and drive somewhere was too much for me. My boss became very angry when she saw I didn't want to make that delivery for her. She said that every day that week I had come to work looking like death; it was not good for business for people to see me sitting there looking like that. Just hearing one more person yelling at me was all I needed — and I broke down. My boss shouted that I was fired. She said if I was that sick, I ought to be in a hospital. I couldn't stand to hear any more of this. I grabbed my purse and quickly walked out to my car, leaving her standing there yelling at me in a rage. At that point, I didn't care what she thought about me. I knew I didn't belong there; I didn't feel safe there. But where could I go? I knew I wouldn't feel safe by myself at home, either. I was only a few steps across the street from Zane's office, and all I could think about was seeing him. If only I could talk with him, everything would be all right. He would take care of me; he had always said he would take care of me and he would always be there.

I drove over to Bettie Shepherd's. I knocked on the door and when she answered, I blurted out that I had been fired and asked if I could talk with her. She was so comforting and calming. She fixed us each a cup of tea and then we sat at her kitchen table talking. Bettie and Gary Shepherd had come to be more like family to me than my real family had ever been. They were always there when I needed them, and they seemed to love and support me without judging constantly what I was doing. Bettie said nothing that might alarm me, of course, but I could see the concern etched in her eyes as she listened to me. Over and over, I asked her if she thought I would ever be all right. I guess I meant, was I ever going to get well — although I was not rational enough to put the question in such blunt language. Bettie listened and then spoke calmly. She said the important thing for me right now was to get well. I had to get some rest and I had to eat something. Just talking with her had calmed me down, and after a while, I felt I should go back to my apartment.

Going out to my car, I passed by the shrubs and flowers I had planted in what was once my own yard next door — that place where I had spent so many busy, happy hours making a home for my husband and our two sons. They were all part of my past now. I had lost them long ago, as Zane had always told me. I had lost them and now I was losing him, but I couldn't bring myself to think of that.

Alone again in my apartment, I couldn't sit still or relax enough to lie down. I began pacing back and forth, back and forth; the memory came back of that awful weekend when I went through withdrawal from all the drugs Zane had given me.

Some time later, Gary called to see how I was doing. Bettie had told him about my losing my job and about my not being able to sleep or eat. Gary said it was very important for me to try to eat something and then to sleep. There was nothing on my shelves or in the refrigerator except juice and tea. I decided I should do what Gary said, so I went out for a sandwich and brought it back. As much as I hated being alone in that apartment, I knew there was no way I could sit still in a public place with all those people around me while I tried to eat.

The first bite I swallowed came right back up, and that upset me so much I started crying — which only caused me to start coughing and gagging and vomiting some more. My head was aching so badly that I thought my eyes were going to pop out, the pain was so severe. The dull, nagging pain wouldn't go away as the hours of night dragged on into Saturday — an awful haze of pain and fear and confusion.

On Saturday afternoon I called Bruce and tried to talk with him. Just by hearing me, he could tell my condition had gotten much worse since he had seen me on Monday afternoon. He told me to come have dinner with the boys and him and then spend the night at their house.

I tried to sit at the dinner table as if nothing had happened, but as soon as I swallowed one bite of food, I had to get up and rush to the bathroom and be sick again. I excused myself, went upstairs, closed the door, and went to bed.

The next day, Sunday, I was in an even worse panic. I tried to stay calm, but I couldn't stop shaking. Coming home had been a mistake. I was a guest in my own house. Being so near Bruce, Carl, and Michael only aroused my old shame and guilt. I was more aware than ever of all that I had lost. All I could think about was Zane. Surely if he knew how bad I was, he would try to help me. I asked Bruce if he thought it would be all right for me to call Zane. He said I should do whatever I felt I needed to do. But I didn't know anything, much less what to do. Finally, I decided I had to speak with Zane. Very nervously, I dialed the number of his answering service and left a message for him to call me at Bruce's number. Within minutes, Zane called back. He sounded very low, as though he had a bad cold. I told him I was sorry, but I just had to speak to him. Everything had gotten too hard for me to handle alone. I needed his help. He told me to go back to Doctor Olenik. I explained to him that I didn't want to see Olenik; I was afraid he would put me in a hospital. Then I told Zane I had lost my job at the design shop. He was furious, yelling through the phone at me, "What? You lost your job?" He said that as if I had done it on purpose, just to spite him. I tried to explain to him how upset I had been and that losing the job was not completely my fault, but he wouldn't listen to me. He started yelling at me again. "Evelyn, I'm telling you to go back to Doctor Olenik." "But," I pleaded with him, "he wants to put me on tranquilizers."

"Doctor Olenik is a very good doctor," Zane snapped back. "If he suggests tranquilizers, do what he says." I reminded him that because of my past experience, I was afraid to get back on drugs again. I was afraid to have any pills in the house, especially in my condition now. This made him even more angry with me, and he shouted that I should do exactly as he had told me to do. "Evelyn, I'm not going to tell you again. I will not speak to you or see you until Doctor Olenik says that it is all right to do so. You go back to Doctor Olenik and do exactly what he tells you to do!" I was now crying so hard I couldn't talk. Zane said, "I don't want to talk anymore. I'm going to hang up. Do exactly as I've told you to do."

I couldn't know that this would be the last time we would ever talk. But even if I had, I couldn't have felt more hopeless. I just sat there numbly, holding the receiver to my ear as the dial tone came back after Zane had hung up.

Bruce came into the bedroom and saw me sitting there with the phone still to my ear. He took it out of my hand and put it back on the receiver. Then he sat down beside me. As if I were in a trance, I repeated everything Zane had said to me, word for word. Bruce said maybe I would feel better if I took a nice, long shower. He helped me get undressed and into the shower. While I was drying off, Bruce brought me a cup of tea and casually mentioned that he had plans for the evening. In other words, it was time for me to leave.

I drove very slowly; it seemed like hours before I got back to my apartment. When I opened the door, the phone was ringing. It was Bruce, calling to be sure I'd made it home safely. I called Doctor Olenik, and he was very glad I had changed my mind and decided to come back to him. He made an appointment for the next afternoon,

Monday. Later that night, I regained my composure enough to sit down and write a long letter to Zane. Even if he wouldn't talk to me, I had to try to communicate with him.

▬

By the time Parzen received this letter, Evelyn had been committed to a mental hospital. He passed it on to Olenik with the following note:

Dave
Thought you should have a copy of the latest communication to me. Z

Dear Zane,

I want this letter to be so very right and I'm concerned that the words won't come out correctly.

First of all I feel you think I betrayed a trust between us. This is one reason I didn't want to talk to Dr. Olenik. However, I am seeing him and I am able to talk to him. Because I don't care about him only that he helps now. I don't care that he sees and hears the pain. You see I really knew for a very long time that I should see another doctor. But there was just so much money and it was more important to me to be with you. I'd always hurt to know that it cost money to be with you no matter how it was justified. But I couldn't have both so I stayed where I wanted to be, with you.

Zane, I always knew I could tell you anything. In one way it was so good to tell you what I would never have told anyone but at other times I didn't like you to know how bad things are. I never wanted you to feel sorry for me. I would hate that. Yet I knew inside you knew anyway. Then of course there always was the time factor. How I've grown to hate time.

Zane, I really know that you love and care a great deal. I really know that you don't have to be with me all the time or touch me all the time or tell me you love me. But there was always so little time to be with you that it became very important.

Zane, you asked me to trust you, don't hide from you, don't turn from you, hold on to you, don't *push* you away. At one level this was the doctor but as time went by this was the man in his way asking for my love as well and in my time I knew my trust was turning to a very deep love for you.

Believe this I only turned to Gary because I could trust him & I felt I needed advice and help. Zane, I just wanted to get well faster and above all not to lose you in any way. Gary really cares about *Both* of us don't ever think anything else! He feels you are a fine man and I already explained his reasons for the other doctor. I don't know what happened and I can't stop thinking about it. Yes after this length of time there are a few people I'm close to who could tell I cared for you but if I turned to anyone close it was again in trust and to get advice because our relationship means that much to me. I'm thinking of my friend [Connie] (in Santa Barbara).

Zane, you have shared yourself with me and the things good & bad stay within me. I feel very close to you.

I haven't ever felt ugly about your wife or been unfeeling about your children. They aren't my enemy. It's your sense of responsibility. That's what I really fear. Of course you've shared a great deal with your wife and love your sons. And yes you have feelings about your wife as I would expect. But something is lacking. A man doesn't push himself the way you do just because he likes his work or even the money. It's also to fill a void. Marriage sometimes can become safe, something you're used to and don't have to think about. But children grow up, lead their own lives and then that void is greater. You once told me people sometimes have to settle for things.

You said once that I want you to give up your family, people you care about. I'm not asking you to give up. I'm asking you to see that you can have that and more. Don't you think I would care about your children?

Big changes are very hard to make. *I know.* But it can be worth while. I have so much I want to share with you and I believe in my heart you want my love and caring. I don't see you as a god. You are a warm, loving, strong at times, weak and even frightened stubborn man. You've been hard, loving, cold at times hurtful to me. Made me angry and laugh. I ask you now, turn to me, don't push me away, let me be close to you. I'll never turn my back on you.

It was very un-just of you to say "I got myself fired." When I came back from your office I was in very bad shape. You know how [the shop owner] is, doesn't care about people. I wasn't doing well that week, very shaky and pale, she had a bad day, yelled at me. I broke down and that was it.

During this time I have felt some anger toward you, but mostly deep pain. You pushed me away, turned your back to me. Dr. Olenik told me, professionally there aren't problems for you. That no one can tell you what to do outside your office. He maintains that he can't decide if we can see each other. That's between you and me. Therefore, if you don't see me I can only assume you have betrayed me! This would destroy me. Don't do to me what Bruce has done, don't be foolish and throw away what we could have together. Life is just too short to settle just because it's easier.

Your actions have shown me a deep love and caring. Even when your anger has hurt me, and occasional words have cut into me, your eyes and touch tell the truth and show the confusion within YOU.

You've said at times you do want me, but can't do anything about it. I believe in time you'll see *you can*. Trust me as I have trust in you. Please just don't take forever.

I don't believe that you can work me out of your mind & body for long.

You even told me I do have you or I wouldn't be afraid of losing you.

You've gone through a great deal, lost people you loved. But I'm *alive* where you can reach & be with me.

Zane, I've never wanted anything so much, worked so hard to improve. It's for me I know but all of it has real meaning because of you.

I'm tired, so very tired. I miss you and your touch. I pray you feel the same of me.

Evelyn

■

On Monday, almost exactly one week to the hour from when Zane had shoved me out of his office, I sat in Doctor Olenik's office trying to talk with him. Every time I opened my mouth, I started to cry all over again. I couldn't finish a sentence. I don't remember saying anything at all to him, but I could see through the tears that he was talking to me. But nothing he said was getting through to me and I have no idea what he told me that day. I went back and saw him again later that week, but the only thing I remember is that he gave me a prescription for a mild tranquilizer. Running over and over in my mind was Zane's threat that he would never see me again if I didn't go to Doctor Olenik and pay attention to what he told me to do. I felt I had no choice but to get the prescription filled and take it, as I was told to do. For the first time in 6½ months, I had a bottle of pills in my hand.

I sat on my bed with a glass of juice and opened the bottle, ready to take one as directed. But then the thought of taking the whole bottle kept coming to my mind. I pushed the thoughts back and remembered my promise to Zane. Also, there weren't enough pills to kill me anyhow. But I decided I didn't want to take even one — I had been through so much hell trying to get off them I was afraid I'd never be able to stop if I ever started again. I felt so hopeless. I was thinking, Why not get it over with? Then I would remember Zane's words and my promise to him. And, again, there was the practical thought that these were a mere twenty-five milligrams, and I had once been used to taking sixty or more pills of at least fifty milligrams each. One of these wouldn't do anything, I reasoned, but the whole bottle might calm me down. But I made up my mind not to take any of the pills. And then I started to cry again. I was so weak from not eating and so confused and so tired — so very, very tired.

Sitting there with that bottle of tranquilizers, I felt the old horror return to my mind. The terrifying memory came back of all those times I had taken overdoses, and of those times I woke up sore and humiliated after failing at suicide again, and of that awful weekend of withdrawal from drugs. I couldn't stop crying; I was out of control, and even I knew that now.

I called Bruce and asked him to please come and be with me. When he arrived, I put my arms around him and told him about seeing the doctor that day and about getting the prescription for tranquilizers. I explained to him I couldn't take the drug, I just couldn't get hooked on drugs again. Then, I started back over why I felt this way, what Zane had told me, what I had promised him. To Bruce, it must have sounded like a broken record; how many times had he heard me say all this before? I was becoming more and more hysterical as we talked. Bruce didn't know what to do with me; I didn't know what to do with me. I started getting sick, and then I couldn't stop gagging and retching. Finally, I asked him to call Gary Shepherd — he would know what to do. Bruce made the call and then said he was taking me over to Gary's.

All the way over, I was coughing and trembling. I congratulated myself on not vomiting, but there was nothing in my stomach to throw up. Gary opened the door and hugged me, then we all went into their family room. Gary took his place in his big overstuffed arm-chair and I sat on the floor beside him. As he began talking, Gary reached down and took my hand and held it the whole time he was talking to me.

Gary said, "Evelyn, you've got to go into a hospital. You have to be taken care of." I started crying and telling him how afraid I was of going into a psychiatric hospital. Gary spoke calmly, but he was still very firm, gently insistent about what I had to do. "Evelyn, you are very ill. You just aren't going to make it if you go on like this. You are suffering from malnutrition, your health is getting dangerously poor. You've gone far too long without proper care. It just isn't safe for you to be alone in that apartment."

I kept crying, but I was trying to hear him and understand what he was saying and figure out what I should do, what I could do. All this time, Gary kept explaining what I had to do. "I can understand that you are afraid, but everybody will be very good to you at the hospital." I never took my eyes off Gary as he continued to talk to me. I tried to answer what he was saying. I said I would be all right if I could just eat. I didn't want to go into the hospital. Finally, Gary said, "Evelyn, you must go into a hospital. You don't have any choice if you want to live. And you have to live."

Now the horrible truth finally got through to me: Gary was telling me I was dying. I looked over at Bruce and he told me he wanted me to go into the hospital. I looked back at Gary and saw that he had tears in his eyes. I told Gary I would do it; I would go into Mesa Vista psychiatric hospital.

Gary called Doctor Olenik and they talked for several minutes. Then, Gary asked me to come to the phone. Doctor Olenik asked if I was ready to go into the hospital immediately. Gary told me to say yes. Then he asked if I wanted to go to Mesa Vista. Again, Gary told me to answer yes. [The law requires that the patient must voluntarily agree to go into the hospital and must specify which hospital he or she wants to go to. Since Evelyn and Bruce were legally separated and her two sons were underage, the only people who could have signed papers committing Evelyn were her parents.] Gary spoke briefly to Doctor Olenik and hung up. He explained to me that all the arrangements were being made for me to go into the hospital that very night. He told me everything was going to be all right; I mustn't be afraid; he would talk with me later. He asked Bruce if he could take me to the hospital, and Bruce said he would. Gary put his arms around me and kissed me on the cheek. "Don't be afraid," he said again. "The people are very nice at Mesa Vista; they'll take good care of you." I asked him about Zane; would he know I was in the hospital? Gary said I should not worry about Zane now; the only thing that mattered was that I be cared for and get well.

Bruce took me to my apartment. I was so confused I couldn't think what I should take. I picked out a nightgown and some toiletries and I remembered to take a piece of needlepoint I had been working on. Then we were in the car on the way to the hospital. As the Mesa Vista buildings appeared ahead, I started sobbing again, and I told Bruce I had changed my mind — I didn't want to go through with it, I just couldn't go to a psychiatric hospital. Bruce reminded me that I had promised Gary I would do it, that I needed to be somewhere where I would be taken care of. I begged him not to park the car. "I can take care of myself," I cried. "I won't bother anyone." No, Bruce said, I could not take care of myself, I was too sick for that. I remembered the tears in Gary's eyes and I knew I had to keep my word to him.

At the registration desk, Bruce helped me answer the mostly routine questions about name, age, address; I was so confused I couldn't be sure of anything. The woman at the desk typed up an identification bracelet and tied it around my wrist. Then she had a stack of forms I had to read and sign. Some of them had to do with insurance, others with hospital rules. Then I came to a form involving medication and the kinds of treatment used for mentally ill patients. I had to check off what I would and would not permit them to do to me. I scanned the list until I came to the two words I most feared: SHOCK TREATMENT. I glared at the woman behind the desk and almost shouted, "I won't let you give me shock treatments. I'll leave right now if I have to go through that." I was crying and trembling; my blouse was soaked with perspiration.

I looked desperately at Bruce. I wanted him to say he wouldn't leave me in a place like that; he would take me home and take care of me himself. But he didn't say a word. The woman reassured me that the hospital staff could not do anything I didn't want them to do. They even had to have my permission to give me medication. "You mean, no one can force me to take shock treatment?" I asked. "That's right. No one. Mrs. Walker, you are voluntarily coming into the hospital; no one can do anything without your permission."

"Does that mean I can leave when I want to?" I asked. "Yes, it does," she said. "My doctor can't force me to have shock treatment either?" "No, he would have to get your permission if he had thoughts about such treatment for you."

I read the instructions at the top of this form again. I was to check off only those forms of treatment I would allow. The only one I checked was MEDICATION. I figured that in a hospital it would be safe for me to take whatever the doctor prescribed. Before I would agree to sign the form, I made Bruce read it very carefully and assure me it said what the woman said it did. And still I wrote in block letters that I did not give my permission to have shock treatment — and underlined it.

A woman came and introduced herself as a nurse, and Bruce took my hand and tugged at me to get up and follow. I was thinking: They are taking me away. Going down the long hallway, I hung back and stayed several steps behind Bruce and the nurse. The hallway seemed endless. I could hear keys jingling at the nurse's waist, and she kept talking about something, I didn't know what.

At the end of the hallway, we came to some stairs. I stopped cold and started crying; then I backed away from the two of them. I wasn't going up those stairs. "I've changed my mind," I told Bruce. I felt so weak, I was afraid I might fall; I backed up against the wall and kept inching away from the stairs. "You'll see it really isn't so bad being here," the nurse said to me. "How would you know, working in an office?" I asked her. She said she was one of the nurses who would be taking care of me; I wondered why she wasn't wearing a uniform. Bruce told her I hadn't had anything to eat, so she said as soon as we got up the stairs to my room, she would get me a tray and sit with me while I ate. She seemed so nice and I was so tired that I took Bruce's arm and followed her up the stairs to the room.

It was a large room, designed for two people. There were twin beds and, on the opposite wall, built-in closets and drawers for two. Over the drawer space was a mirror. The walls and furnishings were plain and sterile, as you would expect in a hospital. The nurse suggested it was time for Bruce to leave so that I could unpack and get undressed. I held on to him and whispered to him to please take me with him. I didn't want to stay; I was almost numb with the fear of being left in that place. Yet I knew I had no choice but to stay there. Bruce said I had to stay; it was very late; we both needed some sleep. He kissed me on the forehead, turned, and walked out the door.

When I opened my suitcase, the nurse said she would have to go over my things with me. She asked if I had any jewelry, and I told her no. Then she explained that there were some things that would have to be checked at the office — and when I needed them, I could speak with the nurse and get them just long enough to use them. I couldn't believe what she was saying. Then she emptied out my toiletries bag and picked up my razor, the tweezers, a small pair of scissors I used for my needlepoint, my birth control pills, a tin of aspirin, my stomach medicine. When I pulled out my needlepoint, she said I wouldn't be able to keep the needle in my room — that would have to be checked at the office too. I was furious. I told her I had no intention of hurting myself, and even if I did, what would I be able to do with a dull-tipped needlepoint needle? She explained that the rules were not just for my own safety. If other patients knew about these things, they might try to steal them and use them to hurt themselves or somebody else.

"Are there people here who would hurt another patient?" I asked.

"Don't worry about that," she said. "The hospital has to have these rules. Any and all items that could possibly cause harm have to be kept safely out of reach." Again I had no choice. I handed over the needle and the nurse said she'd get my dinner tray.

I sat on the bed staring at nothing. I was so embarrassed and ashamed about ending up in a place like this. I was thinking I had hit absolute rock bottom. I hoped nobody would ever know I had ever been here. Zane had always told me I wasn't crazy. But if that was true, what was I doing in a mental hospital?

The nurse came back with a cup of coffee for herself and a tray of food for me. The sight of the food made me ill. I told her I didn't think I'd be able to eat anything. She asked me to try. I managed to eat some of the pudding. She started making conversation and asked how long I had been married, not realizing Bruce and I were separated. I said fifteen years, without explaining anything else. She asked if we had children, and I said we had two sons. She kept asking what must have seemed innocent questions to her, but they reminded me of one unhappy scene after another. I started crying; I didn't want to talk anymore. I was very tired. I didn't want to talk, I didn't want to eat, I didn't want to be alive. She came over and sat beside me on the bed and said I should undress and someone would bring my sleeping medication. The nurse told me not to move around or try to leave the room after taking the medication, because it was rather strong.

As I was undressing, I happened to look in the mirror. It was the first time I had looked at myself in days. I was shocked. The face looking back at me seemed like that of a total stranger. I looked like a starving poster person needing a CARE package. My eyes were red and swollen, with dark circles around them; my face was incredibly pale in contrast with my black hair. I was thin and drawn. Even I could see that here was the face and body of a very sick woman. I turned away from the mirror, put on my nightgown, and sat on the edge of my bed, feeling numb and lost. I vaguely heard someone saying my name and looked up to see a woman I assumed was a nurse (like the other one, she wore no uniform). I obediently took the pills she handed me — and fell into a deep sleep.

In his report on Evelyn's stay at Mesa Vista, January 15–29, 1977, Olenik noted that she was "referred to me by her previous psychotherapist, who insisted that she transfer to me because of the development of an apparent psychotic-like transference. She quite reluctantly came to see me the first time, refused hospitalization, and refused to consider medication. It apparently had taken her a long time to get off medication, and she did not want to go back on it. She agreed to see me for three sessions of evaluation. By the end of the third session there appeared to be some semblance of a therapeutic alliance. She did have signs of impaired reality testing when I saw her on an outpatient basis. Two days after my last office visit with her, I received a call from a friend of hers, a psychiatrist, who insisted that she be hospitalized. I spoke with her over the phone; she was willing and was so regressed that she could not make much sense. She was poorly integrated. Her husband apparently brought her to the hospital."

In recording her psychiatric history, Olenik also noted that Evelyn "has a history of suicide gestures, apparently around arguments with her psychotherapist." She was now haunted by a dream, he said, in which she would never be let out of the hospital. As to her mental status at that time, Olenik concluded: "Mrs. Walker is whining and crying in her affect, but I do not see any tears. The thought content is highly critical of the facility, obsessed with the feeling that 'no one wants me; I want someone to hold me,' and continues to move around in her chair, with bizarre facial contortions and a blank look in her eye and bizarre stare. This fluctuates with periods of apparently appropriate smiling affect. Her reality testing is impaired. Her judgment seems poor. Her impulse control is somewhat questionable. IQ is well above average. Motivation for therapy is fair, with some magical expectation existing that I can do things for her that are not within the realm of therapy. She has some difficulty understanding a therapeutic alliance and relationship."

In psychiatric terms, Olenik described Evelyn's condition as "schizophrenia, latent type (borderline personality disorder, severe)." She was a "5.5 in DSM-3." That is, in the American Psychiatric Association's *Diagnostic and Statistic Manual,* her characteristics fit under the category of "Schizophrenia, latent type." At that time there was no separate category for borderline cases such as Evelyn's. Newer editions of the *Manual* list "borderline" as a separate and distinct category all its own. This new diagnosis has been one of the most widely discussed issues in recent psychiatric history, producing scores of controversial papers and books and seminars at nearly every professional meeting.

Writing in the August 22, 1982, *New York Times Magazine,* psychology professor Louis Sass listed several common characteristics of the borderline patient: "Difficulty being alone, manipulative and self-destructive (often self-mutilating) behavior, and — perhaps most important — extreme instability and unpredictability." The borderline patient, according to Sass, is "erratic and quixotic, they tend to perceive the world in extreme dichotomies of good and evil, and they are often intolerant of routine and social convention." He said the diagnosis could apply to a disparate assortment of personalities — from Marilyn Monroe to Adolf Hitler, Lawrence of Arabia, Zelda Fitzgerald, and the novelist Thomas Wolfe. It covers what once was called "the artistic temperament." But, Sass explained, "the term is much more often used to define people whose desperation is less celebrated." Sass suggests that as much as seven to ten percent of the population of the United States suffers from this disorder, and twenty-five percent of all those who receive any kind of psychiatric or psychological treatment could be classed as borderline.

Mental health professionals, Sass says, "believe that we live in an era of borderline pathology. Just as the historical neurotic of Freud's time—plagued by conflicts of conscience and desire—exemplified the repressive Western culture at the turn of the century, so certain disturbances in an individual sense of identity and difficulties in maintaining stable human relationships—characteristics attributed to the borderline personality—may reflect the fragmentation of contemporary society."

The real key to Olenik's diagnosis of Evelyn Walker was whether or not he believed she was telling the truth. It is not merely a question of separating fact from falsehood. From a medical standpoint, it involved the difference between reality and delusion. In sworn testimony four years later, Olenik would say that he did believe Evelyn when she told him she had had a sexual affair with Zane Parzen. However, his admission report on Evelyn at Mesa Vista would indicate that he had accepted Parzen's opinion that she had a "psychotic-like transference"—in other words, that she was fantasizing the sexual involvement with Parzen. Olenik took only very sketchy notes, and these usually covered changes in medication. He defended this by saying that the note-taking process interfered with his eye-to-eye method of treatment.

At the time he was treating Evelyn, Olenik was a "clinical associate," or student, at the San Diego Psychoanalytic Institute. As part of his program to be certified as a psychoanalyst himself, Olenik was in the process of going through eight years of personal analysis with Sanford Izner, then director of the Institute. When Olenik testified, he was asked if he talked to his analyst about what he was hearing from Evelyn about Parzen. Of course he did, Olenik said. Didn't they discuss doing something about this clear-cut violation of professional ethics? To answer that, Olenik said, would violate his right of confidentiality with his doctor.

As a student at the Institute, Olenik's instructor in three courses was Zane Parzen. Asked, after the fact, if he had ever talked with Parzen about his involvement with Evelyn, Olenik said no, that was not his job. He defended this by saying it would have been a violation of his obligation of confidentiality with Evelyn, his patient. He did say that he had mentioned Evelyn to Parzen only twice when they ran into each other at the Institute, but, he said, it was only a casual comment like, "Your patient is doing better."

I have a vague memory of being awakened another time that first night at Mesa Vista and taking more pills. Then, the next morning, another nurse woke me up for breakfast. I was under such heavy sedation those first days that I quietly did what I was told, and I don't clearly remember much of anything. I tried to focus on the new nurse, but I couldn't tell whether it was the same one I had talked with the night before. It wasn't, but I couldn't remember anything about the previous one.

The nurse helped me sit up in bed and put the tray in front of me. I told her the food looked awful to me. She said it was very important for me to eat. I tried to nibble on some toast, but I couldn't swallow it. I drank my juice and some tea. I wanted to go to the bathroom, but it seemed so far away and I felt so weak and drowsy that I knew I couldn't make it by myself, and I didn't want to ask the nurse to help me. I hated to think of myself as an invalid. But the nurse did help me, and once I was back in bed, I was fast asleep as soon as my head hit the pillow.

Doctor Olenik came to see me that afternoon. I was so drowsy from the medication that I couldn't understand at first that he was telling me he was going out of town, and another doctor would be checking on me while he was away. I was upset by this — I hardly knew Doctor Olenik, but Zane had recommended him and I had accepted him. Now, just as I was beginning to feel safe with him, I was being transferred to yet another new doctor. Again, I knew I had no choice, but I was under such heavy medication that I wasn't aware enough to worry about much of anything.

I guess I had been there for three or four days before there was anything that I remember. At 7 A.M., a nurse knocked on the door and said, "Time to rise and shine." I rolled over and discovered I had gained a roommate at some time during the night. While we were making our beds, she told me she had been admitted around 10 P.M. He husband and family didn't know she was there. She felt she couldn't cope with her problems and depressions. I wondered how she got there without her family knowing, but I just listened and didn't ask any questions. I was afraid if I inquired about her problems, she'd feel free to ask me about mine — and I knew I didn't want that.

I normally don't eat much for breakfast, but this particular morning I was suddenly very hungry, a feeling I hadn't known in a very long time. I had toast and tea and half a grapefruit, and everything stayed down — another first. Patients had breakfast in the hospital cafeteria. I hadn't been among so many people in I-couldn't-remember-how-many months. The low noise of other people laughing, talking, and coughing seemed overwhelming to me.

After breakfast, the nurse who had first shown me to my room took me on a guided tour of the hospital. I didn't remember her at all from that first night. As she explained it, there was a busy schedule, from wake-up call at 7 A.M. through "evening medications" at 11 P.M. But I was to learn that the physical and occupational therapy sessions were few and far between. Twice a week there were "group encounter" sessions, and for the stronger patients there were outings to the movies or on picnics. There was a television and entertainment room downstairs, as well as a little shop where you could buy anything from junk food to nightgowns. The shop was only open a brief time each day, and getting to buy something there became a very special treat to break up the boring routine. Off the sitting room, there were four telephones that patients could use — our main link to the outside world, to family and friends, to whomever we had left behind.

My guide smiled as we finished the tour and said, "Now, this isn't so bad after all, is it?" I tried very hard to see it her way — but I was incarcerated; she'd be going home when her shift was over. She also told me the replacement doctor would be coming to see me later that day.

That afternoon, someone woke me and took me to the "therapy room," a stuffy little office with no windows. It was sparsely furnished with only two chairs, a desk, and an examining table. I have no memory of what the doctor looked like; I just remember the way he conducted this session and some of the things he said. I felt like I was in some kind of inquisition. The room was drab and cheerless; if you weren't depressed when you came in, you surely would be when you left.

The doctor sat across from me, not saying anything for a long time. I had the feeling that he was looking not so much at me as through me. He seemed utterly bored with what he had to do, and he seemed to have no interest in my answers to his questions. He was also chewing gum as he listlessly rattled off his questions.

I had been crying in my sleep, he noted on my chart. Did I know what I was dreaming or what might be causing me to cry like that? No,

I had no idea. He opened up my file and started scanning it. I explained that I was only a temporary patient of Doctor Olenik's.

"Why did you leave the other doctor?" he wanted to know. "What was the problem? How is it that you are a temporary transfer? Do you plan to leave Doctor Olenik too? What was wrong with Doctor Parzen, didn't you like him?"

I didn't answer any of these questions. I insisted that these matters were personal ones between Doctor Olenik and me and I would not discuss them with his replacement. "We would get along better if you would try to be more cooperative," he said. I bided my time until the interview was over. I kept telling myself that Olenik would be back in just one week. I am an intelligent person; I am not insane; I can put up with anything they tell me to do because I am only going to be here a short time. I had to get out of that place; I had to get better. That was the only way I would ever see Zane again.

In the TV room, one or two of the other patients spoke to me, but I just politely said hello and went on to the counter where boiling water was available for tea. I sat down with my tea and finally saw the hospital for what it was — a drab, depressing, colorless place. The furniture all looked used and abused, some of it really shabby. The whole time I was there, I was constantly redecorating the place in my mind. It never left my consciousness that I was in a kind of prison where the only crime was being mentally ill. As in a prison, there was little or no privacy. The public rooms for patients had big windows through which the nurses could always watch from their stations. You would see people scrunched up to the telephones, trying desperately to keep their conversations private. And a sound I'll never forget was the jingling of the nurses' keys as they walked busily about their duties.

Sitting alone with my tea that day, I suddenly realized that someone was talking to me. A young woman introduced herself, sat down next to me, and started talking nonstop. She said she'd been in the hospital a long time but she was getting out any day now. She said she didn't mean to try to kill her children, and she swore she would never do that again. She grabbed my arm and begged me to believe her. "I really wouldn't hurt them; it's just that children cry so much and they were making me so nervous . . . ," she said. "Do you believe me?" I was so terrified, I would have told her anything. I said I thought everything would work out fine for her. And I agreed that at times children can be very trying.

In the days that followed, I tried to keep my distance from this woman and most of the other patients. I cried frequently, and I would try to get to my room whenever that started. But one day I couldn't help it; I started crying while I was in the sitting room. In seconds, the nurses swooped down on me and removed me to the therapy room. "We don't want to upset the other patients, do we?"

I didn't like Doctor Olenik's replacement at all, and his daily visits only seemed to add to my depression. I missed Zane, and in my mind I kept reliving that last day with him. It was an ugly, frightening picture that kept flashing in my brain.

I came to hate everything about the hospital. There were constant reminders that this was a mental hospital, after all, and not the real world. Everything about the daily routine was humiliating. We had to stand in line for our daily doses of pills. Then we had to take them in front of a staff member so that they could be sure we weren't hoarding the pills or throwing them away. Every time I wanted to bathe, I had to go to the office and ask for my personal toilet articles, which had to be returned as soon as I finished my bath. It was as if I had to make a public announcement every time I wanted to do anything that should be private and personal.

I couldn't work on my needlepoint without going to the office and signing for my scissors and needle; and they, too, had to be returned as soon as I was through with them.

Over and over, I would tell myself I was not as sick as the others. I was an intelligent human being who had to put up with these kindergarten rules for a while. Doctor Olenik would soon be back, and I had to get better so that he would tell Zane I could see him again.

When visiting hours came and went and no friends came by, I felt more alone than ever. My friend Connie Martin wrote me a long, supportive letter that I read and reread on many a sleepless night.

Few of my friends knew that I was in the hospital. I told those who did know that I didn't want any visitors, I didn't want anybody to see me in a situation where — like a child or a servant — I was known only by my first name, though the nurses had to be called "Miss" or "Mrs." But my friend Ellen Hayes ignored my "paranoid request," as she put it, and came to see me anyway — and of course I was thrilled to see her.

At long last, Doctor Olenik sent word that he had returned and he was waiting to see me in the therapy room. The nurse brought in the ugliest pair of one-size-fits-all, brown-green muslin pajamas I had ever seen. I was humiliated to be seen in such a hideous outfit, and to get to the examining room, I had to walk down the hall past many of the other patients and nurses. I was furious. I told the nurse I was not going to wear that thing. The nurse said it would only be for a little while and the doctor was waiting. I threw the pajamas on the bed and asked why I couldn't wear my robe. "Don't fight the rules," she said patiently. "Everyone has to wear hospital pajamas when they go for their checkup." Again, I felt I had no choice.

Doctor Olenik greeted me warmly, but I was so embarrassed by the way I looked in that huge sack that I could only muster a weak "Hello." After the routine physical examination, he asked how I felt in general. I told him I didn't like the hospital and I wanted to go home. I said I'd recover better in my own environment. Being in the hospital was just keeping me down, making my condition even worse.

He said he could understand that I didn't like the hospital, but he wanted me to stay a while longer. I had to give it more time. He wanted me to put on some more weight and get stronger physically and mentally before I went home.

I asked if Zane knew I was in the hospital. He said he had not talked with Zane, but he was pretty certain that Zane knew I had been hospitalized. He said he might be talking to Zane sometime soon, but I wasn't to think about that. Olenik said goodby, he would see me again in the morning. I almost ran back to my room, where I showered and put on a fresh pair of slacks, trying to erase the memory of those awful pajamas.

I was happy that Doctor Olenik was back; I felt something might happen now. I would get better and he would help me through this awful period of waiting to get back together with Zane.

Meanwhile, I began to get involved in the hospital program. I liked the twice-a-week group sessions and found it interesting to hear about the problems others had gone through and overcome. I was learning firsthand that I wasn't such a freak. I had great difficulty talking about myself, but I felt better after hearing others speak freely about their suicide attempts and other failures we all had in common. There were even some very humorous moments in these encounter sessions. Sometimes, it seemed, there was a kind of one-upmanship at work, as patients tried to outdo each other with their horror stories.

What hit home hardest with me was a session during which several people talked about going through drug withdrawal. Until that moment, I don't think I completely understood that it was drug withdrawal that I had been through that weekend in July the year before. I couldn't help but notice that nearly every one of them spoke of going through withdrawal in a hospital under a doctor's care.

The most frightening talk was about shock treatment. For some reason, this had always been something I was terrified would happen to me. It sent chills down my spine to think of being strapped down and having electrical currents running through my body.

Meaningless, disconnected days passed. I tried to relax and stay interested in the program and be at ease within the confined space of the hospital. I found that I liked Doctor Olenik and looked forward to his brief visits each day. And, on an individual basis, there were several other patients who were very nice to talk to, learn about, share private moments with.

On the whole, however, I hated each new day more and more. I felt more and more like a caged animal. The other patients' stories had seemed interesting at first, but with repetition I came to realize how hopeless they were. I was determined not to become a lifetime patient; I would not let this hospital routine and the depressing environment rob me of all spirit and fight. I would not become another of the walking dead. I was afraid of going back to the outside world, but I was a hundred times more frightened of accepting this world.

One day, before Doctor Olenik arrived, I had made up my mind. I knew they couldn't keep me there against my will, and I wanted out. The first thing I said when I saw him was that I wanted to go home right away. He advised me that he thought it was too soon for me to leave the hospital. I reminded him that I entered voluntarily and therefore could leave whenever I wanted to. He agreed that this was my legal right, but he added it was against his medical advice. I didn't care. I wanted out.

He made the arrangements for me to be discharged in two days.

At long last I was back in my own little space. It seemed that I'd been in the hospital for months, although it was only two weeks. I didn't know what to do first. I reveled in the feeling that I could do anything I wanted to do, any time of the day or night. I filled the tub with bubble bath and luxuriated in a long, refreshing, and relaxing soak. I got out and put a towel around me and fixed a cup of tea. A close friend soon arrived with arms full of grocery bags. She had brought enough for dinner and for my meals through another week. We talked about everything but my stay in the hospital. I didn't want to think about that, and my friend understood. But, of course, our conversation eventually got around to how much I missed Zane. I told my friend that I liked Doctor Olenik and could get along with him for six months, but I was only living for the day when I could be back with Zane.

After my friend left, I turned on the television and tried to concentrate on the program. But all I could think about was Zane. If I could not see him or talk to him, at least I could write him a letter.

Dear Zane,

It's now six weeks since we've seen or spoken to each other. [Actually, it had been closer to four weeks.] It's been a very difficult time for me. The thought of not seeing you again is very painful. However, I'll wait out the time *you've* set until we can be together.

Dr. Olenik again today said that he saw no reason that we can't see each other. So it's all up to you now. I'm going this Wednesday to see about my new job. The job is already mine, it's just a question of beginning work. I'm somewhat nervous about starting a new job but I will work that out somehow.

Zane, I feel I have done what you asked me to do, I'm seeing Dr. Olenik. We worked out a fee that I can deal with, therefore I'm seeing him twice a week, Monday and Thursdays at 3:30. I'm not holding back with him. I talk quite freely. I like him. Zane, don't hold back from me. You said you would contact me if Dr. Olenik said it was alright. Well, it's alright. I would hope you will keep your word to me.

I miss you very much.

Love, Evelyn

■

Parzen received this letter on February 9, 1977, and promptly sent it to Olenik with this note: "Dave — I think she's biding her time with the suppressed or repressed fantasy of I'll run off w/her if she's good & does what I want. — Z"

Two days later, on February 11, 1977, Parzen received another letter from Evelyn about the new job her friend Ellen Hayes had helped her get at another design shop in a suburb farther inland from San Diego.

Dear Zane,

I've started my new job. The people I'm working with are very nice. It's a small group (4), three of which including me are the designers. It's a much more pleasant atmosphere. My hours are 10 A.M. to 5 P.M. (except Monday and Thursday) because of my doctor appointment. Then I leave at 3 P.M. What I'm really saying is that if you wanted to call me, after five or before 9:30 A.M. is a good time.

Zane, please contact me. I can work, try to keep busy, even date. However, this changes nothing in my feelings for you.

Things in my life haven't the full meaning without you to share them with.

I know you could see and talk to me if you want to. Dr. Olenik has pointed this out to me on several occasions. I pray that you want and will see me. I know you need time — I'm waiting.

I love you deeply.

Evelyn

Parzen sent this letter to Olenik with another note, this one written on a full sheet headed: "From the desk of ZANE D. PARZEN, M.D., A Professional Corporation. . . ."

The note reads: "It seems that the unconscious fantasy is still quite active, & undifferentiated from reality.

"Do you feel the therapeutic alliance you have with her is 'strong' enough to handle a confrontation with the reality, if she sees me at this time. Or would it be better for you to continue to point out to her that I could see her, but that I'm not, as an invisible form of confrontation. Z"

■

I had talked with my new boss at some length before I went to work in the design shop. She knew my situation and I told her that it would be some time before I felt strong enough to take on a full-scale design job.

But she already had heard this from my friend Ellen, and she seemed willing to give me a chance.

I felt good about my new coworkers, and of course I was happy to be so close to Ellen. I began to learn about the various suppliers and the different lines of products sold in the showroom. However, I was always tired. The drive to work was thirty minutes each way, and sometimes the traffic was so heavy when I'd be driving home that it would take me forty-five minutes. My new boss had seemed understanding of my condition at first, but she was very aggressive and ambitious. And each day she was applying more and more pressure on me to produce. I wasn't at all familiar with this area of San Diego County, and it was an effort for me to find my way around. One miserably hot day, when I was tired and horribly confused, I was sent to yet another unfamiliar address. I was afraid I just couldn't handle the job — especially since I couldn't even find my way around. I had to pull off the road and talk to myself, trying to calm down. When I finally found the house, it was still under construction, and I would have been in the way trying to work on interior design plans. I had wasted nearly three hours for nothing.

I was so upset by the time I got back to the shop, I knew I couldn't handle the job anymore. As much as I hated to admit that Doctor Olenik had been right, I realized I had been released from the hospital too soon. It became clear to me that I couldn't handle the pressures of a full-time job. I told my boss — of less than a month — that I had to quit.

After that, I tried to occupy my time reading, doing needlepoint, and watching television. But nothing seemed to take my mind off Zane. He was in my every waking thought and very much in my dreams. And this got worse every day.

My sessions with Doctor Olenik didn't seem to be doing any good at all. I just sat there and cried uncontrollably. Again I wasn't eating, and no matter how tired I felt, I wasn't able to sleep. The thoughts of suicide were coming more and more frequently. Rather than trying to get rid of the thoughts quickly when they would surface, I was beginning to think about how I could obtain enough pills to kill myself.

One day, as I sat in Doctor Olenik's office, I didn't want to leave; I couldn't face going back to that apartment. But I couldn't think clearly about what I should do. I wanted Doctor Olenik to do something. I wanted him to call Zane, but he refused to do that for me. He kept saying I should go back into Mesa Vista Hospital; it wasn't healthy for me to be living alone. I reminded him of how unhappy I had been there, how much I hated and feared that place. But I began to choke on my words, coughing and crying and feeling like I was going to vomit. I knew I couldn't go on living alone; I told Olenik I would go back in the hospital, but only if it was understood that I would be there only for a short time. He immediately picked up the phone and made arrangements for me to go back into Mesa Vista that night.

Not a word was spoken this time as Bruce drove me back to the hospital. I sat there in anguished silence. I was like a defeated warrior being led into the enemy camp. But this time, I was determined to win no matter what it took or how long. I was trying to convince myself that I would get well. I couldn't allow myself to think about never getting well. I had to find a way up and out of all this.

I was depressed by the familiarity of it all — I knew the hallways and where to go, and there were familiar faces greeting me, faces I had hoped never to see again. The nurse I had liked most saw my name on the roster and came and talked with me. She said maybe I had pushed myself too hard; everything would work out for me, but it would take time. The important thing right now, she said, was for me to get some sleep. She gave me my sleeping pills and left. As I dozed off, I prayed to God to help me get well. I didn't want to go on living like this — half-alive, a burden to everyone around me. But I told myself I would do it this time; I would get well no matter what.

▬

In both his admission and discharge reports on Evelyn Walker, Olenik for the first time refers to her involvement with Parzen as an actual event in her life. The reason she had to be readmitted to Mesa Vista Hospital on February 17, 1977, he said, was, "She began to gradually get more depressed over the loss of her relationship with a previous therapist."

In his discharge report a week later, on February 23, 1977, Olenik added some details to this but, oddly, masked the identity of Evelyn's "relationship."

She continued to be depressed about the loss of a previous relationship. It became clear that the party involved would not contact

her as she wished, and she began to mourn and grieve the relationship. She became more grief-stricken, sad and decompensated in her ego functions and her reality testing began to be impaired. There was suicidal ideation. There was some implication that if her husband would not take her back and allow her to live with him and the two boys, that she would not be willing to go back to an apartment to live alone. And indeed, there was some implication that she might kill herself. This was why arrangements were made for her to come back to the hospital.

Having accepted the reality that she would never be able to go back and live with Bruce and that she could not live alone, Evelyn was faced with the question of where on earth she would live outside the hospital. There was only one place for her to go — her parents' house, a place she thought she had left forever.

Olenik was the first of Evelyn's doctors to involve her parents in her therapy. He had talked to both parents several times on the telephone and he had learned a great deal about Evelyn's early childhood and problems she had had in the past.

Olenik would later read in court the notes from a telephone conversation he had at this time with Evelyn's mother (dated February 19, 1977):

Spoke with patient's mother, who said she does not know how much of what patient says is fantasy or not. Describes her as a perfectionist in all areas of her life. Describes "playboy" like life that patient and . . . executive husband lived. Describes idealizing of her husband. Mother says that patient was shy, quiet seclusive child at home. Describes that patient had idealized her father, her husband, and then her therapist to the point of near delusions. Mother also described patient's undying need for perfection in everything. Also described patient's spouse (object choice) as completely selfish person.

Much to Evelyn's amazement, her parents had been receptive and cooperative with Olenik. For the first time, she felt they were genuinely concerned about her welfare and wanted to do something to help her. It was one thing for them to assume that their little girl was playing sick just to get attention. It was quite another to have a doctor, a total stranger, call and say their daughter was seriously mentally ill.

They needed no degrees in psychiatry to understand that he was also saying that they were partly to blame and should accept their responsibility. Her father also had time on his hands now. He had come close to death with Hodgkin's disease, but he had overcome that. Now he had nothing to do but sit at home while his wife went about a busy club life with the neighborhood women.

Olenik arranged a "test run" with Evelyn's parents to be sure the plan would work. Evelyn was happy to see her father when she found him waiting for her in the hospital sitting room on the day of the first test visit. At home, her mother seemed very happy to see Evelyn and busied herself fixing a nice lunch for the three of them. They sat in the backyard for most of the day, having light but pleasant conversation. Late in the afternoon, Evelyn even felt relaxed enough to go inside and take a nap. After dinner, her father took her back to the hospital.

A second daylong visit with her parents also proceeded without incident, and so, after only six days in the hospital, Evelyn was released on February 23 to go home. Whatever mixed feelings she had about going back to her parents were offset by the memory of the bitter feelings of loneliness she had known in her little apartment.

In the next few weeks, she ate well and slept better than she had in a long time. The only time she would allow herself to cry was in her twice-a-week sessions with Olenik. She would start talking about how she missed her Zane and how she couldn't understand why he couldn't talk to her, and then the tears would start again.

In late April 1977, Evelyn wrote Parzen another update on her life without him:

Dear Zane,
    This morning I went to court. I was there from 10:15 A.M. to 1:30 P.M. Most of the time was spent with the lawyer. There was a lot of paper work to be signed. I think the judge was there at the most 15 minutes.
    I miss you all the time but some days are much harder than others, this was one of those days. I did see Olenik today but it certainly wasn't the same and never will be.
    It's very hard to see that (16) years of your life are now only a stack of papers to be signed.
    These past months have been and still are very difficult for me. I see Olenik twice a week, most of the time I start out or end up

crying. I still do a lot of crying. However he is a nice man and I feel comfortable talking to him.

As for work — I stopped working when I had to go to the hospital the second time. I am planning to go back sometime before May. Since I still feel very shaky most of the time Dr. Olenik agreed with my thought of not having to deal with any additional pressure. However I have been in (2) classes through UCSD extension.

Bruce has been very hard to deal with. It's not really that different than in the past but it is harder for me since I don't see you. Bruce wanted Olenik to keep me in the hospital. He also wanted to talk with Olenik without my being there. But Olenik wouldn't do this, it made Bruce very angry.

Then in court my lawyer, Bruce's lawyer and finally the judge told him that he *had* to let me see the boys. That I wasn't un-fit. Since January I've seen the boys (3) times that's all. I talk to them on the phone but that's all. By the way, the (3) times I saw them Bruce came too.

Zane, I must tell you since January my parents have really come around. For the first time I think they were willing to see what was really happening with me. They in their own way have been very good. This is a pleasant surprise. I feel that they see Bruce in a different light. They always felt I was very foolish leaving him, now they can see some of what I was going through with him.

I want you to know I am trying to cope with what has happened. Zane, you said (6) months until you could see me so I wait to hear from you. Even though I know what I must do for my life, find some one *free* to share my life with. I can't believe that the caring and friendship we built over these past years just flatly ends. No-one can tell you that YOU can't *call* or even see me occasionally.

Over the last (2) months I have been dating some, two men in particular. It's hard for me at times. I tend to feel I shouldn't be doing this because I love you. This is something Olenik is working out with me.

You're on my mind most of the time, and I love you all of the time.

Evelyn

Two months later, Evelyn wrote yet another letter to Parzen, who received it on June 6, 1977. He had done nothing meanwhile to encourage her, but her love, her obsession, was, if anything, made stronger by his silence.

Dear Zane,

It's very important to me that I write you tonight. It's been a very difficult few weeks and for some reason today seemed especially hard. I saw Dr. Olenik today. I cried the full hour. Between the divorce & losing you I'm a real mess. Dr. Olenik continually tells me that I should call you but I'm afraid to do that.

I just don't seem to be able to get out of a depressed state.

Bruce is not willing to sign the final papers (for tax reasons) he wants to keep me as his wife. I can't do anything if he doesn't sign. Then Bruce says he still loves me and wants me back, then the next minute he is very mean to me.

Then there is the fact that I haven't heard from you at all. This hurts a great deal. It's the first time I know of that you said one thing then went back on your word. I feel lied to. When I said on the phone I didn't think you'd call me, you got angry, said I don't listen. I heard what you said but I felt the negative part.

I don't know how to stop hurting and loving. Nothing has any real meaning to me. I feel very alone.

January of 76 Eric died — one year later, January of 77, I lost you. The two men that I loved the deepest both gone from me, one year apart to the month. It seems like a bad turn of affairs.

My existing is just that. I date it means nothing, just seems to be the thing to do. I've given up fighting with Bruce about seeing the boys. When he brings them fine and I enjoy seeing them, but I can't fight Bruce any more.

I'm just tired of living and wish it would end.

Not hearing from you or seeing you is the most difficult thing I ever had to go through.

I hope you're well.

All my love,

Evelyn

In those first weeks back at home [February and March 1977], life had never seemed so pleasant between me and my parents. But gradually I began to sense that something was still wrong — not with them or us, but again with me. I was one of those people who had never lived alone; I couldn't — I didn't want to — live alone. It was just not right for a person to live without a husband or wife.

My first step outward was one that I might have laughed at in earlier days. I heard about a singles group at the local synagogue. Even in this, my mother was very supportive. She encouraged me to join, saying yes, this might be a first step for me.

I paid my $2 at the door and was given a big name tag. I was telling myself what a mistake I had made as I wandered around lost in the huge, open room. I felt conspicuous and ill at ease. I moved to a far corner and took a seat, thinking I would be safe there. No sooner had I sat down than a man appeared at my side with a drink for me and a story of his own to tell. He had just been through a divorce and nothing was going to stop him from telling me every gory detail about it.

I was feeling trapped when suddenly another voice — warm and friendly — said hello to me. This second man rescued me and served as my guide through the rest of the evening. We didn't talk much about our pasts. We didn't talk about much of anything. We just enjoyed each other's company. At the end of the evening, I gave the man my parents' telephone number, and we made plans to meet again. I smiled and felt good about my success. I had made a first step back into the social world. I was thinking that maybe I would be able to make a new life for myself.

But the most fateful of my encounters happened not long after this in a nice little restaurant in downtown La Jolla. The place was Botsford's, located diagonally across from the building where Zane had his office. If he were out watering his roses on the rooftop terrace, I could see him from a window seat at Botsford's. Quite often, I would leave my session with Doctor Olenik and walk up the street to Botsford's and sit there sipping coffee, hoping to catch a glimpse of Zane.

One day, a man came over to me and introduced himself. He said he had seen me sitting there alone several times, but I had never noticed him. He was not somebody I would ever before have paid attention to, but now I was so desperately lonely for somebody, anybody, to notice me, to need me, that I smiled and said hello. In the days and weeks ahead, I would come to see in Bob Simmons some hope for comfort and security and maybe even love in my life.

Looking back now, I can see that the place where we met held the key to the violent disagreements that would plague our relationship from beginning to end. The first few times we met at Botsford's, Bob Simmons had no idea he was interrupting my reverie, my vigil for Zane. No matter how good things would seem between us, I was always looking over Bob's shoulder, hoping to see my Zane.

━

In a letter that Evelyn wrote to Parzen about her involvement with Bob Simmons, there were a number of exaggerations and distortions that would puzzle her later. Most were the result of Simmons's misrepresenting himself to Evelyn, but others were Evelyn's own misrepresentations to Parzen. Evelyn did not date her letters, and Parzen has incorrectly dated receipt of this one as "2/9/77." Possibly he had just inverted the day and month, so that he actually received it on September 2, 1977 — which would correspond to Evelyn's memory of the time she wrote the letter.

Dear Zane:
When I wrote you in July I mentioned one man in particular, [Bob Simmons]. [Bob] asked me three times to marry him. Each time I said no yet I wanted to continue to see him. Of all the men I'd been seeing I was very drawn to [Bob]. When he asked the fourth time I decided to give this serious thought and asked for a month's time to think.
I met [Bob] in March [1977]. He is a large, heavyset man always smoking a cigar, very good to me yet like you has been very hard on me. Determined to pull me out of the depression I was in. Forced me to make decisions. With other men I could cover up a great deal, with [Bob] it didn't work. He has been very patient with me. I found it easier to talk to him. [Bob] knew that I cared for someone else but didn't ask too many questions, after several months I told him some about my relationship with you. It was the first time he had ever seen me cry.
[Bob] is a very successful business man, he owns the [a real estate franchise] chain and is part owner of [a nationwide department store chain] plus other involvements.
He is 17 years older than I am but this isn't a problem in the

relationship. So, after much thought I decided to marry [Bob]. I feel good with him, he makes me laugh again and most important — he loves me a great deal. I believe [Bob] is very good for me. I am relaxed. My work is the best I've ever done — not just because it's selling but I know it's good. I feel safe with [Bob]. I believe you would approve. I'm also working as a designer again in La Jolla.

It took me a long time to write this letter, I kept putting it off because I knew it had to be my last. I knew when we last spoke that I would never see or speak to you again but I needed to let you know what was going on in this difficult year.

Zane, I love you more than anything in my life. Nothing that has or will happen will ever change that. There will always be a part of me that loves & misses you and still hurts. You combine the best and the worst thing that ever happened to me.

Even though I knew you would never be in my life again it was very hard to let another man in. The thought of someone else touching me didn't sit well, again [Bob] was very patient.

When I told Bruce that I was going to marry he started shaking me and slapped me saying he wasn't going to let me do this. However, when I told the boys they both said they wanted to be there when we got married, which was a pleasant surprise. We were married at the rabbi's home. [Bob] will not be alone with Bruce. Both boys really like [Bob] and that is so important.

I feel that things are going & will continue to go well. I get very lonely for you and I hope that no matter what happens to you or how busy you get somehow you always keep me within you.

I hate ending this letter it's *so final*. I wish for you all that is *good in life*. All my love,

Evelyn

It seems obvious that Evelyn was exaggerating a bit because she wanted Parzen to think that she was happier and more successful than she actually was and that this marriage was a far better match than it was. If *he* didn't appreciate her, she was saying, then there were others who did. In fact, she says now, she did not get that job in La Jolla; her artwork was selling, but it was far from her best. And, most important, her first husband Bruce was greatly relieved that she was getting married. He was never angry, never struck her; he encouraged the match.

As for Simmons, the facts about him would come out later in court. He was born in 1921, so he was nineteen — not seventeen — years older than Evelyn. He did not own a chain of real estate offices; he was one-fourth owner of one office in a small town north of San Diego, and that office had gone bankrupt. And he was not related in any way to the family with his name that owned the department stores.

Although it lasted for several months, the marriage was a mismatch from the very first hours. They were not sexually compatible. This time, however, Evelyn didn't see that there was anything wrong with her. Moreover, she couldn't stand to let him touch her. And — he would later testify — all she could talk about was "Zane, Zane, Zane."

In spite of their incompatibility, Evelyn still allowed her second husband to make all her decisions. He told her to give her car to her oldest son and he would buy her a new Pinto. (He never got around to putting the new car in her name, however, and kept it after their divorce.) He also told her to stop seeing Doctor Olenik, and she did that too. Simmons didn't believe in psychiatrists.

But if he didn't believe in psychiatry, Simmons had a handy substitute in hypnosis. As a hostile witness in Evelyn's trial against Parzen four years later, Simmons would explain his reasoning.

My reason for asking her to go to a hypnotist friend of mine was twofold; number one, I am a student of hypnosis myself, understand what it can do for people, and she had explained to me that she had been going to this other doctor in La Jolla, and she had told me what had transpired. And, to me, it was a waste of time. She would attend sessions with him, and she was supposed to venge her problems, whatever it is, whatever came in her mind, and he would sit in the background and say, "Uh-huh, uh-huh, uh-huh, uh-huh"; then, when the session was over, he'd say, "Fine, I'll see you next week," and that's the total sum of each session.

Some psychologists believe in venging. I'm not a psychologist, but I don't believe in venging. And so this is the reason I suggested that she go to a hypnotist, because they do and have made cures in this field.

Simmons said the reason he suggested that Evelyn see his hypnotist friend was because of her continuing obsession with Zane Parzen. "She kept bringing up the subject of Zane. . . . So I figured, well, to get it out of her mind and put it into perspective, she's got a life to live ahead of her, and if she's going to jeopardize her life by saying that this guy is the greatest, and nobody can replace him, she's not going to have much of a life ahead of her."

The hypnotist Simmons sent Evelyn to had been trained at the Hypnosis Motivation Institute in Los Angeles. He had then moved to San Diego in hopes of founding a branch of the Institute there. The hypnotist's recollections of Evelyn's visits were almost as confused and contradictory as were those of Simmons. He didn't know when he did what, much less why. In one place, he says Evelyn Walker did submit to hypnosis; in another, he says she did not. In fact, Evelyn vehemently refused to go under hypnosis, but for two or three months, at her husband's urging, she would go twice a week to the hypnotist's office and sit there and talk with him as if he had the credentials of a psychiatrist.

At first, the hypnotist testified, she was so "nervous, upset, distraught, depressed" that all he tried to do was calm her down and relieve her of some of the tension, but after the second or third visit, he said she began to talk. "That's mainly what I let her do, mainly, just kind of ventilate out," he testified.

Somehow, this dreadful marriage dragged on, bitter month after bitter month. Like so many people trapped in a mismatch, Evelyn and Simmons could not stand the life they were living together, but neither could they make the move to change it. They traveled a great deal — once to Haiti and several times to Las Vegas.

On one trip to Las Vegas, Simmons became desperately ill with a kidney infection. He testified that his temperature rose to 107, "when 105 is supposed to kill you." He also testified that when they returned to San Diego, Evelyn attempted suicide just to draw attention away from his illness. It was a ludicrous charge, easily disproved by Evelyn's lawyer. Of all her attempts at suicide, this was the most serious, the closest she came to death: Evelyn "took everything I could get my hands on" out of Simmons's rather extensive stock of tranquilizers and sleeping pills. Her family doctor testified that she was unconscious for several days, and when she finally woke up, she was still "out of it" for quite a long time.

Evelyn was in the hospital for eleven days, starting March 28, 1978. There was no longer any question about the survival of her marriage to Simmons. They quarreled constantly. In their last fight after her suicide attempt, they became so loud and violent that the neighbors called the police. A neighbor also brought charges of assault against Simmons, and he spent a night in jail.

Evelyn wanted a simple annulment to get out of the marriage as quickly as possible. However, her lawyer felt that she was due alimony and that this man (from all he had said) could easily afford to pay.

In late October 1978, Evelyn wrote an after-action report to Zane Parzen:

You have been on my mind for the past few days and the need to write you was there.

First of all, I am at the end of a long trying divorce from [Bob]. Two days after I married him I realized I had made a terrible mistake. It was eight months of hell. I didn't love the man and found that I just couldn't stand to have him touch me. Plus there were so many other problems. He was jealous beyond words, wouldn't let me out of his sight. It got so bad that he began to conduct much of his business from our home so that he could be with me more.

Because he has a lot of money he felt that would hold me. He used it in many ways to in his thinking keep me happy. We traveled quite often. He is big on expensive gifts.

At any rate, I left him and filed for divorce. This time I have a very good lawyer. [Bob] has fought me, we've gone to court so far nine times but this Friday is the trial court. There is a lot of money involved so the fight is worthwhile. It's been long and hard, but I've held up because for the first time something has really made me mad. I really thought that [Bob] was going to be good for me and that I could grow to care for him, but this was far from the case.

Now things are taking some shape. I have setbacks at times but they don't last as long. [Bob] has been a very difficult man to get away from. He still wants me back but that is out of the question.

Until this is resolved I won't be completely at ease but the end is near, and I have good people helping. . . . I am teaching again. I have two classes. On the whole I feel pretty good. Still have trouble with my stomach but it's getting better. I now weigh 123 pounds but at least I'm holding it.

You are still very much with me. I have seen you three times. Once walking down Girard [Avenue, in La Jolla], twice on Prospect

[Street]. It was very hard not to walk up to you but I would not. I couldn't have taken it if you had been cold or even worse, just kept walking.

You've never written me or called. I guess it was a relief to get me out of your life. I think you would like me now. I am holding my own, still frightened but I am doing it. I did have quite a setback in [March and] April. I overdosed and really did a job that time. I was unconscious for five days, in a hospital for eleven. Dr. [Fournier] said he really didn't feel I was going to pull through but I did and when I woke up first I was angry then felt guilty because I broke my word to you. [Fournier] and I talked a great deal and it was clear I had to get out of the marriage.

So that's where I am now. I am very pleased with my new apartment and look forward to present problems ending. I've dropped the name [Simmons], went back to Walker — it's like it never happened.

I miss you and wish you missed me. How I would like to hear from you. All my love,

Evelyn

There was little that was positive in Evelyn's life at this time — the few good things she mentions in her letter turned out to be not quite as rosy as she described. Those art classes she mentions ended soon afterward because she couldn't cope. And all that talk of money from her second husband turned out to be nothing more than talk. If he had any money at all, Bob Simmons was not about to share it with Evelyn. The court ordered him to support her during the time of their separation, and he was also ordered to pay alimony under the terms of their divorce. But Simmons elected to go to jail rather than forfeit one penny to Evelyn Walker.

Meanwhile, the separation had freed Evelyn to date other men. Much later, long after her successful trial against Zane Parzen, Evelyn was appalled to learn that her own lawyer had characterized her behavior during this time as "going from man to man to man." Hearing the words, she broke down and cried. "I am not a whore," she said. Her lawyer was making an extremely important point in the case. Here was a woman who had been almost Victorian in her prudishness. Prior to her marriage to Bruce Walker, she had hardly even kissed a man. She had never had sex with any man but Bruce

Walker until she met Zane Parzen. After that, she was still remarkably faithful to her man, although that man was no longer her husband. Then, when Parzen had thrown her out of his office and his life, it seemed she would go with any man who (like Simmons) offered a pretense of security and love and affection.

In fact, there were only three men she was involved with between 1978 and 1980 before she met and fell in love with her third husband. By current standards that number hardly reflects any kind of promiscuity — but, as her lawyer pointed out, it certainly reflected a change in Evelyn. What she was seeking in these relationships, her psychologist would later explain, was a very basic "infantile" need. In other words, sex had little or nothing to do with why she was going out with these men. Over and over, the child in the mature woman's body would plead, "I want somebody to hold me." It was the kind of cuddling and caressing a parent gives a child. Evelyn had never gotten this kind of physical affection from her parents or from her first husband. This crying need of hers had been instantly identified — and satisfied — by Parzen, who, after all, had been trained expertly to diagnose and analyze just such needs.

The first man Evelyn became involved with was the "ex-FBI man" her lawyer had hired as a private investigator to check up on Bob Simmons's financial claims. (As it turned out, this so-called ex-FBI man was an ex-convict who had no valid license to work as a private investigator.) Although they dated often, he was never there when Evelyn needed him most. She didn't consider it a serious involvement.

The second man was a Mexican-American politician, a leading figure in Republican politics in San Diego County. He was the most genuine of the three. He would talk with Evelyn and, more important, he would listen and try to help her overcome her problems. He liked the way she looked and he was proud to be seen with her. They went to several Republican Party functions and made a handsome couple. Evelyn liked being with the politician; she especially liked being able to go out in public with him, something that had always been missing in her long involvement with Parzen. But theirs was not a passionate love relationship.

The third involvement was serious. It lasted — on again, off again — for almost two years. In many tragic ways, this relationship was only a repetition of what Evelyn had gone through with Zane Parzen. The man who suddenly announced to her that he had been in love with her for a long time was none other than the family physician, Robert Fournier. Years earlier, Parzen had correctly sensed that Fournier was a competitor for Evelyn's attentions not just on a professional level but also on a private and sexual level. That can be the only explanation for Parzen's violent reaction whenever Evelyn mentioned Fournier's name — or for the vehemence of that long, long letter of October 1975 in which Parzen laid down the parameters of what Fournier should and should not be doing for Evelyn.

Subpoenaed as a witness in the trial of *Walker v. Parzen,* Fournier would angrily deny that he had ever had anything but a professional relationship with his patient, Evelyn Walker. And furthermore, he almost shouted, he had been called to give expert medical testimony, not to talk about his private life. As if he himself were a psychiatrist, Fournier had arranged for Evelyn to come in for counseling twice a week after her suicide attempt in March 1978. Asked at the trial if it weren't a little unusual for a general practitioner to be counseling a patient in this manner twice a week in his office, Fournier was indignant again. No, he said, it was not unusual at all. He said that any time a patient was in pain, he wanted to see him or her every four days.

Evelyn's relationship with Fournier became as much a delusion for her as her involvement with Parzen had been. The sexual, affectional part of it was real, but, once again, the doctor had no intention of leaving his wife for Evelyn. At the time, Fournier told Evelyn that his wife was very ill and not expected to live. Evelyn never found out whether this was true or not — but she did see them together on one occasion, and the wife appeared to be in good health.

There were many differences, however, between this relationship and the one Evelyn had with Parzen. Fournier kept the office visits on a professional basis; the personal relationship developed in her apartment, where he visited almost every day. They spent many pleasant hours together — talking, making love, just being together. Fournier would occasionally take Evelyn out to dinner — not often, but it did happen. Fournier and Evelyn would sometimes decide not to see each other and Evelyn would begin dating other men, but Fournier would always come back and break up whatever relationship she had established. And so she began to think — as with Parzen — that somehow, some way, she and Fournier eventually would live together as man and wife.

By November 1978, Evelyn had not yet become so involved with her family physician for that to have pushed aside her obsession with Zane Parzen. She was still preoccupied with thoughts of Parzen, and she still wanted desperately somehow to get through to him. None of her loving correspondence had drawn any kind of reaction from Parzen, so she finally wrote him a long, bitterly angry letter, denouncing him and his lies and all he had done to hurt her. Parzen noted that the letter was received on November 3, 1978. In passing it on to "Dave" Olenik, Parzen wrote:

> Latest letter —
> Be care — as she dethrones me she will probably idealize you & then you be on the hot spot —
> Her splitting is probably going to be necessary to some extent —
> I had hoped she hold together better — but the object hunger (ambivalent as it may be) seems too great still. Z

Evelyn's letter — to her exasperation and horror — would later turn up as the key evidence against her as Parzen's lawyers tried in the later hearings and trial to dismiss her claims as the frenzied rantings of a jilted lover. It is quoted in full here.

Dear Zane,
This is a letter that should have been written almost two years ago. But it has taken me this long to get angry, to see things clearly.
I recently wrote you. Would it have been such an effort to take a few minutes of your valuable time to reply?
Ever since you turned your back on me and dropped any and all responsibility you had to me, leaving the mess you helped create to anyone else. In this time I've been asked continually when I would finally get angry and see you for what you are. But it didn't happen. I always could justify you.
Dr. Olenik still asks on the occasions I see him if I'm angry yet, and up until now still the answer is no.
I don't really know why now it hits me. Maybe the recent divorce, I finally woke up.
Zane, I put more trust and love in you than I have ever known. I was willing to work harder than I've ever known and although I

gained in some ways the end result has been a nightmare.

I see you now to be a shallow man. You allowed things to happen not really ever considering what in the end this would do to me.

You counted on the fact that I would protect you no matter what price I had to pay. Believe me, I've more than paid.

You accepted my love and caring with no intention of seeing the relationship go anywhere. You knew that my feelings and trust cut me off from anyone else.

Your words were lies. You'd never abandon me. <u>You'd never turn your back on me.</u> You'd always love me. You'd always be true. You'd never turn me out. And the biggest lie, you made love to me for me.

If that was the case, <u>why didn't you ever try to wait and</u> please me as well?

You used me pure and simple—and I have the power to ruin you. I always did. I was advised more than once to use that power. But as always I continued to protect you, to see that no one else hurt you, to protect your family. The question is what in the Hell did you ever do to protect me? You didn't even keep your word to me that if I went to Olenik you would call me—that I would at least get to talk to you during this difficult time. To feel that you were there to care. You lied. You told me 6 months then I would be with you again. I waited—all the time in the hospital I waited. I couldn't believe you would just ignore what in fact was happening to me.

Zane, you're a coward, I could forgive that but it's how you did things that I can't forgive and for that I hate you. To protect yourself and your plain little wife you could have cared less about me.

I know one thing. You also had and probably still have a void in your life. You also needed love and I gave you more than you'll <u>ever</u> get from anyone. I stuck it out under the most difficult of situations.

You continue to hide in that office playing god with people's lives. It gives you purpose.

With me, you became a cruel man. I doubt you've really ever given to anyone.

All this time without you has been <u>Hell</u>, a constant struggle. In all the writing to you not one lousy letter from you. It would have meant something but god forbid you could have been that thoughtful. You weren't even a <u>friend</u>.

How many times have you done this before. You should be

stopped from hurting anyone again.

Your ego is so big that you believed you could be everything, doctor, so called lover and you failed it all. But how it must have amused you to know you had a woman so in love with you that she would go to any lengths for that love. And of course it put money in the pocket let's not forget that.

All the pain I've known, all the investing in you that I did, always being afraid, afraid to get angry, afraid of losing you, afraid of your anger, afraid you wouldn't like me or care any more. Afraid all my life — I didn't deserve all of it.

Left with no one to care, no one who really knew me, no one to really turn to, to trust. Eric was dead, you dropped me, Bruce could care less, Olenik didn't even know me plus right away left for a trip. If it hadn't been for Gary & Bettie god only knows what would have happened.

How do you live with yourself? I feel sorry for you, you're an empty man. And yet still with all this I still love you and hurt inside for your pains. But what you didn't [sic] will never go away. It has marked me in many ways far more than anything of the past because it meant everything to me. You should know the effect is still strong — it has left a fear in me that affects my trust in other men.

I feel something must be done. I'm at this point not completely sure how yet, but something so that you can't damage someone again.

You can't just take a person's life and then throw it away like so much trash.

To save yourself you lie about me, making me out to be some sick woman who didn't know what was going on. Well, I've got news for you, you weren't believed, only protected. There are people you didn't fool, whose respect you haven't got.

Well instead of protecting, what happened almost killed me. To this day I still have dreams about that last day with you. I wake up frightened and cold.

You'll hurt someone again. Maybe this doesn't bother YOU. Maybe YOU can live with that —

I can't.

Evelyn

Under cross-examination from Parzen's lawyers in the later hearings and trials, Evelyn would be interrogated at length about the radical change in mood against Parzen reflected in this letter. His lawyers would claim that her motivation was jealousy and revenge, pure and simple. They would try — in vain — to prove that the letter was written after Parzen's colleagues learned (and informed Evelyn) about another woman Parzen was abusing in his office even more severely than he had done to Evelyn. But the facts support Evelyn's contention ("the God's honest truth") that she had no knowledge of this other woman or the professional steps being taken against Parzen at the time she wrote the angry letter.

Parzen himself had no knowledge of any moves against him at that time — as the tone of his own accompanying note to his colleague Dave Olenik clearly indicates. In his own mind, Parzen was still the respected professional. He held on to his copy of Evelyn's angry letter because he seemed to think it was his "smoking gun," the sensational piece of evidence that would prove Evelyn was distorting everything she said in order to get even with him for dropping her. In a succession of hearings and in the two-part public trial, Parzen's lawyers kept introducing this letter as proof positive that *he* was the victim — that Evelyn was the villain pursuing this upstanding professional and trying to ruin his career over her delusions of love and marriage with him. In one of the more brilliant strokes in her trial, Evelyn's lawyer would simply take Parzen's smoking gun and turn it right back on him.

II. Legal Remedies

Chapter 8

In fact, when the turning point came against Zane Parzen, the actions that precipitated his downfall were not initiated by Evelyn Walker — nor did they begin with anything said or done by Gary Shepherd. A woman patient from Chicago was the one whose behavior — unknown to her — led to Parzen's public disgrace. And it was not Parzen's worst enemy among his psychiatric colleagues who would lead the fight against him; it was his closest friend and neighbor, Al Robbins.

Alvin Robbins was born in 1940 in Detroit, Michigan. He completed his undergraduate and medical school degrees at Wayne State University. He did his internship at the USC Medical Center in Los Angeles and his residency at the Detroit Psychiatric Institute, followed by a year's fellowship in child psychiatry at Cedars Sinai Medical Center in Los Angeles. He spent two years as a lieutenant and lieutenant commander in the United States Navy, and that took him to the huge Navy hospital complex in Balboa Park in San Diego, where he worked with Gary Shepherd, among others involved in this story. He was among the first students at the San Diego Psychoanalytic Institute, and he graduated from there in 1975.

His favorite instructor at the Institute was Zane Parzen, a man not unlike himself in many ways. They even look alike; Robbins has the same Eastern European olive complexion, thinning dark hair, and dark eyes. But there the comparison stops. For even approaching middle age, Robbins still has a boyish twinkle in his eye and a kind of youthful vigor and innocence in his manner. There is none of the dark, brooding suspicion that shows in the face of Parzen. However, the two became colleagues and friends — that is, they became as close as was possible with Parzen, who had few friends.

They were both Jewish, although Parzen was more devout than Robbins, and the two families lived only a block away from each other. Their sons were members of the same soccer team at the high school.

Since Robbins was also a friend of Gary Shepherd, he also had heard the rumors about Parzen and Evelyn Walker. Like so many others at the time, Robbins simply dismissed this as a human failing of Parzen's — he had never seen Evelyn, but Shepherd assured him she was "a looker." Nonetheless, Robbins was among those at the Institute who did not feel Parzen should be promoted to senior training analyst.

However, there was another patient of Parzen's about whom Robbins slowly but surely became concerned. This was Pat Stern. She had been Parzen's patient in Chicago and had followed him to California. She was the woman Evelyn had heard one day screaming and crying hysterically in Parzen's office. Evelyn had looked out the door to see if the person needed help and had glimpsed the thin, blonde woman running down the hall.

La Jolla was, in those days at least, still something of a village. Robbins needed some help in the office, and Parzen's patient Pat Stern needed a job. Stern came to work for Robbins, and she would do routine clerical tasks, such as filing and mailing. Sometimes, while doing her work, Stern would talk to Robbins. Once she asked him if it were right for a psychiatrist to hit a patient. She said her doctor (Parzen) had thrown her against the wall and then explained to her that this was part of the treatment recommended by the famous psychiatrist Bruno Bettelheim.

Robbins was shocked by what Pat Stern said, but when he asked her to explain further, she just laughed it off. Robbins, however, could not dismiss the way the woman looked. Everybody who saw her during this time agrees that she was a ghastly sight: the most frequently used description was that she looked like a concentration camp victim. Stern suffered from anorexia nervosa — a condition that is often misunderstood or oversimplified in the popular press. It is usually described as a kind of frivolous disease occurring among women so fearful of becoming fat and ugly that they eventually refuse to eat anything at all. In fact, anorexia nervosa is a serious, and potentially deadly, condition. Evelyn Walker and Pat Stern — and, it would later be revealed, other patients of Parzen's — suffered from anorexia nervosa at least partly because they had reached such nervous states that they simply could not hold food in their stomachs. They would go for incredible lengths of time without eating anything solid at all.

That peculiar mention of Bettelheim stuck in Robbins's memory, and he recalled it early in November of 1978, when Gary Shepherd told him that Pat Stern had called him on yet another weekend when Parzen was out of town. What had disturbed Shepherd was that Stern had said she was taking a combination of the drugs Parnate and Ritalin. In the language of the profession, "such a combination is contraindicated unless the patient is hospitalized and under close supervision, because of the danger of provoking a fatal hypertensive crisis." In other words, if the drugs are prescribed together except in extreme cases and under hospital supervision they could cause a fatal heart attack. Shepherd told Stern to flush the Parnate down the toilet.

Perhaps that was why Stern didn't call Shepherd the next time she was in trouble; instead, she called Robbins. This was on November 25, a Saturday, and Robbins's wife answered the phone. Over the previous few months, she had talked several times with Pat Stern over the telephone, but this time Stern sounded out of control. Robbins returned the call immediately and tried to talk with Stern, but she was so confused and disoriented that he could make very little sense out of what she was saying. She wanted desperately to talk with her own doctor, Parzen, but she said she was terrified of bothering him after hours or on weekends. He had been angry with her recently, and that made it all the more upsetting for her.

Robbins had made plans for an elegant dinner at a restaurant with his wife, so he told Stern that she should call Parzen. During one of their talks at his office, Stern had mentioned a friend of hers named Mary Sutton, an American Airlines stewardess, who later said that she had no choice but to get involved with Pat Stern — she would see her out at the pool in their apartment complex and she seemed so pathetic, so helpless, so in need of someone to talk with. Robbins suggested that Stern get her friend Mary to come over to the apartment and stay with her. After he finished dinner, he said, he would call her again and see how she was.

As always, Robbins left with the babysitter the telephone number of the restaurant where he would be in case there was an emergency with a patient. Sure enough, about halfway through their meal, the waiter informed them that there was a call for Doctor Robbins. The phone was brought to the table and plugged into a jack there, and Robbins took the call. In six years of casual acquaintance with Pat Stern, this was the worst Robbins had ever heard her. She said she had called Parzen, and he had told her to take even more Ritalin and not to talk with either her friend Mary or Robbins. Still, she begged Robbins to call her after he finished dinner.

Robbins and his wife went to his office, where he called Stern and began to hear her horror story. She said her weight was down to ninety-five pounds, maybe less. She had seen her grandmother wither and die a year earlier in Chicago, and she kept saying that her own legs were like that. She said her body was "concentration camp-like." She said there were things she had told her friend Mary that she could never tell Robbins, but she still wanted him to be her friend. As if talking to a child, Robbins asked Stern what there was to eat in the apartment and convinced her to try to get down a bowl of Rice Krispies. Then he asked her for Mary Sutton's telephone number. Robbins finally had to face a reality he had suspected about Parzen and Pat Stern for some time: there was something wrong in this treatment relationship. He would later testify, "I knew the relationship with Zane was enormously intense. There seemed to be a fusion involved. She — every word that came out of her mouth referred to her relationship with Doctor Parzen. She saw him five times a week — sometimes more than once a day, she would tell me; yet on the weekends or whatever, she couldn't see him. She also told me in the course of my seeing her that Doctor Parzen had physically restrained her and thrown her up against the wall on a number of occasions." The word *fusion* in this context, Robbins explained, meant "an excessively intense attachment between people; that it's very difficult to perceive one from the other at that point."

On Monday, Robbins called Mary Sutton, explaining that he was very concerned about Pat Stern. "So am I," Sutton said. "You do think she is in good hands, don't you?" Sutton asked him.

"I don't know," Robbins answered.

"Well, I don't," Sutton said, "and I would like to talk to you about it."

Robbins went to Sutton's apartment that Monday night, November 27, 1978, and was shocked by what he heard. He had some suspicion that Stern might have been physically abused, but the idea of a sexual relationship had never occurred to him — chiefly because Pat looked so ghastly he couldn't imagine anybody being sexually attracted to her. As Sutton began to tell what she knew about Pat Stern's relationship with Parzen, Robbins realized the problem was even more serious than he had imagined. He asked if he could come back on Thursday and make a tape recording of what she was telling, and Sutton agreed.

Meanwhile, Robbins spoke with Allan D. Rosenblatt, who was then director of the Psychoanalytic Institute, and with several other doctors who were involved with the ethics committees of the various professional organizations. Although he knew he was dealing with a situation that was not only unethical but illegal according to state law, Robbins's personal bias had always been, as he later put it, "to try to treat a problem rather than report it . . . try to deal with the problem so long as it didn't present a danger to patients and avoid unnecessarily blowing the whistle." He was himself the chairman (and only member) of the Impaired Physicians Committee of the San Diego Psychiatric Society; therefore, if any action were taken, it would be his responsibility to initiate it.

Robbins also spoke with Perry Bach, president of the San Diego Psychiatric Society and a former patient of Parzen's, who told him to go ahead. In the tape, Mary Sutton is asked what Pat Stern had told her about her relationship with Parzen.

ROBBINS: What has she told you about it?

SUTTON: Him having intercourse with her to make her feel, because she is so afraid of men and because she doesn't feel and he wants her to begin to feel.

ROBBINS: What did you think about that?

SUTTON: I thought it was sick, but then again, I thought that he was a doctor and knew what he was doing and I'm not a psychiatrist and —

ROBBINS: Well, you know that [Pat] has a difficult time emotionally — what makes you feel that what she was telling you was real?

SUTTON: Well, because of the details she went into and because I knew she had an abortion.

ROBBINS: How do you know this abortion really occurred?

SUTTON: Because she told me that — well, I knew she was pregnant because of the way she is built and her boobs got a lot bigger and her stomach got bigger and she went into detail about what she wanted to do — she wanted to have a baby and she wanted to have Zane's baby because she is so in love with Zane. He's her whole life. . . .

ROBBINS: Where was this abortion supposed to have taken place?

SUTTON: I am not sure, because I turn myself off, but I think at Scripps for some reason, I know Zane helped her with this and got her the doctor and the hospital and the whole bit. . . .

ROBBINS: What else has she told you about the nature of her relationship with Doctor Parzen recently that referred to sexuality?

SUTTON: She told me recently that Zane wanted to take pictures of her nude, from the front and the back, so she could see just how skinny she was because she looks in the mirror she doesn't feel that she is all that thin, and if she could see it — because your eyes only see what you want them to see and that Zane said if she saw the pictures of herself nude she would be able to see just how skinny she was.

ROBBINS: What did you think about that?

SUTTON: I thought it was sick, yet to be honest with you I thought that — I don't know, I just thought that maybe if she did see herself in a picture, not thinking that this guy could be into it for other reasons, that it might help.

ROBBINS: What do you think about what you knew all along, at this point what's your impression now?

SUTTON: It blows me away. I thought all along that it was sick and — the way she depended on him, and I tried to say to her that someday, you know, you are going to be well and you know you're not going to have this closeness with Zane and you know he's not going to be your whole life any more, he's going to have to cut you loose. And I discussed this, never into detail, with my parents about her having intercourse with Zane, but just things that went on, and just my parents seeing [Pat] and the way she looked and knew something wasn't right, but I figured he was a doctor and he knew what he was doing.

ROBBINS: You figure doctors always know what they are doing?

SUTTON: I figure a psychiatrist knows what he is doing but —

ROBBINS: What about now?

SUTTON: No. Everything I had doubts about — I mean, I saw it, my eyes were open, but I guess I didn't want to believe it. I wanted to think that she was being taken care of.

ROBBINS: . . . What do you know about how frequently she saw Doctor Parzen. . . . What would she tell you about this?

SUTTON: Well, I knew for a while she saw him five days a week, for a long time, and then —

ROBBINS: How many times a day?

SUTTON: Several. And I knew she hated Wednesdays, because in the past — I don't know, six or eight months, she doesn't see him on Wednesdays, and Wednesdays would upset her, we'd try to get together for lunch that day just to fill in the gap, and I would — we'd meet for breakfast, that way I'd know she'd have something to eat, and she would go to have something to eat if I was there with her. And I know she hated weekends because on weekends she wouldn't see Zane or hear from him, and I know whenever he goes away that weeks in advance she starts dwelling on it and being upset about it and trying to track down my schedule and where I'll be and —

ROBBINS: . . . How would this sex take place, did she tell you?

SUTTON: In the office. They would lay on the couch and usually leave their clothes on, which I thought was kind of strange, because I wouldn't want it that way. But he's obviously seen her breasts, because she has mentioned in detail about several times she was going to go up to L.A. and see this specialist that he recommended about getting a boob job.

ROBBINS: What else do you know about the nature of their sexual relationship?

SUTTON: I know at one point that [Pat] did go down on Zane, or in my terms give him a blow job because we discussed it, because I was going through something at the same time that I could relate to and tell her my feelings on it and what I had done and —

ROBBINS: Why did she say that she was doing this?

SUTTON: Because she was so terribly afraid of men and sex in every way, shape and form that this was now something else that she had done or tried to do —

ROBBINS: And this was prescribed for her?

SUTTON: Yeah.

ROBBINS: As a form of getting over her feelings?

SUTTON: . . . Yes. And I remember her telling me it's not bad and it's all right if you really love somebody because I remember saying yes I could only do it with somebody I loved and her saying that — and she said that it was all right because she really loves Zane.

Robbins concluded the questioning by asking Sutton if she thought Pat was dying. Sutton answered, "Yes, I really do." She also said that she would be willing to cooperate with the Ethics Committee of the Psychiatric Society in filing a formal complaint.

Parzen's colleagues finally had the evidence — they could no longer deny how serious the rumors were about his private practice. But Mary Sutton was not one of Parzen's patients. She had talked to him over the phone, but she had never met Parzen. Her testimony was, in lawyers' language, second-person "hearsay." It formed the basis for all the actions that would come later, but Mary Sutton herself was never called upon to testify.

Al Robbins and Gary Shepherd both knew Pat Stern well enough to know that she would never testify against her Zane. "She was the kind who would say, 'I may kill him, but don't you say a bad word about him or I will kill you,'" Shepherd said. Also, Stern was in such a visibly disturbed condition that her testimony could easily have been discredited in a court of law.

In other words, all their hopes lay in Evelyn Walker, and nobody could be sure about her. She had just endured a noisy, traumatic divorce from her second husband, and Gary Shepherd was still faced with the dilemma that if he explained exactly what Parzen had been doing with her, Evelyn might take her own life. But the doctors had no choice. Shepherd and Robbins talked and agreed that Evelyn had to be the one.

One night, Evelyn visited the Shepherds, and Gary Shepherd took her home. Evelyn had already told Bettie Shepherd about the angry letter she had recently written Parzen, and Bettie had relayed this information to her husband. Maybe, Gary Shepherd thought then, Evelyn really was ready to do something about Parzen. That night they got all the way to Evelyn's apartment before Shepherd could bring himself to ask the question. He was nervous and perspiring as he struggled for the right words that would convince Evelyn to help the committee to help Parzen. He said that Zane was having problems, and therefore might be using poor judgment with his patients, mainly with regard to medications. Evelyn said, "Well, if he is having problems, wouldn't it be better if I contacted him directly?" Shepherd said no, what she should do was write a letter to Al Robbins, head of the Impaired Physicians Committee, and tell him just how much she cared for Zane and what had gone on during their relationship. As Shepherd explained it to her, this committee was set up to help doctors who were having problems in their own lives. Shepherd explained to Evelyn that Parzen was having trouble with one patient whose friend had contacted Robbins.

Evelyn's immediate response was, how could this woman know, how could anybody know whether this patient was telling the truth? But when Gary mentioned that the patient was from Chicago, Evelyn asked him if the patient's name was Pat, the name she remembered Parzen using after she had seen the woman fleeing from his office four years earlier. He said it was. Evelyn promised Gary that she would do her duty — that she would write a letter to help Zane.

Evelyn went on into her apartment and went to bed, but she could not sleep for thinking about the letter she would write. After some time, she got up and sat down and wrote it.

Dear Dr. Alvin Robbins,
    This letter is being written in the hope that I will help you both Dr. Zane Parzen and patients that he in fact deals with. I was seeing Dr. Parzen for approximately three and one-half years. About six months after I went to him, slowly a relationship developed between us that ultimately became a sexual love relationship.
    During that time together our time was spent in conversations where we both learned about each other where Dr. Parzen spoke of his life at times, his pain and problems, as much to me as I felt I could to him.
    Dr. Parzen constantly assured me how I was loved and cared for by him and him alone. That I in fact would never lose him, he would never turn his back on me. He would always be with me, he would never turn me out.
    In time I turned more and more to Dr. Parzen and finally left my husband and then I divorced him. Besides the divorce, my husband's anger took form in seeing that I did not get community

property. So I lost a large amount of money as well. Dr. Parzen was aware of this.

The stress of this relationship was made even more difficult because Dr. Parzen would not see me outside the office at any time, although he mentioned a desire to.

Yet when I would want to stop seeing him, he would not let this happen, even though at one point I took poison partly because of him. Therefore I believed that in time we would be together. He gave me no reason in many ways to think otherwise.

Finally, on January 3, 1977, Dr. Parzen simply dropped me. Someone found out about us and he said I had to see Dr. David Olenik, that this would help him. That when Dr. Olenik told Dr. Parzen it was all right he would see and speak to me. And that in six months we would be together again.

What followed that day for me was living hell. I saw Dr. Olenik and was frightened to talk for fear something would happen to Dr. Parzen. Within days I lost my job. When I called Dr. Parzen he was angry and hung up on me. With the help of Dr. Gary Shepherd, I finally went to Mesa Vista. If I had not had his help, there is no question I would have died.

In the almost two years since that day in January I still am badly marked by all of this. I have horrible nightmares of that last day with Dr. Parzen when he turned me away in total rejection. I relive the fears of the past. The type of fears that brought me to Dr. Parzen in the first place. I am afraid in present relationships that I will again be dropped and not wanted. I live with it daily. There are times it gets so bad that I am shaky and vomit.

I have over the years written to Dr. Parzen in hopes that he would at least show some interest in my well-being. But never one single word. The struggle is long, lonely and painful.

This has been a difficult letter to write. If I can be of further help, please let me know.

Sincerely,
Evelyn Walker

P.S. I would appreciate it if I was kept informed as to what in fact happens with Dr. Zane Parzen. Thank you.

Evelyn wrote this letter at the request of Gary Shepherd (who was acting on behalf of Robbins and the other doctors at the San Diego

Psychoanalytic Institute), but was later told by these doctors that whenever she was questioned she should not say anything about why she wrote that letter about Parzen. This detail seemed unimportant at the time, but later could easily have lost her the malpractice case against Parzen. These instructions later made it difficult for Evelyn to answer Parzen's lawyer's questions about why she wrote the letter. But, more significantly, these instructions resulted in the record showing — incorrectly — that Evelyn was fully aware at the time she wrote this letter of the fact that what Parzen had done with her in his office was malpractice. As a result, the first and most important part of the trial of *Walker v. Parzen* concerned only this legal question: Precisely when was Evelyn aware that she had been mistreated, and, based on that determination, whether she had filed suit before the statute of limitations had expired.

The doctors also presented Mary Sutton's tape as if it had been Sutton's idea to bring charges against Parzen. The doctors did this because they did not want Parzen to think they were acting in collusion by going out and getting these witnesses to testify against him. "I guess I was a part of that," says Gary Shepherd, "and I'll tell you exactly why we did it. Because we were scared. We didn't know what Parzen was going to do."

The doctors now had their evidence from two different sources and they could no longer postpone the confrontation with Parzen himself. During this time, Al Robbins had talked with Shepherd and three other doctors associated with the Institute, but none of them had said anything to Parzen about what was going on. He was summoned to a meeting in the office of Allan Rosenblatt, director of the Institute, on December 6, 1978. Joining Rosenblatt and Robbins was James Thickstun, assistant director of the Institute. It was an informal but very tense meeting. Three professionals facing one of their own, accusing him of charges so serious that they could end up destroying the career he had spent a lifetime building.

In the weeks and months that followed, the case against Parzen would seem to the casual observer to have meandered through a confused bureaucractic maze of committees and organizations. But all the doctors were members of the very same organizations, and many of them sat on the very same committees, so although the meeting might be called under the auspices of Institute, Society, or Association, the very same people were involved. It had begun when Robbins took action as the chairman and only member of the Psychiatric Society's Impaired Physicians Committee, but as soon as Robbins talked it over with Allan David Rosenblatt, Rosenblatt assumed command.

Rosenblatt was born June 18, 1926, in St. Louis, Missouri, and earned his B.S. and M.D. at the University of Chicago in 1945 and 1948. He also earned an M.S. in Neurophysiology at Chicago. He did his internship at Los Angeles County General Hospital in 1948 and 1949 and his psychiatric residency at Bellevue Hospital in New York in 1949-50. His psychoanalytic training was at Columbia Psychoanalytic Institute at Columbia University in New York. He moved to San Diego in 1954 and to La Jolla in 1975.

Rosenblatt later testified that he had three major concerns when he called this informal meeting with Parzen: "My first concern was protection of the patient, my second concern was protection of the Institute, and my third concern was protection of Dr. Parzen." He then corrected himself. "Actually, I could reverse those — the latter two. The protection of the Institute came third." The three doctors would all remember that Parzen seemed incredibly calm as they laid out their case against him.

Thickstun took very little part in the proceedings; the accusations were all made by Rosenblatt and Robbins. They referred to his "sexual misconduct with two patients," but their main focus was on what they had just heard about his involvement with Pat Stern. They repeated that she had told her friend about the sexual activities, the abortion, being slammed against the wall, having nude pictures taken of her, and of the improper medication. Here Robbins explained that he had talked at length with Gary Shepherd, who had been most concerned about Pat Stern taking the drugs Parnate and Ritalin in combination.

Parzen dismissed the claims about Ritalin and Parnate and said he knew a lot more about that than Gary Shepherd did. He had been at the Michael Reese Hospital in Chicago when the first tests were done on the incompatibility of the two drugs, and he said that the dangerous side effects were exaggerated and overemphasized. Likewise, he said all of this talk by these women patients about sexual involvement was not true. He said that he did occasionally hold a patient during therapy and that there was a particular kind of female patient he had trouble with. However, he said all these other charges about sex, abortions, and nude pictures were products of the patients' imaginations.

Both Rosenblatt and Robbins would say later that they pleaded with Parzen to level with them. If the charges were false, Parzen should by all means say so, but if they were true, he had to come forward with that information, or they would be required to take steps. Robbins outlined the course he would have to take. He said that he had not informed the state Board of Medical Quality Assurance (BMQA), which controlled Parzen's license to practice. He said that he would like to keep the problem within the professional community, although he would have no choice but to go to the state board if Parzen did not cooperate and admit that he was an impaired physician.

At some point in the meeting, Parzen did admit that he had problems. His "grandiosity" was a bit larger than normal, he said. He also asked Thickstun if he could see him for "consultation," not therapy. Thickstun agreed, and thereby earned the disdain of his fellow San Diego psychiatrists. Thickstun's agreeing to talk with Parzen might seem to be a humanitarian gesture, but the others felt that Thickstun jumped at the chance to remove himself from the dirty and time-consuming business that would cause Parzen eventually to lose his license to practice medicine. In fact, Thickstun was able to get out of any further committee meetings or hearings about Parzen by the medical societies, but he was subpoenaed as a witness in a preliminary stage of the later trial.

Parzen agreed during the forty-five-minute meeting in Rosenblatt's office to return to a second meeting on December 21. At the end of this first meeting, Parzen asked if he could have a private word with Robbins in his office just down the hall.

Robbins later testified about this conversation.

I told him that if he was innocent — I told him a number of things. If he was innocent, say so. That if he does not acknowledge these things and he does not say he is an impaired physician, this thing will probably have to be reported. But if he is innocent, despite the fact that BMQA is one hell of a tough organization and they frequently go for the jugular, that if you are innocent you have to say so; that if it were me, I spent that many years and Zane spent that many years building up a career, that he has to stick up for himself.

On the other hand, if he in fact did these things — and if he did these things he is impaired — he should also say so; and at that point we would try to do what we can to avoid reporting to BMQA and avoid potential difficulty with his licensure. And he says, "Okay. Well, even if you won't report it to BMQA, how do I know that these women won't report it to BMQA?"

And I said, "I can't say for sure. What if I ask them to put it in writing, that if you get help they won't report it?"

He says, "See what you can get in writing."

On December 8, two days after that first meeting, Parzen wrote what he apparently thought was a full confession to Rosenblatt, agreeing both to transferring all his women patients and to going into treatment with Thickstun. In the letter, he spoke about "the growing depression I've been struggling with for the last 3–5 years." Without naming Pat Stern, he said she had already been transferred to another doctor "without danger to the patient." He said he would continue to see three "classical" analytic cases, two male and one female. And, he said he would continue "face-to-face psychotherapy (including chemotherapy" with transsexuals, although he did not cite the number. Except for the transsexuals, he said he would not treat any other female patients.

His level of "impairment and dysfunction" had become "too painfully apparent" to him. These steps he was taking would protect "present and future" patients and also protect the profession, he added. "Whether or not they protect me remains to be seen. Maybe I'm acting out to get publicly hung."

Parzen concluded this letter by thanking Rosenblatt, adding poignantly that he offers these thanks feeling as he did when he thanked a friend who spoke to him "when 1 son died: 'Thanks, but I'm not sure I'd rather not still be able to repress and deny. I don't know if I can handle it.'"

The letter did not mention Pat Stern, Evelyn Walker, or any other patients by name. In fact, Parzen had skillfully avoided any mention of the misconduct he had been accused of at the informal meeting in Rosenblatt's office. He was merely "depressed"; he was not impaired.

For the second meeting with Parzen, Sanford Myron Izner was

named to replace Thickstun. Izner was a founder and the director of the Institute for eight years before Rosenblatt was named to that position. Born in Chicago on August 17, 1920, he earned a B.S. at Northwestern in 1941, an M.S. at Purdue in 1943, and another B.S. and his M.D. at the University of Illinois in 1947 and 1949. He did his internship at Wayne County General Hospital in Eloise, Michigan, 1949–50, and his psychiatric residency at Wayne County General Hospital, 1950–53. He completed his psychoanalytic work at the Chicago Psychoanalytic Institute in 1959. He moved to California in the late 1960s and was a faculty member of the Los Angeles Psychoanalytic Institute from 1969 to 1971, when he moved to San Diego. He was named to several medical advisory boards by Governors Romney in Michigan and Reagan in California, and he was also cited for medical advisory service by President Richard Nixon in 1969 and again in 1973.

If the first meeting had been a calm, polite discussion among colleagues and friends, the second, on December 21, was a deadly serious showdown. Rosenblatt, Izner, and Robbins had made up their minds. They had heard the charges against Parzen and they believed they were true. Parzen, they felt, was not leveling with them.

Rosenblatt opened the meeting by accusing Parzen of just that. He said that if Parzen continued to deny the charges, his colleagues would have no choice but to hold a hearing and refer the matter to the state BMQA. Parzen, who had already talked with a lawyer, said he did not feel he was getting due process, but Rosenblatt informed him that this was not a formal hearing but merely an advisory committee meeting. Parzen said, "Well, I'm not interested in due process at this point. I admit I did these things. I felt that the letter I sent you would make it clear that I have already confessed."

Rosenblatt said, "Well, the letter is one thing. I would like to hear it from you. Did you in fact do the things . . . that were alleged at the last meeting?"

Parzen answered, "Yes, I did."

The committee now was faced with a complicated situation. Parzen had admitted to the charges against him, but in his letter he had also proposed that he be allowed to continue in practice provided he transfer his women patients.

Robbins later testified about the meeting.

We felt and Dr. Rosenblatt suggested that Dr. Parzen wind down his practice and — I think it was a three-month period of time under supervision — that he resign from the professional societies that he was a member of and seek treatment. His response was that he didn't give a damn about the professional societies but he wanted to practice and he wanted to practice in La Jolla and he wanted to practice now.

In fact, it wasn't a hard statement. I think that Zane referred to it as pleading, and it was — it was difficult to hear, and I think any one of us can identify with it. It was a very difficult spot that Dr. Parzen was in, one that was very uncomfortable for us. He used the term "plead," to keep his practice going at this point now.

Dr. Rosenblatt suggested that if he were to follow this there would be no reporting necessary, no uncomfortable dealings that his family might be subjected to, the notoriety won't be there, the license would still be there. He could still teach, administrate; or research I think was used.

Robbins said these weren't the only possibilities pointed out to Parzen. It was, at first, a congenial give-and-take about how they were all going to deal with the situation. Parzen even talked about his "pathology," Robbins recalled. "He talked about it in the sense of involving women of a particular stature; thin, tall; he talked about it involving women of deep pathology. He recognized the fact that he was impaired and said so." But at the same time, Parzen had still not made any arrangements to begin treatment with Thickstun. In fact, he said he "wasn't sure that his situation was treatable."

The discussion had grown more and more tense, and concluded with a very angry exchange. Robbins told Parzen that he had to think of the future. He explained that if he acknowledged these problems and dealt with them, the future would still be there and he could one day resume practice. But Parzen snapped back, "To some people the future isn't important."

Rosenblatt joined in, "Zane, you really ought to think of the future."

Parzen asked angrily, "What do you expect me to do, sell real estate?" Izner replied, "Well, you could sell real estate if you like. You can build, you can do whatever you like."

Parzen then said, "I'm better off trying to beat this thing in court. You never know what's going to happen with the courts, and I'm probably better off that way."

As he got up to leave the meeting, Parzen made this parting shot: "People should do a lot of things, like cover their ass when they're trying to help people."

As he had done with Evelyn Walker, Parzen once again acted abruptly in transferring Pat Stern. He had already done this on December 8, as he mentions in the letter he wrote less than forty-eight hours after his first meeting in Rosenblatt's office. Pat Stern naturally was very upset, but she did as he told her to do. She went in for a talk with Al Robbins and she agreed to transfer to another psychiatrist whom Robbins recommended. In the next two weeks, Robbins talked with her once or twice on the telephone, and he also received a friendly Christmas card from her. But Stern's mood took a radical turn following Parzen's heated exchange with the committee on December 21. Apparently Parzen had called Stern and told her all about the meeting.

The next day, around noon, Pat Stern stormed into the building where all the doctors had offices. She was enraged, and determined to find Rosenblatt, Izner, and Robbins before they could destroy her Zane. Izner was out of the office, Rosenblatt was seeing a patient, and Robbins had gone home. Stern called Robbins and said she knew all about what had taken place the previous night, and she knew the names of the other committee members. She said they were killing her, that Robbins was killing her, that she would be dead by evening if they didn't stop what they were doing, and she would leave a note saying he was personally responsible for her death. She said Robbins had taken her world away from her and she would kill herself if he didn't stop the proceedings against Parzen.

When Robbins called Parzen, out of concern for his patient, he could hear Stern screaming and crying in the background. (Stern apparently had been using the phone in Parzen's office.) Robbins was appalled: "Zane, did you tell her about the specifics of the meeting last night?"

"You're goddamned right I did," Parzen answered.

Robbins said, "Well, why would you do such a thing? You know how disruptive it could be, how devastating it could be to her?"

"My lawyer told me to do that," Parzen answered.

Robbins said, "You know better than that. Your lawyer tells you to tell her the specifics of a meeting and you know what it's going to do to her? You should never have done that."

"Don't give me that crap," Parzen said. "You guys aren't really out to help me at all. I've got my lawyer and some other people working on it." And all the while he was talking with Parzen, Robbins could hear Pat crying in the background, "Tell him he's killing me, that I'll be dead by tonight."

In his testimony about it later, Robbins was asked, "Was that the last contact you had with Dr. Parzen in this context?" and Robbins answered, "I think in any context it is." Parzen would never speak with Al Robbins again — and Robbins had been the only person close to being a friend that Parzen had ever had in San Diego. From then on it was war. If Parzen wanted to fight it out in the courts, that is what they would do — at enormous expense that would come close to bankrupting the San Diego Psychoanalytic Institute in the coming months and years. A lawyer was hired to represent the doctors and the Institute. From all that Parzen had threatened, the doctors fully expected Parzen to sue them. They would have to get their evidence in order and prepare for the long, complicated legal battle.

Pat Stern was obviously out of the question as a source of any help to them. It came down once again to the firsthand experience of Evelyn Walker. That was the only hard evidence — evidence that would stand up in court — that the doctors had against Parzen. The rest was all hearsay in legal terms.

During December 1978, Gary Shepherd was talking almost daily with Evelyn. He was trying to keep her abreast of the developments involving Parzen, and he was also trying to explain to her exactly what Parzen had done and how serious the charges were against him. Shepherd carefully asked Evelyn for her cooperation, explaining that she was the only one who could, in effect, force Parzen to help himself. But until this book was being prepared, Evelyn always believed, as Gary had explained to her, that Pat Stern's friend, Mary Sutton, had been the one who started the ball rolling against Parzen. At first Gary did not mention that there had been any kind of sexual involvement between Parzen and Pat Stern, but he did tell Evelyn that there had been improper use of drugs and that the other patient's friend had become very concerned about it and had threatened to go to the state licensing board with a formal complaint against Parzen.

In fact, a taped interview with Evelyn Walker that Gary Shepherd arranged was the first step in the long, slow process of removing Parzen from the Institute, the various professional groups, and eventually the profession itself. When Al Robbins met with Evelyn Walker to tape her statement on December 24, 1978, two days after his last angry telephone exchange with Parzen, he sounded very much like a lawyer himself. As far as Evelyn was concerned, she was doing something to help Parzen; she understood none of the legal implications that seemed so important to Robbins. Robbins explained every step of the process to her in careful detail, however. Robbins especially wanted it explained on the tape, for the record, that the evidence Evelyn was giving might be used against Parzen in a hearing before the state licensing board.

Robbins was totally out of his element, nervous in this new role as private investigator. An odd-looking moustache of sweat beads formed above his upper lip and stayed there throughout the interview with Evelyn that day. Although he felt compelled to explain to her that what she said might be used against Parzen, he still had to couch everything in terms of her helping her former lover and psychiatrist.

Even so, Evelyn would probably never have talked with him if the arrangements had not been made by her friend Gary Shepherd, and if Shepherd had not been sitting beside her as she talked with Robbins.

WALKER: My name is Evelyn Walker, and I am helping Dr. Robbins in order to help Dr. Zane Parzen.
ROBBINS: For purposes of identification, I am Dr. Alvin Robbins and I am Chairman of the [Impaired] Physicians Committee of the San Diego Psychiatric Society. I have asked Mrs. Evelyn Walker to record this information on tape so as to document the nature of the treatment relationship with Dr. Zane Parzen over a period of—
WALKER: Three-and-a-half years.
ROBBINS: This information is being gathered in an attempt to present Dr. Parzen with an understanding of the kind of information that is available in this matter so as to preclude presenting this material to the quality assurance people in Sacramento, which inevitably

might cost him his license and his opportunity to practice. It is understood, however, by Mrs. Walker that this material may in fact be turned over to the Board of Medical Quality Assurance. . . . Can you tell me something about your experience and treatment with Dr. Parzen? Why did you go to see him initially and — why don't we start with that, why did you go to see him initially?

WALKER: I have had a very long history of emotional problems that I was not able to deal with. I was pretty, well — I was in very bad shape. There were difficulties within myself that went all the way back to childhood, tremendous fears that I couldn't deal with, and it became increasingly apparent that I needed help and Dr. Parzen was recommended to me and that's how I initially started to go to him.

ROBBINS: What happened in the first six months of treatment?

WALKER: In the beginning there was a lot of difficulty for me. I had never really opened up to anybody, I had never really told a living person ninety percent of my life, and I was very fearful. I had a long-time history of fears of abandonment, nightmares, a desire not to live, very strong desires not to live, and there was something about Dr. Parzen that to a certain extent it was important to me that he was not important. [In other words, that he was a detached, uninvolved, clinical audience.] So in the beginning there was a lot of talk from his side that there must be something — when he wanted me to talk about my marriage and I continually felt there was nothing wrong with my marriage. I was not willing to accept that there could be anything wrong there, so basically for six months it was partly an unwillingness on my part to trust him, and yet I did trust him. I trusted him from the first day I really started to talk to him. I felt in a strange sort of way comfortable with him even though I did fight talking to him, but that changed very drastically in one day.

ROBBINS: What happened?

WALKER: I had never broken down in his office. In fact, I virtually wore my sunglasses the whole time that I was there. I tolerated being there, which sometimes I think annoyed him, which I liked. But something had happened at home one night that was obviously hitting off that it was more than I was capable of taking. I lived in a household where I was constantly told I was wrong and crazy and put-upon, so I had talked to Dr. Parzen that day about it, and for the very first time, even though I tried to control it, I broke down in a way I have never broken down in my life. And he came over to sit very close to me and he kind of held my arms in a supportive way, and it was really the first time that I was willing to talk to him, really talk to him, and my statement at the beginning was, "This is what you were waiting for," and that was the beginning of what then became the relationship that for me was not a doctor anymore.

ROBBINS: How do you mean that?

WALKER: How do I mean he wasn't a doctor anymore?

ROBBINS: Yes.

WALKER: He became, first and foremost, someone I trusted. Gradually, more and more, he became a friend, and ultimately, with the combination of both of us, he became the man that I loved, and he maintained and said and showed that he loved me.

ROBBINS: How did he show it?

WALKER: He said it. I remember the first day that he said it, and in physical ways he showed it and in caring ways he showed it.

ROBBINS: Can you tell me what you mean by physical ways?

WALKER: We had a relationship like a man has with a woman that you care about and as the months and then the years went by, it became always increased until ultimately we had a total sexual relationship.

ROBBINS: Where was this sexual relationship taking place?

WALKER: Always in the office. In 3½ years, with the exception of the times that I was in the hospital, I never saw him outside the office, never. He was totally unwilling to see me outside of the office, although on various occasions he mentioned a desire to see me outside of the office, but it never took place.

ROBBINS: What about phone conversations outside of your regular appointment hours? Were there frequent phone conversations?

WALKER: Oh, yes. Yes, there was always the phone — when I needed anything and so forth. Yes, that took place. Once, on a combination trip and vacation, he wrote me two short cards which I have. That was — there was the constant assurance that he loved me, that he cared about me, that he was the only one that cared about me, that no one else cared about me, that he would never abandon me, he would never throw me out of the office, he would always be there, that he never would be out of my life.

ROBBINS: Never?

WALKER: Never. And he lied.

ROBBINS: You mentioned that you had a sexual relationship with Dr. Parzen over a period of time and it gradually became a full sexual relationship. Can you give me some of the details of the sexual relationship that you had with Dr. Parzen over that period of time? For example, how did the sexual relationship begin?

WALKER: The first day there was actual physical contact that was not just comforting kind of contact, my husband had come into the office to give a list of things that were wrong with me, and I do mean a list, and during that time I finally asked him to leave the office because I could see — I could see what was happening. He left the office; I was sitting on the couch, and after Zane relocked the door he came over to the couch and sat with me, and I was upset, and he said, "Hold on to me," and I can't say it was him, I can't say it was just me, all I know was that at one point it just happened that I was kissing him. I think I was actually flabbergasted, it never occurred to me that that would ever happen with another man, in fact the next time when I saw him I commented that I was shocked at myself. But from that point on, ultimately I would be on the couch —

ROBBINS: Lying down?

WALKER: Not initially. Sitting. And we would talk, and there would be some talk and eventually he would come over, in the beginning much more of the time just on his own, and ultimately I would ask sometimes. He would — and it was very involved, laying on the couch and touching. He — at one point he wanted to touch me in such a fashion that I stopped him and he said why and I could not think of a reason. Anyway, from there it went on — it went on.

ROBBINS: I know it's going to be difficult for you but —

WALKER: You want to know what we did?

ROBBINS: Yes. I think it's significant for the tape and if you can tell me what he's doing — if you can't just tell me you can't.

WALKER: I will tell you that at no time in that relationship were we totally nude. Never. Partially exposed, undressed, whatever, but never totally nude, which drove me crazy. . . . At any rate, we were never totally nude but there was certainly clothing that was lowered and removed. There was a lot of general fondling, feeling, that type of thing —

ROBBINS: What about intercourse itself?

WALKER: Intercourse did not take place for 2½ years.

ROBBINS: What other kinds of sex—

WALKER: It was all oral sex.

ROBBINS: Oral sex on his part?

WALKER: Both. Predominantly me, my performing oral sex on Zane. He—

ROBBINS: Did he tell you why?

WALKER: I suppose Zane told me why, but Zane has an ability of answering a question and I never knew what the answer was. Zane has a tremendous ability of saying something that has the potential of many meanings and that was a very big factor in feeling I never knew what that man meant, I never actually knew what something he said meant completely. It was the very problem for me that made it necessary for me to turn among, if no one else, to Dr. Gary Shepherd, because I found that I needed an analyst to explain my analyst. I did not understand why I never completely knew what Zane meant because—an example: he knew that I was absolutely terrified of losing him, of abandonment. This is the fear that initially brought me to therapy because this is the fear I've had since childhood, because it's a fear that I have lived with. I have been abandoned by a number of people. He was the only human being that ever knew that I had tried to kill myself when I was 8½ years old; that's how much I trusted him. I told him things that no human being ever knew. He knew how paranoid I was about being abandoned, about losing him, and one example of what he would say is, "If you knew you had me, you wouldn't be afraid of losing me," and then I would say, "Well, does that mean I have you?" and he would say, "What do you think?" and I never really knew and I would go away from the office and it would go over and over and over, "Well, am I afraid because I haven't got him, am I afraid because I know I haven't got him, do I have him so why am I afraid?" and it just went round and round and round to the point that I got sick over things that were similar to that and constant and yet he would promise me, he would look me square in the eye and promise me things but when it really came to the bottom line never were true.

ROBBINS: You mentioned earlier that in the sexual relationship—which I'm afraid we're going to have to focus on just a little bit more—that it was oral sex for a long period of time?

WALKER: Uh-huh.

ROBBINS: And then eventually it became intercourse. How did that change, how did that come about?

WALKER: One day — this was a major problem, I could not understand why we weren't doing this, why we were doing virtually everything that a man and woman do together but we did not have intercourse. I make no bones about it, I absolutely wanted it; I loved the man, he maintained he loved me, it was to me a healthy, normal thing and it was also making me a nervous wreck that we would not — he certainly saw to it that I did have orgasms, that he was very good about, that was no problem. . . . Zane decided everything about what was going to happen between he and I.

ROBBINS: Why did you go along?

WALKER: Because I love him.

ROBBINS: Love or loved?

WALKER: Both. I still care about that man.

Aside from the sexual misconduct, what was most shocking to Robbins was Evelyn's involvement with drugs and then her abrupt withdrawal, all at Parzen's direction. Up to that point his face showed the clinical detachment he wanted, but as he asked her about the drugs and giving them up, Evelyn could see that he was visibly disturbed, even angry, as he was trying to phrase the questions. "You name it, I took it," she said in answer to his question about what pills she was taking. She said she didn't even know their names. "I ate them like candy. I find out from friends later that apparently for almost three years I was on a cloud. I didn't know it, I liked it better than reality, I guess." Evelyn described how she went through withdrawal all alone in her apartment. Robbins asked, "Did you convulse? Did you have convulsions?"

"Yes," Evelyn answered. "I thought that I just wouldn't sleep for a few nights, that's all I thought it would be. I thought it would just be that I'm going to be worn out. . . . Monday morning I called him first thing in the morning and he called, and I guess it was the only time that I came close to hating him, because I went through that not knowing what it was going to be and nobody was with me."

Hadn't she called Parzen at home over the weekend, Robbins wanted to know. "I never bothered Zane at home." Robbins asked why. "I was afraid to make him angry. . . . If you love a man it's not very pleasant to know that you're talking to him in the house that he's living with his wife. So I didn't bother him. But he also did not call me, and the difference was that he knew what I'd go through, I didn't know what I was going to go through. But he also knew that I had nobody to be with me, and it was not until I was in Mesa Vista Hospital, because Dr. Shepherd brought me to Mesa Vista Hospital, that I had really realized that people, when they go through withdrawal, were usually taken care of in a hospital with somebody with them. I had nobody."

Slowly, incredibly slowly, Robbins's words and questions cut through the haze of delusion Evelyn had lived with about her Zane for three years now. After he had finished the official portion of his tape, he turned off the recorder and told Evelyn bluntly that she easily could have died that weekend when she went through withdrawal. She had, of course, heard the word "withdrawal," but she had not understood that that was what she had gone through that weekend, until Robbins spelled it out for her.

Although she had not seen Parzen in all this time, except for brief glimpses once or twice on the street, Evelyn still held to the obsessive hope that her prince would come back and take her away. On a conscious, practical level she could see that what she had with Parzen was no storybook romance of love and marriage, but on the deeper level where she really lived, she still saw it that way. She could believe that Parzen had "problems," because he had talked to her many times about his depression over the many deaths in his family, but she could not deal with the fact that the man she loved so much might have tried deliberately to hurt her.

After Robbins and Shepherd left, Evelyn sat there utterly alone and totally confused about what to think, what to do.

The day after the taped interview with Al Robbins, Evelyn and Gary Shepherd had a long talk about the whole situation. Evelyn asked many detailed questions. It was then that she learned for the first time about Parzen's sexual involvement with the other woman patient.

In the days that followed, Shepherd told Evelyn that Parzen was not cooperating with the other doctors and that they would have to go ahead with the hearings. Upon learning this, Evelyn wrote a personal letter to Parzen, which she sent to Al Robbins with a cover letter asking Robbins to read the letter and pass it along if he thought it all right. Robbins did so.

Dear Zane:

I fully realize that right now you probably dislike me very much. But please believe what I say in this letter to you. In all our years together I've never lied to you and you know my word is good. So please believe that no matter how it seems to you now, I want only to help you.

Zane, you have many people who care. Really care. There is no shame in needing help from those that are able to help. Why turn your back on those people and especially those that love and need you. You are frightened and I understand. But fear is making you do foolish things.

Zane, if you don't stop fighting those that are trying so hard to help you, you and you alone will ruin everything for yourself and drag your family down with you. I beg you please see what you are doing.

Yes, there is a price you must pay now, but you are young and there is a future and it can be a good future. Oh! Zane, please don't shut people out, give them a chance. I love you and care what happens to you.

This is a painful situation for all those who care. Show some trust. You asked me not to turn my back on you and trust you. You may think I stabbed you in the back. I didn't. I want to help you and I don't know what else to do for you. Please trust me. I haven't turned my back on you.

You've never answered me before and I don't expect that will change. But I just had to try one last time to reach you. You will always be special to me no matter what has or will happen.

If there was a way to spare you all of this, believe me I would take your pain and worry. But now you must work and we both know the work is hard. But I believe in you and pray for you. I work hard for me and because I did not want to fail you. I hope you love someone that much that you don't want to fail them. You know where I am if you need me. All my love,

Evelyn

This would, in fact, be Evelyn's last letter to Parzen. And, as with the others, he would never acknowledge it. In fact, because of the loving, helpful tone of this one, he would not even make use of it in the later hearings and trial. He would leave that to the one angry, threatening letter he had received a month earlier.

Although Evelyn urged Parzen in her letter to accept the help of others, she was not at all surprised to learn that he had decided to fight. Deep inside, she still regarded him as her Zane, believed he had done nothing wrong, no matter what the others said. She thought the others were just jealous of her Zane, who was smarter than they were anyway. She was reminded of the time when Parzen told her a person should always fight to defend himself or herself: When Bruce beat her once, Parzen had said she should not take this from him ever again, she should always try to fight back. When Evelyn protested that she was not strong enough to go against a man Bruce's size, Parzen had said she should fight dirty, do whatever she had to do to save herself. He said if he was ever caught in an alley by three men bigger and stronger than he was, he would become the dirtiest street fighter there ever was. Even if he lost, he would never stop fighting. It seemed to Evelyn that Parzen was now caught in that alleyway with his fellow doctors, all bigger and stronger, and closing in on him. On one level she admired him for fighting back, but on another level she had become convinced by Gary Shepherd and the other doctors that what he was doing would only cause him more harm. On one level she could see she was taking a course with no turning back, a course that would permanently sever her ties with Parzen. On another level she held to the obsession that somehow they would one day be together again. From a purely practical view, her actions were the one sure way she would get to see him face-to-face again. In a matter of weeks, she would sit across from him again — not as a lover or even patient, but this time as his accuser with evidence that would destroy his career.

After the directors of the Institute had called for a hearing to be held January 29, 1979, three of them met with Evelyn. Also present were the lawyer hired by the Institute and Evelyn's own San Diego lawyer. The doctors and lawyers explained to her why her testimony was so important. They knew by this time that Pat Stern would never testify against Parzen, and if Mary Sutton did testify, everything she said would be regarded as hearsay.

Evelyn sat and listened during most of the meeting, but she and her lawyer had some important practical considerations to clear up. She wanted to know what legal protections she would have if she testified in the hearing. Maybe Parzen was so disturbed himself by now that he might try to sue her. The lawyer for the Institute and her own attorney assured her that there was no danger of that, that she would be taken care of. She also wanted to know what would happen if she suffered some kind of mental collapse or breakdown as a result of what happened during the hearing. Again, the doctors assured her they would take care of her. (And later they did, as promised, arrange for her to be treated by Sydney Smith, even though she had no money to pay for it at the time.) In summary, the doctors and the two lawyers told her there was nothing anybody could do to her if she simply told the truth about what happened and answered all questions honestly. They also explained to her that this was not an official court proceeding, so she did not have to answer any questions at all and she could leave whenever she wanted to; her testimony was strictly voluntary.

As the doctors and lawyers spoke to her, Evelyn sat looking at her hands, which lay clasped in her lap. At the end of the session, she asked Gary Shepherd if she could talk privately with him. They walked away from the group and she asked him if he really believed this was what she should do. Shepherd said simply, "Yes." They walked back to the group. Evelyn looked at her lawyer and he also nodded in agreement. Evelyn spoke up then and said yes, she would do whatever they asked of her.

Evelyn remembers saying at one point that she didn't like any of these people very much. All of this was tearing her apart inside. In cold, clinical terms, these men had told her that the love of her life was not that at all; everything she had believed in and hoped for all these years was shattered.

In the days before the hearing, Gary Shepherd tried to prepare Evelyn for her first face-to-face encounter with Parzen in two years and twenty-six days. He told her that Parzen was no longer the man she had known. Shepherd's words held little meaning for Evelyn until she saw Zane Parzen at the hearing — a sick, broken man.

On January 29, 1979, as the time for the hearing drew near, Evelyn became more and more anxious. She paced back and forth and back and forth in her apartment. She would shower and then go back to her pacing and then would shower again. She was torn by conflicting emotions of fear and longing, hope and dread. She was terrified of what might happen and what it all meant, but she was thrilled at the prospect of seeing her Zane after all this time, no matter what the conditions were.

The hearing was held in what was designed as the main board room of the new office building at 1200 Prospect Street in La Jolla. By 1979, the psychoanalysts and the Institute were being eased out of the building because a richer corporation with enormous government consulting contracts had begun moving in as the major tenant. Shepherd and Parzen, still sharing the rent on adjacent offices, had moved down from the penthouse to a darkened corner on the first floor. The Institute's offices were behind a glass-walled reception area at the center of the lobby. In the main conference room, behind the receptionist's space, tables had been arranged in the shape of a T. The members of the Ethics Committee of the Board of Directors of the San Diego Psychoanalytic Institute were seated at the top of the T. Parzen, his wife, and his lawyer were on one side of the long part of the T; the Institute's lawyer and the witness who was testifying would be on the other side. Parzen and his wife sat on either side of his lawyer, but several times during the tense hours that followed, Mrs. Parzen reached around behind the lawyer and touched her husband or grabbed his hand to reassure him. Until called upon to speak, the witnesses were seated in two rows at the foot of the T-shaped table. Allan Rosenblatt, Sanford Izner, and Al Robbins were in the first row; Evelyn Walker sat behind them between her lawyer and Gary Shepherd. Unlike a courtroom, where the witness faces the entire audience, this was a peculiar arrangement that had "plaintiff" and "defendant," accuser and accused, sitting face-to-face, literally within arm's reach.

Before the hearing was called to order, Evelyn and Gary Shepherd sat talking in his office at the end of a hallway off the lobby. Above all, Shepherd tried to be supportive and help her to remain calm. Then his telephone rang and they were told the hearing was ready to begin. Shepherd took Evelyn's arm and told her that whatever happened, she was not to go anywhere near Parzen. He told her not to reach out to him under any condition, and not to allow him to reach out to her. "But," Evelyn asked in a childlike plea, "what if Zane needs me?" Shepherd became firm with her, speaking as a doctor now, "Don't go near Zane. He might try to hurt you."

As they walked down the hallway toward the big door to the conference room, Evelyn was almost numb with fear and anxiety. She was terrified of what she was about to do, but thrilled about finally seeing Zane. They reached the door and knocked. Shepherd looked at Evelyn and asked, "Are you ready?" Evelyn nodded yes. He opened the door. She walked in as a witness for the prosecution of the man she still loved and yearned for.

Judith Bailie Parzen looked up as Evelyn entered the room. Her eyes never left the woman whose testimony would change all their lives forever.

In a little alcove behind where the committee sat, Evelyn could see a bulletin board covered with cartoons about psychiatrists, notes about meetings, and two memos "from the desk of Zane Parzen," reminding her of his position of importance at the Institute and in the community. She took her seat against the wall among the witnesses and watched Parzen's face as the preliminary legal wrangles opened the hearing. He was no longer the man of strength and knowledge she had known: Once proud and erect, he was now caved in, defeated. There was something oddly distorted about his face. His lower lip was pushed way out, as children look when pouting.

Evelyn's first impulse was to go to the man she still loved and put her arms around him, and she had a fleeting fantasy of the two of them leaving this place forever and living happily ever after. But, looking at Parzen, she could see clearly that the man before her was a very disturbed person — like some of the more severe cases she had seen in the mental hospital.

Even though the American Psychoanalytic Association did have a provision in its charter for such a hearing, when the local members tried to get some sort of instruction from the national office, they ran into a blank wall. There had been numerous cases over the years where a psychoanalyst had been censured for unethical behavior and been treated within the community as an impaired physician; however, this was the first time in America that a hearing was being held to order a psychoanalyst out of the organization. Parzen's lawyer, Dirk T. Metzger, was aware of the unique situation and made the most of it. Born in San Diego, January 5, 1944, the son of a general in the Marine Corps, Metzger did his undergraduate work at Stanford. A former Marine captain, Metzger earned his law degree at the University of Virginia in 1968 and was admitted to the bar in 1969 in California.

The hearing began at 8:15 P.M. and would not be completed until after 12:30 A.M. This was largely because of long, complicated arguments by Metzger regarding "due process." While this was a private committee meeting of a private organization, everyone in the room understood that a man's career was being judged. This was the first court of inquiry, and whatever came out as evidence or was decided here would lead to other, far more serious decisions elsewhere. Whatever the outcome, Parzen's professional life would be seriously affected — could be destroyed. Adding to the tension was the presence of an armed guard beside the locked outer doorway to the room. Pat Stern had been making wild threats against the committee and anyone else who hurt her Zane, and the doctors knew that she might well carry through with them. They were taking no chances.

Although ample evidence had been presented as to the qualifications of the committee members and the legality of their being appointed for this hearing, Metzger undertook a detailed interrogation of each one before he would allow the first witness to be called. When Metzger continued to question the group's legality, the chairman read from the American Psychoanalytic Association's rules: "Each psychoanalyst should endeavor to safeguard the public and the profession of psychoanalysis against psychoanalysts deficient in moral character or professional competence. He should expose, without hesitation, in an ethical fashion and through appropriate channels, illegal or unethical conduct of fellow members of the profession."

There were often heated and sarcastic exchanges between the doctors and Parzen's combative lawyer. One of the doctors spoke of psychoanalysis as an art, and from then on Metzger would question whether a particularly obscure word were "a word of art." Once, the Institute's lawyer replied, "No, it's English — as in 'legalese.'" Metzger's most curious point did not have to do with the testimony of Evelyn Walker but with that involving Pat Stern. A transcript of Al Robbins's interview with Stern's friend, Mary Sutton, and a tape of that interview were entered as evidence in the hearing. Metzger said it was against all rules of due process and legal procedure for the accused not to be able to confront and question his or her accuser. Pat

Stern herself, everyone knew, would not be testifying, so any evidence regarding her would be hearsay. At this point, Allan Rosenblatt spoke out from the witness's corner and said that the committee's own rules allowed for such testimony — especially when it involved a patient whose mental condition was so "fragile."

After what seemed like hours of such legal talk, Evelyn Walker finally was called as the first witness. She took her seat facing Parzen and glanced over to see Judy Parzen proudly staring her down. In a court of law, Metzger could zero in on Evelyn as the chief witness, and relentlessly hammer away with his questions until he had the witness so confused she would begin to contradict herself. But this was not a court of law; Evelyn knew she didn't have to answer any questions if she didn't want to; she also knew she could leave whenever she wanted to. If Metzger pushed too hard, as he would in fact do, Evelyn was fully within her rights to fire right back at him in kind. Metzger's aggressive manner did not succeed; his verbal assault only served to make Evelyn Walker appear more vulnerable — and more believable.

METZGER: In your own mind the problem for you the last couple of years has been the fact that your relationship with Dr. Parzen has been terminated?

WALKER: It's been a 5½-year fight to get to this place.

METZGER: I'm sure it has —

WALKER: I'm doing better, but there are still some very definite problems for me. One of the biggest was that part of my problem in needing therapy was a tremendous fear of abandonment and not being wanted and not being loved, a long history where that was repeatedly proven to me. And in Zane there were the promises and the repeated — that he would never do that to me. I believed in him as I had never believed in a person in my life.

METZGER: And you felt abandoned, even though you understood that he had been either instructed or advised by the Institute to have no further relations with you?

WALKER: The Institute did not tell him that outside of that office he couldn't at least pick up the phone. The Institute didn't tell him that he couldn't put in a note that I care what's happening with you or that I'm sorry. The Institute did not tell him anything pertaining to outside the office.

METZGER: You're sure of that.

WALKER: I know it, because Zane lied.

METZGER: And that made you angry?

WALKER: I have never been really angry at Zane. I have been hurt and I have been greatly disappointed. It's hard to be angry at him.

The most shocking moment in the hearing for Evelyn came when a folder of her letters to Parzen was introduced coldly as evidence. Was she "aware that her letters to Parzen had been turned over to David Olenik?"

"No!" Evelyn cried. She was not aware of that and she was appalled to see these most intimate pleas of hers being handed around to members of the committee and examined by the lawyers. She kept trying to catch Parzen's eye, and when she finally did, he had an embarrassed, sheepish look that told her he knew he had done wrong with the letters. Evelyn now felt betrayed not only by Parzen but by the psychiatrist who had replaced him. Bitterly sarcastic, she said, "At least now I know they were read. I thought they had ended up in the trash."

Seeing her words of love handled so matter-of-factly, hearing her phrases taken out of context and thrown back at her, Evelyn was confused by the anger she was feeling. A part of her was furious with Parzen for doing this, another part held to a desperate hope that he would somehow stand up, stop all the nonsense, and take her away from all the trouble.

Metzger produced the letter Parzen had received from Evelyn on November 3, 1978. He wasted no time getting down to the most damning line in the letter, the first sentence of the third paragraph on the fourth page.

WALKER: I assume you're talking about, "You used me pure and simple — and I have the power to ruin you. I always did."

METZGER: And did you determine some two years later to exercise that power?

WALKER: If you're asking me why did this letter come when it did — I don't —

METZGER: No, I'm just asking you what I'm asking you, Mrs. Walker. Did you determine some two years later to use this power to ruin Dr. Parzen that you thought you always had?

WALKER; No, not really. This letter is exactly what I said. I felt that after all of my trying, all of this stuff, enough was enough.

METZGER: You mean he didn't correspond with you and didn't talk with you and therefore —

WALKER: Did you read the letter?

METZGER: Excuse me. And therefore —

WALKER: Did you read the letter?

METZGER: And therefore —

WALKER: Did you read the letter? If you read the letter, it says it. Do your homework.

METZGER: So you felt that after two years and the fact that he did not communicate with you, that you had then come to the point that you had to ruin him?

WALKER: Did you read the letter?

METZGER: Just answer the question.

WALKER: I will not answer —

The Institute's lawyer interrupted to say that Metzger's line of questioning was argumentative and unfair, but Evelyn persisted in answering, "I would not be here if it wasn't that I cared about what happened with him. Now Zane may feel at this point that I am stabbing him in the back, but I'll tell you something. He has a problem and he needs help, and if I have to blow the whistle on him for him to recognize that, then that's what I'll do."

Metzger continued to badger her, but Evelyn knew she was on solid ground. While she had not been coached on what to say, she had been told that she could not be compelled to answer anything. After a dozen more exchanges involving that line about ruining Parzen, she stopped the questioning by saying she was not going to answer anything more. "That's a ridiculous question."

Metzger then went after her reasons for making the tape recording with Al Robbins. "What was your understanding of the reason the tape was being made?" he asked.

"Because they wanted to help Zane, and I wanted him to have that help." She explained that she had been told that the information she was giving might be turned over to the state licensing board "as a last resort," but it was everybody's hope that Parzen would phase out his practice and seek treatment and avoid this last step. She also mentioned that she had been told before the tape about another "female patient" who had a friend who was very concerned about the way Parzen was treating the woman. Evelyn said that she understood [incorrectly, as she learned much later] that the friend of the other patient had not only made this tape and sent it to the committee, she had also contacted the state board about recalling Parzen's license to practice. Metzger now had further evidence for his claim that Evelyn was acting only out of jealousy. Here was another "other woman" in Parzen's life, and Metzger hammered questions at Evelyn about her feelings regarding this other woman. But Evelyn remained fiercely loyal to her word to Gary Shepherd never to betray the role he and the other doctors played in telling her about Parzen and asking her to write the letter to Al Robbins.

METZGER: How did you learn that Dr. Parzen had had some difficulty regarding another female patient?

WALKER: I don't really think that's important. The point is that I know about it.

METZGER: Who did you learn that from, Mrs. Walker?

WALKER: I don't think that's important.

METZGER: Are you declining to answer the question?

WALKER: Yes.

METZGER: You don't know when you learned that, either?

WALKER: You mean the date?

METZGER: Yes.

WALKER: No.

METZGER: And you were not motivated in any of your actions, either your letter of November 3, 1978, or your letter to Dr. Robbins or your tape, by any feelings of being wronged or jealous or anything like that, is that correct?

WALKER: First of all, there's nothing to be jealous of. I don't know that I ever thought in terms of "I have been wronged." I don't know. You know, there's really — it's really more a question of there's a lot of pain involved in this. I don't know what you think "wronged" — I don't know how you think that way. You know, you put that kind of trust in somebody and they let you down, uh —

METZGER: How did Parzen let you down, Mrs. Walker?

WALKER: I guess for giving me for the first time in my life the feeling of somebody that would never turn his back on me.

After Metzger had finished with Evelyn, each member of the committee was asked in turn if he had any questions of the witness. None of them did. They had heard her and they believed her.

There were three witnesses following Evelyn — the doctors who had first confronted Parzen with the charges about his misconduct. James Thickstun was not among them because, pleading doctor-patient confidentiality as Parzen's therapist, he had excused himself from any involvement in the proceedings. The other three repeated the exchanges that had taken place in Allan Rosenblatt's office. There had been the initial confrontation where Parzen appeared to deny everything, and then the letter where he seemed to confess. Then there had been the second meeting where he bluntly confessed that he had done everything as charged and then suddenly turned on his fellow doctors and, in effect, threatened to sue them if they proceeded against him.

Izner was grilled extensively on the fact that he had had knowledge two years earlier that Parzen had been involved sexually with a patient named Evelyn Walker. Parzen's lawyer was zeroing in on the obvious point that if these doctors knew at that date about Parzen's unethical conduct, why hadn't they done something then? This is how Izner told the story:

> Someone had come to me and said that they had heard that Dr. Parzen was sexually involved with a patient, and that they knew this woman, and that they had discussed the situation with her and they felt that — I was director of the Institute at the time, and they felt that I should be — that this information should be known to me.
>
> And I discussed this with them, and thanked them for coming in, and then I contacted Dr. Parzen and asked him to meet with me. And I told him of what I had been informed.
>
> I did not discuss at all whether it was true or untrue or anything else; I had no specific evidence. We discussed the situation a little bit, and my recommendation was that if a patient is circulating this kind of material, this kind of information about you, psychotic or not psychotic, the wisest thing to do is to transfer the patient to someone else, that would be my advice.
>
> And we discussed the possibility, and we discussed a few potential people to whom the patient could be transferred, and I said, "Now this is nothing you have to do at the moment, give it some

consideration and get back to me in the next few days, see what you think about it."

And from the next information I got was that within a few moments' time Dr. Parzen was on the phone and had made arrangements to transfer the patient.

Metzger continued his line of questioning by asking Izner if he did not also recommend later that same year that Parzen withdraw his application for certification as a senior training analyst, the highest rank for a psychoanalyst. Izner had to admit that yes, he had done this, because he had found that other members of the Education Committee had learned of Parzen's involvement with Evelyn Walker and that they would never approve his application, no matter how good it appeared on the surface. Metzger would suggest later in the hearing that as director of the Institute, Izner's recommendations often sounded more like absolute orders or commands. In other words, Parzen had had no choice but to transfer Evelyn Walker and to follow Izner's advice about not applying for consideration as a senior training analyst. Metzger persisted with a line of questioning that produced the disturbing confession that Evelyn Walker's case was not the first "rumor" that had come to Izner's attention about Parzen.

METZGER: Did you cause any investigation to be conducted into these allegations or rumors concerning Dr. Parzen and Mrs. Walker?
IZNER: No, because I had no direct evidence of anything at that time.
METZGER: Did you attempt to determine whether there was any direct evidence?
IZNER: I had no way to go about that.
METZGER: You could have talked to Mrs. Walker, couldn't you?
IZNER: I had no reason to contact her. She had made no complaint to the Institute. And I didn't feel that that was — she was a patient in treatment, I didn't feel that was my prerogative.
METZGER: Is that your criteria for investigation, whether the patient in therapy made a complaint?
IZNER: Well, I think that's possibly one; there could be others. Certainly if enough of the analytic community is involved and we have serious enough information, I think there's evidence for going ahead with some investigation. We didn't have anything of that

order at that time. In fact, that wasn't the first thing that had come up about Dr. Parzen. There had been something some years before, on the order of a rumor. And I didn't pursue that either.

METZGER: Well, you had the order of a rumor in January of '77 when you discussed with Dr. Parzen the advisability of transferring the patient.

IZNER: Yes.

METZGER: You felt it was serious enough that he ought to transfer the patient.

IZNER: Well, I felt it was serious enough that he should consider that.

METZGER: Yes.

IZNER: I didn't say that he had to transfer the patient. I called him in for his own protection, and my concern was for him.

After the three doctors had been questioned, the lawyer for the Institute routinely said, "Dr. Parzen, I call you as my next witness."

But Metzger quickly interceded, "No, I don't think so."

"On what basis, counsel?" he was asked.

Metzger answered, "Well, any basis is sufficient, because as you have so artfully stated . . . you don't have the power to compel the testimony of anybody, including my client. It is sufficient that I don't believe that it is in my client's best interests at this time to submit to examination by you."

At the end of the hearing, Metzger delivered a summation of his client's defense. He said he felt that all testimony regarding Pat Stern should be set aside because it was secondhand hearsay. As for Evelyn Walker, he said:

Well, let me tell you first of all that my problem is Mrs. Walker has been in treatment for some time, she has been hospitalized on several occasions, several suicide attempts. I wanted to elicit from her the facts that I felt were important without directly challenging her or attacking her. I believe the situation is this: I believe that in January of 1977 Dr. Parzen terminated his relationship with Mrs. Walker. . . . I think all of the — the frustration, the anger that you saw in Mrs. Walker, was a function of the fact that she didn't like that. . . . So he did the right thing. The problem was, that's not what Mrs. Walker wanted to have happen. I think, very frankly, that Mrs. Walker learned about what [Mary Sutton] may have said about what [Pat Stern] may have told [Mary] and that that triggered something in her. She got angry again. . . . I think she felt wronged by the fact that she had terminated her relationship with Dr. Parzen, I think she felt wronged that someone else may have occupied a central position in Dr. Parzen's life. . . .

Metzger also attacked the informal committee that had first met with Parzen, saying that he had been "willing to do damned near everything but give up his license. And this ad hoc committee said no, whether they told him to go sell real estate or he said maybe I should do that and Dr. Izner said yes, maybe you should. He had no place to go."

Finally Metzger quoted from the American Psychoanalytic Association's rules:

The necessary intensity of the therapeutic relationship and analysis may tend to activate sexual and other needs and fantasies on the part of both patient and therapist, while weakening the objectivity necessary for control. Nevertheless, sexual relationships between analyst and patient are inconsistent with treatment and damaging psychologically to both. If drive regulation and control are not possible for the psychoanalyst under the impact of stimulation in the analytic situation, he should transfer the patient to another analyst and seek treatment himself. The occurrence of sexual activities with the patient is a violation of this principle of ethical conduct and is compounded by failure to take the remedial steps mentioned.

As Metzger saw it, Parzen, when confronted with his misdeeds, had done precisely what the association's own rules required. He had transferred the patient.

After the hearing was held, but before the Ethics Committee announced its decision, James Thickstun sent a letter to Robert Nemiroff, the committee chairman. Dated February 1, 1979, it reads as follows:

Dear Dr. Nemiroff:
    I have been seeing Dr. Zane Parzen in intensive psychotherapy

since December 8, 1978. We plan to begin psychoanalysis as soon as the ambience is more favorable for undertaking such a procedure. I do not foresee an easy analysis, but I do believe Dr. Parzen is analyzable.

At present, Dr. Parzen is depressed and distraught and this does interfere with his capacity to function at his best as a psychotherapist and psychoanalyst. Furthermore, there are certain kinds of patients whose needs and psychopathology resonate with those of Dr. Parzen in such a way that difficulties may ensue. This seems particularly true when Dr. Parzen is significantly depressed, as he has been for the last few years. However, I believe very strongly that these problems can and should be handled in psychoanalysis and not by restrictions imposed from without upon his freedom to practice.

> Sincerely,
> James T. Thickstun, M.D.
> A Medical Corporation

Despite Thickstun's recommendation and Metzger's defense, the members of the committee felt the evidence against Parzen was clear-cut and conclusive. He had violated the association's rules of ethics. Following the hearing they would vote to recommend that the Board of Directors of the Institute dismiss him as a teacher and as a member of the Psychoanalytic association.

What none of the professional men in that room could know at that time was that Walker and Stern were just two of the patients Parzen had been involved with. It would take years before this information would come out in court — and possibly the full story of Parzen's involvement with his patients will never fully be known. But his own friends and colleagues had taken the first all-important step, and the rest would fall like dominoes until Parzen had lost everything he had ever cared about.

Evelyn Walker, meanwhile, resumed her anguished life alone. Before the hearing, Evelyn and those most concerned about her saw this face-to-face confrontation with Parzen and this public declaration of all that had gone on between them as a traumatic but healthy climax to the long, emotionally destructive relationship she had had with him and with his memory. But it was more of an anticlimax than a real turning point. She went there and saw him and said what she had to say and came away feeling good that she had maintained her control, but nothing seemed changed. She could admit, on one level, that this man had wronged her; but on a deeper level, she could not put him out of her mind. She was still obsessed by her longing for him and for the life she had dreamed they would share.

Gary Shepherd and Al Robbins and the others at the Institute were indebted to Evelyn, because without her testimony they would have been powerless to act against Parzen. Shepherd and Robbins were also on a list of people Evelyn would call whenever she was troubled, and she seemed to be troubled twenty-four hours a day during this time. To help Evelyn, they approached Sydney Smith, a newer member of the Institute faculty, and asked him if he would agree to begin treatment of Evelyn, even though she did not have the money to pay him. Smith had served on the committee that had recommended the dismissal of Parzen at the Institute because he had been in La Jolla for only eight months and did not know Parzen or anybody else involved in the case. He would later say that he had sat on many professional committees, but he had never heard of a case involving a physician impaired so severely. "Given simply the overt behavior . . . one could not help wondering if Dr. Parzen was not suffering from a severe disorder of an emotional nature that was leading him to use his patients for the gratification of his own needs in an inappropriate and destructive way."

Although he was a new arrival, and with no medical degree in his background (which meant he could not prescribe drugs for patients), Smith was one of the only members of the Institute with any kind of national reputation. He had earned his Ph.D. in clinical psychology in 1951 at the University of California. He then had a two-year fellowship at the Menninger Foundation in Topeka, Kansas, passing his board examinations in psychology in 1958 and in psychoanalysis in 1976. He was chief psychologist at the Menninger Foundation and editor of the bulletin published by the Menninger Clinic from 1964 until 1978, when he moved back to California.

Smith had the manner of a somewhat eccentric professor — he was always adjusting his wire-rimmed spectacles — but with a genial, kindly air that caused Evelyn to trust and like him more and more as the months and years went by. [She continues to see him for regular treatment.]

As he did with all his patients, Smith took unusually detailed notes on his sessions with patient "Mrs. E.W." Much to his professional embarrassment, these notes were later subpoenaed as evidence in Evelyn Walker's trial, and, because they were virtually illegible to lawyers on both sides, Smith was required to read them very carefully into the record. He felt this was a betrayal of the very private nature of psychotherapy. He said he would never have taken such notes if he had known they would be used in this manner. Because of his years as an editor and because he had great experience as the author of numerous articles on psychology, these notes are especially well written, and they show, as no other document does, just how disturbed Evelyn Walker was during this time.

Evelyn first saw him on February 27, 1979, and he made the following notes:

> Patient tearful, confused, distraught, demanding, hyper-alert, and quick to read more meaning into any comment than intended. Goes over again troubled relationship with Dr. Parzen, indicating she was a battered child, unloved and felt unloveable; and then a married man who similarly did not love her, and then found both her psychotherapist and her husband wished her dead and attempted to suggest her into suicide. Left her husband for relationship with Dr. P. doing it impulsively and self-destructively. Getting no money and having no access to her two sons. Feeling she lost everything. Rushed into second marriage with man she thought wanted to take care of her, but somebody she did not love. This quickly proved unworkable; so, got out, only to discover that the doctor was interested in her, and had been for eight years in love with her, and suddenly let her know of his feelings and moved in on her life.
>
> He [the doctor] is married, unhappily, and wishes out; but his wife threatens him with never seeing his only son again. She worries if they can ever get together and if she will be left alone again. She is chronic depressive with serious problems, re: self-esteem and feared loss of narcissistic supplies. Treatment needs to be aimed at narcissistic and depressive issues.

Evelyn was involved with three different men during the time Smith was treating her, and he would later say—in his pretrial deposition—that he was often confused as to which man she was talking about. The confusion was increased by the fact that two of them had the same first name.

In early March Smith noted, "This woman is terribly lonely, and in her loneliness she begins to have old problems and fears return to her."

On another day in March he wrote:

Patient continues to be emotionally upset over not having any income and hearing only promises from attorneys to finish off her divorce [from her second marriage] which has now taken longer in process than the marriage lasted. She complains of not hearing from boyfriend, but then says she was not home all weekend. I have to raise the question about how boyfriend could reach her in that case. She re-covers some old ground, and I try to link some of current feelings with her past, showing her how on the one hand she can think reasonably about situations she is in and understand it but on the other hand becomes overwhelmed by feelings of abandonment and lack of self-meaning which must blow in from the past relationships since they don't make sense in the current ones. She does not develop much genetic material in this connection except briefly to talk about the miserable punitive treatment of mother. Hard to get this woman off the topic of how needy she is and how badly she has been treated.

On St. Patrick's Day Smith's notes included the following:

Called and asked for special session. Talked of fact nobody needs her. She has nothing to get up for in the morning and thinks she could easily end it. These thoughts frighten her. Get her around these thoughts by indicating to her how happy she would make Dr. Parzen. He would be delighted to have her dead so he could have the suit against him dropped so he could continue doing to others what he did to her. This idea disturbs her and she calls me sneaky for bringing that up and making her want to live to see this through. . . . The patient also disturbed by the fact that her friend Dr. S. [Gary Shepherd] indicated that she should marry an older man who sometimes takes her out. That was confusing to her. I point out that she often makes people feel that they have to come up with immediate solutions for her and people may respond impulsively to make her feel better.

While the hearing in January had served to remove Parzen from his position at the Psychoanalytic Institute, it did not satisfy the requirements of the rules of the parent San Diego Psychoanalytic Society, so a second hearing was scheduled for April 2, 1979, before the Ethics Committee of that group. Evelyn had at first agreed to testify at this hearing as she had at the earlier one, but as the time approached, she became more and more distrustful and anxious about going through the process again.

On March 29, 1979, Smith made the following notes about her:

Very angry with me and everybody. Has discovered going to be two women at the hearing on Monday for the Society membership fight over Dr. P. She does not trust women. Won't have anything to do with them. No woman going to hear her problems and won't go to the hearing.

Wonder what she is angry with me about. She says I'm one of all the others. Only interested in using her and when that is over, then forgets about them. Knows all of us see patients in treatment and when the hour is over, put them out of mind, not caring about her.

Tried to relate this action to what she is seeing as rejection from the boyfriend and she is upset about that, feeling something is wrong with her; that nobody wants her, everybody uses her, throws her away; so, she won't go to the hearing. Then, a lot of anger about the last hearing came out, how the right questions were never asked; how Dr. P.'s attorney wasted time and nobody called him on it; how she was alleged to know the other patient involved with Dr. P. and nobody corrected that; how her one request to listen to the tape was not honored. Talks about how she is all alone in this and that when others go to these hearings, they have somebody to go home to; but she had nobody. Don't know what it takes for her to prepare herself for these meetings, the sleepless nights, the internal agony, walking the floor; so, not sure she would do it.

All ended by my telling her she should make her complaints and her wishes known to Dr. R. [Al Robbins] who had talked with her before, but [she was] angry with him because he ignored her at a party she attended. Finally, arranged that I would tell Dr. R. to call her. Ended by telling her to do what she had to do regarding the hearing and that it made no difference in our relationship.

Evelyn did talk further with Robbins and with Gary Shepherd and finally agreed to go through with her testimony at the hearing. Afterward, Smith noted, she was exultant.

Tells events of the hearing with great pride in how she showed up Dr. P.'s lawyers and how well she handled herself before the group. . . . Went on for three-and-a-half hours and she was exhausted, but thinks she made good points and everybody there praised her for her job. Obviously basking in that praise and tells me the story in a way to draw my praise as well. . . . Demonstrates a good deal of savvy and strength. She is obviously proud of self and looking for kudos from me.

The second hearing, on April 2, was almost a repeat performance of the first. It was held in the same board room of the Psychoanalytic Institute in La Jolla, the same lawyers represented both sides, and the same witnesses presented testimony. The members of the Ethics Committee had been chosen because of their ignorance of the case: None of them knew Parzen or any of the patients involved. None of them had read any of the evidence presented at the previous hearing. It was agreed that they would not go over any of the evidence from the other hearing, but would simply introduce transcripts of the testimony and the committee members could ask questions beyond that. The hearing became more than a little confused, since committee members could not know what had been asked at the previous hearing if they had not read the evidence.

Just before the hearing convened, Evelyn's lawyer told her that she should not trust the private investigator he had hired to help with her divorce proceedings. Since Evelyn had become emotionally involved with the investigator, the news that he couldn't be trusted with money was a severe shock to her. She had already given him $2,000 to invest for her — money that she had received from selling her interest in her first husband's home. She became so distraught over hearing this, that everybody in the room thought she would never be able to go ahead with the hearing. But she calmed down and the hearing was called to order.

Evelyn and Gary Shepherd were asked to leave the room while Dirk Metzger made a preliminary statement on behalf of Parzen. Metzger again said that he felt the hearing was not according to the rules of due process, but this time he added that he had informed the president of the American Psychoanalytic Association that this hearing in San Diego was being carried out in violation of the association's own rules. Again, Metzger went on at some length in objecting to the introduction of anything regarding Parzen's patient Pat Stern. He said none of the evidence regarding her was valid because none of it had come directly from her, all of it was hearsay, and this, he said, violated Parzen's right to due process under the Society's by-laws. "The courts, according to my understanding . . . require that bodies that sit to review this type of charges, these type of charges, and have this type of impact on the life and property of an individual in our society be afforded fundamental due process rights. And I don't believe those rights are being afforded to Dr. Parzen. . . . "

After much wrangling over due process, Metzger then proceeded to examine each member of the committee by asking what they did or did not know about the case. It turned out, as expected, that none of them knew anything. They had been given a simple letter informing them that Parzen had been charged with misconduct of a sexual nature involving two patients, but although they had the minutes of the previous hearing in hand, none of them had read them. Metzger said, "I think the problem is that the members of the panel don't have a context in which to hear that testimony and make any sense out of it, in the absence of a more detailed written charge or charges."

The lawyer for the Society, Norman Allenby, said, "Well, what do you suggest we do at this point?"

METZGER: That's up to the chairman of the committee and you as counsel for the Society. I'm just suggesting that I don't think that they — if what I'm hearing is correct, I don't think that they feel they can properly evaluate the testimony in the blind, as it were.

FELIX LOEB [a member of the committee]: I'm not sure if I understand Dr. Conn's point [that they review the previous testimony and then call witnesses] but perhaps it is that there is a historical context for tonight's situation —

BURTON CONN [committee chairman]: I don't know what's in here.

FELIX LOEB: But there's a lot of material, and it seems we were selected because we did not know this material, and yet it —

NORMAN ALLENBY: Well, we're not expecting —

FELIX LOEB: It seems like we're starting in the middle. I know that there's — we don't know the charges which are here, which we're supposed to know before we see the witnesses or we have no way of judging the witnesses — I'm confused.

Metzger had them confused and running, and he didn't let up. The members of the committee then wanted to hear what the charges were. Allenby, for the Society and the Institute, was trying to get on with the proceedings, trying to call in the witnesses because they were waiting in other rooms. After much long and confused discussion about whether they should hear the witnesses before or after they had read the evidence from the other hearing, the committee finally agreed to call in Evelyn Walker as the first witness, but she had hardly pronounced her name before the proceedings were interrupted by confusion again.

The chairman said, "Excuse me. Before we proceed, I'm sorry, Dr. Shepherd, but this is not an open hearing." There then followed arguments over whether Shepherd, as Evelyn's longtime friend and supporter, should be allowed to remain in the room. Again the air was full of confused exchanges as the doctors tried to talk like lawyers and the lawyers tried to make sense of the proceedings to the doctors.

CONN: Mrs. Walker, I'm Dr. Conn, and I'm the chairperson for the Ethics Committee for the Psychoanalytic Society. I think it's clear that you would like to have Dr. Shepherd here as a friend and as an interested person and that he would like to be here for that reason. Unfortunately, there is an objection by Mr. Metzger who is representing Dr. Parzen who's accused in these proceedings —

WALKER: Well, if that's the case, then I object to Mrs. Parzen being here as his moral support. She has no more cause to be here, if that's the case. I mean, you see, I don't — now if you really want to get down to it, we could say —

CONN: I think that if you wish her to be absent during your testimony that's a valid objection.

WALKER: I have no objection to her being here at all; but I'm just saying that, you know, if I had a husband I would like him to be here. I don't; and I don't object to her presence. I don't really see what his presence — but if it's that big an issue, I can handle it.

CONN: Dr. Shepherd, I am sorry. Would you please excuse yourself? Thank you.

Shepherd said, "Sure," and left the room to wait in his office until Evelyn had finished her testimony.

The first hearing in January had been polite, calm, and restrained when compared to the near-raucous confusion of the second one in April. Everyone in that room could see that Evelyn Walker was nearly frantic, very close to the breaking point. But she had been through all this before. She was not cowed by the situation this time, not terrified by the mere presence of all those doctors, plus Parzen and his wife. She knew the rules — better, in fact, than most of them did. She didn't have to be there. She didn't have to answer any of their questions. She could leave whenever she wanted to leave. But surely one of her prime motivations was that she had some things to tell them. Although Metzger could see her condition as well as anybody else, he continued to push and push and push.

After a long sequence of questions about her suicide attempts, the chairman finally stopped Metzger and said, "I'm a little bit puzzled. Perhaps other members of our committee are also puzzled as to what this has to do with charges and allegations against Dr. Parzen."

Metzger said, "Well, I'm puzzled as to what the suicide attempts have to do with Dr. Parzen at all, and that's the purpose of my questions."

Evelyn didn't need to be asked a question. She blurted out her explanation.

Would you like me to tell you? I would be very happy to tell you. First of all, I got the hell beat out of me, because my husband was very upset about the relationship that I had with Zane, about the money that it was costing. That was already number one.

Okay, I committed suicide attempts because Zane made a lot of promises and then we would have fights and then he would say wonderful things that just, you know, really hurt and cut me down. I came with a problem; I don't deny that. . . .

METZGER: In July of 1975 did you tell Dr. Parzen, "You'll be sorry" for refusing to have sex with you and premise a suicide attempt on that?

WALKER: No, not because of sex. I got ticked off and stormed out one day, yeah. We had arguments. We also had arguments in which I said I didn't like that we had arguments. And he said, you know, "Don't worry, you know, we'll have hundreds more as the years go by."

METZGER: Are you angry with Dr. Parzen?

WALKER: Yes, because I'm going through hell and it's a lot of fun, and he sits there smirking like it's, you know, a big joke.

METZGER: Mrs. Walker, you've been in analysis, one way and another, for a number of years; is that correct?

WALKER: Yes.

METZGER: Do you know what the term "fantasize" means?

WALKER: I do not fantasize. Zane has a wonderful way of using that word. In fact, the last day we were together he explained that he had to tell the doctors that I lived in a fantasy world. And I said, "You made a liar of me by doing that." And his exact words were, "What can I do? I have to watch out for my career."

Metzger asked Evelyn about all those letters she had written to Parzen after he threw her out. She answered:

In the beginning it was a plea for contact. Then it became just a need to let him know I was doing someting. I had hoped that he at least would be concerned about my well-being. I had hoped that there would be some kind of a note, maybe just to say that, you know, he was glad if I was doing okay; something. It was a hope for some kind of contact from the standpoint that I thought maybe he would care what happened to me. It was very hard for me to believe that you have a relationship with somebody that meant that much and a person just cuts you off like you don't exist. . . .

Again, Metzger brought out the angry letter Evelyn had written in November of 1978, and again he tried in vain to show that she had written it out of jealousy after she heard that there were other female patients involved with Parzen. This time Evelyn was ready for him: "You tried to make that accusation the last time. I never heard about those two ladies until the hearing. I never heard their names. I never heard anything about that. The first time I heard anything was when this thing came to the surface."

Metzger hammered away. Why did she write this letter if not out of jealousy? What did she mean by the word *ruin*? But Evelyn stopped him every time: "I don't want to answer that again."

Long after a judge would have stopped Metzger's line of questioning, the chairman finally did stop him and say, "I think she certainly answered that many times already."

Metzger said:

It's our feeling that Mrs. Walker is motivated not by her — by the affirmative aspects of her relationship with Dr. Parzen, but the negative aspects; that it's the fact that Dr. Parzen refused to develop the relationship in a manner, in a fashion that Mrs. Walker wanted; that she attempted to continue that and to seek that during the two years that he was not treating her professionally.

And then all of a sudden this letter comes out of the blue. She maintains that there is coincidence between that fact and the fact that at about the same time there was another charge going around, and I suggest that it's not coincidence.

Metzger said his problem was that "Mrs. Walker has a difficult time giving a straight answer to a straight question." To which Conn replied, "I don't really feel that that's called for. I think she's doing the best that she can, and I think she's answered quite directly on many different occasions certain questions you've put to her; okay?"

This was not okay with Metzger. He said there was only one witness to very serious charges and he had only so much time to examine this witness in representing his client, and he was going to do what he could.

METZGER: Mrs. Walker, on page five of your letter, you tell Dr. Parzen that you hate him, and then you say, "So protect yourself and your plain little wife, you could have cared less about me."

WALKER: I don't think it's very kind to bring that up. I was angry. Why hurt somebody that's sitting in a room? . . . Now, you see — you see, you have a wonderful way. You put "I hate you"; and I didn't do it just "I hate you." "Zane, you're a coward, I could forgive that but

it's how you did things that I can't forgive and for that I hate you."
You pull one sentence. I did not say, "I hate you." I said, "For that."
He can't help that he's a coward, but the way he handles things he
can. I don't hate him, but what he did I hate.

Metzger's questions continued: "What was the purpose of the refer-
ence to Dr. Parzen's wife?"

"I think you're a very unpleasant person," Evelyn answered. "I
wrote a letter to that man in private that you are making public. I was
angry. I have a right to be angry. Why are you being cruel? What I say
in anger in private to him was not intended to be made public. I do not
choose to hurt anybody in this room. And you are cruel."

Metzger then offered an opinion. "Mrs. Walker in this letter more
clearly demonstrates her motivation and her potential for bending the
facts if not breaking them completely." And that was all Evelyn had to
hear. In her whole life, the worst that anybody could ever say about
her was to call her a liar. She was not a liar. She did not need to lie, and
they would hear her out no matter what their rules of law and order.

WALKER: I do not bend facts. How would you like to have—
CONN: Mrs. Walker.
WALKER: Just a second.
CONN: Now I'd like—
WALKER: Now just one— No, just a minute, please.
CONN: Can we take turns?
WALKER: No. How would you like for 3½ years to pour thousands of
   dollars out to a man, hoping to get some help, hoping that what he
   says to you is the truth? Do you know what it has taken in the last
   two years for me to get to this place? Do you know what it is to be
   thrown out, put to a doctor that doesn't know you, that you don't
   know, that within one week's time goes on a trip; that you're put in
   a psychiatric hospital where you don't know anybody and they
   don't know you; where you don't have a husband; where you don't
   have money; where you don't have emotional or financial support;
   and this lies and dumps you and takes thousands of dollars? And
   you dare say I don't have a right to be mad? Well, you go through it
   and see how thrilled you are. If I don't have a right, nobody has a
   right, and I have the guts to sit here. The person that started this [Pat
   Stern] isn't here. I'm here. He didn't have the guts to talk last time.

So he sits there and chews on his pipe and makes funny little faces. Now you tell me where the guts are. Now if I don't have a right to be mad, nobody does. It took me a long time. Now ask your questions and I'll answer them all.

The effect of this emotional outburst was devastating. Parzen was done for, and his lawyer surely recognized that. Throughout the hearing, Parzen had made weird little faces as Evelyn answered the questions put to her. Nobody who sat there and saw him is quite able to describe his facial gestures, but everybody agrees they were what psychiatrists call "inappropriate gestures." He would grin or appear to laugh at a most solemn accusation. Evelyn would recall they were just plain weird distortions of his face that seemed designed to make her feel that he thought she was not telling the truth. Whatever they were, the chairman was forced on one occasion to stop the proceedings and caution Parzen that his gestures were disturbing the witness and he should stop them. It was a telling moment that his lawyer should have paid closer attention to, for in the coming months of litigation against Parzen, the most effective witness against him was the man himself. Everybody would remember that during the most sordid and horrifying testimony about his actions, he would respond by grinning, smiling, or making some other inappropriate gesture.

Similar inappropriate gestures and behavior made the Green Beret officer and physician Jeffrey MacDonald a damning witness against himself. After long years of litigation, MacDonald was convicted of the hideous stabbing deaths of his wife and two young daughters — and, as with Parzen, his lawyers despaired of his grandiosity on the stand. In the face of horrible testimony about his loved ones, he would smirk and grin and even laugh. In the book *Fatal Vision,* written with and about MacDonald, author Joe McGinniss quotes from the 1975 book by Otto Kernberg, *Borderline Conditions and Pathological Narcissism,* to explain MacDonald's behavior.

Although Zane Parzen was never accused or charged with anything as serious as murder, there was mounting expert evidence against him that his method of treatment easily could have killed two of his patients on several occasions. The lines McGinniss quotes from Kernberg fit everything that is known about Parzen. "On the surface [pathologically narcissistic] individuals may not present seriously disturbed behaviors; some of them may function socially very well."

He says these people possess "the capacity for active, consistent work in some area which permits them partially to fulfill their ambition of greatness and of obtaining admiration and approval from other people." Kernberg explains that the main characteristics of such personalities are "grandiosity, extreme self-centeredness, and a remarkable absence of interest and empathy for others in spite of the fact that they are so very eager to obtain admiration and approval. . . . It is as if they feel they have the right to control and possess others and to exploit them without guilt feelings, and, behind a surface which very often is charming and engaging, one senses coldness and ruthlessness. These patients not only lack emotional depth, but fail to understand complex emotion in other people."

The "patient" in Parzen's case was the doctor himself.

There would be one further hearing the next week before the San Diego branch of the American Psychoanalytic Society, but the only witnesses would be Izner, Rosenblatt, and Robbins, repeating the accounts they had given in the first hearing.

Once again, the evidence was overwhelmingly against Parzen, and the committee members would vote almost routinely to reject him as a member of their group. There would be no other professional hearings because they would not be necessary. By this time the state licensing board, the Board of Medical Quality Assurance, had its investigators working on the legal case that could strip Parzen of his license to practice medicine.

At this last hearing of the Society, one person was conspicuous by her absence — Parzen's wife, Judy. She, too, must have made up her mind about the man. In the coming month, she would successfully file for divorce. Parzen, of course, was in no position to fight. Almost in mirror repetition of what had happened to Evelyn, he lost everything. The house was to be sold and the funds put in trust for their sons, and he was forced to move into an apartment in downtown La Jolla. Even his gold bracelet, a gift from his wife's parents, was ordered to be returned to them.

Following the hearings, Sydney Smith's notes document another disturbance that had developed in Evelyn Walker's life. On April 5, 1979, he wrote: "Somebody is calling her through the night, and when she answers the phone, the caller hangs up. . . . She believes it is Dr.

P. because the calls come right on the hour and he is systematic about such things. Also, he has trouble, like her, in sleeping at night." On May 4, he noted, "Patient disturbed by phone call she received from man she didn't recognize who said, 'You're the woman who likes to give doctors trouble. Do you know you can be murdered for that?'"

Another night, Evelyn recalls, she answered the phone and heard a woman saying in a low, sinister voice, "Murderer, murderer." The anonymous calls became even more frequent in late 1979 when the *La Jolla Light* published the first newspaper accounts of Parzen's predicament, mentioning Evelyn Walker. Then, in 1980, Evelyn received an anonymous letter in the mail, with these words fashioned from newspaper and magazine headlines: HAPPY NEW YEAR, WALKER, YOU'RE DEAD.

During his testimony at the January hearing, Al Robbins had said that he had not yet reported Zane Parzen's misconduct to the Board of Medical Quality Assurance. Soon after that, however, he did report to the board and to the investigating attorneys in the state Attorney General's office. With evidence provided by Evelyn Walker and Parzen's fellow psychiatrists, and through their own investigation, the BMQA was able to produce a remarkably detailed accusation against Parzen that was dated October 31, 1979. Parzen held Physician and Surgeon Certificate #C-21583. Under Sections 2360 and 2361 of the Business and Professions Code of California, that certificate could be suspended or revoked if the holder was guilty of unprofessional conduct. Physicians are further regulated by the Medical Practice Act of California. In the accusation, the BMQA accused Parzen of gross negligence, incompetence, and unprofessional conduct under the several acts and sections of the law dealing with the conduct of physicians. Parzen was specifically charged with having engaged in sexual relations with patient "E.W.," which "consisted primarily of manual and oral sexual activities." There were also eight acts of sexual intercourse.

The accusation added that during the time of these relations, the doctor had told the patient that he loved her, was the only person who cared about her, would always be in her life, and would never abandon her, although the patient was married and living with her husband during most of this time. The accusation further stipulated that patient E.W. had attempted to commit suicide on several occasions and at one time the doctor had actually told her to go ahead with it. In July 1976, the BMQA accusation stated, Parzen told patient E.W. to stop taking any drugs and she followed his instructions, "and suffered severe withdrawal symptoms, including convulsions."

In regard to patient E.W., Parzen was charged with being guilty of incompetence and general unprofessional conduct, but regarding patient [initials for Pat Stern] he was accused of being guilty of gross negligence. In regard to patient [P.S.], the accusation stated, Parzen had not only been involved in sexual relations — oral and otherwise — he had also caused her to become pregnant and assisted her in obtaining an abortion, and he had taken pictures of her in the nude.

Parzen was accused of prescribing, in December 1978, the drug Parnate for [P.S.] along with the drug Ritalin. Parzen would now read from the highest legal authority governing physicians in California what his colleague Gary Shepherd had tried to tell him many months earlier: "Such a combination is contraindicated unless the patient is hospitalized and under close supervision, because of the danger of provoking a fatal hypertensive crisis."

The final paragraph of the accusation calls for a hearing to be held on these charges. However, no such hearing was held. Parzen would swear that he was forced to sign a statement agreeing to the truth of all these charges. However, he was offered a choice: He could agree to certain conditions and lose his license for one year with a ten-year probation, or he could go through with the hearing and face the permanent loss of his license. He chose the former, complaining about the injustice of it.

In the stipulations agreed to by Parzen and members of the board, he would lose his license for a period of one year, beginning May 28, 1980. He was also required to undergo an administrative psychiatric evaluation by a psychiatrist designated by the board, and if it was found necessary, he would, within thirty days after notification, submit to psychiatric treatment by a doctor approved by the board. Meanwhile, he was prohibited from practicing medicine and was required to reappear before the board to receive its approval before resuming practice after his license had been restored.

Were his license reissued, Parzen's practice would still be restricted for the duration of the ten-year probation period. In that time, he could not examine or treat any female patients, and he could have nothing to do with prescribing or administering drugs — nor even possess them unless they were administered to him by an authorized physician. He was required to report at various intervals, in writing and in person, to the BMQA's medical consultant. If he left the state, he was required to notify the board, in writing, of the dates of his departure and return, and "periods of residency or practice outside California will not apply to the reduction of this probationary period." Since Parzen moved to Arizona a year after this order went into effect, and has lived there ever since, it appears that he will still be on probation for another nine years if and when he ever decides to resume practice in California.

Parzen would go through the testing and examination by a state-appointed psychiatrist, who determined that he did indeed need regular psychiatric treatment. His old friend and colleague, James Thickstun, was authorized to carry out this treatment, and a year later, in October 1980, Thickstun would write an extraordinary letter about Parzen's case that would help Parzen to regain his license to practice medicine. This letter, quoted extensively earlier in this book, concludes as follows:

> This analysis has moved rapidly, and I believe we have come a long way in the working through of the central core of pathology. . . . It is conceivable that Dr. Parzen may, or may not, decide to return to the practice of medicine in any form, including the practice of psychiatry and psychoanalysis. . . . Dr. Parzen is a very capable person, creative and gifted in many ways. Without the need to preserve himself by abandoning his own desires and needs he may enter another field or he may return to practice without the need to sacrifice himself to his patients — which resulted in damage to himself and to others as well.

None of Thickstun's colleagues was aware of the letter he had written with such high praise for having cured Zane Parzen of his psychopathology (without ever stating clearly what that pathology was) until one of Evelyn Walker's lawyers mentioned it during the trial in mid-1981. After that, one of Thickstun's most distinguished colleagues wrote to the lawyer, saying: "I consider this letter to be an abuse of psychoanalytic dynamics, language and application. I am most concerned with the feeling that much of what is expressed in that letter appears to severely distort and misrepresent the facts in the case, along with what is expectable in a therapeutic situation."

Among the more fascinating documents subpoenaed for the 1981 trial of *Walker v. Parzen* were four psychological tests to which Zane Parzen had submitted. Almost more interesting than the information revealed by the tests themselves are the dates on which he took them — December 27, 1978; January 12, 1979; January 16, 1979; and September 11, 1979. All of these, of course, took place after Parzen was confronted by his colleagues with evidence of his misdeeds. (The first three were taken before the first professional hearing on January 29, 1979. The fourth test was done before Parzen received the detailed accusation from the Board of Medical Quality Assurance but after he knew such an indictment was on its way.) But Parzen submitted to these tests long before he was required to do so by the state. Perhaps he thought they would bolster his original contention that he was sane and his two female patients were only fantasizing about relationships with him. Then again, he might have been seeking evidence to support his contention that he was a disturbed man but he was also taking steps to cure himself.

Whatever his motive in taking them, the evidence in the four separate tests is quite damning. It is a classic case — the doctor was indeed sicker than his patients. In fact, Parzen showed many of the same psychological characteristics of the female patients to whom he was "most attracted."

The earliest of these tests carried the cautionary note that such a test was no substitute "for the clinician's professional judgment and skill." However, the test "can be a useful adjunct in the evaluation and management of emotional disorders." In the case of patient Zane Parzen, the "test results of this patient appear to be valid. He seems to have made an effort to answer the items truthfully and to follow the instructions accurately."

The first part of the test was a sequence of true-false questions; Parzen's answers appear in parentheses below.

Someone has it in for me. (True.)
I have no enemies who really wish to harm me. (False.)
There is something wrong with my mind. (True.)
Sometimes I feel as if I must injure myself or someone else. (True.)

I believe I am a condemned person. (True.)
Most of the time I wish I were dead. (True.)
Most times I think I am no good at all. (True.)

Parzen claimed to have no problems with drugs or alcohol and did not answer the questions in that section. However, under "Depression," the test showed: "He appears to be deeply depressed. He is overwhelmed by guilt feelings and he blames himself for his trouble. Life holds little enjoyment for him and he has difficulty maintaining interest and involvement in his day-to-day responsibilities. He feels isolated from others, sensitive to slights and unworthy of happiness. He expects punishment and feels that he deserves it."

Under "Family Problems," the test showed: "He describes his home life as unpleasant, with parents who were critical of him and unreasonable in their demands. His family was characterized by quarrels, isolation, and a lack of love."

The report concluded:

He appears to be an idealistic, inner-directed person who may be seen as quite socially perceptive and sensitive to interpersonal interactions. His interest patterns are quite different from those of the average male. In a person with a broad educational and cultural background, this is to be expected, and may reflect such characteristics as self-awareness, concern with social issues, and an ability to communicate ideas clearly and effectively. In some men, however, the same interest pattern may reflect a rejection of masculinity accompanied by a relatively passive, effeminate, non-competitive personality.

The test results on this patient are strongly suggestive of a major emotional disorder. The test pattern resembles those of psychiatric outpatients who later require inpatient care. Appropriate professional evaluation and care and continued observation are suggested.

The same test administered three weeks later showed almost identical results but with an even more pessimistic conclusion: "His expressed intentions to improve seem genuine, but the pattern is a persistent one. Assisting him to a better adjustment will probably require a combination of firm limits, warm support and environmental modification. Although improvement may be rapid in a protected environment, the long-term prognosis is poor."

Added to the questions this time was one about sexual concerns and problems: "I have never been in trouble because of my sexual behavior." To that, Parzen had answered, "False."

By this time, Parzen knew that the first professional hearing was scheduled for two weeks later and that his colleagues were lining up against him. Under "Depression," this test said of him: "He is unhappy and discouraged, with the feeling that life is not working out well for him. He is filled with regrets and guilt about the past, and has little hope for the future. He often feels lonely, discouraged and misunderstood. His self-esteem is low and he feels ineffectual and dissatisfied with himself."

The last of these reports was the most damning of all. Dated September 11, 1979, it was compiled after Parzen had been rejected by the professional societies and after he knew his license would surely be suspended, if not revoked. The test results showed:

> This patient appears to be an angry, suspicious person who has difficulty with impulse control. He is evasive and defensive about acknowledging psychological problems. He tends to handle anxieties and conflicts by refusing to recognize their presence, and he utilizes rationalization as a defense mechanism. He resents authority and is likely to be argumentative and irritable in social relations, especially with the opposite sex. This test pattern rarely occurs among normal adults, and its presence suggests the necessity of careful appraisal. Although the patient may appear sociopathic, the possibility of a psychotic or pre-psychotic condition should be considered. Psychiatric patients with this pattern show depression, irritability, suspiciousness, judgment defects, and addictions. They are likely to show little response to psychotherapy, and the prognosis is poor.

The test conclusions seem thoroughly negative, yet other parts of this same test reflect a different Parzen, a new, defiant Parzen. By this time he had lost his family, his career, and virtually everything he had ever cared about. He was cornered in that alleyway, and gearing up for the fight. The other tests had shown his depression level as high; this one showed his depression as average. And under "morale" was this comment: "He seems to be a confident, cheerful person who feels able to deal effectively with his environment. He seems relatively content with himself and is not hypersensitive to the opinions of others. He sees himself as a stable, competent person who stands up well in comparison with other people he knows."

It was this false image of himself that had sustained him in previous years — but had also led to his problems. And it was this same "cheerfulness" that might keep him going in the long years of litigation ahead — but would also be his undoing in court.

Sydney Smith's notes about patient Evelyn Walker are almost as interesting for what they say about the doctor as what they say about the patient. While they are a case study of the hopeless, helpless mental condition of a borderline patient, the notes also show in fine detail how exasperated, indeed helpless, the doctor felt in trying to treat such a person.

On September 29, 1979, Smith noted:

Take up with her the anger she expressed on the phone indicating she was not coming in today because of her negative reaction about me. . . . She catches me up in some joking, bantering interaction, and then decides I am making life miserable for her and she becomes angry and rejecting and decides to withdraw and remove self from me as a patient of me. She has a difficult time getting into this issue, but talks instead of the fact that Dr. P. is the only one who ever loved her and she would go to him even now if he asked her to. I tried to help her see how self-destructive this fantasy is and how needy she is; that she can misperceive his motives, but she does not want that fantasy taken away from her because he is the only person in her life who really loved her.

Another day, it seemed to Evelyn that a great many problems were hitting her at once. Her former lawyer wrote to her, threatening a suit if she didn't pay her bill; her current boyfriend seemed about to abandon her; and there were calls from her ex-husband, who refused to get out of her life. Smith noted: "I point out how all this, like the lawyer's letter, seems to be saying she is wrong, she is bad, and that takes her back to a childhood feeling that she is going to be abandoned. She could realize in some corner of her mind that all this was happening, but couldn't keep it from going on."

On a Sunday, Smith received a call from Evelyn saying she had taken all her pills in another suicide attempt. But this time the medication included an emetic that would cause her to throw up if she overdosed. Smith noted, "She felt that she had been tricked."

After he saw her the next morning, he made these notes: "Get into the issue with her of two sides of herself: the little girl who regresses into helplessness, and the grown woman who can handle a situation."
On November 6, 1979, Smith noted:

> The patient comes to the hour in a drugged state. Her motor coordination was reduced and her speech was occasionally slurred, but she appeared in good enough shape to drive. She refused to tell me what drugs she was taking and spent a quiet hour not talking about much of anything. I attempted to get her to talk about what was on her mind, but the hour was a desultory one. On leaving here, she went home, made several angry phone calls getting people concerned about her suiciding, and finally OD'd and was hospitalized by Dr. G.S. [Gary Shepherd], her good friend, at Scripps.

Three days later, she was out of the hospital and back in Smith's office. He noted: "This hour was a short one because the patient stormed out in anger over my telling her she was late and not treating herself very well." He said she had begun a

> diatribe about how nobody was treating her well, and that's when I made my comment that she was not treating herself very well and she angrily left the office. In talking with her on the phone later, she indicated that I did not understand what she was going through; that she could not stand being alone; that the time with me was not enough. She needed to see me every day, and that there were times even when she saw me she could not talk, but she felt I did not appreciate that. She indicated she had given me repeated warnings that she was in trouble, but I point out to her that on the contrary she had not talked at the last hour despite my repeated efforts to learn what was going on, and she turned on my suggestions that she go to the hospital or we call a friend to stay with her.

A few days later, Smith noted that Evelyn had

> an attack of reality, in that she has thrown the doctor boyfriend out of her life, recognizing at last that he is a superficial, unsubstan-

tial man who uses her like an object and does not want to hear about her troubles. She feels that the Mexican boyfriend was a real man, and it's for this reason she is down about leaving him. Have gone over with her the fact that she became so needy and so controlling and so unable to allow for a separation from herself with men. As the relationship gets more important for her she frightens men away. She recognizes that she does this, calls herself bad, and sees that everything is her fault; so, she takes the position of the bad parent, punishing herself, and also puts me in that position as well.

Although it was nearly three years since Evelyn was thrown out of Parzen's office, he was still very much on her mind. On November 16, 1979, Smith made these notes: "She also talks about how she is controlled by the fantasies of Dr. P. and how he told her that she would never get free of him, and she knows she can't. I told her she didn't want to get rid of them [the fantasies] because in a certain way she enjoys them."

Later, when Smith would be required to read these notes into the record of Evelyn Walker's trial, he would stop at this point and explain:

I think that the idea of being able to come together with him [Parzen] at last, of his finally becoming her rescuer and her savior, that those ideas to her were gratifying and it really is based upon the fact that in her mind, in her unconscious mind, Dr. Parzen had become the loving uncle who was the only male figure in her life from her past who had treated her like a human being and who seemed to love her for herself without any strings attached, and that idea of what a love relationship should be like, she transferred to Dr. Parzen, and I think is one of the reasons that Dr. Parzen had such a hold on her. It was as if Parzen had taken the place of the dead uncle. Now, that inference was confirmed by repeated dreams in which Dr. Parzen and the uncle would appear in a kind of oscillating identification, and in these dreams, she was always a little child in a white dress that she could remember, but it was a repetitious dream in which she would be with the uncle, who would become Dr. Parzen, who would become the uncle, and these dreams also had a frightening quality about them because they had something to do with her fear of death and her fear of loss through death, which, of course, was what had happened to the uncle, and the fear that the same thing was going to happen with Dr. Parzen.

Indeed, these dreams I am telling you about were intertwined with some very frightening nightmares that always involved Dr. Parzen, nightmares in which she either saw him as at first being with her and interested in her, and then he would somehow disappear or he would leave a room or a building or a house or whatever it was in the dream, and she would be held back from following him. She would be contained in some way or restricted, and then the other dream, the other nightmare that she had about Dr. Parzen is that he would murder her, and that dream has been a repetitious nightmare which still occurs from time to time that she will be killed by him.

Sometime later, as Smith was reading his notes into the record and mentioned yet another man in Evelyn's life, the lawyer for Parzen stopped the proceedings by laughing out loud. "I don't mean to laugh because I'm not a feeling person," he said, "but if someone were to film a soap opera. . . . " — and then he went off the record to make the point that he was trying to establish a permissive or promiscuous background for Evelyn. Back on the record, Smith corrected him:

In the first place, not all of these relationships have been sexual relationships. This one I just mentioned was not a sexual relationship at all. The other thing is that considering her pathology, there may not be any relationship that has been a sexual relationship for her. All of these relationships are really a way of finding the good breast. They represent much more oral, the fulfillment of oral needs than they do of sexual needs; and in that sense they represent the regressed infantile part of her, and that sexuality is merely a vehicle for satisfying those oral needs. This kind of statement she made about needing a man to envelop her in his body is not really a sexual statement. It is a statement of the infant's need for protection and care and comfort and warmth and being safeguarded from the dangers of the outside world. So, I think that it really is a mistake to think of her as being a sexual person, certainly not a permissive sexual person. Many of these relationships have not been on those lines, but I think what we have here is a much more regressed personality we are dealing with which we can get fooled by because of what comes out in the record about the times — that there are times when she can suddenly get hold of things, act like a very grown-up person, take charge of her life, suddenly get something done that she has been waiting around in a passive state for everybody else to do for her, and once that's done, she regresses back into the old picture again.

While he was explaining things, Smith continued with an explanation of what he felt Parzen had done to Evelyn Walker.

. . . This is a sick woman and she has been made a great deal more sick as a result of the experiences she has had from, I think, Dr. Parzen, especially. She had difficulties to begin with which this man with all of his psychiatric knowledge and skill had the chance to help her with, and instead he destroyed her, and that's his sickness that he had to do that. It's a tragic situation.

It wasn't that she didn't have problems [when she first went to Parzen] but I think that the problems were workable at that point. I think if she had been able to get with a responsible person who exercised therapeutic integrity with her, that she could have made pretty good gains. She had at that time what the people in my business like to call sublimatory channels; in other words, she had aspects of her life that she could function with which were gratifying. She was an artist who did painting. She did some fantastic macramé work. She did a lot of other kinds of things which is all gone. She has lost it. Those functions aren't there any more. She can't do those things. She can't concentrate on them. She can't get any gratification out of them, and there is no channel of sublimation for her. That's been destroyed, and it's all been replaced by this obsessional stuff on what her needs are, how nobody is meeting those needs, and the creation of this kind of hunger in her.

I think that the chief damage that Dr. Parzen did to her was to allow the fantasy that she was going to have all of these infantile needs fulfilled come into full flower. He nourished that idea in her. He made it clear that he was the only one who could fill those needs. He was the only one who could satisfy her. He played the role of

Svengali in her life, and any sex had a kind of hypnotic influence over her, and she is not free of it yet.

We keep hearing through these hours how she would return to him if he only would smile at her, indicate he needed her, she would go right back into it again, and she has no concept of this man's destructiveness, the horror that he has perpetrated in her life.

She is angry with him, and we talk about the vengeful issues in here, but that's largely because he rejected her. If he took the rejection away, the anger and vengeance would disappear. She would run right back into his arms, and that is not good reality testing. That's the piece of her own craziness.

. . . The job of the psychotherapist is to bring her to a point where she can let go of the past, emerge out of this obsessional preoccupation of how badly she was treated, and therefore escape the necessity of having to repeat that process over and over and over again in every relationship. That's what the hope of psychotherapy could provide for her and is what Dr. Parzen should have provided for her. That's the issue he should have been working on her with. Instead he contributed to it. He made it worse.

He did probably one of the most dastardly things a person in this profession can do to a patient, and that is that he treated her in a way to garner all of her trust, make her believe that all of the dissatisfactions that she had in her life could now be assuaged; that she had at last come home to a safe place, and then he turned her life into a nightmare.

Chapter 9 The original papers in *Walker v. Parzen* were filed in the Superior Court of San Diego County on July 11, 1979, by the local attorney who had represented Evelyn Walker during her second divorce and who had sat with her through the two hearings of the Psychoanalytic Institute and Society.

Gary Shepherd and the other doctors involved in getting Evelyn to testify against Parzen in those hearings had promised to help her in any way she might need. After they arranged for her to begin treatment with Sydney Smith, they recommended that she find another lawyer who had more experience in this kind of litigation.

I think the doctors I had dealt with at the Institute and their lawyer had discussed it among themselves before they talked it over with me. But they felt I should have a lawyer more experienced in personal injury cases than the one I had in San Diego, and I went to see two local lawyers they recommended. The first one read over the documents I had — transcripts of the Institute hearings and Al Robbins's interview of me. He said I obviously had a very good case. But, he added, "I have to live in this town and I really don't want to touch anything like this."

The second lawyer went over the same material very carefully. But he said I needed somebody who was "more a pro" in this specialized field; he felt the case would require more expertise than he had in personal injury cases. Then he asked if it would be all right if he put in a call to a lawyer he knew.

I was getting ready to go into the hospital for very serious surgery, and I was mainly preoccupied with getting through that. But I told the lawyer to use his own judgment, and he went ahead and contacted a

San Francisco lawyer named Marvin Lewis, Sr. Several weeks after I got out of the hospital, this local lawyer contacted me, saying that Marvin Lewis was interested in meeting with me to talk about the case. He wondered whether I could possibly manage to go to San Francisco to see him. Again, the doctors at the Institute and their lawyer helped me get all of the transcripts and documents from their hearings. And I immediately made plans to fly to San Francisco.

I took the elevator up to Lewis's penthouse offices and told the receptionist who I was, that I had an appointment with Mr. Lewis. I don't know what kind of slick appearance I expected, but the famous lawyer dispelled all that when he came barreling out to greet me in person. He was in shirtsleeves, with his tie askew and the top button undone; his hair was in a tangle and he looked like he needed a shave.

Back in his office, I was impressed by the plaques and pictures and framed articles about his career, covering two walls, floor to ceiling. But there was something else about the office that startled and saddened me—it was decorated in masculine shades of beige, with leather furniture, and at the end of his desk were a huge collection of pipes and a humidor of tobacco. It was that smell of tobacco and leather I had always loved, but it reminded me of all those times in Zane's office.

Marvin sat back in his chair across the wide desk from me as I started telling him about my involvement with Zane. Every few minutes, he would interrupt me and ask me another question before I felt I had answered the previous question. At the time, I thought he was simply being rude; only much later did I realize that he had been testing me to see if I'd be able to handle cross-examination by a hostile lawyer. Apparently I passed the test; after about two hours, Marvin clasped his hands, leaned across the desk and asked, "Do you want to call your attorney and release him from the case?"

I asked if that meant he wanted to take my case. He looked me straight in the eye and said, "This is one of the most exciting cases that has come across my desk in quite a while."

He dialed the number and I tried—very nervously—to tell my San Diego lawyer that I was releasing him from the case. The other lawyer started yelling and I felt he was threatening me. He said he'd take me to court over this; he said he'd sue me for the money I owed him, although he knew I had no money at the time. After a barrage of this, Marvin took the phone and helped to calm down the other lawyer and let him know he shouldn't be threatening me over anything.

After our meeting, Marvin was going to drive me to the airport. As we went down to the garage, he explained that he'd just picked up a new car. When we got in, he couldn't find the place to put in the key; I had to show him where it was. We had a good laugh over this — the new client with mental problems helping the expert lawyer start his car.

We had many difficult moments in the months ahead, but I always trusted Marvin Lewis. I always felt he knew what he was doing, and I'm confident, looking back on it, that nobody could have put my case together as well as he did — nobody else could have won that final verdict.

▬

Like Sigmund Freud and many other successful men before him, Marvin Lewis's overachievement in life can be traced directly to the influence of one special woman: his mother. Born July 14, 1907, Lewis remembers constant bickering between his parents when he was a child. They divorced when he was a young boy. When Lewis was seventeen and just entering law school, his father was struck by a car and killed in downtown San Francisco.

Selena Lewis, meanwhile, was not only mother and father to her pride and joy, Marvin, she was also his favorite professor, acting and speech coach, and best friend. Selena Lewis's school of rhetoric and elocution was locally famous. Lewis would spend the regular hours at the local public school and then come home to extra hours of training under his mother.

Once, it seemed Lewis might fulfill the acting career his mother never quite achieved. Mrs. Lewis's old friend Sol Loesser had made it big as a Hollywood film producer, and he called her up and said, "We need you down here." Selena Lewis and her young son moved to Hollywood for a time, where she made a good living coaching actors and actresses for the new sound films. Loesser convinced her to allow young Marvin to take a screen test for a part in a film. Much to his mother's shock, the boy passed the test and — he was always told — would have gotten the role in *Peck's Bad Boys* that made a star of Jackie Cooper. But Selena Lewis felt this was wrong; her son had gone into something because she had pushed him there. She packed up their belongings and they returned to San Francisco. She resumed her speech and acting school and sometimes toured as a one-woman show, assuming ten and fifteen different roles with no props, scenery, costumes, or special lighting.

While studying voice with his mother, Lewis won a state contest in Shakespearean oratory. Lewis saw public speaking as a gift, a talent to be used and not wasted frivolously or insincerely. That seemed naturally to lead him into the study of law. His mother got him a job in the office of a friend who was a lawyer, and Lewis started studying at the San Francisco Law School — five nights a week for four years. During part of this time he supported himself by working at a switchboard and delivering newspapers.

Marvin Lewis tried his first jury case in 1929, a case that he won against the Southern Pacific Railroad. Later, in the 1930s, he joined the law firm of Edgar Levy, then the Speaker of the House in California. One of his first cases, involving the unlawful cremation of a body, first brought Lewis into the spotlight of publicity, and he thrived on the glare from then on.

In 1942, Lewis was elected to the Board of Supervisors in San Francisco; he was reelected twice and served ten years in that position. Otherwise, his political career was less successful. He lost a campaign for State Assemblyman when he was young, and later lost another campaign as a Republican candidate for Congress.

The headline over an early news story about Marvin Lewis reads, TOUGH PROBLEMS CHALLENGE SPIRIT OF YOUNG ATTORNEY. He loved the attention and wasn't afraid of controversy. In one case, Lewis first represented a tenant who had been injured on a faulty staircase, and successfully sued the tenant's landlady for damages. Then, in one of his more famous turnarounds, Lewis promptly brought suit on the landlady's behalf and had the state law, under which she had been sued, overturned. He was always attracted to the more sensational cases, but Lewis ended up a champion of victims of psychic injury almost by default. Many lawyers would refer cases involving mental injuries to Lewis, because they simply could not or would not handle them. They would only represent clients with physical injuries that any jury could see and understand; they left it to Lewis to represent clients who seemed physically healthy but had suffered serious psychological injuries.

The courts were even slower than the rest of society in recognizing mental injuries alongside other diseases and injuries. It was not until

1966 that the U.S. Supreme Court finally recognized psychological injuries as a legitimate cause for damages. So, at a time when many of his legal peers would be thinking of retirement, Marvin Lewis found himself in the young man's role of trailblazer, a pioneer in a very complicated area of law.

Lewis's most notorious success came in 1971, when he won $50,000 in damages for a woman who had been injured during a cable car accident in San Francisco. Her physical injuries healed, but something happened to the woman during that crash — she claimed it was seeing the brake or gearstick as her head smashed into the floor — and she became overnight what the press would call a nymphomaniac. Johnny Carson and every other stand-up comic in America was making jokes about the case, but Lewis was — and remains — deadly serious about it. When she came to him, this woman was clearly suicidal. He was able to prove to the court that she was not a nymphomaniac and that she had never been permissive or promiscuous before the accident — and the jury agreed that she deserved damages.

It takes more than a knowledge of the law to handle such cases, Lewis believes. He looks on it as a kind of art. You begin with clients whose mental injuries may make them extremely difficult to deal with, but, he says, you have to believe in the injury and you have to believe your client is telling the truth. Then you have to be able to prove: one, that the injury definitely occurred and the person is not a malingerer; two, that this injury was in fact caused by the accident in question; and three, that the person has been damaged in specific ways by that injury. None of this is easy to accomplish, which may be why Lewis, a founder and first president of the California Trial Lawyers Association, was honored for his achievements by the national organization of that group as Trial Lawyer of the Year.

Evelyn Walker's case, however, was unusual even for Lewis. He had never handled a case involving psychic injury that originated with a doctor's malpractice. And the case seemed unique because the doctor had already confessed to nearly every one of his unethical and illegal actions. What convinced Lewis to go ahead with Evelyn Walker's case was the close involvement of Gary Shepherd and the other doctors. In fifty-two years at the bar, Lewis had learned that you simply could not get a doctor to testify against another doctor in a malpractice case. But Lewis found that these doctors were willing to go the full route in testifying against their former colleague in court.

On September 21, 1979, Marvin Lewis's firm formally replaced the San Diego lawyer who had first represented Evelyn Walker. On October 1, 1979, Lewis filed his own amended version of the original complaint (July 11, 1979). The usual schedule for such a case would involve a minimum of three years before it came to trial, and often it would be four or five years from the original filing date. But once Lewis met with Evelyn Walker and then with Sydney Smith, he felt that if they had to wait that long for this trial, Evelyn might no longer be alive.

On May 19, 1980, Lewis filed a motion to advance the date of the trial. In it, he said, "There is no denial that Mrs. Walker is currently suicidal and that it is difficult for her to eat and sleep and that the litigation that is now hanging over her is further causing her mental deterioration to the point that she might not even be able to testify at the time of the trial." The court approved Lewis's motion and set the trial date for one year later, May 26, 1981.

By the time the trial date was set, Zane Parzen was represented by Rhoades & Hollywood, the San Diego law firm that represented his insurance company. The firm, in effect, had no choice but to represent Parzen, and Parzen had no choice but to accept the attorney the insurance company assigned to him. Although the insurance company was footing the bill and would be making certain decisions involving the case, the attorney, Michael I. Neil, was viewed by the court as Parzen's personal attorney.

Central casting could not have come up with an opponent more perfectly matched to Evelyn Walker and Marvin Lewis. Everything in Mike Neil's background had produced a stereotypical macho man. Evelyn felt that he could not have been more insensitive to her plight or to that of any woman in her situation. Inside and out, Neil seemed to be almost the exact opposite of Marvin Lewis.

Neil is not only a second-generation Marine Corps officer, he is also a second-generation athlete. His father, Gene Hadley (called "Cheesey") Neil, was a captain in the Marine Corps and a locally famous football player. "Unlike everybody else in this cast of characters," Mike Neil says, smiling, "I had a normal childhood — a strong father figure." Born August 21, 1940, in Long Beach, California, Neil was three when the family moved to San Diego, and, except for his high school years when his father was stationed in Hawaii, all of his youth and most of his adult life have been spent in San Diego. After working his way through college in San Diego, Neil went to the Boalt Hall School of Law at the University of California at Berkeley, where he graduated in 1966.

Those were not the most congenial of times for a young man with a Marine Corps mindset to be at Berkeley. Here was Mike Neil:

> I'm holding down three different jobs, working thirty-five hours a week, and all I want to do is graduate from law school and go out and practice law. There are these constant rallies, university riots, and regular riots, everywhere. Guys felt they should be allowed to stand on a street corner and yell, "Fuck!" What really set me off one day, aside from the people trying to shut down the campus, I saw a sign that advertised Young Socialist Alliance was showing a Vietcong movie. I was interested in seeing it, so I went to the theater. It showed an American helicopter actually being shot down — and the audience cheered when the American helicopter got shot down. It also showed this one guy climbing out of the helicopter, and it showed him just being blown away, and the audience cheered again. I said, "Wait a minute, something is sick here." The next day I went down and joined the Marines.

That summer of 1966, he took and passed the bar exams and loaded 7-Up trucks in San Diego while he waited to be inducted into the Marine Corps. The Marines tried to pressure Neil into serving in their legal section, but he insisted on going into the infantry, where the action was. He got his wish, and in a matter of months, he was in Vietnam, assigned to a small air observer unit on Marble Mountain, six miles southwest of Danang. It was at the edge of an area the GIs called "Mortar Valley" because of the frequent Vietcong mortar and rocket attacks.

In September 1967, Neil was wounded in action, but not seriously enough to be sent home. On December 20, 1967, the young second lieutenant led a twelve-man force to relieve another patrol that had come under heavy enemy fire. The relief force itself was heavily attacked, and Neil emerged a hero. He was later given America's second highest award for bravery in combat, the Navy Cross. Another man involved in that same action was awarded the Congressional Medal of Honor, posthumously.

Until March 1970, Neil stayed on active duty and served as a legal officer at the Marine Corps Recruit Depot in San Diego. Transferring to the Marine Reserves, he worked as a civilian lawyer in partnership with another ex-Marine for 2½ years, before joining Hollywood & Rhoades on December 1, 1972. Much of his work at the firm has involved representing insurance companies and corporations in damage suits, and most of them, he says, he wins.

But the case against Zane Parzen was different in almost every aspect from anything Neil had ever handled. He accepted the case because his firm was on retainer from Parzen's insurance company. He didn't think twice about it; whether Parzen was right or wrong, guilty or innocent, had nothing to do with it. "The guy's got a right to a lawyer, no matter what he's done," Neil explains.

But, it was "the most unusual case I've ever been involved with and I hope ever will be involved with," Neil says. "By the time the case came to us, he [Parzen] had already admitted virtually all of the allegations against him. The case, in part, was already over before we ever got it. Defending him was an uphill battle all the way. . . . Nobody was in love with my client — I guarantee you that."

Although people who attended the trial say that Neil was visibly uncomfortable around Parzen, Neil claims he liked Parzen. "He's a nice guy. He really is. First of all, what he did was wrong and he understands that. He was having problems of his own. He had a son die in an accident who was in a coma for a long time. And basically his problems started with that. He was always cooperative with me, always honest with me. But he did not make a good witness on the witness stand."

Neil admits that Parzen himself may have been the most damaging witness in his case. "I kept trying to tell him all along. I said, 'You *smile* inappropriately.' He would get up there on the witness stand and be describing the most horrendous thing in detail and he would smile. The jury, I'm sure, assumed that he was enjoying it. It was a leering, lecherous type of look — which was not the way he felt."

Prior to their involvement in *Walker v. Parzen*, Mike Neil and Marvin Lewis had never met. In almost every aspect — looks, experience, education, outlook, politics, you-name-it — they were different. The gladiators — to use Lewis's favorite word for himself — came from enemy camps; this would be a fight to the finish, the kind of all-out challenge both men loved.

As a kind of dress rehearsal for the main performance before judge and jury, the opposing lawyers would face each other during the lengthy pretrial "discovery" process. In civil cases in California, both sides must make available a year or more in advance of the actual trial lists of all the witnesses they intend to call. Also at that time, both sides must make available any and all personal, private, confidential records that might bear on the case. In the case of *Walker v. Parzen*, this meant that hundreds — indeed, thousands — of pages of medical and legal documents had to be turned over as part of the public record of this trial. Both sides had to waive the usual privilege of confidentiality that goes with such communications between and about doctor and patient, lawyer and client.

In addition to this voluminous amount of documentation, both sides were allowed to examine the opposing witnesses months in advance of the trial. Although no judge and jury were present for these sessions, the witnesses were under oath and their testimony was transcribed in depositions that were part of the public record and could be entered in part or in whole as evidence during the trial itself. Marvin Lewis left the examination of most of the witnesses to his young assistant, John Winer. Only Zane Parzen was examined by Lewis himself; Lewis was also present during the two days it took Mike Neil to examine Evelyn Walker.

These pretrial sessions serve to ensure that the opposing lawyers know any and every piece of information that might be presented against them in court. But lawyers like Lewis value the opportunity these pretrial sessions offer to see the opposing lawyer in action, to study his manner and method of operating, and to see just which questions he is going to focus on.

There were no real surprises in Neil's examination of Evelyn Walker on May 19 and 20, 1980. By this time, Evelyn had been examined on every fine point of the story of her involvement with Zane Parzen — in the taped interview on Christmas Eve, 1978, and at the two professional hearings in January and April of 1979. Now, however, for the first time, she was under strict rules of court procedure under which she could be compelled to testify about anything and everything. Neil's questioning, incredibly, seemed like a repeat performance of the examination by Parzen's previous lawyer, another ex-Marine, in the two hearings. Perhaps Neil had no choice but to attack Evelyn's credibility, but just as the other lawyer had done, he wound up creating a situation in which he appeared to be a bully picking on somebody who was already down. In most situations of such legal combat, Neil would have come across as an energetic, aggressive lawyer doing a good job defending his client. But his persistent digging and his repetitive questioning did not confuse Evelyn nearly as much as it angered and upset her. The more Neil tried to pick at and tear apart Evelyn's recollections, the more vulnerable — and damaged — she seemed. But Neil pushed ahead in his determination to depict Evelyn as a woman blinded by her own love and caught up in a fantasy romance with her doctor. This lovesick woman, Neil claimed, turned on her doctor only when he did what was professionally right and transferred her. To prove this, he produced that notorious November 1978 letter in which Evelyn had vowed "to destroy" Parzen.

Marvin Lewis could not have been more pleased with the tack his opponent was taking. Even in the informality of these pretrial proceedings, Evelyn was reduced to tears on several occasions, and the examination had to be stopped while she regained her composure. Lewis knew exactly how a jury would see these same scenes if Neil repeated them in the courtroom. Lewis was in an enviable position: No matter what his client did or said on the witness stand, it would probably benefit her case. In fact, the more bizarre her behavior and her testimony, the more it supported Lewis's contention that she had been damaged permanently by Parzen's abuse.

If there were no surprises in Evelyn Walker's pretrial deposition, nearly everything in Zane Parzen's deposition was new. It was, after all, the first time he had said anything for the record about the charges. He had remained silent through the two hearings at the Psychoanalytic Institute, and the state licensing board's accusation and stipulation against him included no explanation or defense from Parzen himself. Now, as Zane Parzen testified for the first time, Evelyn Walker herself was present. It was the first time Evelyn had been in the same room with or had even seen Zane Parzen since the second hearing at the Psychoanalytic Institute in April 1979.

—

I was anxious about the prospect of seeing Zane for days before it actually happened. *Anxious* is not really the right word. I was excited, happy; I was glad that I was finally going to get to see him again. If nothing else, I'd be able to see how he looked, if he was all right or not.

By that time, I had begun to prepare myself for what he might say; I felt he might say things that were not true about me or he might deny things that I knew were true. I was afraid he would say some things out of anger that might be hurtful to me.

I was amazed at myself when it was all over. Marvin had talked to me at length about how important it was that I remain calm. And when I got there, I didn't react on an emotional level at all. Zane looked healthy and confident as he sat across the table and answered Marvin's questions. Sometimes he would laugh or chuckle as if to say, How could anybody be taking all this seriously? At other times he would try to engage in banter with the stenographer, actually flirting with her at times. His nonchalant attitude probably helped strengthen my own will to keep my emotions under control.

Zane and I were not allowed to talk with each other, of course; our lawyers kept us apart throughout the day. But afterward, I remember having a feeling of such sadness and longing. I wanted so desperately to help him. But I was beginning to understand that it wouldn't just be Zane who would be judged. As I had seen during my own deposition and now again during Zane's, nearly all his lawyer's questions were expressed so as to discredit me, to cast doubt on my truthfulness. I knew that I was going to be on trial as much as he.

—

What Marvin Lewis would always remember about Parzen's demeanor was that while the man admitted all the horrendous acts of which he was accused, at no time did he show even a trace of remorse or regret. He had done these things, but he flatly refused to confess to any wrongdoing. Parzen was cocky, arrogant, often sarcastic in his responses, as Lewis — ever so slowly and with exceeding politeness — led him through the sordid details of his illegal and unethical involvement with Evelyn Walker.

From Evelyn, Lewis already knew of Parzen's duplicitous way of answering questions — of seeming to answer without actually doing so. He frequently answered a question with a question, or with a "sometimes," "maybe" "it could be. . . ." He said he had signed the Board of Medical Quality Assurance's accusation because he had no choice; it was a "nothing or all" situation. But, he said he had never told Evelyn Walker to kill herself, had never told her she had used the wrong kind of poison in a suicide attempt. But then again, he said he might have said those things in a kindlier context. He explained that in his view, none of Evelyn's suicide attempts was "serious"; he had never prescribed drugs in a volume or strength sufficient to kill her. But, on further questioning, he had to admit that maybe these same drugs would do the job if taken together. He said he had never told Evelyn that he loved her in the way she took it; what he had meant was love in the sense of caring or concern. Yes, he was aware that to have sex with a patient under any condition was unethical, illegal. Yes, he had had sex with Evelyn Walker on numerous occasions, but not nearly as often as she had claimed.

Had he considered having sex with Evelyn a method of treatment? "Yes and no," Parzen answered.

"What do you mean by 'yes and no'?"

"She wanted to do it and I let her do it and felt that to totally say no to her would have been a problem."

In other circumstances, Parzen's answers would have been the stuff of high comedy. But Marvin Lewis refused to let these ludicrous responses stop him. He pursued Parzen relentlessly about his sexual relations with Evelyn. What about the first time Evelyn performed fellatio on Parzen? Parzen replied that she pushed him to do it by saying, "Let me make you feel good." Parzen, a strapping, physically healthy man, sat there and claimed that a woman he described as "whiny, needy," had bullied him into having sex he really did not desire.

Lewis asked, "When she put her head down on your penis, did you try to push her head away?" Parzen answered, "Initially, yes."

"Were you successful in getting her head away from your penis?" Lewis asked.

"Yes."

"Did you get angry? This woman had forced her mouth on your penis. Did you get angry?"

Mike Neil interrupted, "Just ask the question."

"All right. Did you get angry?"

"Irritated."

"Did you tell her you were irritated?"

"No. I acted as if I was — I said, 'That's not what we are here for.'"

In answer to another question, Parzen said, "She rarely had an orgasm." He knew this, he said petulantly, from "reading her complaint about me, it was that I did not satisfy her."

Lewis asked, "Now, did you ever put your mouth on her vagina?"

"Once she insisted," Parzen answered.

"Did you fight it off?"

"I tried for some time."

"Did she wrestle with you?"

"I was stronger than she was."

"Were you? All right. Now, did she grab your head and force it down on her vagina?"

"Yes."

"Did you try to pull away?"

"Slightly."

"Then, unable to do so —"

"I was able to do so."

"Did you insert your tongue in her vagina?"

"I don't believe so."

"You don't believe so. Do you know whether you did or not?"

"I don't believe so. I don't remember doing so."

Parzen was only giving Lewis the same kind of double-talk that had so upset and frustrated Evelyn Walker, but this time he did not have a captive audience of one emotionally disturbed female patient behind the locked doors of his office. At times, Parzen seemed not to understand the seriousness of the proceedings; once he laughed aloud when Lewis asked him to define *psychoanalysis*.

The most stunning revelation by Parzen came during a routine sequence of questions about his background. Lewis was "just fishing" — throwing in a question deliberately out of context to catch the witness off guard and see how he responds.

Lewis asked, "Where did you go to college?" Parzen answered, "I first went to college at Harvard University." He thus neatly avoided mentioning that he did not graduate from Harvard, but from the University of Indiana.

"Where did you get your medical training?"

"University of Chicago. School of Medicine."

"What year did you start practicing?"

"Nineteen sixty-two."

"Was that in Chicago?"

"Yes."

"Did you continue your practice there until the time you came to California?"

"Yes."

"Was there any particular reason why you left Chicago?"

"No, except for the weather."

"Did you ever have any patients of yours, female patients of yours, commit suicide in Illinois, Doctor?"

"Yes."

"How many?"

"Three."

In the same line of questioning, Parzen further admitted that another female patient in Chicago had attempted suicide, and one woman in California had killed herself after she was no longer under his care. Lewis, of course, had known nothing about any of these suicides, and was delighted to have produced such damning evidence from the accused himself. As it turned out, any mention of these suicides — and most other information about other patients Parzen had abused — would be ruled inadmissible in court by the judge.

But Evelyn Walker had been sitting there, and she knew nothing about court procedure — what could or could not be said. This new information made an indelible impression on her. Not only had other patients gone through what she had, but some had succeeded in killing themselves, as she had tried to do. This would reemerge powerfully during her testimony in the trial, and, curiously, not from anything her own lawyer advised her to say, but from Mike Neil's persistence.

Like any good general or successful politician, a trial lawyer is only as good as his staff. A lawyer as busy as Marvin Lewis simply does not have the time to spend on the extraordinary amount of research and pretrial preparation for a trial as complicated as *Walker v. Parzen*. For this, Lewis depended upon John Winer, a bright and idealistic young man fresh out of Florida State University Law School. Winer had joined the firm only a few months before the papers were filed in this suit.

One important reason why Lewis was able to maintain the friendship and respect of Evelyn Walker through what was for her an exceedingly traumatic period was that he rarely talked with her. That was one of John Winer's most important jobs — before, during, and after the trial. No matter how much was explained to her, Evelyn never seemed to understand what was going on. And Winer felt there was always the veiled, and sometimes the direct, threat of suicide because Evelyn couldn't cope with all the waiting and uncertainty. Twice in the two years before the trial, Evelyn was hospitalized because of the very real danger that she might kill herself.

Winer also handled the examination of all the witnesses (except for Evelyn and Parzen) in the pretrial depositions. And, just as important, he did all of the very complicated psychological research that went into Marvin Lewis's celebrated explanations to the jury.

In the Superior Courts in California, in damage cases such as *Walker v. Parzen,* both sides are required to come before a panel of judges and lawyers and attempt to make a settlement in order to save the time and expense of going through a trial. The two sides met at 2:45 P.M. on May 11, 1981. The written statement for Evelyn Walker summarized the facts of what had happened to her and included long excerpts from her — and Parzen's — pretrial depositions to support these facts. As Lewis and Winer presented it, Evelyn had been a happy housewife and mother with a mild depressive neurosis when she first went to see Parzen; as a result of his treatment, she lost her family and all community property and ended up with permanent and severe mental disorders diagnosed as "borderline psychosis."

Mike Neil was somewhat more colorful in his "Response to Plaintiff's Settlement Conference Statement." He wrote:

Defendant [Parzen] thinks the endeavor to portray plaintiff as the sweet little innocent "Suzy" gobbled up by the big bad wolf psychiatrist is somewhat of a fairy tale. The psychologist currently treating her describes the plaintiff as a "seductive, manipulative, derogating" type person. . . . The public image of plaintiff's marriage to Bruce Walker as being fine and dandy until, enter DR. PARZEN, is probably just that — a public image. Common experience and knowledge tells us that the couple one sees at parties and social gatherings often operates behind the façade erected for the social purpose of the visit, as one day we are shocked to hear news that Mr. and Mrs. Apple Pie are getting divorced. Defendant believes the testimony will show that although plaintiff was happy attending to her home and her children, her depression neurosis was rooted in the relationship she had with her husband, who was obsessed with a job requiring extensive travel, and not with his wife. . . . The

Defendant is not an evil sorcerer who preyed on his patients like a wolf sinks his teeth into sheep.

After four pages of refutation of what Evelyn Walker's lawyers had said, Neil finally got to the heart of the matter: The question of Parzen's guilt or innocence had nothing to do with the upcoming trial. The first and most important legal question had to do with the statute of limitations regarding malpractice. Neil contended that Evelyn Walker had last seen Parzen as a patient on January 3, 1977, and in the ensuing months and years several people had told her that what he had done was wrong. But she had not filed her suit until July 1979. She had filed too late, in other words, under California law. That part of the California malpractice statute of limitations that applied to Evelyn Walker's case specifies that a patient must file suit within one year after the patient discovers the injury — or should have discovered it with reasonable diligence.

These statutes had been more liberal in their time limitations, until they were changed in the mid-1970s at the height of what the American Medical Association saw as a "malpractice crisis." The crisis, of course, as they saw it, was not that patients were being mistreated but that so many suits were being brought against doctors. California had one of the highest rates of malpractice suits, but the vast majority of these cases were decided against the victim, in the doctor's favor.

In 1972, 137 verdicts were returned in California malpractice cases and 60 percent were in favor of the accused doctors or defendants; in 1976, when verdicts reached a high of 226, 74 percent were in the doctors' favor. All of this, the AMA reported, caused increases of from 50 to 200 percent in doctors' insurance. And all of that would be passed on to the consumer. In 1984, the AMA issued a report that said that patients would be paying a whopping $40 billion extra purely because of increased insurance payments by doctors.

In the mid-1970s, the AMA and other medical organizations successfully lobbied in nearly every state to have the statute of limitations in malpractice cases lowered — to one year in many places. But, in California, there is an interesting snare that can trap the unsuspecting doctor who employs the statute of limitations defense: In order to go into court and prove that a patient was aware of malpractice yet failed to file within the required time period, the doctor and his lawyers first have to prove that malpractice actually took place. While the point of

law being argued in such cases as Evelyn Walker's might be precisely
when the patient knew she or he had been the victim of malpractice,
the necessity of introducing all that detailed evidence about the malpractice itself could not help but sway a jury in the victim's favor.
Thus the popular concept of "justice" does not always rest on a
specific reading of the law. In fact, Mike Neil would complain bitterly
after the trial was over that the jury had not done what it was supposed
to do in rendering a verdict in *Walker v. Parzen*. He said the verdict had
nothing to do with the jurors liking Evelyn Walker but had everything
to do with their dislike of Parzen:

> She came across at the time of the trial — of course, I know her
> only as the result of an adversary situation — but she came across
> on the witness stand as a whiner and a complainer. She is not the
> type of person you feel comfortable with or want to be around.
> The verdict was not so much an award because the jury liked
> her — she does not come across as somebody you like. But it was a
> statement against what Parzen had done. There were [supposed to
> be] no punitive damages, but that was a punitive damages verdict
> by the jury. And it should have been reduced by the judge. And
> Marv Lewis expected it to be reduced and every lawyer in this town
> and every judge in this town expected it to be reduced. But the judge
> did not do what he should have done.

Actual damages are just what the words say — the jury simply deter-
mines how much the victim lost in the past or would lose in the future
as a result of the injury. Punitive damages, on the other hand, are
assessed as punishment. Many people do not understand that malpractice, or "professional negligence," is not a criminal offense, but a
civil violation of a state professional code. They read that a doctor was
assessed damages and feel he got off lightly because he was given no
prison sentence. In fact, since malpractice cases are matters of civil
violations, damages are the only punishment a court can give a doctor
who has injured a patient through malpractice. In Evelyn Walker's
case, the jury could only award actual damages, but as Mike Neil saw
it, the jury would never have awarded nearly so high a figure if they
hadn't been wanting to punish Parzen the only way they could.

The position taken by Parzen's insurance company doomed the
pretrial settlement conference for *Walker v. Parzen* to failure. Evelyn

Walker's lawyers were under the mistaken impression that Parzen carried only $1 million in malpractice insurance, so they had asked for an out-of-court settlement of $950,000. The panel of one judge and two lawyers heard both sides and came back with a recommended settlement of $500,000. Long after the trial was over, Mike Neil would say that he had urged the insurance company to settle at this point for $500,000. But the company refused and ordered Neil to go back with a figure so embarrassingly low that the judge said he would not pass it along to Evelyn Walker's lawyers. When Marvin Lewis got back to San Francisco, he received a letter from the insurance company offering a settlement of $300,000. But, by that time, he was confident of his case and refused the offer.

The trial was set to begin two weeks after the settlement conference, on May 26, 1981, before Judge Wesley B. Buttermore. Before the trial started, Judge Buttermore made several decisions regarding evidence and how the trial would proceed. It would be a bifurcated, or two-part, trial, but the same jury would hear both parts of the trial. The first part of the trial would decide the question of law — whether Evelyn Walker had, in fact, filed within the statute of limitations. If the jury were to rule against Evelyn in the first trial, there would be no second trial. But if it were found — as her lawyers contended — that Evelyn had never understood or realized that malpractice had been committed against her, then a second part of the trial would decide if that malpractice had resulted in injuries to her and, if so, just how much compensation she was entitled to.

Before the trial began, Lewis dropped the charges of assault against Parzen — which were based on his forcibly removing Evelyn from his office on January 3, 1977. And he explained why he would be asking only for actual damages and not punitive damages from Parzen. (Actual damages would be paid by Parzen's insurance company, but punitive damages would have to come from Parzen's own funds.) Lewis said he had done this because "the doctor doesn't have the assets and I wouldn't want his meager assets that I've been able to find brought out before the jury."

In another ruling on evidence, Lewis was barred by the judge from mentioning anything but the "bare essentials" about the other female patients known to have been abused by Parzen. Lewis would continue to protest — in the judge's chamber, out of the jury's hearing — that he had a right to counter certain evidence from the defense by producing details from two patients who by that time had themselves initiated legal action against Parzen. (These cases would be settled out of court.) The judge ruled against Lewis — before the trial began and four or five times during the course of the trial — because he said it was comparable to a criminal case in which a defendant's past record or his commission of other similar crimes cannot be used as evidence against him.

One line of evidence that Mike Neil presented at the settlement hearing was not carried over into the trial. This had to do with Parzen's mental state. In the settlement statement, Neil said, "To this day, Dr. Parzen was [sic] suffering from his own mental illness and was at that time operating from an unsound mind. Dr. Parzen may have been in more need of psychiatric care than the plaintiff herself." In the trial, Neil would only touch on this issue by describing Parzen's depressions following the death of his son. He knew well that if he pushed the issue, Marvin Lewis would shoot it down with one quick explanation to the jury: In the eyes of the law, a doctor's mental or physical condition is no defense in a malpractice case.

And about that word *malpractice* — the judge cautioned both sides to avoid the popular term in favor of the legal phrase "professional negligence." Parzen was not accused of any kind of criminal act; rather, he was on trial in a civil action involving a violation of the state's professional code for physicians. But this advisory by the judge would be overturned — unwittingly — by Parzen himself. When he admitted he had committed malpractice and used the word itself on the stand, he freed the plaintiff's lawyers — according to court protocol — to use the word at will. In fifty-two years at the bar, Lewis would tell the judge, "I never heard of a doctor going on the stand and saying, 'I committed malpractice.'"

On one point the judge and lawyers kept agreeing before, during, and after the trial: They had never been involved in a trial with such a complicated and confused set of circumstances as this one.

Evelyn Walker herself was not aware of any of these complex legal exchanges. All she knew was that there would now be two trials instead of one and that meant more days, weeks, months of waiting in frustration. She held to a childlike faith that a favorable verdict in court would change things in her life.

Chapter 10

At 2:10 P.M. May 26, 1981, in Department 31 of the Superior Court of San Diego, Judge Wesley B. Buttermore asked the clerk to call the next case. The clerk then read: "Walker versus Parzen."

In some states, lawyers are given a *venire* of names of prospective jurors well in advance of a trial. They can then prepare elaborate psychological profiles to see whether a person might or might not be favorably disposed toward their case. However, in California, there is no such advance warning. The process of selecting a jury even varies among the several jurisdictions in the state. The way Judge Buttermore handled it was to call in a panel of twelve prospective jurors and talk with them as a group and individually and then let the lawyers question them (in a procedure called *voir dire*) to see if there was anything in their current lives or backgrounds that might cause them to be prejudiced against either side.

Although Marvin Lewis said that the jury selection "was one of the most important parts of a psychiatric case," in fact, the *voir dire* examination of potential jurors — a process that can often take days or even weeks in a trial of this consequence — took less than one day in this case. Neither side even used up its preemptory challenges, which allow an attorney to excuse specific jurors without cause. Ten women and two men were selected for the jury, with two women as alternates (in case something happened to one of the regular jurors before all the evidence was heard).

Although the lawyers and the judge himself would complicate the issue in the long days of the trial ahead, the judge explained at the beginning, in simple concise language, what the jurors were to decide in the first part of the trial:

269

"You are not trying the question of whether or not the doctor did something wrong. You are not trying the question of whether or not the plaintiff is entitled to damages. You are merely deciding whether or not the suit was filed on time. That's a simple approach.

"Now, you are going to hear a lot of evidence about the conduct of the parties, and you may have some value judgments as to what they did, whether it was right, wrong, proper or improper, or what. But, regardless of those feelings, the question will be one before you, a very simple question: Was the lawsuit filed on time?

"Now, the reason you are going to hear all this other evidence is because it relates to the question of the emotional condition of the plaintiff, or the knowledge she may have had as to what transpired, or whether she did in fact discover, or she should have discovered, the harm that is alleged to have resulted from this relationship, and filed her suit thereafter within a year. Now, that in a broad sense, is what we're talking about."

Before the first day of testimony began at 9:08 A.M., May 28, 1981, the judge went further in this explanation of the statute of limitations. "Our law provides that, in an action or an injury based upon a doctor's alleged professional negligence, the time for the commencement of the action — that is, the filing of the complaint appearing in the courthouse — the time to do that is one year after the plaintiff discovers, or through the use of reasonable diligence should have discovered, the injury. The complaint in this case was filed July 11, 1979."

In his opening statement, Marvin Lewis wasted no time in getting right to this very point: "So we are going to show you here in this case by proof that, number one, Mrs. Parzen had no way of knowing—"

The judge interrupted, "You mean Mrs. Walker?"

It was a slip Lewis had made in his pretrial examination of Zane Parzen and it was one he would continue to make throughout the trial. He did it so often, in fact, that Parzen's own lawyer would refer to Evelyn as "Mrs. Parzen" once and to Bruce Walker as "Mr. Parzen." Lewis would explain that he had just handled a case for a Mrs. Parsons and that was the reason for his mistake. However, given the circumstances of this case, one cannot imagine a more devastatingly effective slip of the tongue—or say what effect this might have had on the witnesses (especially Parzen himself) or on the jurors. After all, wasn't this a case involving confusion of roles? And wasn't "Mrs. Parzen" exactly who Evelyn Walker had been led to believe she would become?

Lewis continued: " — that Mrs. Walker had no way of knowing that her injury was being aggravated, and that new mental injuries were being precipitated and triggered by her psychiatrist, Dr. Parzen. And further, that she had no realization and under her state of mind didn't even know that what was being done to her was constituting malpractice on the part of a physician to a patient. Nor did she know the subtleties of the type of acts that were aggravating or were causing this aggravation of condition.

"And even as of today, she does not fully comprehend and fully realize, because of her present mental condition and the mental condition that she has had for a long period of time, either the injury, the full amount of the injury, or the type of actions upon the part of Dr. Parzen that caused that injury to her."

Evelyn Walker was not present in the courtroom as Marvin Lewis described her. Perhaps one of his reasons for choosing not to have her present was so that he would be free to describe her as he wished, without upsetting her. But in his opening statement, and several times later in the trial, he would explain to the jury that Evelyn could not be there because of her unstable mental condition. There is no question that hearing all the evidence for and against her would have been a traumatic ordeal for Evelyn, but there are other, more practical reasons why she wasn't there.

John Winer explains that his boss, Lewis, "literally invented how to try a psychological case." And one of the primary rules Lewis had developed, Winer says, was to keep the victim away, out of sight of the jury except whenever the victim himself or herself is testifying. Lewis reasons that if the jurors see the victim day in and day out, they get used to whatever is supposed to be wrong with the victim. Also, in the boredom of hearing the tedious psychological testimony, the jurors cannot help but examine the victim and play detective or psychologist themselves. They begin to wonder: Is she really damaged or injured? By keeping the victim out of court, the attorney can start conditioning or educating the jury on the very peculiar nature of the case, which is particularly important, Winer says, since the defense attorney is going to try to laugh it out of court. The attorney offers expert testimony from a psychiatrist, who explains why the victim cannot be there, and then, before the victim testifies, explains to the jury that the victim may come up with inappropriate behavior, and they may not like what they see. But, as Lewis would explain to this jury: "The very reasons you don't like her may be exactly why we're here."

Lewis's insistence that Evelyn not be present in court left Evelyn alone at home, anxiously waiting to hear how her life was being described, how her fate was being decided.

I remember going into court with Marvin Lewis the first morning the trial was to begin. Gary Shepherd sat with me and Marvin and John Winer sat at the plaintiff's table up front. The morning was spent on preliminary legal wrangles back and forth over procedures for the trial, all of which utterly confused me.

The four of us — Marvin, John, Gary, and I — had lunch together before the trial was to start that afternoon. Marvin suddenly announced to me that he was not going to bring me into court except for the days that I would be testifying. This was a totally unexpected and devastating blow to me. I was very upset because I had planned and thought about this trial for so long. To me, it was a chance to hear what everybody had to say about me. I had thought that if I heard it all out, maybe I would be able to leave it all behind me and go on to something else. I wanted to hear Zane Parzen in open court; I wanted to know just how he would explain to others what he had done to me; I wanted to hear him say he was sorry for all the hurt and pain he had caused me. And this was going to be denied me. I was so upset I could hardly talk. Logically, I understood Marvin's explanation of why I shouldn't be in the courtroom. But on a deeper emotional level, I felt I was being robbed of something that was very important to me.

But I accepted Marvin's decision; I had to trust him to know what he was doing. Then I had to go home and wait. I had to stay home all those days — it was a very bizarre feeling. I remember nothing but anxious hour after anxious hour — as I tried to keep busy and not think about what was happening, about how my life was in the hands of other people in that courtroom. I could hardly wait for the end of each day when John would call and report to me on what had happened that day in court. My trial was taking place and I wasn't there to know what was being said; more important, I wasn't there to see and hear Zane.

I had arranged my life without Zane. I had been living with a wonderful man, Paul Adams, for some months, and we were very much in love and very happy. But there was still a part of me that belonged to Zane—I knew or felt that I was never going to be out of reach of him, he could call me back at any time. And yet, underneath that emotional attachment to his memory, there was within me a core of reality that knew this trial was the absolute end of everything between us. I knew I would never see him and certainly never speak with him again. It was a dramatic conclusion—and it was taking place without me. I sat home waiting, waiting, waiting.

━

Lewis traced Evelyn Walker's history for the jurors—from her parents' escape from Nazi Austria through her troubled childhood in Chicago, from her happy marriage to Bruce Walker through the birth of her two sons, whom she loved and cared for, and on up to when she started psychotherapy with Zane Parzen.

Lewis said, "The doctors will tell you, that during this type of psychotherapy, where the doctor is questioning the patient, he should become almost like a blank wall. His personality should be completely out of it because normally what takes place is a transference phenomena that is well known to psychiatrists and well known to psychologists."

That word, *transference,* and a confusing array of different definitions of it, would be tossed around throughout the trial. As Lewis first defined it, transference was when "the patient who sits there in the office and is being treated starts transferring whatever their affection, or whatever their needs are from some person or persons, to the doctor who is the treating doctor. And there becomes this bond that is being established under the transference phenomena between the doctor who is giving the psychoanalysis and the patient. . . . The doctors will also testify that psychiatrists and psychologists are taught, as one of their first fundamental lessons, that this transference phenomena is an explosive type of thing that can be so dangerous in the hands of a psychiatrist, a psychologist, if it isn't used properly, the psychiatrist can then use it and manipulate it more even than hypnosis. It's in his power to do so.

"They will also tell you that another well-known problem in this type of psychotherapy treatment is what is known as 'countertransference,' and they will tell you that countertransference is when the psychiatrist—and this is normal—starts to get feelings about his patient that are maybe personal feelings. He may think, 'Now that patient is attractive. She's kind of cute,' or 'I don't like her,' or 'I think she's a whiny type of woman,' or miserable or whatever it may be. And because he's human, he starts getting these thoughts in his head. That's all right, the doctors will say, up to a point.

"But no psychiatrist is permitted or allowed to act upon that transference and the doctors will testify that in their opinion what Dr. Zane Parzen did, he not only misused the transference phenomena but he used and misused and acted upon the countertransference phenomena and all of this.

"We will prove that Mrs. Walker never knew what a transference phenomena was. Mrs. Walker never knew what a countertransference was. Mrs. Walker had no idea that it was explosive in nature, if not handled properly . . . and what this was doing to her, where he was becoming — it was more than love. It was a Svengali type of ideation for this doctor, where it became almost a master/slave relationship, and all of this time the doctor now is reemphasizing, as the evidence will show, the fact that she's got to get away from her husband and those children as soon as possible because this is a very dangerous situation for her."

Evelyn Walker decided to bring suit, according to Lewis, after "learning that there had been other women patients who had been so abused, for the first time it dawns on her that possibly there is a cause of action and to sue Dr. Parzen for malpractice. And for the first time, she's starting to see that this is malpractice and not just a love affair where a woman has been scorned by her lover."

She had this realization, Lewis contended, after hearing the evidence at the two hearings of the Psychoanalytic Institute and Society in January and April of 1979 — either of which would put her well within the one-year limit for filing a suit.

Lewis concluded that not only had Evelyn Walker not realized the extent or even the fact of the damage done to her within the statute of limitations, she *still* did not know or understand. He said if Zane Parzen tomorrow "would snap his fingers, she would come running back into his arms, feeling that the two of them could go off into the sunset."

In his opening statement, Mike Neil rambled on in a long, disjointed speech. He made no mention of any kind of character witnesses for the defendant—because there were none. In other words, there would be no defense of the man himself or what he had done— for the simple reason that he had already confessed to nearly every one of the acts in question. There was disagreement as to "exactly what took place all the time" between Parzen and Evelyn Walker, but, he added, "there is no question that sex was involved." He emphasized here and continued to do so throughout the trial that whether Parzen was right or wrong was not a question for the jury to decide. "The question you have to decide is whether or not this case was timely filed after she quit seeing Dr. Parzen on January 3, 1977." Neil told the jurors that several witnesses would testify that they had told Evelyn Walker that what had been done to her was wrong and that she was fully intelligent and able to understand what was being said to her. These witnesses would include Evelyn's second husband, a hypnotist she went to see with him, a woman psychologist who directed a Gestalt therapy program that Evelyn enrolled in, and the psychiatrist who saw her immediately after she left Parzen. Neil also said Evelyn's family physician explained to her just how and why what Parzen had done was wrong—and he added that Evelyn had become involved sexually with this same physician as she had been involved with Parzen two years earlier.

Neil said Evelyn Walker had filed this lawsuit for one reason only —"financial gain." The judge stopped him and said, "I think you are arguing your case now; just tell them what the evidence will show." Neil apologized to the court and told the jury once again that "any value judgments as to what was right or wrong should play no role in your decision here, and I'm sure they won't."

Gary Shepherd was the first witness for Evelyn Walker. Lewis would use him not only as a key eyewitness to what had happened to Evelyn under Parzen's care, but also as an expert witness in the whole field of psychiatry and analysis.

"What is psychoanalysis?" Lewis asked.

"Psychoanalysis is a—well, it's two things. One, it's a body of knowledge, a psychology [sic] way of understanding human behavior; and secondly, it's a method of treatment. It's a type of psychotherapy.

"The nature of the therapy process is one in which you see a patient several times a week, usually with them lying on a couch. You withhold any significant information about yourself, your personal life—

sort of a blank screen concept—that encourages the patient to develop feelings about you that relate to feelings and experiences they have had towards important people in their own past—mother, father, grandparents, uncles—but very significant people from their early life."

"Does that have a medical term for it?"

"It's called *transference*."

"And is there a term known as *transference phenomena*?" Lewis asked.

"Yes."

"And would you explain to us what is transference phenomena."

"Well, it's a phenomena of transferring those feelings toward someone in the past onto the person of the analyst in the present situation, so that you begin to have feelings toward the analyst like you had towards that important person in the past. . . . And in their being able to realize that the feelings they are having toward the analyst really represent the feelings from the past, and to work those through — in other words, to develop them—that's the curative process that comes about, and freeing them, in a sense, from childhood, or early experiences that still are shadows in their lives at the time they come into treatment."

"Now, Doctor, you mentioned, while this is going on, the doctor should keep his own life, while with the patient, blank. What is the reason for that?" Lewis asked.

"The reason for that is because you're trying to create an atmosphere for the patient to believe about you whatever they wish; to develop whatever kinds of feelings they want to.

"Now, if they know a lot about you, if they know about your politics, if they know about your interests in music and art, and how many kids you have, and that kind of thing, it's going to be a lot more difficult for them to make you into someone from their past, because they know too much about you."

"Now, Doctor, can this transference phenomena, if used or misused by the doctor who is conducting this type of therapy—can it be harmful or explosive?"

"Yes, it can."

"And will you explain to us what is the danger if this transference phenomena is not used properly, and why?"

"Yes. That's really a large part of what my nine years of training was about. It is enough of a problem that I feel, as an analyst, and as do all analysts, that the reason for such long training is that you're dealing with a very explosive or powerful phenomena, and if you don't know how to use it appropriately, it can be damaging."

Lewis then said, "Well, would you give us — I know it's difficult in this short time, and we're all lay people, and in a courtroom, and you've taken nine years — but can you, as best you can, in a simplified way, give us the mechanics of how this becomes detrimental or harmful, and how it comes about?"

"Yes, I think I can do that.

"One of the very prominent kinds of transference phenomena that will develop is that a patient in this situation, after a period of time, very likely will develop feelings of love toward you.

"Now, this wouldn't necessarily be romantic love. It might be the love a child would have for a mother — it could also be a father, an uncle, whoever — that they can develop very, very strong very positive feelings toward you that are neurotic, but that's really what you're trying to develop in the analysis, so it can be treated.

"They develop these feelings, and initially have the expectation that somehow their wishes and desires are going to be fulfilled.

"Well, of course, then the analyst has the patient in an extremely vulnerable position, in that they have neurotic feelings towards him of a very powerful nature, of seeing him as a very powerful father or mother, or uncle, or combination of all three. And because of their sort of idealization, then, of the analyst, he has a lot of power in his hands, and if he isn't careful in what he does, I think you can see he has the power and the potential to cause them harm because of the fact that they're so needy at that point, and so reliant upon what he does and says, and there is so much idealization that goes on that it's a very tricky situation.

"So that's why the training is needed, to know how to handle that appropriately, and not cause problems for the patient.

"An aspect of the problem and the reasons why psychoanalytic training is as long as it is is that the analyst has to have his own psychoanalysis to try and deal with his own neurotic problems, his own distortions, and sort of get his psychological life straightened out. The reason for that is because he's also a person who had parents, important people in his earlier life, or in her earlier life, and in the course of this very intensive kind of treatment modality, he can also develop feelings that really have origins, let's say, in his own past."

"Doctor, does this have a name to it in psychiatry?"

"Countertransference. . . ."

"And what is countertransference?"

"Well, it's the development of feelings on the part of the analyst — and you see this not just in psychoanalysis, but in other forms of psychotherapy as well. It's the development on the part of the analyst of feelings that really have origins in the analyst's own past and don't necessarily relate to the patient, let's say, in the present, but he's responding to something in the patient that sort of strikes a chord with something in his own past and he can develop transference.

"But if it's the analyst doing it, then we call it countertransference phenomena, and those feelings can be a feeling of disliking a patient intensely for no logical reason. It may be even having a sexual feeling, whatever. Any kind of feeling is possible.

"By virtue of the training of an analyst, in his own analysis and the fact that there's always consultation available from other analysts, if you feel you're having a problem with a case, he should be in a position to observe his own countertransference feelings, and, because of his own analysis and training, remove those from the treatment situation, so that his feelings about the patient do not become a part of what's going on between them, so that his actions aren't based upon his needs, his feelings, his wants, so that what he does in the therapy process is really going to be something that's helpful to the patient. And it certainly isn't going to be helpful to the patient if he's trying to use them, in a sense, to get gratification for himself of whatever kind. . . ."

"And are you saying that the psychiatrist, psychoanalyst, should not act upon the countertransference feelings?"

"Absolutely not."

"And, if he does act upon these countertransference feelings, what, if anything, can he do to the mind of the patient he's treating?"

"He can precipitate psychotic episodes. Some patients are a little sicker than others. He can certainly increase the severity of the mental illness.

"There are certainly instances where suicide has resulted from the mishandling of countertransference or a psychiatrist acting on his countertransference, either in a positive kind of way, or in a negative way. Where he conveys in some fashion to the patient that he doesn't like them, whether he actually uses the words or not, his feelings get out and interfere and the patient acts out. It increases the severity of pathology. It can really destroy their life. It can destroy their ability to trust.

"There's no — except maybe with a mother and child, and then only for a few years of life — there's probably no greater, in a sense, a trusting relationship that develops in the course of an analysis when you're talking about several years of therapy, in which as a patient, you are telling your analyst the deepest, darkest secrets of your life, from childhood, things that probably you've never told your husband, friends, or anyone else. In order for the process to work, you really have to open up and let him know everything.

"Now, when you open yourself up to that degree, you've made yourself pretty vulnerable, so that the psychiatrist, the psychoanalyst, has a real responsibility to be sure that, with all this information, he doesn't cause the patient harm through his actions or through his inactions, and certainly not through any actions on his part that are based on his own needs, or his own wishes or desires."

Lewis then led Shepherd through a slow and careful definition of the other terms that would come out in the trial. He explained what the unconscious is and the difference between a neurosis and a psychosis. After this brief summary of psychoanalysis, Shepherd was then asked to tell on a personal level about his former neighbor Evelyn Walker and what he saw happen to her.

When he first knew her — before she started seeing Parzen — he said, "She was very outgoing, verbal on the occasions, let's say, where there were people over   like a party, some sort of get-together. She could play a prominent role in talking to people, being the life of the party kind of thing. As I say, very outgoing. She was very active as an artist. . . . She was very talented, she did all kinds of crafts, some very artistic kinds of weaving, she did a lot of pottery, she sold a lot of it. Very good stuff. . . . She was busy doing that, busy being a housewife, mother, and seemed like a reasonably happy, active, involved person."

Then, after she had been seeing Parzen for several months, Shepherd said, he saw her becoming more and more moody, going out of the house less. Then, in 1975, Shepherd said he learned, first from others and then from Evelyn herself, that she was in fact having a sexual relationship with her psychiatrist.

Lewis asked, "generally speaking," if it were harmful for a psychiatrist to have sex with his patients in the office.

Shepherd replied, "The reason has to do with transference kind of reasons I detailed earlier. The code of medical ethics, the code of psychiatric ethics, the code of psychological ethics, or psychologists or any health profession, that's a strictly and absolutely forbidden activity on the part of the physician because there's almost no instance where that wouldn't cause harm."

Shepherd further described the changes he saw in Evelyn. "I saw a lady who, up to that time, I had seen as a pretty outgoing, reasonably happy, capable person, functioning in the world, become extremely moody, depressed. She began to spend a good portion of the day in bed. There were times when I'm not sure she got dressed or maybe even got out of the bed except twice a week when she went to see Dr. Parzen."

Shepherd was asked why he had not tried to explain to Evelyn that what Parzen was doing was malpractice and not good for her. He explained that "her mental state was such, in terms of her level of disorganization, impairment of reality testing, her complete belief in the integrity and honesty and goodness of Dr. Parzen, that she wouldn't have believed it and probably would then have not talked to me anymore, which would not have been helpful to her either."

The key question, of course, was whether Shepherd felt that Evelyn Walker "right up to the present time . . . has any true understanding of what Dr. Parzen did to her, and how or the mechanics of how that was done, or that it was done?"

"A few months — this is the best way to answer it that I can think of. A few months ago, maybe three or four months ago, I got a call — and it wasn't the only time I ever got that kind of a call — but I got a call from her, in which, again, she was sounding very much like a little girl, very distraught and very upset, and was saying that she thought that maybe all this [the case against Parzen] was wrong, and this was untrue, that Zane really had never done anything to her, that maybe it was just everybody else that was saying that he had — and that she thought she could go out and find him. Which scared the hell out of me."

In answer to another question, Shepherd explained, "I know she's filed a lawsuit, but there is no question in my mind that if he appeared at her door and said, 'I love you, come with me,' that she would drop whatever she was doing and go."

Mike Neil did not waste time educating the jury on psychoanalysis or on polite questions about Shepherd's qualifications. He said Shepherd knew about the statute of limitations and that that was the key to this trial. He implied that Shepherd had met and talked about all this many times with Evelyn Walker and her lawyers—and he further implied that Shepherd might say anything that would help his friend's case.

But Shepherd felt he had nothing to hide and answered strongly in the affirmative to all of Neil's accusatory questions—until he came to this one: "And are you being paid to testify here today?"

"No."

Later, Neil asked, "Doctor, do you not have guilt feelings about the fact that you did not stop this relationship back when it was first brought to your attention and allowed it to continue in the—"

Shepherd interrupted to answer, "No, I don't."

Neil's questioning got even more pointed. "Doctor, do you blame yourself for what her present condition is?"

"No, I don't."

"Have you ever considered that you yourself might probably be sued by Evelyn Walker for malpractice should she—"

"Never entered—"

"—lose this lawsuit?"

"—my mind."

After questioning Shepherd about his own motives, Neil later asked Shepherd about Evelyn Walker's motives: "Doctor, isn't it true that the real reason why Mrs. Walker went forward with her complaint against Dr. Parzen with the Psychoanalytic Society was that she had no source of income, and she felt, by proceeding against Dr. Parzen, she would guarantee herself income in some form, either by way of a malpractice action or by way of some payment by Dr. Parzen to keep her quiet?"

"Absolutely not," Shepherd replied.

After Gary Shepherd stepped down, Marvin Lewis called Zane Dribin Parzen as an adversary witness for Evelyn Walker. More than anybody in that courtroom, Zane Parzen stood alone. There were no members of his family, no friends or colleagues there to give him moral support. Even his own lawyer seemed to distance himself from his client. In a case involving lengthy questioning, it is not unusual for a lawyer to spend most of the periodic recesses together with his client, discussing what's been said and what might be asked next. But Parzen and his lawyer were rarely seen having such conferences. During one recess, John Winer left the plaintiff's table and went over and chatted with Parzen out of pity for any man left so alone. It was small talk of the most shallow kind, but a grand gesture in that setting — the only kind words Parzen would hear in the course of the trial.

Ironically, whatever preparation Parzen's lawyer may have provided Parzen for the intensive questioning from Marvin Lewis, it was Parzen himself who offered the most conclusive evidence — much of it needlessly volunteered by him — that would seal the case against him.

The routine opening questions elicited the bare facts of the recent tragedies in Parzen's life and career.

"Are you a practicing doctor?" Lewis asked.

"No."

"And are you a married man, Doctor?"

"No."

Yes, he had been a practicing psychiatrist from 1962 to 1980, and yes, he had been married, but the divorce was finalized just two weeks earlier.

The questioning was following a routine pattern — with Lewis asking expected questions, such as when Parzen first started seeing Evelyn Walker, and how she appeared at that time. Then, Lewis threw a curve: "Now, Doctor, prior to this time that you saw her, you had been having sexual relations with other patients of yours in your office — isn't that true?"

Mike Neil jumped to his feet in protest. "Your Honor, may we approach the bench on that question?" The lawyers squared off in front of the judge out of the hearing of the jury.

Neil said, "I wish to cite Mr. Lewis for misconduct in asking what is clearly an improper question." He said it had been decided before the trial began that there would be no mention of Parzen's involvement with other patients, except in bare detail to explain when and why Evelyn Walker filed the suit. Neil said the jury should be admonished not to consider the question because it was improper. Lewis fired back, "No, it's perfectly proper for this — "

The judge said, "Keep your voice down." Then Lewis said his question was proper because it established Evelyn's state of mind when she filed the suit. The judge admonished Lewis to lower his voice again and sustained Neil's objection.

In legal textbook fashion, Lewis asked Parzen about proper ethics and proper treatment in psychiatry and analysis — and then promptly asked a question that showed that what Parzen had done with Evelyn Walker was improper by his own definitions.

Lewis used Parzen to prove Evelyn Walker's claims of injury. "Doctor, would you say that a person who has the type of neurosis that you said Mrs. Evelyn Walker had when she went to you as a patient, if they were not properly treated by either a psychiatrist or a psychoanalyst, they could have the mental injury aggravated by a doctor?"

"Yes," Parzen answered.

Lewis used Parzen himself to contradict points made by Parzen's own lawyer. Neil had tried to show that because Evelyn had been "lucid" in the two days it took to take her pretrial deposition, and in the time during and after she was seeing Parzen, that one could assume she had also been lucid enough to understand that a malpractice had been committed against her. However, Lewis asked Parzen to corroborate that "a person who has a borderline psychosis can be out of touch with reality with a particular subject, and yet be perfectly lucid on other subjects; isn't that true?"

Parzen answered, "Yes."

"And by the time that Mrs. Parzen left your office, you believed, did you not, that she had a borderline psychosis?"

"For the record, you meant Mrs. Walker," Parzen said, and then answered, "Yes."

In one of the more tedious but effective parts of his questioning, Lewis took almost a half hour to read slowly, carefully, into the record all of Parzen's own notes on the drugs that he had prescribed for Evelyn Walker. The cumulative impact was devastating. Starting with a mild prescription for two Empirin for a headache on her first visit, the prescriptions steadily escalated to heavier and heavier strengths and numbers — of Seconal, Valium, Noludar, Elavil, Talwin, Placidyl. And, repeating the words over and over, twice a week, through 1975 and 1976, more and more Elavil, Valium, Noludar. . . .

Lewis spent some time questioning Parzen about the office notes and longer reports he had made on patient Evelyn Walker. "Now, when you prepared these kind of reports, Doctor, that I've been reading from, did you believe at some time that maybe these reports would be seen by other psychiatrists or other psychoanalysts who might be possibly judging what had gone on between you and your patient?"

"No."

"In other words, were you preparing self-serving reports?"

"No."

"Never had that in mind?"

"Never."

Parzen then explained that "every report—except the one dated January 3, the last report, the other reports were all for my own information and were part of the patient's records, and were confidential. They could not have been shown to anyone except under these circumstances."

The January 3 report was after "my kicking her out" (as Parzen himself phrased it on the stand), about which Lewis questioned him at length because he had clearly lied in that report. In it, Parzen had said that Evelyn was suffering from a "psychoticlike transference" in which she fantasized about having sex with him and being married to him. He sent her off for treatment with another psychiatrist, in other words, based on this false report that she was fantasizing about her relationship with him. About the lies contained in that report, Parzen volunteered, "That had some—I don't know if I would use the word *self-serving*, but it had some documentation effect at a different level." A convoluted way of saying, yes, he had lied to protect himself.

Lewis went into even more detail on the sexual misconduct of Parzen with Evelyn Walker. He asked if it would not be harmful for a doctor to perform "acts of sex with that patient in his office, such as masturbating her, or putting his mouth on her privates, or vice versa, or sexual intercourse?"

Parzen answered indirectly, as he had so often to Evelyn Walker's questions, "I don't believe that would necessarily substantiate the other."

"Would you say that would be unethical, in your opinion, Doctor?"

"Yes."

"And would you say that you've been taught that that's harmful to do to a patient?"

"Yes."

"And why, Doctor, why is it harmful?"

"It's harmful, according to some people, most people teach that it's harmful because it leads to intensification of feelings."

"And in your opinion, there was a severe intensification of feelings caused by sexual relations you had with Mrs. Walker in your office, isn't that true?"

"I believe the intensification was there, aside from the sexual activities."

"You did have acts of sex with her, did you not?"

"Yes."

Parzen was consistent in saying that while he had engaged in sexual acts he claimed Evelyn initiated, he had never told her that he loved her or that he would marry her. He said, "I believe, if you would follow those notes, there is a statement there that I was not going to — actually tried to tell her that I did not love her. I was not going to run off with her."

"But you continued to have sexual relations with her — "

"Yes."

" — didn't you? Did you think that continuing to have sexual relations with this patient was going to help to alleviate these feelings that she had about you?"

"May I explain myself?"

"Yes."

"My feeling was that she could not tolerate rejection; she could not tolerate the rage that she felt any time she got rejected, and that to prematurely stop something, whether it was good or bad, would have driven her to suicide attempts that may have been really serious.

"At that point, I felt her suicide attempts were to try and manipulate me to continue to give more to her, and more of what she wanted, and I thought it was too dangerous to stop at that point."

In answer to other questions, Parzen explained that he had a long-range plan for patient Evelyn Walker of "giving to her for a short period of time. And with the idea of slowly, over a period of time, weaning her from me."

"Did you feel that having sex with her was weaning her from you?"

"At that point I didn't feel she could tolerate the wean. At some point I felt that would be what would have to happen."

Lewis then got Parzen to admit that the "closeness" they developed between them was as much his fault as hers. Parzen answered, "I believe I allowed it to happen, yes."

"And did you feel that by allowing it to happen in the way you did that was malpractice, Doctor?"

"In terms of the law, yes, that was malpractice."

"And not only in terms of the law, but in terms of medicine, it was malpractice?"

"In terms of standard psychiatric psychoanalytic ethics, that was malpractice."

Lewis continued to push for permission to introduce evidence about the other women patients Parzen had abused in his office. In one session in the judge's chamber, he said, "There's another reason now why these other women should come in. He [Parzen] has said that the reason he had sex with her in her particular situation was because he felt that if he didn't have sex with her, she'd commit suicide, and I think it's only proper to point out that the real reason he had sex with her is because, as he said later, she was tall, thin, and the type that he would have sex with. And, in fact, he asked permission to practice as a psychiatrist, but not to see these patients, women that were tall and thin and weighed the amount of pounds that Mrs. Walker weighed."

But, once again, the judge ruled that Parzen's malpractice was not the issue in this trial; the only question involved was the statute of limitations — so this other evidence about other patients was not admissible.

Like a bulldog after a bone on the other side of a fence, Lewis kept after it, but he never quite got the evidence included. His questions — although objected to and ruled out by the judge — let the jurors know that it was possible there were other women abused by Parzen. When the information about these women — and the suicides in Chicago — did emerge in a dramatic moment before the jury, it was Parzen's own lawyer who brought it about.

Lewis was just fishing when he got an extraordinary confession out of Parzen on the witness stand.

"Doctor, at any time while she was a patient of yours, or at any subsequent time, did you ever advise her that you had committed a malpractice on her?"

"No."

"Did you ever tell her that she should consult a doctor, or make inquiry of anyone to ascertain whether you had committed a malpractice on her?"

"No."

"And, in your opinion, do you believe now that you have committed a malpractice on her?"

"Yes."

"And when did you first have that realization or belief?"

"I don't know if I could really answer exactly when. I mean, certainly over the last two years, but I don't know when I would say that I really came to a full awareness of it."

"Well, could it have been sometime around July of 1978?" [A year before Evelyn Walker filed suit, the key date in the trial; if she had known before this, then the suit was improperly filed.]

"Well, could it have been sometime around July of 1978?"

"I don't know about July of 1978 particularly."

"Or somewhere around the middle of '78?"

"It could be," Parzen answered.

"Why do you believe that it was so late in time that you yourself realized that you committed a malpractice on her?"

"I think the issue has to do with my own particular state of mind during various parts of what's happened over the last five, six — almost nine years."

"Well, then, do you believe, Doctor, that because of a state of mind, someone would be unable, like you, to even realize that they had committed an act of malpractice?"

"I think — if at a certain point some of my colleagues had confronted me, I would have had to face it."

"But you hadn't faced it yourself?"

"At that point, I hadn't. No."

"I see," said Lewis.

"That's one of the paradoxes of any problem," Parzen added.

"And that's because of your — all right. Let it go at that," said Lewis. He could let it go, all right, because Parzen had unwittingly brought up, answered, and resolved the key question of this trial. Parzen's state of mind was not an issue; the issue was whether a person like Evelyn Walker could have known when and if a malpractice was committed against her. If her doctor, with all his years of training, didn't know, how could she — diagnosed as a borderline psychotic — be expected to know when and if it had happened?

Then it was Mike Neil's turn to lead Parzen through a more positive description of the same events. Neil went over Parzen's educational training in detail — especially the thirteen years of postgraduate training in medicine, psychiatry, and psychoanalysis. And then he brought Parzen's biography up to California in 1971 and asked about the following year. "Did you experience a tragedy in your own life, sir?"

"My oldest son, a fifteen-year-old, was killed in an auto accident after — he was in a coma for two months and then died."

The son's death, Parzen would explain further, "affected me very deeply. When my son was dying, and my wife felt that she could not continue to be a mother to the other children, so I had to make all the decisions about my son — life, death, what-have-you — on my own. I went to the hospital daily for those two months, and I don't think I ever quite got over having to make the decision that we had to end things; that there was no hope. . . . We took him off life support."

There were other tragedies in addition to his son's death that Parzen was asked to enumerate — his stepfather, his only brother, and his mother had also died in recent years.

"Doctor, during the years 1974, 75, 76, do you have any opinion as to whether you yourself were laboring under any mental incapacity or disability?"

"I think there's a lot of evidence that I was."

And then, through his lawyer's friendly questions, Parzen was finally able to give his version of the events that Evelyn Walker had described:

"She [Evelyn Walker] came in and she sat mutely in the chair with glasses on, and I believe she had the dark glasses at one point, and she wouldn't talk. And I said, 'You've got to say what's on your mind, or what's bothering you.' And I asked her is there anything in her marriage, and she said, 'No, no. Everything is perfect.' And I said, 'It sounds like you are protesting everything too much.' And she said, 'I won't say anything negative about my husband.'

"And she persisted for two or three sessions. She wouldn't say anything negative. And I finally pointed out to her, by her not saying anything negative, it was obvious that there were a lot of negatives there that she couldn't deal with, with her anger at him, and then she began to talk about a lot of the marital difficulties that had been going on: his affairs, relationships, the feeling that he was just using her, and so on. Then the marital problem became only too evident. . . .

"She would come into the office and cry, and not talk, and she literally spent two or three sessions just sobbing.

"My office was set up with the patient's chair, my chair, and an ottoman footstool in between, and I got up and I sat on the ottoman, on her side of the ottoman, and put my hand on her shoulder and said, 'I know something is hurting you. You've got to talk about it, though. Maybe you'll feel better if you'll talk about it.'"

Neil interrupted here to ask, "Now, going back to your training back in Chicago, this type of contact of touching a patient, perhaps putting your arm around a patient, was this taught as an acceptable technique in psychiatric counseling or treatment?"

Parzen answered, "At the time that I was in Chicago, certainly with children it was done all the time, holding the child even on your lap, if they were scared.

"We began using this technique very routinely with patients with medical illness within the time that I was — I believe for four years I was running an inpatient service at Michael Reese Hospital, the psychiatric unit. It was a closed unit for disturbed patients. The holding of a patient, the walking down with an arm around someone's waist, or if someone got bad news and was scared, to hold them at that point was fairly acceptable."

Neil asked, "And the medical reason, or the psychiatric reason for doing so is what, aside from just being a human being about it?"

Parzen answered, "Well, there are two aspects that go into being a psychiatrist, or doctor: One is a technician, or the so-called blank screen that just reflects back; but the other part is the real relationship that seems to make it possible for people to expose the painful part of themselves. And if you are going through enough pain, whether it's something purely psychiatric, or if it's something like you've just been told you have cancer, it had become, even in the early seventies and the late sixties, a very important thing to have physical contact with the person at that point. It's a way of not feeling as alone. . . . it has to do with recognizing that when a person is in pain, you have to do something to help at that moment. And if being held helps, then they can go on."

"Doctor, during the time that you cared for and treated Mrs. Walker, was it always your intent to help her?"

"Yes."

"Was it ever your intent to harm her, or to hurt her in any manner?" Neil asked.

Parzen answered, with a curious qualification, "During the time I was seeing her, I never had that intention."

"Now, did you see the movie *Ordinary People*, by the way?" Neil asked.

"I saw part of it."

"And did you see the scene where the psychiatrist puts his arm around the boy in the movie? Is this the type of touching that you are talking about?"

"Yeah."

Returning to his narration of his relationship with Evelyn Walker, Parzen explained that one day Evelyn was crying and he came and sat on the ottoman in front of her, "and I put my hand on her shoulder and held her. . . . To let her feel when she was obviously feeling scared and frightened, to give her some sense of security at that moment, so that maybe she could then relate a little more about what was the problem. . . . The relationship got out of hand because she wanted more, and I couldn't say no. . . . It started off with just my holding her, and then her wanting me to kiss her on the cheek, and then she began to move to kiss her on the mouth, and then moved from one rank of things in sexuality order, to higher and higher degrees of intimacy, which she looked at as acceptance. If I did not have sex with her, she felt I really didn't care for her; or I was not accepting her; I didn't really care for her, and so on. And, from my own problems at that point, I did not set the limits and say no. . . .

"She would ask me to do something, and I would try and say no, no. And she—and she would—one time she stormed out when I wouldn't have intercourse with her—'You'll be sorry,' and she made a suicidal attempt at that point, or took an overdose, I guess would be more correct. . . . She would shout and scream at me. I remember once she threw the Kleenex box at me. She kicked over the ottoman. There was a pillow on the couch—she never laid on the couch and free-associated, but there was a little pillow there for people that did, and she threw that at me several times. . . . it shows that she knew what was going on, and I wasn't giving her enough, and she was able to assess things very accurately. . . .

"It must have been in December of '74 or maybe it was '75, when I was having to cancel appointments at a moment's notice. It looked like my stepfather was going to die, and I was having to go back East like at a moment's notice, and I must have gone back four times every other week.

"And I felt it was, you know, just—it looked like I was goofing off, or what-have-you, and I felt that it was important that she knew that I was doing it for a reason. And then we'd come back and, you know, things would stabilize back where I grew up. And then she'd say, 'How are things?' I'd say, 'Well, it looks like everything will be all right for a while. I'm still concerned, and I may have to cancel appointments.' And I would tell her if he had a coronary, or if my brother got sick, or what-have-you. . . .

"I never tried to exercise any power over her, other than to try and convince her not to try to take overdoses, or not to act out. I believe one of the testimonies was I did try and use my influence to get her to not just run off and divorce her husband, that her new sense of independence should be taken carefully. . . . Mr. Walker at one point went through a big thing with her, aside from — well, there were a number of different things in which I was concerned. I used the term 'gaslighting,' but I spelled out more to her, too, that he was doing things, such as telling her, 'I didn't love you then, but I love you now, but I'm having an affair.' He beat her up one day to the point where I was concerned enough that she was going to have internal bleeding and I made her immediately go to the hospital, or see Dr. [Fournier], because I was concerned enough about this. This happened a number of times.

"The thing that got me most routinely is that with almost all these overdoses, she was the one — he was the one that called me. And, like I would have to persuade him [Bruce Walker] to take her into the hospital. You almost had the feeling like he was waiting and waiting to see if something would happen. And I remember getting — I said, 'You've got to take her into the hospital now.' And I related to her that she has to be careful that she doesn't overreact to what he is doing, 'because he may be trying to get you to kill yourself.'

". . . I remember I believe one time he called me and said she had taken pills two hours ago, when he was home, and I said, 'Where is she now?' I presumed she was in the hospital. And he says, 'Well, she's in bed.' And I said, 'Well, can you arouse her?' 'I don't know.' And I said, 'Well, go up and see if you can.' So it was two hours after he knew she had taken pills before he called me. . . .

"Oh, part of the memory comes back at this point. He [Bruce Walker] had become impotent at some point, in one of my notes, that since he had for the first time begun to have an internal psychiatric or psychologic problem with impotency, at a point he came to see me once and I referred him to someone for marital counseling, and I believe he went to him once or twice." [Bruce Walker would testify that he talked on numerous occasions with Parzen about Evelyn, but never about himself or any problems he might have been having; he never consulted Parzen about "impotency," and never was referred to "someone for marital counseling."]

Neil asked Parzen to explain further what he meant when he kept saying that Evelyn Walker's suicide attempts were not "actual" or "serious." Neil asked, ". . . why don't you tell us what, in your opinion, is an actual suicide attempt, as opposed to, for example, an attention-getting device?"

Parzen responded, "Where a person with at least a certain amount of knowledge takes what could in fact be a fatal dose — it would be by popular knowledge. For example, there's been enough over the years of how many pills of taking Valium with alcohol; how much of what — to me, is a suicide attempt, rather than a manipulative or an attention-getting device. . . . The only one [of Evelyn Walker's] I really had questions about as to whether it might be a, quote, suicide attempt, rather than an attention-getting device, was the one that she did take the rat poison, and I was quite concerned about that.

"In retrospect, when she didn't have any liver impairment, or any of the other side effects that would come from even a significant dose of whatever the poison was — I don't remember — I think was even not a full-blown one. She was smart enough to have known better as to what one would have to take."

Neil asked why Parzen felt Evelyn "would act out in this manner towards other people?"

"Well, I think this goes into the essence of her pathology that had existed since childhood.

"It's always kind of popular in psychotherapy, or psychoanalysis: Everyone's parents are terrible. In fact, her parents were not terrible. They weren't the best parents in the world. They did physically abuse her at times. They did certainly psychologically abuse her. And things that go into the notes, that everyone remembers, is always the horribles and negatives.

"On the other hand, she came through a fairly traumatic life fairly well in many ways. She didn't fall apart, so on and so forth. There were times that she did, but overall what happened in her childhood is her parents would give something to her — attention, love, whatever —

and then, for either the parents' reasons, the parents' problems, or whatever, she would then experience deprivation. Her rage, her childhood rage, would then come out in the temper tantrum way, and her parents responded to her temper tantrum by spanking her or beating her more. She didn't give in, so they would give a little, and then she would be spanked, or beaten type of thing, and she had a tendency to repeat this pattern.

"This is actually what transference is all about, how you relate to someone else in their presence. You begin to want something from them, and then it's not enough. 'I want more.' If the person doesn't give more, you have the temper tantrum. If they do give more, you still have to make it not enough, and it's an ongoing thing."

In further questioning, Neil attempted to show through the notes taken by doctors who later treated Evelyn Walker that she had a similar, if not precisely the same, diagnosis when she left Parzen as when she first saw him — although this contradicted Parzen's own notes. Neil also tried to make light of the descriptions of Evelyn's going off drugs and suffering withdrawal. It was not withdrawal, he said, but "like tremors, like sometimes we're a little hung over, we're a little nervous type of thing. . . . Maybe plaintiff's counsel doesn't get hung over, but some of us do once in a while."

Toward the end of his examination of his client, Neil asked Parzen for a summary opinion. "Now, based on your training and experience, and your personal care and treatment of the plaintiff, and your personal observations of her, and based on the material that you've read, in your medical opinion, was Mrs. Walker mentally capable of understanding, assuming it to be true, that she had been injured by you during the year 1977?"

"I would have to answer yes, she was capable of it."

"And was she further mentally capable, sir, of understanding that it was you, the person who had sex with her — "

"Yes."

" — in his office, that had caused the injury?"

"Yes."

It was an extraordinary admission, and Marvin Lewis seized on it; he could hardly wait for his turn to come again to ask Parzen: "Doctor, you just told your counsel that you believe that my client, Evelyn Walker, knows, or should have known, that you injured her. Doctor, how did you injure Mrs. Evelyn Walker?"

"By having sex with — "

The incriminating line was almost out before Mike Neil finally objected and said it had been a hypothetical question, and he and his client had never admitted that there was, in fact, an injury. The judge overruled Neil's objection and Lewis asked his question again.

"Doctor, in what manner do you believe that you injured Evelyn Walker?"

"By having sexual relations with her."

"And what type of an injury did you cause her by having sexual relations with her?"

"It made her feelings of attachment being greater, and made for the separation being more painful."

So there it was: The accused himself had more or less answered the major questions not only in part one but also part two of the trial. Regarding the statute of limitations, Parzen had admitted that even he would never have known that what he was doing was malpractice; regarding the malpractice itself, yes, he had committed that, and yes, he was the cause of Evelyn's injury. The only thing left was to settle how much in damages Evelyn was entitled to. But a jury was not swayed as easily as that. Marvin Lewis had a number of other points to make, and others to reemphasize.

In fact, he still had a few points to settle with Parzen. Being a devout Jew and family man himself, Lewis was not about to let slide the vulgarity of Parzen's mentioning the death of a beloved son as an excuse for having adulterous sexual relations.

Said Lewis: "Well, now, Doctor, are you telling us that because of the unfortunate tragedy of the death of your son in 1972, and the death of your stepfather in '74, and the death of your brother at a later period of time, that that's why you couldn't say no to the sexual advances of Mrs. Walker?"

"Not entirely."

Lewis rephrased it and asked again, "Are you going to blame, in any way, you having masturbated Mrs. Walker, and having put your mouth down on her vagina, and having her put her mouth on your penis, and you inserting your penis into her vagina and having sex, on the death of your son in the year 1972, in any way?"

"You asked two different questions. Was I going to blame her in any way for the death of my son?"

"Are you going to attribute in any way, shape or manner, to the death of your boy in 1972, any of those actions I have just related in my question?"

Parzen would not be cowed by Lewis's moral outrage. He answered firmly, "Yes."

This led Lewis into a repetition of the line of questions that had produced Parzen's ludicrous descriptions — in the pretrial depositions — of how he had been forced by Evelyn Walker to have sex.

"In order to engage in this oral copulation, you took your pants off, didn't you?"

"She took them off."

"Did you fight her?"

"Sometimes."

"Did you struggle?"

"Sometimes I held her away."

"And was it difficult? Would you say she raped you?"

"I never said she raped me."

"Yes; but you were struggling to keep your pants on, and she was pulling your pants off. Is that what you are saying?"

"She would try and take my pants off. I would try and stop her, and she would say, 'You have to let me. You have to let me love you.'"

"Did you ever voluntarily take your pants off?"

"I don't believe so."

"Doctor, then did you ever remove any of her articles of clothing?"

"No."

"Doctor, at times you were the one that was the aggressor; that is, you were the one that put your mouth on her vagina, isn't that right, and kissed her?"

"She insisted that I do."

"Well, did she take your head and forcibly put it there?"

"Several times."

"Did you fight to get away?"

"I tried to talk to her."

"Did this irritate you, that she was doing this with your head?"

"Yes."

"You weren't enjoying it?"

"Sometimes I did, but I still — I still was irritated by it."

That was the admission Lewis had been looking for. He had gotten the doctor himself to admit that he had indulged in sexual relations with Evelyn Walker at least partly for his own pleasure and not as some last-ditch gesture to save her from suicide. And in so doing, Lewis had also brought some comic relief into the courtroom — and allowed Parzen to make a laughingstock of himself and his case.

Zane Parzen was excused and Sydney Smith was called as the next witness for Evelyn Walker. After giving his background in psychology and analysis, Smith went on to describe his treatment of Evelyn Walker and how Zane Parzen's abuse of her had opened up old mental problems from her childhood.

Lewis thus set the stage for the key question before the court. "In your opinion, Doctor, could the plaintiff, Evelyn Walker, in your opinion, have discovered malpractice that had been practiced upon her by Zane Parzen, at any time prior to July 12, 1979, or should she, in your opinion, reasonably have discovered or made inquiry that such malpractice had been committed, and the injury resulting that she suffered by it?"

"No," Smith answered, "I don't think she had an appreciation of it."

Smith explained that a major part of his treatment of her was to consistently confront her with the reality of her relationship with Parzen. He added that she could be lucid on other issues, but she simply could not see the reality of this one. "She was unaware of all the damage that he had done to her, all the injury it had done to her, despite my efforts to help her see that this was one of the things that was impeding the progress that she was making in her present treatment. She was, in a sense, obsessed with that relationship. . . . She was entranced with it. She was taken up with it. It had set off in her a neediness, which she had not experienced for years, in the sense that this relationship could, above all, fulfill every wish and every hope and every desire she ever had, and that was the promise of the relationship, and that's what she hoped to have fulfilled. She could not give it up."

Lewis asked, "Can a person, even who is psychotic, and believes that he is Napoleon Bonaparte, and madly in love with Josephine, appear lucid on other matters?"

Smith said, "That's true."

"And, as long as she had this fantasy, Doctor, do you believe that there was either any psychiatrist or psychologist, or any lay people that could reach her and get through to her, so that she might start an inquiry to make a discovery of this type of malpractice that had been practiced upon her, and the results of it?"

"No," Smith replied.

"Well, Doctor, do you have an opinion as to whether it was Zane Parzen who, by his malpractice, caused this fantasy that no one could get through to her?"

"Yes," said Smith.

And just how and why did he do this? Lewis continued. "Well, I think what he did was that he set out to create a relationship with her that would make her totally dependent upon him. . . . I think he did it through constant insinuations that he loved her, and that she was the most important person in his life, and that he was going to fulfill her needs. He would fulfill all of these fantasies that she had. That was appealing to the infantile wish in her, and it's a very strong—it's a very strong appeal that had to be made.

"But I think that what happened was that she became controlled by this kind of interaction between them, so that she, in a sense, had no life of her own, outside of his. She was willing to discard everybody and everything around her for the sake of this one relationship. It was, in a sense, a kind of Svengali-like relationship that was going on."

"Well, maybe we're not all familiar with Svengali. Can you tell us what you mean by 'Svengali'?" Lewis asked.

"Yes. He was a kind of hypnoticlike person, who influenced others."

"Is he the one who made Trilby sing?" Lewis asked.

"Yes, right."

"All right."

Mike Neil interrupted to ask, "Who is Trilby? Tell us who Trilby is."

Lewis answered: "Trilby and Svengali is quite a well-known story that I will tell you about sometime when we have time, Counsel."

"Did he serve with Napoleon?" asked Neil.

"What's your next question?" asked the judge.

Asked if he thought Evelyn would go back to Parzen if he "would just give her the nod," Smith said, "I'm afraid that's exactly what would happen." He said that in his opinion, Evelyn began to understand at the hearings in 1979 that Parzen had done something wrong with her, but what brought that home to her was the fact that the Board of Medical Quality Assurance took away Parzen's license. (All three of these events still put Evelyn well within the proper time to file her suit.) When the state took Parzen's license, Smith said, that "brought home to her that he must have done something dreadful to her, or that wouldn't have happened to him."

Smith testified that at the time she first went to Parzen, Evelyn could have been cured, because she was suffering only from "a depressive disorder, with certain narcissistic features." Now, however, he said, she would appear lucid one minute and the next be suffering from "dissociative experiences," where she didn't even know where or who she was.

Lewis himself had been dealing with Evelyn Walker's unpredictable moods, and he was surely worried about how she might behave on the witness stand. In a brilliant stroke, he set the stage by asking an expert, "Well, Doctor, if I was to ask you to tell this Court and jury how they can expect to find Evelyn Walker when she walks into this courtroom and goes up there and takes that stand, and while she's testifying, would you, yourself, know what we would expect to see by way of responses, or how she acts, or how she appears at that time, while she's a witness?"

"No," Smith answered.

"Is there any way of predicting how she is going to be as a witness?"

"Well, no," Smith replied. "I think it's a very difficult thing to predict that."

When his turn came for cross-examination, Neil came down on Smith with a sledgehammer of a question that began: "Dr. Smith, do you want this jury to believe that a woman. . . ." The question went on for almost five minutes, giving Evelyn Walker's history in brief, but attempting to show she was making all kinds of other competent decisions, and why wouldn't she know what happened with Parzen. But it concluded on a note that brought Marvin Lewis straight out of his chair: ". . . and finally had to go to San Francisco to find an attorney to take the case, who is presently representing her— Is it your opinion and are you asking this jury to believe that this woman did not have the common sense during the year 1977, and up until July of 1978, to recognize that she had been injured by Dr. Parzen's alleged misconduct?"

Lewis said he was shocked by the question, which was "so obviously objectionable." The judge agreed that it was objectionable — compound and argumentative. Over Lewis's strenuous objections, Neil kept trying to get in his question that "this woman did not have the plain, old basic common sense. . . ." Finally the judge allowed it.

By then, Smith was ready for it. He answered, "Well, what I have, I think, suggested to you already is that not only did she not know it then, I don't think that she even knows it now. I think this is a mentally ill woman who is going to continue to need treatment for a long period of time, and she does not recognize the consequences of what is happening with her now."

Neil then read from Smith's office notes about Evelyn's initial meeting with Marvin Lewis: "Patient frightened because has appointment to go see most important attorney in personal injury cases in country. She flies to San Francisco and taking a lot of stuff with her including audiotape I arranged for her." Neil then asked, "Now, Doctor, coming back to my earlier question: Is it your testimony that a plaintiff, or patient, such as Mrs. Walker, who would go to the lengths of flying to San Francisco to retain an attorney to represent her in this case, is this the type of person that you want us to believe did not recognize that she had been harmed by Dr. Parzen?"

Smith answered, "Well, you are ascribing much more independence of action to her than was actually the case. These attorneys were found for her by her friends. She was talked to by her friends about the importance of going to see them. . . . If all of this had not happened by friends and doctors who were working with her, she would probably still be with [the local attorney]."

At 9 A.M. on June 3, 1981, the sixth day of the trial, Marvin Lewis asked to address the court before the jury was called in to resume hearing testimony from Sydney Smith.

He said, "Dr. Gary Shepherd phoned me somewhere around 6:30, 7 o'clock last night, at my hotel room, and he advised me that there was a woman patient, and her name was [Pat Stern], and that she had been the first of the patients of Dr. Parzen that had been reporting mistreatment and sexual abuses of the doctor, while a patient.

"It seems, as she had said, that when he came out here to this area from Chicago, where he had been practicing, at the same time that he brought his family, surreptitiously he had brought [Pat] out with him from the Chicago area, and she's been living here and been his patient up to the time this happened in San Diego, which was a continuation of her treatment in Chicago. . . .

"He said that, in his opinion, she's a very dangerous hysterical woman, that she has threatened to — that she says she madly loves Dr. Parzen, but that she is going to kill him, and it's only a question of time when she will kill him.

"And when, last night, she called Dr. Shepherd, she said, 'I intend to do something about this. I saw it in the paper, and heard on the TV that this trial is going on against Dr. Parzen, and I was promised by you and promised by everyone' — which isn't true, according to Dr. Shepherd — 'assurances were given me that his reputation would never be affected, and that no litigation would ever be taken against him.'

"She's the one that has never — she's the only one that hasn't filed a suit. So he said, 'I'm merely calling you because,' he said, 'I feel in my opinion that she could be a danger; that she's the type of woman that could come into a courtroom shooting,' and he said, 'I just feel that you should be notified and use the information for whatever purpose you want to use it.'"

The judge thanked Lewis for the information and then Lewis moved once again to get in evidence that Parzen had been having sex with other female patients. Once again, the judge stipulated that only the bare facts of those other cases could be mentioned. Meanwhile, Pat Stern did not show up at the courthouse and there were no other threats from her.

When the trial resumed, Mike Neil's questions of Sydney Smith got more and more pointed. "Do you consider yourself an advocate for her in this lawsuit?"

"No, I do not."

"Is it your desire that she recover money in this lawsuit?"

"Yes. I would like to see her recover some money in this lawsuit, because she is going to be in need of extensive treatment, and she needs a way to pay for it."

"Doctor, does she owe you some money?"

"Yes, she does."

"How much does she owe you?"

"Oh, I think approximately $8,000."

"And if she doesn't recover some money in this lawsuit, you are not going to get paid, are you?"

"No, but it's not going to break me, either. I would like to say, in that regard, that even before there was the lawsuit at stake, in regard to her condition, that I agreed, along with the Institute, to defer payments in her case because she was unable to pay for this treatment, and yet was desperately in need of it, and it's not the first time I've done that in my career."

Neil would not let up on the money question. "Doctor, is it still your testimony that she was not obsessed with financial gain from this lawsuit?"

"I do not think that it's really fair to say that she is obsessed with money. She is not obsessed with money. She's never been obsessed with money. She's had money under her first husband, and she hasn't had money now. I think that the only thing that she's ever asked for is enough to live on."

When it came his turn again for re-direct examination of Smith, Marvin Lewis spent almost a half hour going over Evelyn Walker's admission records from Mesa Vista Hospital in early 1977. This might seem an irrelevant line of questioning, since Smith was not treating her at that time and had never heard of her then. But Lewis was aiming here for a direct blow at Mike Neil's earlier presentation. Neil had gone over this same history, but in doing so, he asked Smith to confirm that this report showed Evelyn had been diagnosed a "borderline psychotic" when she first began seeing Zane Parzen. The point of that, of course, was that her diagnosis was the same, and Parzen had not caused her condition to worsen.

Slowly, slowly, Marvin Lewis repeated the very same line of questions Neil had gone over. Pointing to the hospital records in Smith's hands, Lewis asked: "Do you see, anywhere in that record, Doctor, a diagnosis of any psychosis prior to 1977?"

"No," Smith answered.

"And when Mr. Neil asked you to assume that that was in the record, Doctor, now you see the record, and you know there is no such assumption, correct?"

"Correct."

It was a powerful blow to Neil's presentation, casting doubt on all the other "assumptions" he had made to the jury. Neil lost no time trying to correct that impression. "Doctor, I want to apologize to you if for any reason I misspoke myself in reading from this record; and if I led you to believe that that was the final diagnosis, it certainly was foolish on my part, because the record is right here to speak for itself. And with these two fine gentlemen [Lewis and Winer] sitting here, there's no way you could ever get away with something like that."

After Smith, Lewis called his next witness, David Anthony Olenik, the psychiatrist who treated Evelyn immediately after she left Parzen. Olenik explained how he knew Parzen through the Institute and how he had agreed to take Evelyn Walker as a patient after Parzen asked him to do so.

In his opinion, Olenik said, Parzen had committed malpractice with Evelyn because it is "not ethical or standard practice to involve one's self physically in a relationship with the patient. You don't respond to those kinds of thoughts and feelings by getting involved physically. . . . a relatively healthy patient might walk away from a situation like that. A relatively neurotic patient might be terribly anxious and depressed, and a borderline kind of patient, or somebody with a barely compensated borderline personality, might become psychotic.

"So you have to understand patients on a continuum, and I think that in this particular case Mrs. Walker developed a transference psychosis. She lost touch with reality."

Olenik would not comment on the drugs Parzen had prescribed, except to say that "in a sophisticated community like San Diego," he should have referred her to a neurologist for treatment of her migraine headaches.

He was more outspoken on the subject of Parzen's talking about his private life with a patient. "That has no place whatever in psychotherapy with this kind of patient. Often that's done with adolescent patients to share a little bit of yourself, but you don't share your internal problems with a patient. . . . The patient has enough to do, struggling with their own problems, much less their therapist's problems, and it adds to the confusion of differentiating self from non-self.

"The patient is there to work on their own problems. I presume she went there for help with her problems. She didn't go looking for a bartender, or a love affair, or whatever the case was. She went for help, so she didn't go to hear Dr. Parzen's problems."

Lewis asked, "Did the borderline psychosis you've testified that, in your opinion, came from medical errors of Dr. Parzen prevent her from discovering that there was this medical negligence of Dr. Parzen that had caused this injury, and prevented her from discovering the injury that was caused thereby, at least through the month of July of 1978?"

Neil objected but was overruled, and Olenik answered, "I find it a complex question to answer, but I think I would have to say yes, sir."

Lewis continued to reinforce his contention that Evelyn was in fact injured by Parzen and that because of this she could not have known that what he was doing was wrong. When Lewis went over the misuse of transference yet another time, and then said, "Doctor, that answers my question" in response to Olenik, Neil took the floor. "Your Honor, counsel has indicated this before, and I would ask the court to also admonish counsel to not comment upon answers given by witnesses to his questions, as he just did, 'That answers my question,' or words to that effect."

"My goodness!" said Lewis.

The judge's impatience with the lawyers' bickering spilled out: "You know, it's difficult enough for me to rule on the objections and the issues at law that are raised by the objections, rather than trying to rule on whether or not some style that a practitioner may have is proper or improper. I think you both can assume some responsibility for side comments that I alluded to yesterday. . . . I feel the two of you should get on with the business at hand."

In his cross-examination, Neil persisted in asking over and over if Olenik had not told Evelyn Walker that Parzen's involvement with her was shocking and wrong. In one reply, Olenik said, "I think I expressed some amazement that perhaps, even by my gestures or expressions, that I was surprised that a respected colleague would carry on this way with a patient. But again, I was not critical of her, nor of him, and again tried to deal with her feelings about it.

"I didn't make any overt statements about it being a malpractice or that she should report him to anybody, or anything like that, because that would be outside of the realm of therapy. I couldn't treat her as a patient if I was making moral admonishments to her, or telling her to seek counsel, or anything like that. That's not the role of a psychotherapist." Once again, Neil had persisted with a line of questioning that could only end up supporting and strengthening the arguments of his opponent.

When Neil questioned Olenik about Parzen's initial diagnosis, Neil was led straight into an incredibly damning conclusion about his client.

"Now, Doctor, you don't have any reason, I would assume, to disagree with Dr. Parzen's initial evaluation of her as a borderline personality, do you, on the first one or two visits that he had with her, his initial diagnosis, since we know there's no sex going on, or anything else?"

Olenik answered, "Well, quite honestly, I have difficulty with any of the communications from Dr. Parzen, because my understanding of what some of the things that he admitted to in this courtroom are different than what he has said on paper in the past. So I can't put any stock in what he has said in his clinical reports."

"His initial diagnosis?" asked Neil.

"Well, I probably wouldn't take much issue with his initial diagnostic impression, but some of the later reports appear to be very self-serving and defensive."

"He was trying to cover himself later on?"

"I believe so, sir."

And later, after Neil continued to assert that Evelyn's condition had been diagnosed as "borderline" from the beginning, Olenik volunteered a correction: "So he [Parzen] does not diagnose her as borderline personality disorder after he initially saw her, for the record." The record of this trial was beginning to show that Mike Neil may very well not have grasped the details in the complicated testimony.

Perhaps it was Neil's growing frustration at seeing his case fall apart that led to an explosive confrontation with Marvin Lewis in the courtroom after the jury had been excused for the day. The incident began as an apology to the court for Neil's own outburst, but it quickly became an insult to Marvin Lewis instead.

Said Neil: "This gentleman is a — I was warned about this before I started this trial — a past master of making ad lib comments and statements, and histrionics in front of the jury, and I find it very

difficult to sit back and continually take this, and from time to time —
and I appreciate the Court's position also . . . but I feel it necessary to respond because that's simply not my nature to be pushed
around."

Lewis was spluttering words of protest of his own by this time. Even
though this was being said out of the presence of the jury, the court
was still in session and everything was being transcribed and would be
part of the record if the case were ever appealed. Lewis said, "I resent
what's being said."

The judge tried to calm down both of them so he could say something of his own. But first, Lewis insisted on a few words. "I feel that I
have acted and tried to act, as I always have over the years, as a
gentleman, with full respect to the Court. I have not been disrespectful
before this court, or to counsel, and I've tried to act at all times —
there's been no histrionics on my part. There's been no wisecracks.
I'm sure that I have acted in a dignified manner, and if I thought I had
anything to apologize for, I would, but I do not."

The judge then said he did not like "the nature of the comments"
being exchanged between Neil and Lewis. "I think a little of that is all
right in levity, but I don't think any of it has been in that spirit. And I
think, frankly, that the effectiveness of your cases, respective cases, is
substantially diminished when the jury observes this. You are not
helping your client, I think, in doing that. . . . You [Lewis] do have a
tendency to be a very strong advocate. You tell me you tried your first
jury trial when I was three years old. . . . I don't think you've been
discourteous with this court at all, but I do think there's too much of
these collateral side remarks between counsel, and they are totally
irrelevant. . . . Now, I'm not accusing anyone of anything, other
than both of you, in my judgment, are losing the jury, and it's because
this case is beginning to drag, and it's because these side comments are
not humorous. They are rather strong, I would think. . . ."

Lewis was still fuming. "I do not apologize for the way in which I'm
conducting myself; no, sir . . . it's been put in the record that he
[Neil] had been warned of my snide remarks, of my histrionics. . . .
And I don't like it in the record that I'm acting that way, and I'm
putting in the record, for whatever good it is, that it is a deliberate
lie. . . . My client is being well represented, in my opinion."

The judge said both men were now on record saying how they felt
about each other, that from then on, there would be "no speeches to

the jury," and that applied to both lawyers. He concluded, "I'm not going to put up with any more of this monkey business. See you at 9:30 tomorrow."

Russell Bruce Hubbard was the next witness for Evelyn Walker. He had been the admitting psychiatrist at Mercy Hospital in March 1980 when Evelyn Walker's psychologist, Sydney Smith, felt she might carry through with a suicide attempt. Hubbard had also been hired by Lewis's firm to supervise a series of psychological tests to show Evelyn's current condition and also to show how she had been injured by Parzen.

As he did with the other doctors, Lewis led Hubbard through definitions of the major terms in psychiatry — *depression, suppression, repression, the unconscious.* But, by this time, Lewis was talking like an expert himself, and many of his questions were designed to get the doctor to agree with his own commonsense explanations of the difficult-sounding terms. Dreams, Lewis said, are a "keyhole into the unconscious." Hubbard said, "That's a very elegant way of putting it." Repression, Lewis said, is like a "bolt on the door of the dark closet of the unconscious." Hubbard added that it's "a fairly weak bolt sometimes." A psychotic, Lewis explained, was a person who believed that two and two makes five; a neurotic "knows that two and two makes four, but he worries about it; is that true?" The witness answered, "Yes."

Lewis was well into his examination of Hubbard before he stopped to go over his educational background. Hubbard earned his M.D. at Vanderbilt University, then came to the University of California/San Diego in 1972 for his residency in psychiatry. After completing his residency, he stayed on at UCSD as a teacher and researcher. He is the author of nineteen books and articles, most of them dealing with his specialty, "psychopharmacology," the study of drugs used in psychiatry.

Although Parzen had steadfastly refused to show any regret — much less remorse — for what he had done to Evelyn Walker, he had at least admitted to the fact of his malpractice in having sexual relations with her. However, when it came to his overprescription of drugs and to her abrupt withdrawal from drugs, he was adamant: He had not overprescribed, she had not gone through withdrawal, and only one of her suicide attempts (or overdoses) was "actual" or "serious" enough to have killed her.

Hubbard would, line by line, contradict nearly everything Parzen and his lawyers had tried to say about drugs. Hubbard was first asked if he didn't find it strange that the records of Evelyn's several overdoses on drugs were mysteriously missing from Scripps Hospital files when they were subpoenaed. "I found it quite remarkable that this was missing," said Hubbard. The subject was never mentioned again, but the point had been made that somebody might have been tampering with the records.

In one "hypothetical" question, Lewis spent forty-five minutes going over Evelyn's history before he asked Hubbard if Evelyn could have known what Parzen had done to her. Hubbard replied that "up until very late 1978 and early 1979, she did not have the capacity to discover that she had received bad medical treatment, or had been injured by it. . . . This woman was captivated by Dr. Parzen, almost like a slave. She wouldn't do virtually anything unless Dr. Parzen told her to. He was a Godlike figure to her. And this, combined with her mental illness, this feeling for him and love for him, she simply could not appreciate that he had hurt her as a patient."

Hubbard explained that almost none of the drugs Parzen was using to treat Evelyn Walker were proper for her condition.

"Of particular concern to me are some of the sleeping pills that he gave her, and what concerns me is both the type of medicine he gave and the quantities he gave it in.

"First of all, I want to address the type of medicine. We're talking about medicines like Nembutal, Seconal, Placidyl. These are strong sleeping medicines, and ones that can become addicting if a person takes enough of them over certain periods of time, addicting as much as alcohol can be. There were alternative drugs available for sleeping pills that were not addicting, which he did not use.

"Of particular concern to me is a pattern of his prescribing, beginning in about February of 1976, through early July of 1976. Dr. Parzen was prescribing for her increasing quantities of these sleeping medicines, so that she had great amounts available to her to take, up to six a day, eight a day. He did not prescribe her to take it that frequently, but she had sufficient quantities that she could, and in my mind did take them that frequently. In those quantities, they can become addicting, and, under their influence, a person acts as if they're intoxicated, which I've read in the depositions she was appearing during that period of time.

"These drugs are also of a concern to me in that, since they are addicting in the quantities she was apparently taking them, they can produce a medically very dangerous withdrawal syndrome when they are stopped. . . . When a person is addicted to a drug or to a medicine, they have to increase the amounts of the drug they take to achieve the same psychological effect. This is true of heroin; this is true of alcohol; and this is true of these barbiturate-type drugs.

"So after a person has been increasing their amounts to achieve the same psychological effect, the body physiologically becomes dependent upon these drugs. In other words, it needs a certain amount of that drug to come in each day to stay in balance.

"If the drug is suddenly stopped, a person's physiologic systems can go out of kilter, and that is a withdrawal syndrome — anxiousness, nervousness, disorientation, confusion, extreme fears, insomnia — and if the addiction is severe enough, the withdrawal can end in convulsions and death. That's the withdrawal syndrome. And from the depositions I've read, Mrs. Walker did have a withdrawal syndrome, so the addiction was my first concern with the drugs that Dr. Parzen prescribed.

"The second issue is that many of these drugs, such as Noludar, Seconal, and Nembutal, are very toxic medications. One pill or two pills at bedtime is a safe amount, if taken alone, to produce sleep. But six or eight pills taken at one time can produce a fatal overdose."

"Was he giving her those kinds of amounts?"

"Oh, yes."

"Will you illustrate where he was giving her fatal amounts of drugs?"

"Well, specifically, in June of 1976, there were four prescriptions for Noludar, which is one of these very potent sleeping pills. The total number of pills that he prescribed during one month were — let me total this quickly — 105 pills. . . . These were for the Noludar, which is a very strong sleeping medicine. It's also favored by people who want to kill themselves, because it produces a relatively painless death.

"So she was receiving very large quantities of this type of medicine that not only was very toxic, if taken in overdose, but could produce addiction.

"In addition, there were some other medicines, specifically Elavil . . . that were prescribed in quantities that could produce a serious overdose, and in a patient who is potentially suicidal, a doctor doesn't give them those quantities of medicines at one time."

"Would you consider this malpractice, Doctor?"

"Yes, I would."

In answer to the most relevant question as to whether Evelyn could "reasonably be expected to discover that malpractice was being committed upon her," Hubbard said, "During the time she was taking the barbiturate drugs, I am virtually convinced her judgment was impaired. They are like alcohol, and staying drunk all of the time impairs one's judgment, certainly."

Three other witnesses called by Lewis corroborated and explained further that Evelyn Walker had been damaged by Zane Parzen and that she was never aware of the fact that his treatment of her constituted malpractice. Alvin Robbins testified that even as Evelyn was giving him evidence against Parzen in a taped interview, her complaints against Parzen were only that he had deserted her. "She was shocked and dismayed and felt betrayed" when she heard about the other woman, Robbins said. He also said that in referring to Parzen as "doctor" when speaking to Evelyn, that "I was angrily greeted by a response saying to me, 'He was Zane. He was not my doctor. We were a man and a woman.'" The taped interview Robbins had done with Evelyn on December 24, 1978, was entered as evidence for the jury to hear.

Marvin Lewis called his last witness. The clerk instructed: "Will you state your name for the record, please."

"Evelyn Barbara Walker."

Some of the jurors may have caught a glimpse of Evelyn on the opening day of the trial, but she had not been there since that morning. Lewis had explained to the judge in private that he couldn't deal with her and plead the case too. But it was also a tactic Lewis had developed — the less the jury saw of the victim in these cases, the better.

For her part, Evelyn Walker was finally having her day in court. All those months and years she had suffered quietly. And then when she did begin speaking out, she found that her word was contradicted at almost every turn. This day in court she had so yearned for she knew would be yet another ordeal.

—

The night before I was to testify in court was a nightmare for me. I couldn't decide what I should wear — I must have tried on every piece of clothing I owned. I didn't have much of a wardrobe at the time, and I was so thin, the few things I had didn't fit very well. I was lucky to have Paul there to calm me down. He was so wonderful; he just kept reassuring me that I would look fine and I'd do all right on the witness stand.

But, once in bed, I could hardly sleep. And when I did sleep, I had a nightmare involving Zane, a nightmare that I had been having night after night in the days before and during the trial. In the dream, I am in court on the witness stand when I suddenly hear him whisper my name. I stand up and see him beckoning toward me. I get up from the witness chair and start walking toward him. Then, he pulls out a pistol and shoots me and then he shoots himself. It was so real I'd wake up tense and exhausted.

That morning, I got up and dressed and told Paul to go to work as he usually did. I had tried to keep the trial and my involvement with Zane out of our life. That was all in the past, and I tried to concentrate on us and on the present.

I drove alone to the courthouse, and met Gary. We went up on the elevators and were walking down the long hallway to the courtroom. Gary was telling me to relax, that everything was going to be all right. Turning a corner into another corridor, I could see in the distance a small group of people talking to each other. One by one, they turned to look at me, and suddenly they were all silent and staring straight at me. I could feel all of these people examining me from the top of my head on down to my feet. Gary whispered, "This is your jury." Without a word, they seemed to sense that I was the woman they had been hearing so much about.

Marvin met us outside the courtroom and escorted me up to the plaintiff's table, where John Winer was sitting. As we sat waiting for the judge to enter, I looked around and realized with great disappointment that once again Zane was not going to be here to hear me.

My name was called, and, as I sat there looking at the witness box to which I was being called, I remember thinking that my legs would never hold me up those few steps. It seemed like the longest and most frightening walk I'd ever made.

I swore to tell the truth and then sat down. I tried not to look at the jury—I had become frightened when I saw how many women were on the jury. I was thinking they would blame me as the bad woman in all this; I had never denied that I had loved Zane or that I had committed adultery. Maybe they would think I deserved what had happened. I had felt so guilty about everything that had happened, and now I just felt truly unworthy. I just wasn't as good as anybody sitting in that room, as good as those who would be judging me.

I kept control by concentrating on Marvin and his questions. And I drew strength from knowing that Paul loved me and was with me in spirit. And every now and then I would look over and be reassured by seeing Gary sitting there. The questioning by Marvin and then by Zane's lawyer went on for two exhausting days—but, except for one or two breaks, I managed to maintain control and answer all the questions calmly.

—

When Evelyn was called to the stand, she looked weary, haggard, and drawn, but as Lewis gently led the way, she told her story in a calm, assured manner, with an occasional break or slip that only made her seem all the more believable. Starting with her parents fleeing Nazi Austria, she began at the beginning and left out nothing. Almost with a novelist's eye for interesting detail, she kept the narrative flowing, and if she did lag, Lewis was quick to liven the pace again.

"My father was thirty-two when he married my mother, who was sixteen. . . . She became pregnant, which she resented—she hated children—and blamed him for everything that ever went, in her mind, wrong, including that she was taken away from her family, where, realistically, she probably would have been killed too, if he had left her behind.

"I'm apparently very, very much like my father and his side of the family, and that was probably the undoing. I was sort of the end result of everything that she disliked and hated in him. She was a verbally and physically abusive person, and it was a very rough going . . . at one time my mother screamed at me that, if it wasn't for me, they'd have money, and they'd have food in the house, and that it was because of me that she — you know, they had a terrible life, and this type of thing. When all else failed, you know, I was physically knocked around. . . ."

"Did you try to please your mother?"

"I was as good as human nature could make a person, because I was scared to death to be anything else, 'cause I never knew what would happen if I didn't behave perfectly. . . . One time she had a folding bed, where the springs are out when the bed is closed, and she knocked me around. And in the process, I fell back accidentally and hit that, and got cut somewhere back here, and I got blood on the mattress, and then I was punished because there was blood on the mattress. . . ."

"Does the verbal abuse of your mother continue up to the present time?"

"I have not seen or spoken to my parents in almost a year, because I can't handle it. And I decided that nothing will ever change. But a few months ago, I got a letter from her that was verbally abusive from beginning to end, and I finally recognized that as long as I live, as long as they live, it will never change, and I can't handle it to this day. . . ."

Slowly, Lewis let her tell her story in careful detail — about the family's moving to California and her marriage to Bruce Walker when she was twenty years old.

"Would you say, when you were married, did you go to your husband a virgin?"

"Oh, yes."

She told about working in the launch control division at Convair Astronautics and about art courses she took after finishing high school. She related the moves that she and Bruce had made — from their apartment in the Point Loma section of San Diego, to Riverside, then back to La Jolla, then to a new house in nearby Clairemont, and then to their last house, next door to the Shepherds in University City. She never had any help with the housework; she loved cleaning and cooking and making things for her husband and their two boys. But, in Riverside, she said, she started having headaches, and a medical doctor could find no cause for them, so eventually she went to see a psychiatrist named Dr. Philip Lawler. She liked him and felt he helped her; no, she never once felt her husband was to blame for any of her headaches.

Back in San Diego, she went on, she was too busy with the new houses to worry much about headaches. But once the comparatively huge house in University City was all decorated and the boys were off to school, the headaches and depressions returned. "I had a good relationship with Bruce, but I didn't have one in which I could turn to him to talk to him about anything. . . . I don't totally understand it myself. It just is part of what I didn't — you know, nothing is perfect in life, and I had a lot of other things with him, but I didn't happen to have that. He just isn't that type of person. He doesn't like problems. And if it's not a piece of equipment, he doesn't want to deal with it. I don't think he knows how. . . . I would just have days that I felt really bad, and trying to talk to Bruce didn't help. He would leave the room. He'd walk out. He'd say, 'I'll talk to you when you are feeling better.' "

Then Evelyn told how she and Bruce finally agreed she should begin seeing a psychiatrist again. "Our neighbor there was Dr. Gary Shepherd, and his wife, Bettie, and we were very good friends. . . . Bruce and I asked Gary if he could possibly recommend somebody, and he asked for a few weeks to think about it because he wanted to pick somebody that he felt would be right for me. And he gave me a list of three names. He didn't say anything about any one of them in particular. He just said these are three people that he felt would be good for me to work with, and that they were considered very fine in the profession. . . . One of the names on the list was Dr. Zane Parzen, and I picked that name first to call because I liked the name."

Lewis wanted to know every little detail Evelyn remembered about those first meetings with Parzen — where they sat, what was said. "The only thing I can tell you about my appearance was that in the first six months that I was there, I never was in there that I didn't keep my sunglasses on."

". . . why did you just happen to tell me now, and the Court, that you had sunglasses on?"

"Because it was significant to, after six months, things changing."

Evelyn couldn't know it, of course, since she wasn't there, but Lewis was taking Parzen's own testimony about these same events and contradicting him line by line by line. Ironically, Parzen himself had corroborated nearly everything Evelyn would say, although he was giving the details — about the sunglasses, for example — for his own reasons. Still, in nearly every incident, enough of his details coincided with hers to give greater credibility to what she was saying.

"I would come to a session, and it started rather early, probably within the first month that I would come, and he would ask me what I think about him; what did I think about while I was getting dressed to come and see him, and I never thought anything about him.

"And then he would — he would ask me — He didn't ask me. He would phrase it that — he was making a statement that he would point out things that should be wrong with my marriage, and I continually told him that the problems I felt I was having had to do with my insecurity, my not feeling good about me, about things that had been said to me over a period of my childhood that I believed were true, but he wouldn't let go of that.

"And eventually, it became almost a constant thing, what did I think about him, and he would tell a little bit, little things about himself, so that I would — "

"Like what?"

"Well, we both came from Chicago, so he would talk about things pertaining to — oh, like one time he talked about something — how in Chicago you can go to a lot of the delicatessens, and you buy sausage by the foot. You don't buy it by the pound; you buy it by the foot. And he would talk about how he used to go, and his favorite thing was to buy so many feet of sausage, and stuff, which had nothing to do with anything that was why I was there, but it did bring about that he would enter something in, so that now, if I saw sausage again, it would make me think of Zane. That doesn't make any sense, does it?"

Lewis didn't answer that question. Whether or not his star witness was making sense didn't matter; she sounded real — those were the kinds of details — however irrelevant — that nobody could just make up.

Moving on into the relationship, and with Parzen's own descriptions in mind as he asked every question, Lewis had Evelyn tell about the first time Parzen touched her. It was identical to Parzen's own testimony — except for the interesting detail that he had touched not her shoulder, but her leg.

And then, after that day when Bruce went to Parzen's office with her and coldly read a long list of her faults and problems, she and Parzen held each other on the couch. "And Zane came over, after he'd locked the door, and he sat on the couch facing me, sort of like this, and he said that he wanted me to hold on to him, that I was to lean on him and hold on to him. But he meant physically hold on, not, you know — and he sat extremely close, and he has a way of staring at you that you don't look anywhere but at him. You don't listen to anything else but him. The traffic outside doesn't have any meaning anymore. . . ."

Lewis was especially interested in who took the initiative in their sexual activity in Parzen's office. Evelyn explained that she was not one to handle rejection very well, so that if Parzen had held back even the slightest, she would never have gone ahead with the sex acts. "I mean, that day, let's say, I stopped him from opening my blouse, but the next week, maybe he tried to — to touch me, and I was a little less — you know, I'm not a machine, and all of a sudden somebody was paying attention to me. That was different than I — it never occurred to me that anybody would do that. So, you know, he was very insistent on the physical contact.

"Zane is a very strong man. Now, I'm tall, but I'm not an Amazon, and he would do things, like he would pull me kind of with him on the couch, and he — he liked very much to wrap his legs around mine, and lock his feet, so that I couldn't move away from him. And this was a — this was a commonplace thing for him to do this, to lock me with his arms and his legs around me, so that I physically could not move away from him and I could not look anywhere. If I tried to turn around, he would pull me around. I never — I never could get away from him.

"I used to say he was like an octopus. I never — he was just all over the place.

"And one day he tried to rub me between the legs, and I wouldn't let him do that. And he said, 'Why not? After all, you know, why not?' And the truth of the matter is I didn't have a good answer. All I knew was that nice girls don't do that. . . . He had put my hand on him to touch him between the legs, and at one point he had loosened his belt and partially opened the top part of his slacks, and put my hand inside for me to touch him."

Lewis stopped her to ask, "Pardon me. Dr. Zane Parzen has testified in this case that when his pants were down, that you were the one that undressed him and grabbed his pants off; is that true?"

"You know, after a — after, let's say, maybe eight, nine months, a year of the relationship, there were times I took the initiative, but not what we're talking about then. I mean, after a period of time, this was a relationship of two adults, where, you know, he had started something that I grew to then like, you know."

"But initially did you try to rape Dr. Parzen, or forcibly take his clothes off?"

"That's a silly question. Of course not. . . . No, I did not."

The narrative slowly moved on through the developing sexual relationship and into the subject of drugs. Evelyn said she used to joke with Parzen that he was "my supplier." She said she had only "foggy memories" of the several times she overdosed, but that Parzen himself "knew everything." After a certain point, she said, "I was doped up all the time; it was chaos in our household."

As for the suicide attempts, Evelyn said, "I didn't want attention; I wanted to die." As for that horrible weekend of withdrawal, she flatly contradicted Parzen's most important point: He had never suggested that she go into the hospital that weekend; he gave no indication of what she might go through alone.

Then Evelyn described how, after Parzen had thrown her out, she had met Bob Simmons. ". . . I got to thinking, well, he seems to love me so much, that maybe it's better for me to be with somebody who loves me, even though I don't love him, because maybe I could grow to like him. And I was so afraid out there, I just — I didn't have Zane physically with me. He was with me all the time, but he wasn't physically with me. And I had waited and waited and waited, and my thinking wasn't all that clear. . . . And [Bob] then started really, you know, saying, you know, he could take care of me and protect me from everything that was ugly; and I needed to be safe, I felt, so I married him. . . ."

After her second marriage ended in divorce, she had dated other men, she said. "I've had the problem that sometimes I would get the men confused in my mind. I would have a problem, and I would get it confused, that it was still Zane." In fact, once during her testimony in court, Evelyn slipped and said "Zane" when she meant Bob Simmons.

Lewis then went through the slow, laborious process of producing every letter Evelyn had written to Parzen after he threw her out, identifying each one through Evelyn and marking them as evidence and then reading them slowly into the record. There were ten long letters and a birthday card. None of this was rehearsed with Evelyn: Lewis wanted to elicit a particular spontaneous reaction. The most damning evidence against her was the November 3, 1978, letter in which she threatened to destroy Parzen. Lewis knew that if he didn't use it first and defuse the issue, Mike Neil would rub it in their faces.

So Lewis himself began reading: "Dear Zane, This is a letter that should have been written almost two years ago. . . ." He read on, but stumbled over nearly every word. "You accepted my love and—"

Finally, Evelyn stopped him and said, "Would it help if I read it?" [Later, Lewis would confess to her, "I thought you were never going to ask."]

And then Evelyn took this deeply, bitterly personal letter written from her own heart and — choking back the tears — read it as she had written it. . . . "You accepted my love and caring with no intention of seeing the relationship go anywhere. You knew that my feelings and trust cut me off from anyone else. . . ."

These were truly words of hurt and confusion, maybe even anger, but the jury could see and hear they were not words of hate; they were words of bitterly disappointed love.

"How do you live with yourself? I feel sorry for you, you're an empty man. And yet still with all this I still love you and hurt inside for your pains. But what you didn't . . . [Here she broke down for a moment and then continued, correcting a mistake in her original letter.] But what you did will never go away. It has marked me in many ways far more than anything of the past because it meant everything to me. You should know the effect is still strong—it has left a fear in me that affects my trust in other men. . . . What happened almost killed me. To this day I still have dreams about that last day with you. I wake up frightened and cold. . . ."

Lewis then asked, "Now, what prompted this letter?"

"I had gone through a lengthy, hard divorce with [Bob]. In the process of the divorce, I learned that the man had virtually lied to me about—just about everything. . . . And I guess after that long divorce I started thinking of [Bob], that [Bob] had lied to me so much, and I believed him. Was it possible that Zane had lied to me?"

Lewis — again anticipating questions Neil would raise — asked, "Let me ask you this question: When you wrote in this letter, 'I have the power to ruin you. I always did,' what did you mean by that?"

"I meant that I knew that two people being married, having an affair, if that got out, it could be bad. There are patients that wouldn't approve of their doctor getting a divorce. There are children involved. There are finances involved. I know that in my own divorce, to protect my children and not cause any problem, I sacrificed, because I had no choice in the matter, because I knew a divorce could be ugly if one of the partners wanted to make a mess of it. . . ."

"At the time you wrote this letter, did you still love Dr. Parzen?"

"Yes."

"Do you love him today?"

"Yes."

As expected, Mike Neil grabbed that same letter and ran with it in his cross-examination of Evelyn. "Mrs. Walker, at the time that you wrote the November 3 letter in 1978 to Mr. Parzen, or Dr. Parzen, in which you said the many angry things to him that you described for us yesterday, you knew as of that date that Mr. [Simmons] had stated under oath to the court that he was penniless and had no money, and couldn't pay you any alimony or support, did you not?"

"I knew he said that, and we also knew he was lying."

"Well, I understand that. But isn't it true that on November 2, 1978, under oath in the Superior Court of the County of San Diego, Mr. [Simmons] took the witness stand and said he had no money to pay you any support?"

"That has nothing to do with what's going on presently."

Neil continued to hammer away on this point, and Evelyn accused him of "putting words in my mouth."

"Mrs. Walker, I think the question can be answered yes or no, if you know. If you don't know, there's no sense in your and my arguing over this." No matter how gentlemanly his words, Neil was still pushing, and there was a mountain of evidence already before the jury that this was a fragile, defenseless woman that he was pushing. At any moment, she just might break, and nobody could say when that would happen or what she might say when she did.

Neil asked, ". . . you turned to Dr. Parzen as a means of gaining some support in the future, and you wrote that letter, which was marked November 3, 1978?"

"First of all, I did not mark the date; Zane did.

"Secondly, if I was a materialistic person, do you really think that I would have forfeited everything that I had for one human being? I could have stayed married to a very affluent man and kept up a relationship. Money had no meaning then, and it had no meaning in the relationship. . . ."

"Isn't it true that the reason that you've initiated any action against

Dr. Parzen was to assist you in bringing this malpractice suit in which you have filed against Dr. Parzen for $10 million?"

"What?"

"Isn't that true?"

"Is what true?"

[The court reporter reread the question.]

"Are you asking me if I did this for money?"

"Yes."

"That's ridiculous."

Neil then tried to show that Evelyn was competent in other areas and should have recognized Parzen's malpractice. But she continued to shoot down his suppositions one by one. She could drive a car, couldn't she? Well, yes, but she had had one bad accident. She had a checking account, didn't she? Well, yes, sometimes, but usually she used money orders to pay bills. Doctor Olenik told her that having sex with Parzen was inappropriate. "I'm sorry," Evelyn snapped back. "That's not true."

Neil refused to give up, and his questioning went on for hours. There was evidence that Neil himself was getting flustered. More than once, he referred to her as Mrs. Parzen, as Lewis had done. As he pushed on with his questions, Evelyn was consistent. "I'd be with Zane today," she said, if events in 1977 had turned out as she had wanted. Later, she answered Neil by saying, "I will always love Zane."

Evelyn had been on the stand for almost two full days as Neil — oblivious to the hazards of pushing such a fragile witness too far — kept after her to say that it was her need of money that caused her to file this lawsuit. Finally, Evelyn had had enough. She took the floor and explained exactly why she'd filed the suit.

"When the discussion of a lawsuit came up, it took a lot of talking of other people to convince me. I weighed this thing very heavily, because I recognized that if I did this, I was starting — there was no choice. There was no choice. I couldn't ignore what was made for me to see." Here, her voice began to break and she was crying openly. "I didn't know until he confessed about all the other women. I didn't [know] about the dead ones in Chicago. I couldn't ignore it anymore. I had to do something. I had to. And I — I did what I was advised to do by people I trusted. I didn't have a lawyer at the time to advise me until this all came about." The court transcript here reads: "[Witness sobbing.]"

The judge called a ten-minute recess. In the confusion, Mike Neil either hadn't heard or had missed the significance of what Evelyn had just blurted out about "all the other women . . . the dead ones in Chicago."

"What dead ones in Chicago?" a reporter from the *Los Angeles Times* would ask Marvin Lewis during the break. And Lewis explained that in his pretrial deposition, Parzen had admitted that some women in Chicago had killed themselves while under his care.

Mike Neil, meanwhile, completed his questioning after the recess as if nothing had happened. Marvin Lewis announced, "The plaintiff rests." But the next morning Neil, having seen the *Los Angeles Times*, came storming into the judge's chamber, demanding a mistrial. Once again, he hadn't done his homework and (in his words) ended up "with egg on my face."

Neil read from the *Times* article: "She [Evelyn Walker] said the decision to sue Dr. Parzen was prompted when she learned that previous female patients of his had committed suicide, something that Walker said she had tried fifteen or more times herself. Those suicides were acknowledged by Parzen in a sworn deposition taken last September, in which he said three of his female patients killed themselves when he practiced psychiatry in Chicago, and, Your Honor, that's not true.

"I have brought Dr. Parzen's deposition down here, and if opposing counsel disagrees with me, I would invite them to direct my attention, the court's attention, to where Dr. Parzen ever acknowledged anything to that effect. . . .

"Now, they have been talking to the reporters at length in the courtroom, in the hallway, and to the television media, and they have been filmed in the hallway, and this information came from them.

"Now, the fact that it came up in front of the jury is bad enough. I know Your Honor has been advising this jury not to read anything that has been going on about this trial. I cannot believe that in some manner this is not going to get to one of those jurors. And if it's there, and in the deposition, I would like counsel to show it to me, because I have no idea where this information could have come from, and it's not true, and at this time I would move for—"

"Well, what are you requesting?" asked the judge.

"I would move for a mistrial in this lawsuit."

Meanwhile, John Winer found the page in Parzen's deposition where he talked about the suicides in Chicago, and Marvin Lewis carefully read every word of it for the judge.

Neil interrupted the reading: "Well, I've got egg all over my face then. You can stop. . . . I've got egg all over my face, and I apologize for that portion of what I've said here today, and I apologize to Mr. Lewis, Mr. Winer, and the Court.

"However, I still move for a mistrial based on the plaintiff's statement on the witness stand, which was totally nonresponsive and inadmissible in this court, and has nothing to do with this lawsuit. It is extremely inflammatory. . . ."

Lewis then said, "Your Honor, please, I explained to this jury, even through a doctor, that there was no way I could ever tell what my client would do on that witness stand from one minute to the next. It's a type of situation where I can't even sit down with Mrs. Walker. I had to let her go on the stand without even talking to her. If I call her, she'll hang up, and she'll talk irrationally on the phone. The next minute, she'll be perfectly calm and controlled, as she was most of the time on that stand. Another time, there's just no knowing what she's going to say.

"I have, in my opinion, a psychotic client. I can't control what this woman is going to say; nobody can. And if it's true she is psychotic, it speaks for itself. There's no way of knowing what she's going to say on the stand, and the jury is going to have to take it into consideration. Either they don't believe me, or they don't believe her, or that she's not psychotic and making it up, or she is faking it.

"If this is true, she's going to hurt herself more than anything by the display. If they believe her, it's going to substantiate her case."

The judge asked what the question had been that provoked the outburst. He said if it was the general question, "Why did you bring the lawsuit?", then Evelyn's response "is the answer to the question." He thus ruled against a mistrial, but he agreed to interview each of the jurors to determine whether any of them had read the newspaper article. Not only had none of the twelve read this particular article, they all said they never read that newspaper. "Somebody should tell the *L.A. Times* they don't have any readers in San Diego," cracked the judge to the last of the jurors.

Mike Neil called only three witnesses to testify in Zane Parzen's defense: Bob Simmons, Evelyn Walker's second husband; Robert Fournier, her family physician; and Joseph J. Bailey, a psychiatrist who would give expert medical testimony. All three men ended up giving testimony that was damaging to Parzen's case while strengthening nearly every point made by Evelyn Walker and her attorneys.

In the case of Bob Simmons, Neil himself did a superb job of discrediting — or "impeaching," as it is called in court — his own witness. Neil asked Simmons, "While you were dating her, did she ever tell you about Dr. Parzen, or anything about Dr. Parzen?"

Simmons answered, "No, not that I remember."

Then Neil read from Simmons's pretrial deposition, in which Simmons was asked a similar question. "Did she ever tell you, before you were married, that she engaged in any sexual relations with the defendant Parzen?"

At that time, Simmons had answered, "Oh, yes."

Later, Neil asked, "Did she ever tell you why she had attempted to commit suicide?"

Simmons replied, "No. I would just — I reached the conclusion myself."

Again, Neil asked if it would "assist you in refreshing your recollection" if he read from Simmons's deposition. At this point, Marvin Lewis objected that the questioning was irrelevant, but the judge interposed by saying, "The Evidence Code allows one to impeach his own witness. The objections are overruled."

Lewis said, "Well, if that's what counsel is doing, impeaching his witness, then — "

The judge said, "You may proceed."

And, incredibly, Neil did, showing, once again, that what Simmons had said earlier was in flat contradiction to what he was saying in court. One of the questions from the deposition was: "Did she ever say why she had attempted to commit suicide?" Simmons had answered, "For two reasons; one, she stated she didn't want to grow old, and the other was for attention."

Neil continued to read more questions and answers from the deposition. "Did she give any reasons in relation to these other times that she told you she tried to commit suicide as to why she had attempted such on prior occasions?" Simmons had said, "Just felt there wasn't any point in her life. . . . And that she missed Zane so much, that her life had gone by, and she didn't feel there was much point in living."

In the course of answering Neil's questions, Simmons said he met Evelyn Walker through an ad she had placed in the *San Diego Union*'s personal column. When his deposition was taken, Simmons had been questioned at length about how they met, and he had made no mention of any newspaper ad. After reading from the deposition and going over this point in fine detail, Neil left the clear impression that Simmons had made up this one on the spot. But, by that time, the jury had heard this witness contradict his own testimony so many times that it hardly mattered. He was obviously called to show that Evelyn was "obsessed with money," but he also testified that he had gone to jail rather than pay any of the alimony he had owed her. And he had also been jailed another time for assault and battery against Evelyn and a woman neighbor. He reaffirmed Marvin Lewis's contention that Parzen maintained a "Svengali-like hold" over her even after she was not seeing him. An unspoken point that this witness also confirmed was that Evelyn must have been very desperate in those days to have ever become involved with a man such as this.

The most interesting point about Neil's examination of the Walker family physician was the questions he did not ask. In his opening statement, and in questioning two other witnesses, Neil had gone into explicit detail—using Fournier's name—about the doctor's sexual involvement with Evelyn Walker. However, when he faced the doctor himself, he said not one word about that. Rather, his main point with Fournier was to show that Evelyn Walker was not nearly as unaccustomed to drugs as Marvin Lewis had tried to show she was.

Fournier said he first started seeing Evelyn as a patient in January 1973. In March of that year, he performed a complete physical and wrote down the patient's history. He said she "gave a history of having migraine headaches, as she termed them, seven years prior to that, and she was treated with Demerol three times a week, according to her history, for three years. . . ." He also prescribed the tranquilizer Stelazine for her, and she "volunteered that she had taken as many as six Stelazine a day. She was prescribed two."

But, as before, Neil went beyond this routine questioning, until his witness was giving more weight to the other side. Neil had been arguing that none of Evelyn Walker's suicide attempts had been "actual" or "serious," but in answer to one of his questions, Fournier told about "the time she was in a relatively comatose state for two or three days after an OD. . . ."

When it was his turn, Marvin Lewis again took the same points Neil had tried to make and turned them around. He showed that nearly all of Evelyn's serious physical problems in the late 1970s were a direct result of her emotional turmoil involving the relationship with Parzen. He said that just one such diagnosis was anorexia nervosa, which Evelyn had suffered and which was clearly a physical condition tied to emotional anxiety.

Lewis also entered as evidence the long letter Parzen had written Fournier on October 8, 1975, telling him, in effect, not to prescribe "psychiatric drugs" for Evelyn. And then Lewis read from Fournier's office notes that patient Evelyn Walker had called Fournier and asked for refills. "Referred to Dr. Parzen to refill her medicine. Felt there were too many doctors spoiled the broth; so, all these things were renewed by him, theoretically, gave her 100 of this, 100 of that. I don't know why he gave her 100 of anything."

Finally, Lewis went down the list of times Evelyn had overdosed on drugs — once on Valium, another time on Seconal, again on Elavil, and once on Triavil. Fournier had never prescribed any of those.

The most important of the three witnesses called by Neil was Joseph J. Bailey, a paid expert witness on psychiatry and drugs. In answer to routine questions about his educational background, Bailey volunteered some details that must have galled the short-haired Marine Reserve colonel who had hired him. He said that among the reasons he'd gone to medical school was to get out of the service three months early. Then, he'd gone to school in Geneva, Switzerland, because (in 1954), "there were a lot of various political issues in the United States, which I really didn't — I didn't really want to come back to. . . ." In another setting, these would be innocent, even sensible explanations — but on cross-examination, Marvin Lewis made it all sound vaguely anti-American.

Bailey said he was fifty-one years old and had been in private practice in psychiatry in San Diego since 1964. He said he had written "several hundred" psychiatric reports about patients involved in trials where insanity was a question. Anticipating a line of questions by his opponent, Neil pointed out with questions that, yes, Bailey had been asked to testify for Parzen as an expert, and "of course, we will pay you for your services."

Neil's questioning hit an early and devastating snag when he asked, "As a result of your review of the records and the depositions that were taken in this lawsuit, Doctor, did you form an opinion as to any label or diagnosis or terminology that should be applied to, or could be applied to, Mrs. Walker during the year 1977?"

Lewis objected loudly and clearly. ". . . There has been no testimony here that this gentleman has at any time ever talked to Mrs. Walker; that he's ever interviewed her; that he's ever examined her; that's he's ever seen her; and I trust that he's not going to attempt to give this type of answer based on that situation. . . ." The judge sustained Lewis's objection time and again as Neil persisted in trying to get a medical opinion from Bailey regarding Evelyn Walker. Along the way, Lewis made it clear through his objections that Bailey should have and could have examined Evelyn Walker prior to the trial if he and Neil had only requested such an examination.

At one point, after Neil had finally gotten his question allowed as a "hypothetical" — assuming certain facts about Evelyn Walker — Lewis objected again and the jury was dismissed while the two lawyers argued before the judge. The judge himself got involved, and asked Bailey, ". . . do you even know, in terms of psychiatry, why she saw the first doctor that was referred to back in 1965 and '66? You don't even know what she was seeing him about, do you?"

The judge finally ruled that Bailey could give an opinion based on the records he had read and in answer to Neil's hypothetical question. But all this back-and-forth might well have suggested to the jurors that there was something wrong about Bailey's testimony.

Bailey said, "In reviewing the records of Dr. Olenik, it was my opinion that there was nothing so disordered about her mental state that she would not have been able to be aware and understand that what had transpired in treatment with Dr. Parzen was not the usual and customary treatment, and would have been able to act on that."

In his cross-examination, Lewis went straight for the jugular. "Doctor, for the last few years, isn't it true that most of your income comes from attorneys who have cases in court, whether criminal or civil?" And, after a few more clarifying questions and answers, Bailey would admit that "most of my income . . . has come from the courts or from attorneys, or from insurance companies."

Lewis kept coming back to the fact that Bailey had never seen or examined Evelyn Walker, yet he was attempting to offer expert testimony about her condition. "Would you say that it's very unusual for a psychiatrist to be able to tell the extent or the type of thought processes that are distorted of a patient when they've never talked to that patient in their life, never seen that patient, never examined that patient, Doctor?"

Lewis was including his own answers in the way he phrased his questions. "Would you feel more comfortable as a psychiatrist giving your opinion, Doctor, as to any individual's thought processes if you had had the opportunity of at least once to have talked to that person, and examined them, and given them some scientific psychiatric examination? Isn't that true?" Bailey admitted, "I would feel more comfortable. . . ."

Long after the trial, Lewis would express amazement that Neil had put a witness on the stand under such conditions, and had not asked for a pretrial examination of Evelyn Walker by Bailey. If he had done so, Lewis would have had to produce her for such an examination — just as she had had no choice but to be present for the pretrial cross-examination.

Lewis attacked Bailey's qualifications to give an opinion on Evelyn Walker in general and then went after his specific opinions. As for the drugs Parzen prescribed, Bailey said, "I would not have used barbiturates for sleep. I would rather use a different medication, such as Dalmane."

And, Lewis asked, didn't Bailey think that Parzen had written "too many of the prescriptions at one time"? Bailey agreed with Lewis again. "That was my — my impression."

Even on the subject of withdrawal, Bailey countered his own testimony by saying, "I really wouldn't discontinue medications abruptly with that kind of patient . . . what one generally does is reduce the medication in a step-wise fashion."

Bailey further testified that Parzen's sexual involvement with Evelyn did constitute malpractice; and he volunteered the opinion that his abrupt transferral of Evelyn to another doctor also was malpractice.

Line by line, Bailey supported, even reinforced, nearly every point of Marvin Lewis's case for Evelyn Walker. He had been an excellent witness, but not for the people who were paying him. Still, he persisted in saying (when Mike Neil's turn came again) that "exercising reasonable diligence," Evelyn Walker should have known what had happened to her, and she was capable of making a "rational decision."

Then Marvin Lewis came back with a parting shot. "Doctor, before you make a rational decision, you have to be rational, correct?"

"That's true."

"And before you make a rational decision as to what happened to you, and what you wanted to do about it, you have to know that there's been malpractice, and you've been hurt by it, don't you?"

"Yes."

"No further questions," Lewis said.

The judge said, "Thank you, Doctor. You may step down. You are excused."

There would be no further witnesses in this first part of the trial. The jurors would hear the two lawyers' final arguments on the evidence, and then the decision would be up to them.

In his closing arguments, Lewis maintained that this first part of the trial was an obstruction to Evelyn Walker's right to a fair trial. He said the defense—using the statute of limitations—had put up a roadblock and said, "Look, you have to prove first that you've got a right to be in court. . . .

"Now, I am stating here that this case on its face is almost ridiculous. Here we are claiming not only that the malpractice in this case was so subtle and so complicated and so imperceptible to the average, normal patient, particularly one who's coming to a doctor for a mental illness to start with—to start with, she has a mental illness, admittedly, and we claim that because of this malpractice, she gets what is known as a borderline psychosis, where every psychiatrist and psychologist that's come into this courtroom has said no way would Evelyn Walker ever have been able to have acted as a reasonable and prudent person, and no matter what advice was given to her, it couldn't get through. And the reason was because the malpractice did this to her. . . .

". . . And she went to a doctor who abused her, admittedly, admittedly, and has confessed admittedly to what he did, and now he wants to say, 'All right. I brazenly have admitted that I misused this sick patient of mine, but, aha, because of her illness, she should have sued me earlier than she did, and because she sued me too late, there'll be no damages because of that.'"

During a recess, Mike Neil requested that the judge tell the jury in his final instruction that they disregard the "hearsay" evidence Evelyn Walker blurted out about the other female patients and "those dead ones in Chicago." Neil, of course, had not objected when this happened. But, in making this request, he offered a bit of revisionism. ". . . Your Honor allowed certain hearsay evidence to come in to show her state of mind; i.e., the statement that there were other patients, and also, over my objection, she blurted out on the witness stand — on my later objection she blurted out on the witness stand there were some patients in Chicago, and this is the reason why — or deaths in Chicago, words to that effect — and that's the reason she filed the lawsuit."

"Well, now, just a moment," the judge stopped him. "It came in — It didn't come in under the questioning by Mr. Lewis. It came in under your questioning, and I assume the answer was not anticipated, but it is before the jury. So it wasn't let in for a limited purpose, and the jury was not so advised. However, as a matter of law, it's only admissible in this trial for the purpose of showing what her state of mind is, and that's what the whole trial is about. All of the evidence before this jury relates to that issue: Did she know, or should she have known?"

In his final argument, Neil repeated his earlier warning that Parzen's behavior was not at issue in the trial; the only question for the jury to decide was whether Evelyn Walker had complied with the law in filing the suit. But he didn't stop with this simple explanation; he pressed on into the murky evidence at hand.

"We have some claim of transference, this magic term, and a lot of fancy psychiatric terms bantered around here. I assume, when a man is courting a woman, he's practicing some transference on her. Maybe some gal is trying to get the attention of a guy, and she's practicing some transference on him. I don't think these terms are restricted solely to psychiatry. . . . This is part of life. . . . Transference means confidence built up in a person. . . ."

Neil said that "Dr. Parzen has attempted to make a clean bill of health, or at least set the record straight as to what he has done. . . . Dr. Parzen has paid for that. You are not here for any purposes associated with punishing Dr. Parzen, and that's not the question to be decided. . . ."

Evelyn Walker's second husband was depicted by Neil as "this nice gentleman. . . . I came away with a feeling that he was a rather pathetic character. . . . I felt sorry for the guy, and I think he'd been taken advantage of, and despite the fact that there's a claim that he lied at his deposition, I don't think he did. . . . I mean, you may think he's lying. I don't think he is. I think he's telling the truth." Neil, of course, was the one who had pointed out the discrepancies in Bob Simmons's testimony — and now he was highlighting it by using the word *lie*, which Lewis had never done.

Neil insisted that Evelyn Walker had decided to sue Zane Parzen when she realized she wasn't going to get any money out of Simmons.

"Now, she files a lawsuit for $10 million after going around to several attorneys and finally changing attorneys, apparently, and being referred to San Francisco, she had dollar signs in her eyes. She had dollar signs in her eyes. This woman did not have any money, and that's plain and simple, and maybe that's something to feel sorry for — it's sad she didn't have any money, in a sense. I mean, everybody should have some, in a sense. I think she has to take some responsibility for her actions and her conduct and what transpired. . . . She was responsible, and therefore, she had to be held responsible. She can't be excused. She can't pick and choose in her life what she wants to do, and therefore evade the requirements of the law. 'I am psychotic about one thing, and that's Dr. Parzen, and therefore, I'm excused for anything I might do with respect to him.'. . .

"You are the judges of what Dr. Parzen appears to be. I would suggest to you that he appears rather to be a pathetic individual, hardly capable of being diabolical. . . ."

In his rebuttal argument, Lewis rose to a point of moral outrage over such a man as Parzen, who "to make sure and lock it up, he addicted her to these drugs; and to lock it up, he started to arouse her passions; and then he played with her like a cat would play with a mouse, to the disgusting, vile situation — one of the worst things a man can do — to position his body on top of a woman and let him have his orgasm and leave her, knowing she's a mentally ill woman, completely frustrated for two-and-a-half years. And it was over that period of time that he was driving her absolutely crazy, and he drove her psychotic, and today this woman lives in a fantasy world; that nobody can really talk to her, and no matter how this case ends or what happens, I don't know who can pull her out of it. . . .

"The point is: If a statute of limitations has been violated, if a person is so negligent to sleep on their rights, they do not deserve to have their case heard in the courts, but that wasn't the case with this poor, sick woman.

"She's done everything to protect her rights under the illness of her mind, and the circumstances of the case, and the very tragedy that has been brought upon her, and the illness to her mind, which has been increased by the viciousness of the admitted confessions of Dr. Parzen in this case. And I, from the bottom of my heart, on behalf of my client, who unfortunately — she would have loved to have been here, rather than to have been ill and have to stay home and have to hear it from me at the end of the day, what's going on, but I know that she has all the faith in the justice system, and in you and the courts, and I know that after you hear the instructions tomorrow, and you consider the evidence in this case, although it may have seemed complicated, it isn't. It should be a very simple matter for you in a very short period of time to bring in a verdict that the statute of limitations has not barred this action, so that we may continue with this trial. Thank you so much."

In fact, John Winer would explain later, Evelyn Walker was not in the courtroom that day not because she was ill, but because her lawyers felt that there was a good chance the jury would decide against them. Lewis and Winer had told Evelyn Walker to stay near her telephone the day this first verdict was awaited. But she made other arrangements that day.

Paul and his brother had planned a full day to keep me busy. We were going to lunch, and the two of them kept me talking about anything and everything except the trial.

Because Paul had gone ahead in his car to pick up his brother, and I met them later at the restaurant, Paul and I were in two cars at the end of the day as we were going home.

We had just turned onto one of San Diego's main thoroughfares when the news came on the radio. We both had the same station on our car radios, and both of us heard the news at the same moment — that the jury had returned a verdict in my favor. Paul was honking his horn and waving his hands and yelling at me. I pulled over and got into his car to hear the rest of the news about the trial. We laughed and hugged each other; tears of joy were spilling down my face.

Here we were, in a car miles from the scene, hearing the news like any other John Doe Citizen — and this was news that would change my life.

The testimony of twelve different witnesses had taken up nine full days in court, and it had taken the two lawyers a full day to present their final arguments. Yet the jury had apparently agreed with Marvin Lewis that the case was not all that complicated. After hearing the judge's instructions on the law, the jurors had been excused at 9:25 A.M., June 12, 1981, to begin deliberations on a verdict. At 11:55, the jury had returned to the courtroom with a verdict. The presiding juror, Jane Martin, had handed the verdict papers to the bailiff, who passed them to the judge, who read them and passed them on to the clerk to read.

"We, the jury in the above-entitled action, find that the statute of limitations is not a bar to the plaintiff's cause of action against the defendant."

The judge had told them that the verdict in this case did not have to be unanimous, that they were to come back in as soon as nine or more jurors had agreed. When they were polled, it turned out that two of the women jurors had felt that Evelyn Walker had not filed her suit in time; but the majority, the other ten, had voted in Evelyn's favor.

The second part of the trial would thus proceed — with the same judge and jury, plaintiff and defendant, lawyers, and even many of the same witnesses called back to repeat or expand on their earlier testimony. Meanwhile, the trial would be recessed for two weeks while Mike Neil went off to summer camp as commander of a Marine tank battalion.

Chapter II

After the first part of the trial, it seemed that anything that could happen in the second part would be anti-climactic. But, in spite of all the dramatic evidence, the first trial had merely determined a point of law — that the case for damages would be heard. The real issues at stake would be resolved in the second part of the bifurcated trial: whether Parzen had in fact committed malpractice; whether that malpractice had damaged Evelyn Walker; and, finally, how much if anything she was entitled to in damages.

In his second opening statement, made on June 30, 1981, Lewis said that further testimony from Doctors Shepherd, Smith, and Hubbard would prove exactly what Evelyn Walker's condition had been before she went to see Parzen and would show how Parzen had turned her mild depression neurosis into a borderline psychosis. He would also use testimony from Evelyn's friends to describe in everyday language how they saw a woman who was the life of the party turn into a suicidal recluse. Most important, he said, the jury would now hear from Evelyn's first husband, Bruce Walker.

Shepherd and Smith essentially repeated the testimony they had given in the first part of the trial. But there were some dramatic additions to the testimony of Lewis's medical expert, Russell Bruce Hubbard.

Hubbard said he had examined Evelyn as recently as the day before, and she was "very, very depressed" and paranoid to the point where "she wasn't trusting anyone. . . . Dr. Shepherd, who has been continually supportive to her for a long, long time, beginning at the time she went into therapy with Dr. Parzen — that's a long relationship. I know Dr. Shepherd, and I know he has very much gone out of his way, as a friend and former neighbor, to help her out, has done a lot for her; and yesterday she was mentioning she didn't trust him. She wondered if he might harm her in some way or was letting her down again. And there's no evidence that Dr. Shepherd would do something like that. She wasn't trusting you," he added, looking at Lewis.

"That's nice," said Lewis.

"She wasn't trusting Mr. Winer."

"Why? Did she say that?" Lewis asked.

"Yes," Hubbard answered.

"Did she bring that up?"

"Yes, she did."

"What did she say?"

"You mistreat her."

"I mistreat her," said Lewis.

"Uh-huh."

"Did she say how I mistreat her?"

"Ignoring her."

When he had examined her a week before that, Hubbard said, Evelyn was "one of the most depressed people I've seen . . . she was feeling as if everything in her life was hopeless; that the outcome of this trial, whether it was decided in her favor or not, was really hopeless; that her illness was hopeless, and why go on."

Hubbard said from all he knew, Evelyn was suffering only from a depressive neurosis when she went to see Parzen; now, he said he would diagnose her condition as borderline psychotic. In his mind there was no question that this was caused by Parzen's treatment of her. In his opinion, Hubbard noted, Parzen approached her problems from the absolute wrong direction. "Instead of telling her about her husband's 'gaslighting' and dislike of her and things like that, which drove her further from her husband, Dr. Parzen should have enabled her or assisted her to obtain more supporting relationships in the community; just the opposite of what he did. . . . Had she been treated correctly from the time she began to see Dr. Parzen she would probably still be married, probably be productive in terms of artwork, or whatever she had chosen to follow, and would not be in this incredible mess that she's in now."

Lewis then asked the key question he would use in setting the amount of money Evelyn was due in damages. "Do you feel that there's any medical care that she should have in the future that you would recommend, and its possible cost?"

"Yes. I feel that she would be best treated with very long-term hospitalization in a psychiatric hospital, not of any type that we have even in San Diego. There are several in the United States that work particularly with this type of patient. . . . Minimum time, I would say one to two years; maximum four, five . . . the hospitalization alone would not suffice. She would need individual, one-to-one therapy during that period of time. . . . In my opinion, Mrs. Walker will need psychiatric care the rest of her life."

Lewis then called, one at a time, four people who were friends of the Walkers before and during the time she was seeing Parzen. All would agree Evelyn had been the life of the party, outgoing, a meticulous housekeeper, a loving mother, and a devoted wife. The most articulate of these witnesses was also the one who had been the closest to Evelyn and known her the longest — from just after the Walkers' first son was born until dinner the previous evening.

This was Connie Martin, who had flown in from her current home in McLean, Virginia, just to testify for her friend. Her husband was in the Navy, and the couples had been friends since 1962, when the Martins had moved into an apartment two doors down from the Walkers. With Lewis's guidance, Martin provided the jury with an incredibly moving narrative on Evelyn Walker's life up to the time it was shattered by her treating psychiatrist.

"She was a new mother, and she was a very proud mother. She was fun to be around. She and Bruce were both — they were an interesting couple. We did things like had parties together. We attended parties. We went out to dinner together. We went swimming together. We had picnics. We went to the beach together. This is oftentimes on the weekends with her family; and we just generally had fun together. She was, by the way, very interested in my work also. . . . [Evelyn] was very gregarious, and oftentimes I can remember kidding, saying that if it weren't for Evelyn, Bruce wouldn't have many friends because Bruce was very quiet, and Bruce is reserved. . . . I would say Bruce was a typically professional engineer, whatever that means. And Evelyn was very outgoing and friendly and loved to — and she was very talented, very creative.

". . . She was a wonderful mother. I — it was — I'll never forget the time she had a party for her — a birthday party for her older child, and she made really elaborate decorations for this out of oranges. She made things that looked like Mickey Mouse and had them decorated with felt and so on, and these were supposed to be favors for the other children in attendance. She also sewed. She made her children's clothes. . . .

"She was a a good cook. She was a gourmet cook. . . . [She also did] all kinds of artwork. I, in fact, own several of the things that she's done. She did woodcuts, woodblock prints, weavings, pottery, that kind of thing; painting. She even — she did watercolors, too."

"When you would visit in the home," Lewis asked, "what type of home did she keep?"

"Meticulous."

"And how did the boys dress?"

"Oh, beautifully. I mean, she took very good care of them. They were typical boys; and I knew them from the time they were babies, over the years 'til they — 'til they were teenagers."

"And did you see any — what would appear to you, any rift between her husband Bruce and herself?"

"No. Evelyn idolized Bruce."

By the time the Walkers moved to Riverside, Martin said, she and her husband had also moved north to Garden Grove, "and we got together quite often there because it was just a short drive from Garden Grove to Riverside. And they came to visit us and stayed with us in our home, and we did the same thing." She knew that Evelyn was seeing a psychiatrist when they lived in Riverside, but Martin said she could not see any severe depression in Evelyn. "I think she probably had an underlying desire to want to maybe understand her parents better, her mother. . . . I do remember one thing she said that stands out in my mind clearly is that Dr. Lawler told her that she was married to the best person in the world for her, and she really — and she believed that."

Lewis asked Martin if — up to the time she went to see Parzen in September 1974 — Evelyn was "the type that would be a complainer, complaining of aches in her body?"

"No. Evelyn was fun."

And then when her friend started seeing Zane Parzen, Connie Martin testified, everything changed. They visited only once or twice in the next four years, but Evelyn called Martin "sometimes daily . . . which was a new thing." After several months under Parzen's care, Evelyn visited the Martins, and Connie Martin recalled:

"She was strange . . . she was unsure of herself. She was shaky. She wasn't confident about what she would do, or she couldn't make a decision, and she didn't even want to do something like go shopping. That was a big chore, for her to do that. . . . She was very weepy. She cried a lot."

"Had she been weepy and cried a lot before seeing Dr. Parzen?"

"No. She laughed a lot then."

And, for the first time, Evelyn and Bruce were having trouble. "She was no longer the outgoing, fun-loving person that I knew or that my husband and I knew, actually. . . . She was very sad. She had a kind of a bland, sometimes very bland expression on her face. Sometimes a lot of quivering, I noticed, not only in her — her facial expressions, but in her gait. . . ."

In the phone conversations, she talked of nothing but Zane Parzen. "It was almost like she had no direction other than Zane, who was — who promised her that he would — and these are the words; I remember very clearly because they were used over and over again — 'He would always be with me, and he would never abandon me.' "

Connie Martin never knew exactly what medications Evelyn was taking, but "I knew she must have been taking a whole lot of something. . . . She sounded, oh, very weepy, cried, sometimes would call and would be in tears on the phone. She would sometimes ramble and not make much sense. She would not remember conversations, whole conversations that we would have."

Martin added a new and important slant to the harsh testimony from Evelyn's second husband. He had gone on and on about how he almost died in Las Vegas. But Evelyn had called Connie Martin at the time, and Martin told the court: ". . . her husband had contracted some type of virus and was very ill and didn't want to go to the hospital and it was through Evelyn's efforts that his life was saved."

Martin said Evelyn still called her and talked about Zane. And how was Evelyn's condition when Martin saw her last, at dinner the night before? "She was wound up like a top, like if you just said anything, she'd fly off the edge."

Mike Neil had no questions for the witness, and she was excused. In fact, Martin's testimony would have been nearly impossible for Neil to discredit. Never mind all that complicated expert testimony about transference and countertransference, Connie Martin was a real person speaking a language any juror could understand. There was no impeaching her testimony: She spoke the simple truth.

By far the most impressive and most important witness for Evelyn Walker in the second part of the trial was her first husband, Bruce Walker. Lawyers for both sides would agree that his testimony was a turning point. Long after the trial, Neil would say that Bruce Walker's testimony "absolutely devastated the jury. It removed the last shadow of doubt as to the destructiveness of what happened. It left the impression that what everybody else had said was right. If she had not seen Parzen, they would still be living happily ever after together and she'd still be the mother of his children."

Although Bruce Walker had been subpoenaed for cross-examination before the trial began, Marvin Lewis had decided not to call him for the first part of the trial. When the decision was made to call him in the second part, Walker was on a camping trip in Oregon with his second wife. But Lewis's wife, Freddie, got on the phone and stayed on the phone until she tracked him down and convinced him that he owed it to his children and to the happy times he and Evelyn had once shared to come testify in her behalf now.

Marvin Lewis went into elaborate detail about Walker's current financial situation, explaining to the judge (after Neil objected) that "it is our position that if it had not been for the malpractice, there would have been no separation and therefore no divorce."

Walker said the equity on his house was then $160,000. He also had $10,000 worth of furnishings, company stock worth $10,000, $5,000 in a profit-sharing plan, and a pension valued at $50,000. His salary at the time he married Evelyn was $14,000 a year, and it had risen to $35,000 when they separated. He had earned $900 a week, or $52,000, in 1980, the year before the trial.

He was asked to describe Evelyn before she went to Parzen. "She was very active, had a lot of friends, was interested in art, was working on, I believe, at that time, painting, a little bit of weaving, involved with doing things in the house, and involved with . . . raising our children, very much so. . . . She was a very conscientious mother, a very loving mother."

"Had there been the slightest indication that she'd ever been having an affair with any other man, other than outside of the marriage circle, prior to seeing Zane Parzen?" Lewis asked.

"No. I don't think it ever occurred to her to do that, and it never occurred to me that she would do that either."

They had no problems in their sex life, he said, and she kept the house "immaculately" and was a very good cook. "I was very happy," Bruce Walker stated.

And then slowly, Lewis led Walker through the changes that took place in Evelyn's behavior after she began seeing Zane Parzen. ". . . she seemed to get more and more depressed, lethargic. The children irritated her. She frequently was not interested in going out or taking care of things in the house or cooking. Ultimately, it got to the point where she spent almost all her time in the bedroom, sleeping or trying to sleep, except when she went to see Dr. Parzen."

When she first told him she was involved with Parzen, Walker said, "I thought she was fantasizing, and I talked to Dr. Parzen about it a couple times on the phone, and he said she was fantasizing. . . . I thought it was strange, but I also realized that she was using a lot of drugs, and I didn't know very much about psychology or psychiatry at the time. And some of the things she said, I thought, perhaps were a normal function of the relationship of the psychiatrist, like falling in love with your psychiatrist, you know."

"Now, did you ever get angry at her because she would tell you that the doctor was having sex with her and she loved another man? Did you ever hit her because of that?"

"I hit her once, yes."

"And that's the only time you ever struck your wife?"

"That I recall. There were a couple of other times where I handled her rather roughly because she was acting out in the kitchen, with the children around, and I wanted her in bed, and she didn't want to go up there, so I had to drag her into the bedroom."

In his pretrial deposition, Bruce Walker had made what seemed like a peculiar admission: He said that his sex life with Evelyn had actually improved after she became involved with Zane Parzen. It is hard to imagine how Marvin Lewis thought this might improve her case, but he pursued the question in open court to defuse any use Mike Neil might try to make of it.

"Now, after she had told you that Dr. Parzen was having these sexual relations with her in his office, did those sexual relations that were infrequent become more frequent between you and Evelyn?"

"Yes, they did. Her whole attitude towards sex changed . . . she was very, very interested in sex; and we had sexual intercourse much more frequently than we had before, and she talked about sex a lot. She really seemed to enjoy it. . . . [Before] she was timid, fearful, just did not enjoy sex very much."

Lewis concluded his examination of Bruce Walker by going into fine detail about all that Evelyn lost through her first divorce. Walker went on to explain that the divorce was not his idea. "In fact, I didn't seek a divorce from her. She wanted to divorce me so she could marry Dr. Parzen. I felt that she was such a pathetic person, so unable to take care of herself, that I felt like I was taking care of a child during a lot of that time; and I was not going to divorce, or at least I was not going to be the one that initiated proceedings. I felt she was too fragile to handle that right then."

In his cross-examination, Neil asked if Walker hadn't discussed this trial with his former wife. Walker said yes, he had, but she had hoped it would be settled out of court and that there wouldn't be a trial. Neil asked if Walker hadn't once threatened to go public about Evelyn and Zane at the time of the Walkers' divorce. Bruce answered, "Well, for one thing, making public the affair wouldn't do any less for me than for her. It wouldn't be a reasonable thing to do."

Neil also questioned him at length about his being involved with another woman and how upset Evelyn had been over this. But Lewis was quick to jump right back on this one when his turn came again. "Did you have the affair only after you learned she was having sex with Dr. Parzen?" "Yes," said Walker. And no, he had never been involved with another woman before that.

"Had you ever had any inkling of divorce or any problems of leaving each other prior to her going to Dr. Parzen?"

"No. I fully expected to spend the rest of my life with Evelyn."

"Thank you, sir. No further questions."

Neil had no further questions either.

Lewis then called Goetz M. Wentzel, Evelyn's gynecologist, who testified that in his opinion Evelyn's many serious physical problems were a direct result of her psychological condition resulting from her mistreatment by Parzen.

After calling Bettie Shepherd to testify about her firsthand knowledge of the changes that took place in her next-door neighbor after she started seeing Zane Parzen, Marvin Lewis rested the plaintiff's case.

The first two witnesses whom Neil called for Parzen's defense were female interior decorators who had employed Evelyn Walker at the height of her troubles over Parzen. They were both cold, hard career women — one even volunteered, "I'm tough" — who were not about to be shoved around by anybody or show sympathy for a woman who couldn't make it as they had. They showed not one trace of compassion for Evelyn's plight. And, incredibly, they testified that they had seen nothing wrong with Evelyn except that she just didn't work out. Evelyn had been involved in a long fight to get her commissions out of one of the women, but she denied everything when Lewis asked her about that in court. They weren't giving Evelyn an inch, and the jury could see that the women were straining hard to assert their own strength — at Evelyn's expense.

Neil's third witness was Evelyn's former mother-in-law, Margaret Walker, who had to be helped on and off the witness stand. Margaret Walker had not wanted to testify. In the corridor outside the court, she had pleaded with Neil to allow her not to testify. But Neil insisted. Neil apparently wanted to use Margaret Walker's testimony to show again that people had told Evelyn Walker that what Parzen was doing was wrong and she had understood. Margaret Walker said, "I tried to talk to her and suggest a few things that might help, and she just ignored it."

As he had with the two interior decorators, Marvin Lewis established in cross-examination that Margaret had been contacted by a private detective sent by Neil and that she had not appeared in court voluntarily but had been subpoenaed. He also got her to admit that Evelyn was an "excellent" housekeeper who kept her home "beautifully" and had been a good wife to her son and mother to his children "until this trouble started." Once again, a witness called by Neil had ended up testifying for Marvin Lewis's case.

The next witness called by Neil was Paul Adams, the man Evelyn was currently living with on a boat docked in the Mission Bay Marina, just north of San Diego.

Neil would attempt to depict this 46-foot Chris-Craft in need of repairs as some sort of yacht. He would also attempt to show that Evelyn was not in nearly as bad a shape as Marvin Lewis and his witnesses had said she was. She had a lover and they had this idyllic life on a boat, didn't they? Also, he elicited the fact that they had taken two trips together to Mexico and Las Vegas.

Adams was asked about Evelyn's personality. "Well, she's a very kindly person. She's a kindly, friendly, witty, talented person. She's subject to some tantrums, but — or moderate tantrums. She's upset easily. She's, I think, best described as — she's upset easily."

Neil asked what Evelyn was doing now. Adams said, "Well, she's doing a lot on the boat. I bought a boat that requires some maintenance and some upkeep and some care and some renovation, and I consider it some therapy to get her involved in it. She's been working on it, and doing a lot of things."

Neil quipped, "Somebody described a boat to me one time as a hole in the ocean that you just pour money into." It was a nonchalant way of suggesting a playboy lifestyle, which simply was not the case.

Marvin Lewis got right to specifics in his cross-examination. "You and I met for the first time last night," he said, and then went on to ask Adams about the dinner they had shared with Evelyn. During that dinner, hadn't Adams noticed, "while we were talking at various times and having a pleasant conversation, that you observed tears come into the eyes of Evelyn, and she had to leave the table?"

"Yes."

Lewis said this went on three or four times. Evelyn would start to cry, leave the table, and then come back. "And at one time she just couldn't stay any longer and said, 'We've got to leave,' and she left and went into the bathroom, and then we all departed. Is that true?"

"That's true," Adams agreed.

When Lewis persisted in questioning him about Evelyn's condition, Adams said, "If I may say, she's a — I like the lady, and I'm glad I met her, and I — I like her. . . . And after I realized that she was involved in this to the extent and it was affecting her and emotionally she was very upset, I couldn't — because I do like the lady, I couldn't throw her off the boat. If such a thought occurred to me, I couldn't throw her off the boat because I really feel she needs the type of thing that she's doing right now."

Adams would later tell Evelyn he "had to say some things" just to help her case; in fact, as the coming days would show, he loved her very much and they would eventually be married.

Neil called Evelyn B. Walker as his next witness. Lewis had tried unsuccessfully to keep Evelyn from being called in the second part of the trial. He explained to the judge and Neil in chambers that she was not in any condition to go through the ordeal of another cross-examination. But the judge reminded him that it was a basic point of law that a man had a right to face — and examine — his accuser in court.

Instead of calling her himself, Lewis had read quite a lengthy excerpt from Evelyn's pretrial deposition. In it, Mike Neil had questioned her in minute detail about her artwork and about every job she had ever had. His point, of course, had been to show how capable she was. But once again, Lewis took the very same evidence and turned it around — for it also showed how many times she'd tried to work and couldn't; how much of her talent and success had been lost as a result of her treatment by Parzen.

Now Neil questioned Evelyn about her last job at the Rik-Sha Boy, a Chinese carry-out place where she worked as a counter girl for four or five months before she got into a rehabilitation program, where she was being trained to work as a medical assistant.

Neil pushed for details about the fast-food counter job, and Evelyn gave them. "That was a tremendous strain because I'm not used to being around a lot of people. I've been isolated. So all of a sudden, I was inundated with people all those hours, four-and-a-half, five hours. That was very fearful — you know, I was frightened of that."

When Neil pushed for more details about the rehabilitation program, he learned from Evelyn that she had been taken out of her first "internship" assignment by the school itself, and although she had completed the six-month course, she was not sure she'd be able to get a job as a result of it.

Inexplicably, Neil began to ask about another job Evelyn had had as a receptionist for a chiropractor. Again, he got a response that went against his client and in favor of Evelyn Walker. "I was fired . . . because I couldn't — it wasn't an ugly kind of firing. . . . I couldn't handle any pressure, and they were aware of it . . . it was just too much for me. I — I easily broke down and cried, and I couldn't control what my moods would be. It's hard, putting on a front."

"Well, why would you break down and cry at work?"

"I don't know."

And then it became obvious why Neil had insisted on bringing Evelyn Walker back to testify in the second part of the trial — it was purely for "impeachment" purposes. He had come across a résumé that a friend of Evelyn's who ran an employment agency had prepared for Evelyn and it was full of inaccurate statements about her background. But when Evelyn haltingly explained why she had made up all these jobs for a résumé, it only reinforced her own lawyer's contention that she had been desperate to get a job during this period. "I virtually had no résumé or anything except for art jobs; and that really wasn't going to be very helpful. So in order to get some work that could help get something, 'cause virtually, other than when I worked at Astronautics, I had no office experience . . . so I used . . . Dr. Lawler's name . . . and I used my uncle's name because there was no way to get a job. . . . When you need to work, you do whatever it is you can. . . . I know it doesn't sound always on the up-and-up, but it isn't exactly unusual. When you are divorced and you haven't been in the job market for so long and you are over 40, you are not wanted unless you've got experience."

Neil went over the list of the boyfriends Evelyn had had since Parzen, and again, she explained that she was only seeking him through them; with every one of them, she only realized how much she needed and missed him.

And then he got to the man she lived with at present. He was trying to show that she had recovered and was functioning as a normal, healthy woman in that situation. But it was a touching love story as Evelyn told it. "I'm doing better all the time. I do the laundry now, which I couldn't do before. I'm pretty much that I can do a full marketing now. But then he's really helpful. If I start sinking, he won't let that happen. Paul will get me out, and we will go to dinner, or we'll go out with his brother or friends or something. We go to the Brigantine about once a week. I understand the bartender is a good friend of yours, at the Brigantine — Skip?"

Neil said, "I know a lot of bartenders. You are not supposed to bring these things out, see?"

Again speaking of her current love, Evelyn said, "He won't let me — because I tend — if things go bad for me, I tend to retreat to the stateroom; and he won't let that happen; and he can make me laugh, and that's important. And he makes hurting sometimes not hurt as bad. He listens to me. He's a very alive person. He's taught me how to fish. He seems to care."

Marvin Lewis went back over the areas Neil had covered, but he showed that Evelyn had hardly recovered to the point Neil was trying to show she had. She would go to convenience stores instead of supermarkets because she was afraid of all the choices in the bigger stores.

She confessed, "I'm afraid out there. I'm afraid."

Incredibly, Neil next called Evelyn's co-worker, the manager at the Rik-Sha Boy. The young man obviously had liked Evelyn and didn't want to do anything to hurt her cause. He explained that she had worked as a counter girl at the minimum wage, $3.15. And there were many times when she was nervous and some times when she cried. When Lewis asked about the day the paramedics were called because Evelyn had passed out at work, the young man said he wasn't there that day but he had heard about it.

Apparently it had not occurred to Neil that the more details he produced about this job, the more the jury was reminded of just how low this woman had sunk — from a $160,000 house in the suburbs to a $3.15-an-hour job as a counter girl.

Neil's last witness was his medical expert, Joseph J. Bailey. Once again, Bailey attempted to contradict everything the other doctors had said in Evelyn's defense. When Neil questioned Bailey about Russell Hubbard's contention that Evelyn should be hospitalized for an extended period, Bailey said he did not think she "exhibits that degree of mental illness that would warrant hospitalization."

Once again, Lewis neatly shot down everything Bailey had said with the commonsense observation that he had never examined Evelyn Walker, so how could he deliver an expert opinion on whether or not she should be hospitalized. It reached a ludicrous point this time when Bailey said, "I've seen her. I've never spoken to her."

"You've never spoken to her?"

"No, I have not."

"The only place you've seen her is here in this courtroom, just like the judge and jury have seen her."

"That's right, or outside in the hallway, but only here in court."

"Did you talk to her out in the hall?"

"No, I did not."

"Stand close to her to hear what she was saying?"

"I didn't overhear anything that she was saying in the hallway."

And then Lewis went through a long sequence of questions about how a doctor diagnoses a patient properly for hospitalization.

"Now, how do you evaluate a patient's problem to make that determination as to hospitalization, Doctor?"

"You interview. You review the kinds of things that have gone on in their life. . . . You determine how they appear nonverbally and what — in other words, how they evidence any kind of — whatever kinds of feelings that they are evidencing not verbally; in other words, body tone and body language. You assess their resources, resources outside the hospital. You assess the degree of dangerousness for that person or for some other person. . . . And then you make a decision as to whether or not that you want to hospitalize that person."

And then Lewis delivered the coup de grace. "Right. And you did none of that in this case of Evelyn Walker, did you?"

"No. But I reviewed the records."

Lewis rephrased the question. "Did you do any of those five elements that you've just talked about in coming to your conclusion that Evelyn Walker doesn't need the type of hospitalization other doctors have said in this case she needs?"

"At the present time?"

"Yes."

"No. I did not do any of those."

Even Mike Neil would later pay tribute to Marvin Lewis's handling of Evelyn Walker's case, especially his final argument to the jury on July 6, 1981. Said Neil: "I have nothing but admiration and respect for him. It was a tension-filled trial. He's a brawler and I'm a brawler. My back was against the wall. Keep in mind that Marvin Lewis was trying lawsuits in 1929 and I wasn't born until 1940. I learned a lot from this guy. He is brilliant. Nobody could have won the verdict he did in this case. His argument on damages was the best I've ever heard."

Although his final argument and rebuttal read like polished speeches, Lewis, in fact, was speaking from his own brand of notes. He and John Winer spent every free hour away from the trial planning this final speech — going over every piece of evidence and deciding just what sequence would be most effective to a jury. Lewis appeared with huge stacks of transcripts — mainly from the pretrial depositions. On these he had big circles around page numbers — a system only he could follow. This meant that he was in constant motion as he argued before the jury. Picking up this or that page from the table, putting his glasses on, and then taking them off — all for just the right emphasis on whatever point he was making.

In the same low-key, commonsense style that had swayed the jury in the first part of the trial, Lewis reviewed all the evidence, reminding the jurors of the testimony from the witnesses he had called, as well as those witnesses called by Mike Neil. (As Lewis said, sometimes he would go home, after hearing Neil's witnesses, thinking, "I don't know whether they're my witnesses or his," because "I was getting everything that we had said out of the very lips of his witnesses.")

The most important part of his argument dealt with the precise amounts of money he was asking the jury to award Evelyn Walker for damages resulting from Parzen's mistreatment of her. Using big-lettered charts prepared by his wife, Lewis showed that Evelyn was entitled to $6.9 million. Included in that amount was what it would cost for her to spend one year in a hospital and have psychiatric counseling twice a week for the rest of her life. It also compensated her for the community property she lost as a result of her divorce from Bruce Walker — half of his projected salary of $3.8 million (from 1977 until he reaches 65) and half of the value of their house and its furnishings. Lewis also included $2 million to compensate Evelyn for the pain and suffering she had endured.

"That $2 million for pain and suffering is not a gift," he told the jurors. "It's a debt to be paid."

Lewis appealed to the jurors to consider all that Evelyn had lost apart from material things. "Her mind," he said, "this marvelous thing which enables her to be Evelyn Walker is gone. . . . How would you like to spend your life in that type of a mystic maze with no way of getting out? And that's where she is today. She is worse, I tell you, than any case, if you've ever had it before, of any quadriplegic or paraplegic." And he explained why. ". . . when you destroy the mind of a human being and you set them afloat with fear for every moment that the least thing may set them off, when nobody can want them around because they don't want the unpleasantness, nobody wants to look at suffering, when she has to go through the rest of her life with pain that is based on functional causes, and can't be helped, and has to lean and depend, she is the most dependent woman, I think, I've ever seen; a brave woman, but she is in a horrible mess, as the doctors said."

In conclusion, Lewis said, "I've told Mrs. Walker that I will allow her to be here in court and wait here for your verdict. She has, I know, the confidence and the faith in you ultimately. . . . I know that this verdict of yours is going to be a verdict that you are going to live with, and that you are going to be proud of, because it's going to be a verdict that's going to be based on your logic and your empathy and your understanding, and it's going to be ratified by your conscience."

There was no question in any of the jurors' minds at this stage about whether Evelyn was entitled to damages; the only question was precisely how much. It took them less than four hours (and that included a lunch break) to come back with a verdict. Evelyn remembers that Marvin Lewis called her that morning after the jury had gone out to begin the deliberations and told her to come on down to be there when the verdict was returned.

▬

I think I got there around 2 P.M. I know I wasn't there too long before the jury came back in. I drove down by myself and went up to the floor the courtrooms are on; there was nobody in the whole corridor. I felt isolated, alone.

I took a seat toward the back of the room, in front of Marvin's wife, Freddie. The room was so deathly silent. You could hear the wall clock ticking the minutes away; it seemed to get louder and louder, sounding like a dreadful drumbeat marking the minutes off. Every now and then, Marvin would get up and pace back and forth, or come back to whisper something to me and his wife.

The bailiff received word that the jury had reached a verdict, and he walked over and whispered that to Marvin. The bailiff then went over to a telephone and apparently made a call to Zane's lawyer to let him know a verdict had been reached. The judge came in and took his seat and the jurors started filing in. According to the official transcript of the trial, the jury returned at 3:20 P.M., July 7, 1981.

I felt the jurors were all looking at me as they came in; I didn't know what to make of that; I didn't know what to make of anything. I felt very alone.

The judge asked the presiding juror, Jane Martin, "Apparently, you've reached a verdict; is that correct?"

"Yes, sir, we have," she replied, and she handed the verdict form to the bailiff, who handed it to the judge for him to review. "The verdict appears to be in order," he said. "I'll ask that you read it," he said to the clerk, handing him the form.

The clerk read: "In the Superior Court of the State of California, in and for the County of San Diego, Case No. 437641, Evelyn B. Walker versus Zane D. Parzen, M.D.

"Jury verdict: We the jury in the above-entitled action find for the plaintiff, Evelyn B. Walker, and against the defendant, Zane D. Parzen. . . ."

The clerk started to read a number. I just remembered him reading the number "four," and then he paused for what seemed like a long time. I was thinking, well they gave me $4,000. And then he read another number, and I thought, well, maybe they gave me a little bit more than $4,000. There were all these numbers that just kept coming and coming; I couldn't believe what I was hearing: ". . . and assess plaintiff's damages in the sum of $4,631,666." I recognized that what all those numbers meant was that I had won, I won my case — but I was lost in a haze of disbelief. What I remember most was that I felt in tremendous pain; and I felt so alone. I wanted Paul to be there with me, although I had been the one who had insisted that we keep the trial out of our lives. And although all of this was the wish — that even I knew was crazy — that somehow Zane could be with me, too.

Freddie Lewis came around and put her arms around me. She just kept saying over and over, "This is what we hoped for; this is what we worked so hard to get; everything is going to be okay now." I know I was crying, but I can hardly remember anything that was going on. I just heard Freddie saying, "It's okay; it's okay; it's all over, honey."

Suddenly, it really was over. Everybody stood up. The jurors started coming down the aisle. Freddie helped me up and prompted me to go over and greet the jurors. There were people all around me; it seemed like everybody wanted to touch me. The women jurors, whose judgment I had so feared, were hugging and kissing me and talking to me. We all slowly moved out of the courtroom into the hallway, where I was blinded by the lights from the television cameras. Marvin talked with the reporters, and I wasn't sure what I was doing. I just kept thanking people. Two of the women jurors asked where Paul was. And then they talked about how much they wished I would get healthy again and wanted me to get back into doing my artwork again. They said they wanted me to be happy; they didn't want me to be hurt ever again; they wanted to be sure I was going to be able to live. One woman just kept saying, "Now, you go back and you get back doing your artwork, doing things that make you happy."

I turned to Marvin and asked him if he thought Zane knew that this had happened. Out of the corner of my eye, I could see Zane's lawyer angrily pushing his way through the crowd of people and storming down the hallway without saying a word. I went to a phone and called Paul at work and told him about the verdict, and he was so excited and happy I could hear his voice cracking as he tried to talk. I went home to him, and that night, Marvin was our host at a victory dinner at Mister A's, a penthouse restaurant overlooking all of San Diego.

—

But what Evelyn Walker would soon learn was that this verdict in her favor was not the end or the beginning of anything; it only signaled another long period of exasperating waiting in her life. Parzen's lawyer, Mike Neil, initiated a number of delaying tactics. At first, he filed notice of appeal — the court reporter got three-fourths of the way through the appeal transcript when that motion was withdrawn. Then, Neil went into court and asked that the insurance company be allowed to pay the damages in installments.

By September 24, 1981, Marvin Lewis's patience had run out. He fired off a lengthy but blunt warning to Neil, stipulating that Neil agree to a settlement in ten days or face another action for the full amount. Lewis also accused Neil of acting in bad faith throughout the negotiations over a settlement. Neil had refused to provide Lewis with the name of the insurance company that employed him in the case or to answer Lewis's questions about the amount of Parzen's primary coverage. "Only a few days ago," Lewis wrote, "I learned that American Home Insurance Company was the primary insurance carrier in this case, and that Industrial Indemnity carried the excess insurance."

In his letter, Lewis informed Neil that there were precedent cases in which an insurance company, having failed to pay damages in one verdict, had found itself sued and forced to pay an even larger award. He reviewed the facts of the case and said there was never any question of Parzen's guilt of malpractice or his liability for damages. The only question was how much would be paid — and the jury decided that.

All of this litigation had further aggravated Evelyn Walker's mental condition, Lewis wrote. "The plaintiff is badly in need of the full amount of the settlement, and she is entitled to it. The insurance company knows that they have no realistic legitimate reason to appeal this case, but that the only point of the appeal would be to put a pistol to the head of the plaintiff, knowing she lacks the funds and is mentally ill. They also know that this appeal would be no hardship to them because they can put their money out and receive high interest rates and they will only have to pay the plaintiff's seven percent, which would be far below the interest rate at which they will invest the money. This had been admitted by all the attorneys for the insurance companies and is a well-known fact."

Lewis finally hired an expert in such insurance settlement negotiations, Victor Leavitt of Los Angeles, and a settlement of $2.5 million eventually was agreed to. But Evelyn Walker's money would not reach her until mid-December 1981, nearly six months after the jury had said she was entitled to more than $4.6 million in damages. The amount she actually received was $1.25 million; the other half of the settlement went to Marvin Lewis. That was a payment Evelyn would never begrudge: Without Lewis's brilliant handling of her case, she would never have gotten anywhere near that amount, and she could easily have ended up with nothing at all.

Epilogue   Just as there is no complete cure for mental illness, there are no truly happy endings to stories about the mentally ill. It is, after all, little more than a decade since that day Evelyn Walker first walked into Zane Parzen's office in the fall of 1974. Nobody who knew Evelyn Walker during most of that time would ever have believed that she would still be alive and able to tell her story ten years later.

Although the tragic events of this story left several lives in ruins, most of the people have gone on to healthier, happier lives. Young John Winer is now a full partner in the prestigious firm of Lewis, Lewis and Winer in San Francisco. No longer the leg man for Marvin Lewis, Sr., Winer has a full caseload of his own, many of them dealing with psychic abuse, many of them referred to him by people who first contacted Evelyn Walker. But Winer remains the uncompromising idealist that he was when he first joined the firm. Like his famous mentor, Winer says he will never take a case he does not believe in and he will never represent anybody but the victim.

Marvin Lewis continues to live his life at the same fast pace he has always enjoyed. Recently, he began dictating his memoirs in hopes of publishing a book about his life. Even alone with a tape recorder, he is still addressing a jury. He remains the consummate actor-lawyer quoting Shakespeare, gesturing with his hands — whatever it takes to hold people's attention. His final argument in *Walker v. Parzen* was recorded for historians and other lawyers in the "Million Dollar Cases" series of tape cassettes.

As for Mike Neil, he remains the self-assured Marine. His highly publicized loss in the Parzen case did not cause his world to fall apart. In fact, business has never been better. Neil handled three more cases involving Parzen — all of which were settled out of court. Neil's name was added to that of one of San Diego's richest law firms not long after the *Walker v. Parzen* trial, and he also became president of the firm of Rhoades, Hollywood & Neil. In interviews and seminars on malpractice cases, Neil has nothing but the highest praise for his old adversary "Marv" Lewis, and at legal conferences he greets him with the bear hug of a lifetime pal. After all, Lewis got Neil's name in the newspapers and made him a star of sorts.

The lives of Gary and Bettie Shepherd have remained the same — more so than anybody else mentioned in this book. Gary Shepherd has less and less to do with the San Diego Psychoanalytic Institute. And he no longer has a strictly private practice. He is director of a massive ongoing study for CHAMPAS, the civilian health insurance for dependents of military personnel. This, again, has earned him few friends among his fellow doctors, because part of his job is to set rates and limits on how much may be paid for psychiatric treatment by CHAMPAS, the major insurance company in the area. Gary Shepherd was also coauthor of the American Psychiatric Association's manual on peer review. Bettie Shepherd, after analysis, enjoys a calmer life than she ever knew before. She has a graduate degree in public health administration and plans to pursue a career in that field. The Shepherds continue to live in the same house in University City, though after Evelyn moved out of that house, the Shepherds became more and more estranged from Bruce Walker.

Bruce and Evelyn Walker's sons are among the most unfortunate victims at the heart of this story. They were only ten and twelve years old when their mother first became involved with Zane Parzen. Neither of them knew that it was a sexual relationship until that aspect was revealed in the newspapers during the trial. When Evelyn Walker moved out, Bruce Walker decided that their sons would stay with him. However, in the ensuing months they lived almost without supervision, and the neighbors speak of raucous all-night parties and carryings-on that left no time for studies or schoolwork or any kind of serious pursuits.

After Bruce Walker remarried, the boys suddenly were subjected to strict rules they had not lived by in several years. Among other new laws of the household, the sons were told they would be expected to get jobs and earn their own keep as soon as they reached the age of eighteen. The two sons did get jobs when they reached eighteen, and both moved out of the house as soon as they graduated from high school.

When the Walkers moved out of the house Bruce had once shared with Evelyn, they put up for sale the art objects Evelyn had left behind. Evelyn happened to be visiting the Shepherds that day, and she saw all of her paintings and wall hangings piled up in the garage. There was one especially fine portrait of the boys that she had always treasured. She went over and asked her younger son what was going on, and he explained that it was a garage sale. The son went in and brought out his father. Bruce allowed Evelyn to pick out the most important pieces, which had been hers to begin with. As she was putting them in her car, Bruce said, "Well, you know, we had planned to sell these things." Evelyn turned and left without answering.

In one of the more ironic twists of this story, Bruce Walker and his old nemesis, Zane Parzen, made a dramatic swap of careers. The psychoanalyst went into computer consulting work and Walker began studying toward a career in clinical psychology. After his initial experiences with est, Walker moved on to more serious studies. He took courses in San Diego and then went to a tiny college in the Southeast. These courses bear little resemblance to the degrees in engineering he had earned at MIT and UCLA. When asked to explain why he had left engineering to pursue a course in psychology, Walker wrote:

> The fact that I am now pursuing a doctorate in clinical psychology has little or nothing to do with Evelyn's extremely unfortunate experience with a psychiatrist. I decided to make this career change several years after our divorce, after a rather thorough personal evaluation of my contributions as an engineer. I chose to see if I could use whatever abilities I had, and whatever skills I could learn, in spending the rest of my life in helping those less fortunate than myself. Hopefully, I will be able to help by making a contribution to the science of psychology. It is likely that, after completing my training, I will work in a combined research, educational and clinical setting.

Zane Parzen, meanwhile, has been able to carve out a new life for himself. No criminal charges were ever brought against him. He was convicted only of violating the professional code for physicians in

California. He has remarried and works as a computer specialist in an aircraft plant in a southwestern state, where he has lived since shortly after the *Walker v. Parzen* trial. There were three other cases involving him. These cases were settled out of court by Parzen's insurance company. One of them was brought by a fellow psychiatrist of Parzen's who claimed that his marriage was destroyed by Parzen's involvement with his wife.

When Marvin Lewis took Parzen's deposition a final time for one of the other cases, Lewis reported that Parzen seemed, if anything, even more arrogant and unrepentant than he had been before the first trial. While admitting to the basic facts of the charges against him, he continued to swear that he had done nothing wrong; he was only trying to help these women. He still used those inappropriate gestures that infuriated his lawyer in the Walker trial. As the hideous details of another patient's mistreatment by him were read into the record, he grinned or smiled again and again — as if to ask what all the fuss was about.

More than any of his former patients, Parzen himself now seems the farthest from a cure. He is living proof that "the talking cure" is only a very small first step toward mental health. Talking about a problem, being made aware of its sources, is never in and of itself a cure.

And Evelyn Walker has her own new life.

▬

I now enjoy a kind of independence, comfort, and security I thought were lost to me forever just a few short years ago. Even before the trial in 1981, I had made a total and final break with my parents. I had to accept that there would never be any resolution of this lifelong conflict. It was still a very painful decision. No matter what they had done to me, or had not done for me, they were still my parents. And there was a deep void in my life I knew nobody would ever be able to fill.

One day, long after the trial, I did have a chance encounter with my youngest sister. I had been out shopping when I suddenly felt very hungry. I remembered the delicious Mexican vegetable soup at a nice outdoor café in the heart of San Diego's Old Town. Built over and around the adobe ruins of the tiny nineteenth-century Spanish village that was the original San Diego, Old Town is a nice and cozy village-type collection of shops and restaurants. I knew the couple who had been responsible for this successful development. And one of my very first showings of wall hangings was in a gallery at Old Town's Bazaar del Mundo.

But it was lunchtime, and I was thinking only of how good a bowl of that soup would be. I parked my car in the first space I found—and moved through one of the arched doorways into the main square. I went into the little fenced enclosure of the café and took the first table I came to. I told the waitress not to worry about a menu—all I wanted was a big bowl of their fabulous vegetable soup. She hadn't been gone long enough to get the soup when she came back with a note and handed it to me. "Someone asked me to give this to you," she said.

I looked down at the piece of paper and unfolded it. It was a blunt message signed by my "former sister," who wrote that I had walked past her without speaking to her. Her note said that since I had "divorced" my family, my sister had died of cancer; and that my father was very ill, and why didn't I give him a call.

The waitress had meanwhile brought the soup. I guess she could see the stunned look on my face. I explained to her there was nothing wrong with the soup; I'd just changed my mind about eating. I paid my check and ran back to my car. I didn't look around to see if I could recognize my sister—I doubt if I could have, it seemed so long since I had seen her. There was such a difference in our ages, and we had never been very close. I certainly didn't blame her for any of the bad feelings I harbored about my family. But, still, I had made up my mind—and there was no going back now.

I got in my car and headed straight home. I expected only the worst reaction to this scene—a repetition of a hundred previous scenes in which my family had come crashing down on the little happiness I had been able to make for myself. But the peculiar part of all this was that I didn't feel anything at all. Maybe I had just used up all the feelings I had for my family. But I was still afraid. I called Gary and told him about being in the restaurant and getting that note from my sister. He listened calmly and we talked for quite a long time. He knew me well enough to know when I was really upset; and he knew I was in control, as I told him about reading that note and reacting to it. He said I had done the right thing.

It was a healthy, positive step that I had had this confrontation and had stuck to my decision not to go back to my family. Later, Gary would tell me how proud he was of my handling of that situation—

and he would add, "Five years ago, that would have killed you."

But the best thing that happened to me in those difficult months before, during, and after the trial was meeting and falling in love with Paul Adams. We first met in September 1980 in the bar of a popular steak house where I had gone for dinner with a male friend. I had dated this other man a few times, but we had come to a mutual decision that there wasn't much romantic interest there, although we continued to go out as friends.

At the bar that night, I was struck by this tall, rugged man, and the three of us soon started to talk. I went in to dinner with my date for the evening, but as soon as dinner was finished, I suggested we go back to the bar for another drink. Paul was still standing where we had been, and we resumed our conversation. Paul was tall and gray-haired. An ex-Marine, he had served in both Korea and Vietnam. He was divorced from his wife. Later, I would learn he was born in West Virginia, where his family was among the founders of the town of Parkersburg.

But that night, our pasts didn't seem to matter all that much. We were like two teenagers sparkling with first love. Although my original date was included in the conversation, he quickly realized it was a situation where three was a crowd. And, after a polite interval, he excused himself and went home. Paul thought that was very funny, and he would laugh and remember how another man gave me to him. We were having such a good time at the bar in Miramar, we decided to continue the evening south of the border in Tijuana. We filled up his car with the cheaper Mexican diesel fuel and found a nice place where we could sit and laugh and talk.

After a few hours in Tijuana, we headed north once again, both of us still wide awake with our attraction for each other. A few miles north of the border, we pulled off the highway and went to an apartment that Paul was then sharing with his brother. He said that he was so excited he had to take me home and show me to his brother, the only family he had available at that time. We burst into the apartment and found the brother asleep on the couch. Paul shouted, "Look what I've found. Look here, isn't she wonderful?" His brother rolled over and said, "You can keep her," and then went back to sleep.

For Paul's birthday, I had a T-shirt made with this lettering on the front, "A Guy Gave Her to Me," and on the back, "And my brother said I could keep her."

After dating for five months, Paul and I decided ours was a love that would last. When we first talked about living together, he asked if I'd ever thought about living on a boat. I loved the idea — only later would I learn that to live on a boat had been a dream of his for many years. He already had a small fishing boat he had built himself. We shopped around and found a used 46-foot Chris-Craft; there was plenty of room on board for two people who really wanted to be close to each other. I sewed and hung new curtains, and I felt more at home there than I had anywhere in my life. Many times, Paul would go off and leave me when he had to be out of town on business. I would be on the boat by myself, and I never felt afraid — as I always had been when Bruce went away from home. For once in my life, I felt truly loved and safe — not safe from the usual dangers, but safe from being hurt and being rejected.

At first, the boat was docked at the Harbor Island Marina in San Diego Bay, but eventually we moved it around to Mission Bay. I liked living there. There were all kinds of restaurants and shops in the rolling grassy parklands around the bay. I would take a nice, long walk nearly every day. We didn't dwell on the past; we just tried to be happy with each other in the present. I was terribly worried about the trial — especially when I learned that I would not be in court except for my own testimony. I had to wait for a call from John Winer late every afternoon. Everything Paul did for me during that time was to protect me and make life easier for me. I didn't even know he had been subpoenaed as a witness in the trial until after he came back from the courthouse the day of his testimony.

I had expected that once the jury had reached its verdict and decided on the amount of damages I was to get, I would soon receive a check. As the weeks wore on, I had to face the brutal fact that it might be months or years before a settlement was reached — Zane's lawyer had filed notice of appeal. But Marvin Lewis hired an expert in such matters to negotiate with the lawyers and the insurance company.

Meanwhile, in November 1981, Paul went to the doctor for a thorough physical examination. He had been feeling pain in his shoulder and arm; we thought it was muscle strain from when he had installed a new stern deck on the boat. When we went to get the results of some X-rays he had had done at Scripps Hospital, the doctor said they wanted to do some tissue samples on him, and he would have to check into the hospital for the night. I was leaving the room and going home to get some personal items Paul would need when two of the doctors stopped me and asked to speak with me privately. They said, "There's nothing that can be done; we cannot do any surgery." I don't know why, but for some reason, what they were trying to tell me just didn't sink in. I thought they were just saying there was nothing they could do for him that day. That's when they asked me to sit down on a couch to hear the worst of it: Paul had only two weeks to two months, at the most, to live.

I was numb with shock. Paul seemed so fit and strong and healthy. We had been so happy together — and now this, too, was being taken away from me.

I made it home to our boat at the marina and was just unlocking the door when I heard the phone ringing. It was Marvin Lewis calling to tell me that Zane's insurance company had offered to settle for $2.5 million. I told Marvin about Paul, and that ended our conversation abruptly. Marvin said, "Enough is enough; we'll settle." I don't think I could have taken much more of anything at that time.

Not long after this, Paul was also told by his doctors that his cancer was in too advanced a state for surgery. We decided that however much time we had left together, we would enjoy it right to the last moment. We went to Mexico for the Christmas holidays, and then in January we were married.

Paul's true nobility emerged in this time — all his best qualities seemed to come to the surface. Although we had less than three months together as man and wife, we crammed an amazing amount of living into that short time. Above all, Paul urged me not to grieve over his death. He did say that the hardest part of dying was knowing he was leaving me behind, worrying who would watch out for me, who would take care of me. But he urged me to see our time together as a positive thing. In some ways, he became like a drill sergeant with me. If I was going to have to live alone again, he wanted to be sure I knew everything I'd need to know.

It was important for me to have a place to live. So, we moved off the boat and into a townhouse we bought. But I was the one who had to look for the house, and I had to make all the decisions about it; I was also the one who had to handle our checkbook. I knew his guidance was all done with my best interests at heart, but sometimes I could not understand why he was being so rough on me; some days, I even thought he must not like me any more. Only later would I fully appreciate all that he had done for me.

Another point we talked about at length was the horrible experience I had had with Zane. Paul made me promise that I would do something with that experience — so that I could grow as a result of it and so that others could learn from it.

When Paul died on March 14, 1982, I folded up the T-shirt with the happy slogans from our first night together and put it in the casket beside him. I also put in a bracelet I had given him with these words inscribed: "As deeply as I love you today, so shall I love you all our tomorrows." And then the casket was closed and he was gone and I was alone again.

In many ways, I felt I was burying my last, best hope for a happy life. I couldn't imagine that I would ever find anybody like Paul. But those who were closest to me, especially my therapist, all told me that my having been able to have such a relationship to begin with was a healthy, positive thing, and the fact that I had been able to do it one time might mean I could find somebody to love and to love me and share my life with again.

In fact, that is exactly what happened. In September 1984, I was married again. My husband Earl and I were neighbors; we happened to meet one day in the garage of the condominium I moved to when I could no longer bear to stay in the townhouse Paul and I had shared. Earl is a retired rear admiral; he's a tall, silver-haired, older man — I call him my Silver Fox. By the time Earl and I married, I had reestablished a nice relationship with my two sons. Earl is close to my boys, and he believes in me — I know I can count on him to stand by me.

In spite of all the outward and visible signs of happiness and security, Evelyn Walker remains a troubled woman. There are still times when her obsession with Zane Parzen returns almost with the strength it had over her ten years ago. She still wonders where he is and what he is doing and whether she will ever see and talk with him again. She continues her treatment with Sydney Smith, who sees her as a very different woman from the frantic, out-of-control, suicidal patient he had to deal with in 1979 and 1980. But he also knows that while she is much improved, she is not well and she never will be.